W9-AER-816

PERGAMON INTERNATIONAL LIBRARY
of Science, Technology, Engineering and Social Studies
The 1000-volume original paperback library in aid of education,
industrial training and the enjoyment of leisure
Publisher: Robert Maxwell, M.C.

Soviet Foreign Policy
Since World War II

THE PERGAMON TEXTBOOK
INSPECTION COPY SERVICE

An inspection copy of any book published in the Pergamon International Library
will gladly be sent to academic staff without obligation for their consideration for
course adoption or recommendation. Copies may be retained for a period of 60 days
from receipt and returned if not suitable. When a particular title is adopted or
recommended for adoption for class use and the recommendation results in a sale
of 12 or more copies, the inspection copy may be retained with our compliments.
The Publishers will be pleased to receive suggestions for revised editions and new
titles to be published in this important International Library.

Pergamon Titles of Related Interest

Brezhnev SELECTED SPEECHES AND WRITINGS ON FOREIGN
AFFAIRS
Dismukes/McConnel SOVIET NAVAL DIPLOMACY
Douglass SOVIET MILITARY STRATEGY IN EUROPE
Duncan SOVIET POLICY IN THE THIRD WORLD
Suslov SELECTED SPEECHES AND WRITINGS

Related Journals*

BULLETIN OF SCIENCE, TECHNOLGY AND SOCIETY
INTERNATIONAL JOURNAL OF INTERCULTURAL RELATIONS
TECHNOLOGY IN SOCIETY
WORLD DEVELOPMENT

*Free specimen copies available upon request.

PERGAMON POLICY STUDIES ON INTERNATIONAL POLITICS

Soviet Foreign Policy Since World War II

Joseph L. Nogee
Robert H. Donaldson

Pergamon Press

NEW YORK • OXFORD • TORONTO • SYDNEY • PARIS • FRANKFURT

Pergamon Press Offices:

U.S.A.   Pergamon Press Inc., Maxwell House, Fairview Park,
                  Elmsford, New York 10523, U.S.A.

U.K.   Pergamon Press Ltd., Headington Hill Hall,
                  Oxford OX3 OBW, England

CANADA   Pergamon of Canada, Ltd., Suite 104, 150 Consumers Road,
                  Willowdale, Ontario M2J 1P9, Canada

AUSTRALIA   Pergamon Press (Aust.) Pty. Ltd., P.O. Box 544,
                  Potts Point, NSW 2011, Australia

FRANCE   Pergamon Press SARL, 24 rue des Ecoles,
                  75240 Paris, Cedex 05, France

FEDERAL REPUBLIC   Pergamon Press GmbH, Hammerweg 6, Postfach 1305,
OF GERMANY   6242 Kronberg/Taunus, Federal Republic of Germany

Library of Congress Cataloging in Publication Data

Nogee, Joseph L
    Soviet foreign policy since World War II.

    (Pergamon policy studies on international
politics)
    Bibliography: p.
    Includes index.
    1. Russia-Foreign relations—1945-
I. Donaldson, Robert H., joint author. II. Title.
III. Series.
DK270.N63   1981   327.47   80-21601
ISBN 0-08-025997-9
ISBN 0-08-025996-0 (pbk.)

DK
270
N63
1981

Printed in the United States of America

Contents

Acknowledgments

We thank the following individuals who read a chapter or more of the manuscript and made helpful comments: Edward A. Corcoran, Alex Dragnich, David Kellogg, Robert Kennedy, Paul Marantz, Richard Rowson, John W. Spanier, Alan Stone, and Ivan Volgyes. None of the above are responsible for any of the interpretations of the data. We thank also our wives, Jo and Judy, for the many family accommodations that were required in the preparation of the book.

Chapter 1
Introduction

World War II was a major watershed in Soviet foreign policy. Before the war, the Soviet Union was at best a middle-level power whose overriding concern was the preservation of the Bolshevik Revolution and the protection of the nation's security. Moscow flirted half-heartedly with social revolution abroad for a brief period—a waning legacy of Trotsky's theory of "permanent revolution" and Lenin's "imperalism"—but the ascendancy of Stalin led increasingly to a preoccupation with traditional power politics. World War II radically altered the structure of international politics. Europe no longer dominated world affairs. The great powers of the prewar era (with the exception of the United States) were either vanquished or exhausted. Soviet Russia emerged for the first time in its history as a great power, surpassed in strength only by the United States. Within a short period of time the Soviet Union and the United States acquired a special status in world affairs as not merely great powers, but superpowers. Since 1945, the central focus of Soviet foreign policy has been its relationship with the United States.

The changing character of Soviet-American relations can be illustrated by three statements made by the Soviet leaders at three widely separated points in time. In September 1947, Andrei Zhdanov, Stalin's principal spokesman, informed the founding Congress of the Communist Information Bureau that:

A new alignment of political forces has arisen. The more the war recedes into the past, the more distinct become two major trends in postwar international policy, corresponding to the division of the political forces operating on the international arena into two major camps; the imperialist and antidemocratic camp, on the one hand, and the anti-imperialist and democratic camp, on the other. The principal driving force of the imperialist camp is the USA.[1]

A little over a quarter of a century later, Secretary-General Leonid Brezhnev argued the cause of detente before an American television audience by stating that "I think that those who support a radical improvement in relations between the Soviet Union and the United States may look ahead with optimism, for this

1

goal is in the interests of our two peoples and in the interests of peace-loving people throughout the world."[2] Toward the end of his rule, as Soviet forces were overrunning Afghanistan, Brezhnev described a darker vision of Soviet-American relations: "It has been clear for some time that the leading circles of the United States . . . have embarked on a course hostile to the cause of detente, a course of spiraling the arms race and leading to a growth of the war danger."[3]

These three statements illustrate both the continuity and change in Soviet foreign policy since World War II. Continuity is manifested in the malign view of the United States held by the Soviet leadership. Change is reflected in the fact that antagonism between the superpowers has been broken by periods of peaceful coexistence and detente. This duality in Soviet attitudes and behavior raises a number of questions: What is the nature of Soviet foreign policy? Is the Soviet Union unalterably opposed to the capitalist great powers? Can there be a permanent accommodation between the communist and noncommunist worlds? We are told by commentators that the "cold war" is over, an observation that prompts several other questions: If the cold war is over, when did it end? What produced the change? Indeed, was the Soviet Union ever a real threat to the West or was that dread only a concoction of anticommunist hysteria? During the 1970s the hallmark of Soviet foreign policy was "detente." In the West, a great deal of confusion and controversy revolve around this term. Is detente fundamentally a tactic, a deceptive front designed to catch the United States and the West off guard, or do the Soviets genuinely wish to lay the basis for a permanent coexistence between our different societies? In the early 1980s, can we indeed still use the term detente to describe Soviet relations with the United States?

To answer these questions, we need to examine the forces that produce continuity and change in Soviet politics. In chapter 2, "The Soviet Approach to Foreign Policy," we focus upon the forces giving continuity to Soviet foreign policy. Superpower conflict is explained in part by the global state system that pits state against state, particularly great powers, in the quest for security. To this struggle for survival the Soviet ruling elites bring a particular set of attitudes and ideas. These political values and beliefs are expressed in the ideology of Marxism-Leninism. Soviet communist doctrine reinforces and magnifies those features of the global political system that create conflict between nations. Communist doctrine is a source of continuity in Soviet foreign policy.

It is more difficult to explain the causes of change than of continuity. For one thing, the forces producing change are multiple and are themselves constantly transforming. Change is effected by countless events—some large, others small—that can only with difficulty be evaluated intelligently when they occur. It is easier to interpret the significance of events that influence foreign policy in retrospect because we can at a later period observe some of the consequences of these events more easily. Thus, we need some kind of conceptual framework to organize and give meaning to the multitude of facts that have produced the changes in Soviet foreign policy since the end of the second World War.

Students of foreign policy have traditionally tended to choose either one of two general frameworks for analysis. One focuses upon domestic factors such as the nature of the political and economic system, the various domestic interests seeking advancement, and the ideological preconceptions and perceptions of political elites. An alternative approach examines the influences of the external or international environment such as the international structure, the prevailing balance of power, and specific threats posed by other great powers.[4]

The choice of one or the other of these approaches will influence conclusions regarding the character of Soviet behavior. For example, analysts of the internal or domestic school tend to see Soviet behavior as fixed and undeviating, a product of the authoritarian make-up of the Soviet political system. Not all, but many in this school rely particularly heavily upon ideology as a guiding factor behind Soviet behavior. Thus, the consistency they see is the constancy of Soviet hostility to the West. Communist doctrine induces Soviet leaders to look upon the United States, the citadel of world capitalism, as an implacable foe not because of what it does or may do but because of what it is. Bertram Wolfe, a leading analyst of this approach, warned, "It should be clear then that the men who make policy in the Soviet Union think and act differently from the tsars, and that we neglect their ideology to our peril."[5] The policy prescriptions inherent in such an approach are clear.

Proponents of the external school are less inclined to associate Soviet policy with a fixed line. Soviet behavior is seen as flexible and usually rational. The dominant influences are those of the international environment to which policy-makers are continually forced to react. Since the international environment is in a constant state of flux, the leaders in the Kremlin must be flexible and adaptive in order to meet new challenges. And on the whole they have been. Most observers who look at Soviet policy from this perspective have seen an effective adaptation to the political, military, and technological facts of life. Marshall D. Shulman, for example, in his reappraisal of Stalin's foreign policy challenged the popular view that the cold war was a product of Stalin's paranoid personality or that one had to fathom the "occult characteristics or the psycho-pathology of Soviet leaders" to understand Soviet foreign policy. "One general characteristic of Soviet policy which becomes more evident . . . ," Shulman observed of Stalin's administration, "is the largely rational responsiveness of Soviet policy to changes in the world environment, and particularly changes in power relationships."[6]

Seen in this perspective, Soviet behavior is less unique and perhaps less menacing than it might otherwise be considered. The lodestar of the Soviet ship of state is not so much Lenin as it is the balance of power. And of course in this, the Soviet vessel is no different from nonsocialist crafts. If the balance of power is in fact the central determinant of Soviet foreign policy, we should expect to apply the same modes of analyses to Soviet politics that we use for all great powers, for the balance of power is a universal—if ambiguous—principle of policy.

Which of these two schools are we to choose? Common sense tells us that both have something to offer. It would be the height of folly to ignore completely the domestic structure—the nature of the political system and the political forces operating internally—and to focus exclusively on external forces, just as it would be unwise to see Soviet outward behavior as an emanation of internal pressures and pay no regard to the structure of the state system or the opportunities and threats posed by other nations. At the risk of stating the obvious, therefore, we have to acknowledge that both schools provide necessary pieces for compiling an understandable picture out of the puzzle of Soviet foreign policy.

This study will examine the impact of internal as well as external events upon Soviet foreign policy. It will also provide an analysis of the behavior of the Soviet state as a part of a system of states. The introduction of the concept of system is not intended to suggest an elaborate set of rules of behavior for certain types of states, nor to imply an integrated international system observing certain kinds of functions.[7] It is simply to recognize the fundamental fact that Soviet behavior—like that of all states—is influenced by and reacts to the policies of other states and to the external conditions under which these policies take place. Indeed, the importance of this approach is that, of all the variables that influence the foreign policies of great powers, the most reliable and most consistent is the responsiveness of policy to outside conditions. The Soviet Union has shown a particular sensitivity to power bloc politics since 1945.

Since the end of World War II, the world has been groping for a durable international structure. The defeat of the Axis Powers completed the destruction of the interwar international hierarchy and temporarily produced a global political vacuum. None of the Big Three leaders could envision what kind of a structure the future held in store, although each had a fairly clear idea of what it would like that structure to be. In retrospect, we can say that none of the statesmen of the victorious powers imagined the changes that would take place throughout the world in the ensuing decades. All of the major powers were forced to adapt to unexpected developments such as the collapse of Western colonialism, the rise of Third World nationalism, intercontinental ballistic missiles, the spectacular economic growth of the industrialized nations, the energy crisis, and the failure of the United States in Vietnam. For the Soviet Union, the postwar period was one of unprecedented opportunity to expand its power but, at the same time, it was a period of vulnerabilities and risks of an unparalled magnitude. How and why the USSR responded to these circumstances is the principal concern of this analysis.

Now with the perspective of more than a generation, we can see rather clearly the main outlines of the changes that have operated upon Soviet foreign policy. There are six general variables that stand out as fundamental: four of an external nature and two internal. They are as follows:

1. The change in the structure of the international system from bipolarity to multipolarity;
2. The growth of polycentrism in the international communist movement;
3. The development of a military technology that makes the total destruction of an adversary possible;
4. The achievement of military parity between the Soviet Union and the United States and the change from a regional to a global military power;
5. The change in the Soviet regime from a totalitarian policy to an authoritarian bureaucratic oligarchy; and
6. The differences reflected in the leadership influences of Stalin, Khrushchev, and Brezhnev.

The broadest of the changes has been the decline of the post–World War II international structure and its displacement by a new multipolarity. The international environment has become less tense, more flexible and, in many ways, more complex. During the 1940s and 1950s, international politics were dominated by two giant—though unequal—powers, each of which envisaged the other as a deadly enemy. Through their respective coalitions the United States and the Soviet Union dominated international politics. In the 1960s, there began a disintegration of the two-bloc structure and with it a decline in the capacity of the superpowers to control events throughout the world. New centers of power emerged in Europe, China, and Japan. Militarily, the world of the 1980s remains bipolar but politically, it is multipolar. Both superpowers have had to face the realization that their political influence is not proportionate to their military power. Multipolarity imposes on Soviet policy the constraints of several power centers whereas bipolarity imposed only one.

Soviet foreign policy operates in two distinct though interrelated political frameworks: (1) the international system, which includes all the nations of the globe, and (2) the communist subsystem which today includes 16 states (East Germany, Poland, Czechoslovakia, Hungary, Rumania, Bulgaria, Albania, Yugoslavia, Cuba, Outer Mongolia, China, North Korea, Cambodia, Laos, Vietnam, and Afghanistan), in addition to the Soviet Union, as well as approximately 80 communist parties in noncommunist states. This latter subsystem has become fragmented, or polycentric. In an earlier period (certainly until the defection of Tito), the communist camp could be described as "monolithic." It possessed a unity under the guiding hand of the Communist Party of the Soviet Union either via the mechanism of control such as was exercised over Eastern Europe, or as a result of the deference paid to the Soviet leadership. Yugoslavia's defection in 1948 began the disintegration, but the rupture of the system as such came with the Sino-Soviet schism in the 1960s. No single development has so profoundly affected Soviet foreign policy as the Sino-Soviet split. Soviet leaders now perceive China as more of a long-term threat than the United States.

A third factor is one that has profoundly affected the military doctrines and strategy of both superpowers: changes in the technology of war, changes which have come with unprecedented rapidity since 1945. In the 1960s, Herman Kahn estimated that a revolution in the technology of war occurred every four or five years.[8] In addition to atomic and hydrogen bombs, the postwar period witnessed the development of atomic submarines, liquid fueled and solid fueled ballistic missiles, computer controlled guidance systems, multiple independently targeted vehicles, and television guided missiles. Although the discovery of the atomic bomb had the most dramatic impact on popular thinking about war, it was the invention of the thermonuclear bomb that produced the more radical change in the technology of warfare, for the difference in destructive capability between a megaton warhead and a kiloton is greater than that between a kiloton atomic bomb and the conventional bomb. Thermonuclear weapons have introduced the possibility that one nation can literally destroy another or even all life on earth. As the United States and the Soviet Union acquired stockpiles of these weapons along with delivery systems, each has been deterred from using them against the other out of fear of retaliation. The Soviet Union has come to share the conviction held in the United States that whatever the course of relations between the two nations, a nuclear confrontation must be avoided at all costs.

The change in the technology of war has been paralleled by a change in the strategic military balance between the Soviet Union and the United States. During the 1940s, the United States possessed a monopoly of the atomic weapon. Though the Soviets detonated an atomic bomb in 1949, throughout the 1950s they remained strategically inferior to the United States. But the gap quickly narrowed. The Soviet Union achieved a mastery over the hydrogen bomb in 1953, only about a year after the first successful United States test. As both sides accumulated a stockpile of nuclear weapons, the arms race shifted toward delivery systems, and missiles—their number and sophistication—became the measure of the military balance. Throughout the 1950s and into the 1960s, the United States continued to maintain an overall strategic superiority. In the 1960s the Politburo decided to expand production of strategic missiles, resulting in a numerical superiority over the United States by the early 1970s. At the time of the first Strategic Arms Limitations Agreement in May 1972, each power possessed superiority in some elements of the strategic equation: the United States with a greater number of warheads deliverable to separate targets and the Soviet Union with a greater number of missiles and more powerful warheads.

But, on balance, the overall strategic relationship had become one of parity. The expiration of SALT I in the late 1970s, however, left both powers free to continue the arms race. At the beginning of the 1980s, substantial evidence indicated that the Soviet Union had in fact surpassed the United States in both conventional and nuclear weapons.

The last two of the factors to be noted here concern internal developments in Soviet society. As the external world has changed fundamentally since World War II, so has Soviet society and its political system. The Soviet Union remains an authoritarian state but the character of the regime and the relationship between the state and society are different. Stalin's rule was personal, his objectives total. Through the use of instruments of coercion, he succeeded in transforming the economy and social structure of a vast empire. His revolutionary totalitarianism has become transformed into a postrevolutionary bureaucracy.[9] It is postrevolutionary in the sense that the planned transformation of Soviet society dictated from above has largely ended. The Soviet economy has developed an industrial infrastructure with a dynamic of its own, a dynamic that imposes its own demands upon the ruling elite. No longer does ideology provide a blueprint for action. In its place are the diverse prerequisites for economic growth, science, education, and improvement in the quality of life for the Soviet citizen. Coercion and exhortation have been replaced to a certain degree as the basis of motivation by material incentives, professionalism, and patriotism. Ideology, which in the past was used to transform society, now becomes more an instrument of control, a means simply to suppress dissidence. Under this newer system the principal function of the ruling elite is to administer the enormous, diverse and complex economy under its control in the most rational manner possible. Soviet rulers must arbitrate the demands of the numerous institutional groupings that now exist. To accomplish this task, the ruling elite relies increasingly upon bureaucratic rationality where inspirational leadership or terror had been utilized earlier. One of the consequences of the growth of this postevolutionary bureaucracy for foreign policy is a tendency to downplay the messianic and universal goals inherent in communist ideology and a growing concern with the traditional national interest.

Finally, we must distinguish between the three major leaders who have dominated Soviet postwar foreign policy and who have given their administrations a distinct style and perspective. The Malenkov administration, which succeeded Stalin, was essentially a regime of transition. Khrushchev dominated the leadership from 1955 until the coup in October 1964 led to the emergence of Brezhnev. Each leader stamped his administration with his own personality. Without falling into the error of attributing the aggressiveness of Soviet policy in the postwar period primarily to Stalin's personality, one can reasonably see a connection between Stalin's cynicism and suspiciousness and much of Soviet behavior. Certainly Soviet diplomacy suffered from a high degree of rigidity because of Stalin's refusal to give his representatives any freedom of action. And that same distrust of others led Stalin to impose regimes in Eastern Europe totally subordinate to Soviet (i.e., Stalin's) authority. Nikita Khrushchev brought a change of style as well as objective. Far more open and outgoing, Khrushchev not only moved more freely among his own people, he also shattered the isolationist mold of his predecessor and traveled widely throughout the world. He expanded the scope of active Soviet involvement to Africa, the Middle East, and Latin America, all areas largely ignored by Stalin. More significant than style, though, were Khrushchev's objectives for which the establishment of a long-term stable relationship with the West was central. Khrushchev's successors overthrew him less for the inadequacy of his purposes than because of their dissatisfaction with his methods, so it is not surprising that many of the policies of the Brezhnev team are in substance a continuation of Khrushchev's policies that use different means. Reference is made to the Brezhnev team because, under him, the Soviet leadership has been more "collective" than at any time since the 1920s. Collective leadership has at times led to indecisiveness as factional differences took time to work themselves out. Compared with both his predecessors, Brezhnev has been less imaginative and more conservative.

These six variables are not, of course, the only important changes that have modified the international and Soviet domestic environments during the past 35 years, but they are central for an understanding of the evolution of contemporary Soviet policy. It would simplify our analysis if each of the developments took place *pari passu,* each following a common chronological sequence so that Soviet policy might be conveniently divided into a clearly defined number of stages. Changes in political administration often make the simplest dividing points in describing a nation's foreign policy. Thus, it would be convenient if Stalin's administration coincided with the bipolar world and Khrushchev's with multipolarity, or if polycentrism dominated Leonid Brezhnev's administration while his predecessors were free to operate under monolithic communism. But it did not evolve that way. The modernization of the Soviet polity began while Stalin was alive and continues through the present. The weapons upon which the policies of deterrence are based today and that constitute the basis of Soviet strategic power were developed by Stalin's successors. What we are faced with is a complex interaction of multiple factors, each progressing according to its own dynamic, so that while the initial and terminal periods under study reveal sharply contrasting conditions, the period as a whole does not lend itself to sharply differentiated periods.

NOTES

1. Quoted in Alvin Z. Rubinstein, ed., *The Foreign Policy of the Soviet Union* (New York: Random House, 1960), p. 237.

2. Leonid Brezhnev, *Peace, Detente, and Soviet-American Relations* (New York: Harcourt Brace Jovanovich, 1979), p. 25.
3. *New York Times,* January 13, 1980.
4. For a description of these two approaches and the behavioral characteristics associated with each, see Morton Schwartz, The *Foreign Policy of the USSR: Domestic Factors* (Encino: Dickinson Publishing Co., 1975), pp. 1-4.
5. Bertram D. Wolfe, "Communist Ideology and Soviet Foreign Policy," in *The Realities of World Communism,* ed. William Petersen (Englewood Cliffs, N.J.: Prentice-Hall, 1963), p. 25.
6. Marshall D. Shulman, *Stalin's Foreign Policy Reappraised* (Cambridge, Mass.: Harvard University Press, 1963), p. 3.
7. The classic statement of systems theory applied to international politics is Morton Kaplan, *Systems and Process in International Politics* (New York: John Wiley, 1957). For a criticism of this theory, cf. Stanley Hoffmann, "International Relations—the Long Road to Theory," *World Politics* (April 1961), pp. 356-361; and Hedley Bull, "International Theory: The Case for a Classical Approach," *World Politics* (April 1966), pp. 364-372.
8. Herman Kahn, *On Thermonuclear War* (Princeton, N.J.: Princeton University Press, 1960), pp. 315-316.
9. For an elaboration of this model, see Richard Lowenthal, "The Soviet Union in the Post-Revolutionary Era: An overview," in *Soviet Politics Since Khrushchev,* ed. Alexander Dallin and Thomas B. Larson (Englewood Cliffs, N.J.: Prentice-Hall, 1968), pp. 1-22.

Chapter 2
The Soviet Approach to Foreign Policy

THE INTERNATIONAL SYSTEM

Soviet foreign policy, like that of all governments, operates within the framework of an international system. The structure of the international system—determined by the number of actors and the hierarchical relationships between them—is, of course, constantly changing. The world that confronted the Bolsheviks at the inauguration of Soviet power differed considerably from that inherited by Stalin in the aftermath of the second World War. In 1917, Russia was a weak nation confronted by several powerful potential adversaries in Europe and Asia. Her immediate neighbors to both the east and the west (Poland, Rumania, and Japan) were notably hostile. Because political power was shared by several nations, the post-World War I system is usually described as multi-polar. In contrast, the post-World War II world was bipolar, i.e., political power was concentrated largely in the hands of the United States and the Soviet Union. Europe was devastated in 1945 and Japanese dominance in Asia was destroyed. In spite of its enormous wartime losses, the Soviet Union emerged more powerful than any nation on the Eurasian land mass. A virtual political vacuum existed along the entire international border of the USSR. The opportunities for an expansion of Soviet power in 1945 must have appeared very enticing to Joseph Stalin.

Whatever its structure, however, the international system has certain enduring characteristics that of necessity condition the foreign policy of all nations. Primary among these is its decentralized character. Global politics lack a central political authority like a world government. Ultimately, each nation is free in principle to determine the range of policies it will pursue for itself. This is the idea expressed by the principle of national sovereignty, a concept that rejects the right of any external political authority to control the policies of the state. National sovereignty in effect gives to international politics an anarchic character. There are several important consequences of the decentralized or anarchic character of the international system. Perhaps most significant is the burden placed on each nation to look after its own security. Even more than in the case of the individual, the ultimate value for the nation-state is survival. But unlike the individual within society, the state is unprotected by legal institutions, so the state must look to its own devices—diplomacy, armaments, military alliances, for example—for self-protection. The quest for survival is one of the hallmarks of international politics.

Another is the widespread use of force in relations between states. One can exaggerate the difference between the international system, with its inclination toward violence, and the relative order of domestic state systems; the evidence is overwhelming that some violence exists in all political systems. And the phenomenon of civil war is proof that no society is immune to large-scale war. Yet, while the state may or may not possess an actual monopoly of force in society, it does, as a general rule, control the only legitimate use of force in society. Individuals and groups may wage war upon each other within a nation but they contravene the law to do so. Not so in international politics. The ultimate arbiter of whether a state will or will not resort to the use of force in its relations with its neighbors is the state itself. History provides ample evidence of the willingness of states to resort to war in order to achieve their ends. One explanation for this fact is offered by Kenneth Waltz:

Each state pursues its own interests, however defined, in ways it judges best. Force is a means of achieving the external ends of states because there exists no consistent, reliable process of reconciling the conflicts of interest that inevitably arise among similar units in a condition of anarchy.[1]

A world government that took away from nations the essential prerogative of statehood—national sovereignty—might reduce the incidence of violence between nations. Conceivably, it could substitute for war a political mechanism for reconciling the conflicting interest of states. But no such government exists and the prospects of one arising in the near future are small. Thus, the states of the world inhabit an environment that fosters insecurity and a degree of suspicion and fear.

This leads to another basic characteristic of the international system: the balance of power. In the words of Hans Morgenthau, "The aspiration for power on the part of several nations . . . leads of necessity to a configuration that is called the balance of power and to policies that aim at preserving it . . . (T)he international balance of power is only a particular manifestation of a general social principle to which all societies composed of a number of autonomous units owe the autonomy of their component parts."[2] Stated in a simplified form, the balance of power refers to the tendencies of states to align themselves with others to promote their interests or enhance their security. These alignments may be of a military or political character. For examples of political maneuvering that illustrate the balance of power, one may cite Richard Nixon's dramatic visit to China in 1972 and the Soviet encouragement of "united front" coalitions in the mid-1930s. Both of these policies were strategies designed to enhance the state's political position. These particular examples illustrate how the balance of power operates independently of the ideological predispositions or political structure of the state. Balance-of-power politics are not something practiced only by authoritarian regimes, or for that matter, by "imperialistic" governments. From its inception, the Soviet Union has been an astute, though hardly infallible, player of the game.

There are certain rules that must be observed if balance-of-power politics are indeed to enhance the security of a state or promote its general objectives. First, states must be prepared to mobilize power against any other state seeking hegemony, be it regional, continental, or global. They must be able to assess changing distributions of power so as to be able to act before it is too late. And finally, they must be diplomatically flexible, willing to align with states who share a common enemy irrespective of ideological differences or past animosities. The fundamental object of the balance of power is to juxtapose power against power, to prevent any one nation or coalition from achieving a position of predominance.

Quite obviously, not all balance-of-power politics succeed. There are problems of both theory and practice in the concept.[3] States do underestimate (or exaggerate) the power of an adversary, and they may misinterpret the intentions of another government. Allies may not be available for a weak nation to protect itself. And there is always the possibility that political leaders will act irrationally. The universality of the balance of power in the international system should not therefore be interpreted as meaning that the system itself will necessarily be stable, that peace will predominate over war, or that the weak will always be able to protect themselves against the strong. What it does imply, however, is a pervasive tendency on the part of all nations to respond in a similar manner to changes in the distribution of power.

Soviet foreign policy has been ever aware of the prerequisites of the shifting balance of power. Between the world wars, the USSR was weak and had to pursue a largely defensive course. As the men in the Kremlin perceived the situation, Soviet interests dictated a strategy of keeping the Western powers from uniting against them. In the 1920s, this was accomplished by pursuing a pro-German policy. Thus, in 1922, Soviet Foreign Minister Chicherin brilliantly engineered the Treaty of Rapallo, which kept Germany at odds with Britain and France and prevented a united Western front against the Soviet Union. German-Soviet collaboration in 1925 even extended to secret arrangements whereby the two countries exchanged military information, army experts and munitions.[4] After Hitler came to power, the threat to Soviet security shifted. As the USSR once used Germany to balance Britain and France, so the democracies were now courted to counter the German threat. The year 1935 witnessed Soviet treaties of alliance with France and Czechoslovakia and a new Comintern policy that encouraged an anti-Fascist collaboration between communists and socialists and even bourgeois parties.

Balance-of-power considerations also explain Soviet diplomacy leading up to the second World War. The Nazi-Soviet pact of August 1939 might appear an aberration in view of the United Nations coalition that ultimately fought against the Axis powers. In light of its results, we can see that the Non-aggression Pact was a terrible blunder on Stalin's part, but at the time it appeared a shrewd gamble.[5] Stalin rightly anticipated the impending European war and believed that Soviet interests would be better served by neutrality than by belligerence. If the Soviets were forced to become involved at a later date, he reasoned, they would enter the war under much more advantageous conditions. Stalin's mistake was to overestimate France's ability to keep Hitler at bay so that the Germany that struck Soviet Russia in June 1941 was considerably more powerful than the Germany Russia might have fought in September 1939. The point is that even before the USSR emerged as a superpower, its foreign policies were influenced by the characteristics of the international system and the exigencies of the balance of power. As we shall see, this was no less true of the USSR as a world power.

MARXIST-LENINIST IDEOLOGY

Any study of Soviet foreign policy must quickly come to grips with the issue of the influence of communist doctrine on Soviet behavior. The Soviet Union was the first great power to claim the ideas of Marxism as the basis for all public policy, both domestic and foreign. Every Soviet leader from Lenin to Brezhnev has explained and defended his actions as conforming to the principles of Marxism-Leninism. These principles ostensibly provide a guide for mastering the complexities of international politics. A standard Soviet text in diplomatic history makes the rather extravagant claim that

Soviet diplomacy . . . wields a weapon possessed by none of its rivals or opponents. Soviet diplomacy is fortified by a scientific theory of Marxism-Leninism. This doctrine lays down the unshakeable laws of social development. By revealing these norms, it gives the possibility not only of understanding the current tendencies of international life, but also of permitting the desirable collaboration with the march of events. Such are the special advantages held by Soviet diplomacy. They give it a special position in international life and explain its outstanding successes.[6]

Non-Soviet opinions differ considerably about how reliable a guide communist doctrine actually is toward understanding the foreign policy of states, and they disagree about how seriously the Soviet leaders take that doctrine. Further complicating the picture is the fact that different centers of Communist power—most notably the USSR and China, but also lesser centers such as Yugoslavia and Cuba—have interpreted the doctrine in different ways.

Before attempting to assess the impact of Communist doctrine on Soviet foreign policy, we must examine its content. This is not a simple task because neither Marx nor Engels nor any of their disciples ever attempted to create a comprehensive theory of foreign policy or international relations. The most systematic set of ideas relating to a theory of international relations is Lenin's pamphlet, *Imperialism: The Highest Stage of Capitalism*. But this is a fragmentary theory at best. It explains the behavior of only certain types of capitalist states while it ignores the motivations of the overwhelming majority of states in the world, which were neither capitalist nor advanced industrially. Lenin wrote his *Imperialism*—like many of his theoretical essays—as a polemic. He was criticizing Germany's Social Democrats and the so-called "social chauvinists" of the Second International (i.e., those socialists who supported their government's war effort during the First World War).

As it turns out, the vast bulk of the literature that comprise Communist foreign policy doctrine consists of articles, speeches, and statements made in defense or opposition to the concrete policy issues of the day. Thus, it is not surprising that we find significant contradictions in Lenin between his views before coming to power and those he expressed afterward, or that the political assumptions of Stalin changed as the character of the German threat to Soviet security in the 1930s changed, or that Khrushchev found it expedient to modify theory as a result of the development of nuclear weapons. What we are suggesting is simply that Communist ideology never came to its architects from on high as the Ten Commandments came to Moses; rather, it evolved out of the crucible of the political struggles in which its proponents were engaged.

One further point needs examination before we turn to the substance of Communist ideology. We need a definition of ideology and clarification of where ideologies fit into the total belief systems or thought patterns of the "true believer." Ideology can be defined as a systematic statement of the highest values and ideals of a particular group. This includes a description of the real world that purports to explain the necessity of those values and ideals. As we define it, then, ideology has two distinct features: a set of beliefs about the real world and a complex of attitudes and values (in the language of social science, "cognitive" and "affective" components). Most ideologies are critiques of the world of their times. They either contain or are associated with radical programs for the transformation of society. This distinction between beliefs about reality and attitudes is important because it helps us understand why adherents to an ideology may remain "true believers" even after its propositions about reality have been objectively demonstrated to be false. The underlying values of an ideology may persist long after the facts that purport to justify those values have been disproved. Facts can be demonstrated as true or false by scientific means; not so values. Thus, where the descriptive elements of an ideology conflict with reality, the attitudinal elements will stimulate the believer to revise those propositions and bring them in conformity with reality. The end product of an ideology—its vision, its goals—is the product of the values of the ideology, not of the structure of beliefs about reality. The belief system does not completely define the utopia; it describes the road toward its achievement. So, inevitably, as the real world changes, ideologues are forced to admit that there are different roads to their utopia but the utopia itself need not change.

MARXISM AND FOREIGN POLICY

Marxist ideology, as noted, does not set forth a theory of international relations. Foreign policy develops out of the interaction between nation-states. A theory of foreign policy would attempt to identify and classify the vital actors in world affairs and describe the laws that govern their behavior. It would explain the origins of war and violence in international society. It would assess the nature of international society to determine what if any political structure might unite the world. Marx offered no theory of war or imperialism because the focus of his analysis was the nature of social change within societies, not the interaction or conflict between them. The student of international politics looks at the segmentation of humanity along vertical (national) lines. To Marx, the dynamics of politics were rooted in the horizontal (class) divisions of mankind.

Marx developed an economic theory of history that posited the class struggle as the taproot of all social change. Every society was divided between the haves who possessed wealth and owned the means to produce goods, and the have-nots, the workers. The government, laws and culture of society—which Marx called the "superstructure"—was controlled by the ruling class and used by it to protect its property rights. History moves through a series of stages, each qualitatively higher than the preceding. Each historical stage in every society reflects the struggle between the developing economic forces of society and the entrenched interests of the ruling class. The culmination of this process in Marx's day was capitalism, whose ultimate disintegration he predicted according to a series of inexorable laws.

Although Marxist thought contains no systematic theory of foreign policy, it does analyze two of the factors that are vital to almost all theories of foreign policy: the state and nationalism. Modern international relations theory regards the nation-state as the fundamental unit or actor in international politics, and most theorists look upon nationalism as one of the dynamic causes of conflict between states. Marx disparages both. He describes the state as part of the "superstructure" of society, i.e., one of the instruments by which the bourgeosie exercises its control over the proletariat. After the proletariat has destroyed capitalism and created its own "dictatorship," there will no longer be a class struggle and the state will eventually wither away. Marx himself drew no implications of a stateless world, but since the state is the political unit that wages war, it is possible to assume that a more peaceful world might accompany the demise of capitalism.

National differences and antagonisms are also destined to disappear. Marx saw a clear correlation between nationalistic conflicts and capitalistic exploitation; thus, he noted in the *Communist Manifesto,* "In proportion as the antagonism between classes within the nation vanishes, the hostility of one nation to another will come to an end." These arguments led Marx and Engels to reject the impulses of patriotism and national loyalty. "The workingmen," they said, "have no country."[7]

As a surrogate for the loyalty to the nation or state, Marx introduced the idea of proletarian internationalism. By this he implied that the workers throughout the world had an identity of interest that transcended the particular nationality of which each was a part. The battle cry "Proletarians of the world, unite!" was a call for workers in every country to associate themselves politically in a common effort to overthrow bourgeois rule everywhere. The basis for the unity or internationalism of the world's proletariat lay in the development of capitalist internationalism. Marx saw the world becoming increasingly unified as a result of the expansion of capitalism. The spread of capitalist methods of production led to the growth of a world market and the expansion of trade between peoples who had hitherto had little contact with each other. Thus, the national principle that divided mankind was supplanted by the class principle, which united it.

It is interesting to contrast the politics of Marx and Engels with the principles identified with them. Notwithstanding their disparagement of nationalism and national loyalty in the abstract, both Marx and Engels were passionate nationalists for the German cause. They not only supported Bismarck's wars to unify Germany but argued the cause for a greater Germany that would have included not only Austria but much of the Slavic territories ruled by the Hapsburgs.[8] Unlike Lenin, who was a defeatist for his own country (in 1905 and 1914), Marx and Engels consistently defended the nationalistic position of Germany against all its enemies.

Another contradiction between the abstract principles of socialism and Marx's own politics concerned the issue of war. "Peace is the first and indispensable condition of any emancipation of the working class," declared the founding Congress of the Socialist International in 1889. Though made not by Marx but his epigones, this phrase has become one of the fundamental credos of

Communist doctrine. It was certainly not Marx's credo as editor of *Die Neue Rhenische Zeitung* in the 1840s. One of its central themes was war with Russia as a way to unify and revolutionize Germany. Bismarck's wars with Denmark in 1864, with Austria in 1866, and with France in 1870 were with qualifications endorsed by Marx and Engels. After German unification, however, Marx became less and less sanguine about war as an engine of progress. Toward the end of his life, like Bismarck, Marx became apprehensive about Germany's fate in a two-front war with Russia and France. He came increasingly to believe that socialism, democracy, and European civilization would be served better by peace than by war.

In the period between the passing of Marx and Engels and the coming into being of the first socialist state, the principal vehicle of Socialist thought and action was the Second International, a loose organization of autonomous national socialist parties. The specter of a European war became sharper with the passing of each decade, making the issue of war and militarism the central problem confronting the International. At stake in the bitter debates attending its congresses, notably those of Stuttgart (1907) and Copenhagen (1910 and 1915), was the validity of Marx's assumption that the working classes of all countries had a common interest that would be reflected in a unified program. The question faced by Europe's socialists was what was the obligation of the workers parties in case of war? The answers given revealed that Marx's belief in the unity of the proletariat was more a matter of hope than fact.

Roughly three positions developed among the component parties of the International. On the right were the leaders of Europe's largest socialist parties who asserted the obligation of each party to support its own country's war effort. They were prepared to defend the state, even a capitalist state, in the belief that working-class pressure would reform it. In the center were such leaders as the German Marxist, Karl Kautsky, who stoutly maintained an opposition to the war policies of the capitalistic states, refusing to vote money for military expenditures or for conscription. Unlike the left, however, they were not prepared to support a general strike in order to bring down the government. The most radical position was that of the left.[9] Categorically rejecting war and capitalism, they urged the proletariat to convert a general war into a civil war in order to bring down the capitalist state. Their principal tactic was the general strike. This was the position of Lenin, but it was not the position of the leading parties in the International nor was it the course taken by Europe's workers in 1914. When the war broke out, the pull of national sentiments shattered what remained of the myth of proletarian unity.

LENIN'S THEORY OF IMPERIALISM

For Lenin, World War I posed the problem of making Marxist theory relevant to the 20th century. The failure of Europe's social-democratic parties to act in harmony was only one of several discrepancies between Marx's prognosis and the actual trend of events in Europe. By the turn of the century it had already become apparent that the industrialized nations of the world were not experiencing the revolutionary crises that were expected to follow from Marx's famous "Law of Increasing Misery." The workers, instead of becoming more impoverished and desperate under capitalism, were in fact steadily improving their economic position under bourgeois democratic rule. They were not developing the revolutionary class consciousness anticipated by Marx and Engels. Lenin overcame this theoretical dilemma in 1902 with his pamphlet *What Is To Be Done?* in which he argued that without a revolutionary party constituting the vanguard of the proletariat, the working class would succumb to "trade union consciousness," i.e., it would accept bread and butter gains through unionization rather than pursue its historic mission of revolution. Marx never made a political party the prerequisite for revolution, but Lenin did. In so doing, he was adjusting the theory to fit the facts and at the same time providing a tactical and strategic base for his own ambitions.

Lenin's answer to the socialist crisis of World War I was the pamphlet, *Imperialism, the Highest Stage of Capitalism.* Written in Switzerland in the spring of 1916, it was published in Russia about a year later. The central ideas of this work can be summed up as follows: (1) capitalism in its advanced stages becomes highly monopolistic, permitting banks and financial institutions to acquire huge surpluses of capital; (2) in order to maximize profits this capital is exported to backward countries where capital is scarce and land, raw materials, and labor are cheap; (3) eventually the great capitalist powers divide up the world into colonies where each power is able to exercise exclusive control; and (4) the imperialistic dynamics for expansion ultimately bring the capitalist powers into conflict which brings on war.[10]

By demonstrating that the world war was an imperialistic war on the part of both sides, Lenin was able to establish a theoretical basis for his insistent antiwar position and revolutionary defeatism. In so doing, he added the first cogent theory of international relations to the core of Marxist doctrine. It was, however, an incomplete theory at best—or what today might be called middle-range theory—for it only explains the behavior of one type of state, the advanced capitalistic state, and no other. This theory did not consider the problem of relations between one or more socialist states and capitalist states; nor did it touch on the nature of interstate relations in a world of socialist states. Another of its weaknesses as a theory of international relations was its failure to analyze different kinds of wars conducted by different types of states such as feudal, monarchial, or early capitalist. Not theory but revolution and how to construct the tactical bases for bringing it about were Lenin's principal concerns. The concept of imperialism served a number of functions, some intellectual and some tactical. For one thing, the theory of imperialism explained why revolution had not yet taken place in the advanced capitalist countries. The profits accumulated as a result of colonialism were so substantial that the capitalists were able to distribute a portion of them to the working-class leaders in the home country and thus buy off or bribe enough of the working class to stave off the revolution. In other words, imperialism softened the contradictions of capitalism.

Without formally altering the Marxist model of revolution, Lenin made it at once global and pertinent to the 20th century. Where Marx stressed the clash of classes within industrial societies, Lenin emphasized the conflict between capitalist states. Imperialism provided the means by which the revolutionary cause became not simply a series of disconnected national movements but a global struggle whose ramifications affected the vast majority of nations the world over. In this new paradigm, the main protagonists were no longer classes but states: the powerful industrial nations against the weak backward nations. What Lenin called the backward nations of the world became the 20th-century analog of the 19th-century working class.

We need to be careful to avoid overstatement. Lenin nowhere denied the continuation of the class struggle within societies. He simply enlarged the arena of the battle to include conflicts between nations. Thus, at his suggestion, the Second Congress of the Communist International expanded Marx's best known slogan, "Proletarians of all countries, unite," to read "Proletarians of all countries and oppressed nations, unite!"[11]

The revolutionary implications of this theory were profound. It offered a way out of the constricting formula demanded by orthodox Marxism—namely that the socialist revolution would first take place in advanced capitalist societies and that it would follow a period of bourgeois democratic rule. It offered a rationale for revolutionary movements to take place independently in the underdeveloped, exploited societies of the world. Under imperialism the world became a cohesive, interrelated system with the potential for revolutions in any of its parts. Exactly where revolution would break out would depend upon the total world situation. Using the metaphor of a chain to describe imperialism, Leninists came to identify the area with the greatest potential for revolution as the weakest link in the chain. In 1917, Russia was to be that weak link.

There are many ironies in the fact that the first Marxist revolution took place in Russia, not the least of which is that neither of the two architects of scientific socialism imagined in their wildest dreams that socialism would establish its first roots in the land of Czarist reaction. As we have noted, Marx and Engels looked upon Russia as the most backward nation on the continent and fervently anticipated its defeat in a future war with Germany. Now, virtually overnight, Lenin transformed the Russian people from wielders of the bayonets of reaction to the chosen people whose historical mission would be to lead all mankind along the path of progress.

In time Russia itself would become the surrogate of the working class. Lenin was able to reconcile this shift in the historical position of Germany and Russia with the writings of Marx and Engels because he made imperialism an entirely new epoch different from anything that had existed in past history. Presumably, this is why Lenin insisted on dating the birth of imperialism at 1900 and not earlier. Any date prior to the death of Engels (in 1895) would have been difficult to reconcile with some of the writings of his mentors.[12] If, in exalting Russia to a central place in history, Lenin was guilty of subconscious chauvinism, he did no less than Marx had done in elevating Germany's proletariat as history's foremost carrier of progressive consciousness. The theory of imperialism did more than justify the Bolshevik revolution. Perhaps its most important accomplishment was its reconciliation (and in some cases fusion) of socialism with the most dynamic political trend of the 20th century: nationalism. Although the Soviet regime today no more constitutes a model for the developing countries of Asia and Africa than for the democratic labor movements of the West, the Leninist doctrine of imperialism does continue to find widespread acceptance in what is now called the Third World. This can be explained in part by the fact that imperialism elevates the lowly to a special place in history. Modifying an old principle of Marxism, it asserts that the exploited of this world become the carriers of progressive consciousness. It helps to account for poverty, ignorance, and disease in the Third World while proclaiming the moral superiority of the downtrodden masses.

Antiimperialism has an added appeal to the nationalism born of the disintegration of Western colonialism; it fuses the pro-Western orientations of Marxist thought with the anti-Western orientation of Leninist thought. There is an ambivalence in imperialism toward the West that strikes a very responsive chord among the leaders of the newly emerged countries in the post–World War II period. The contemporary nationalisms of the Third World are torn by their desire to emulate the West, a desire that reflects the condition they aspire to reach and their hatred of the West for what they believe to be its responsibility for the condition in which they find themselves. Alfred G. Meyer, in his analysis of Leninism, offers an illuminating explanation of why the theory of imperialism has found such a ready audience among the proponents of modern nationalism:

Marxism is a product of the industrial age, and all its ideas about society arise from an acceptance of the machine as the most basic fact of modern life. At the same time, it is radically critical of the social institutions and relationships of the industrial age. Transformed into the theory of imperialism, this ambivalence toward industrial capitalism turns into an ambivalence toward the West, and this mixture of hostility and admiration develops naturally among politically conscious men in underdeveloped areas. In espousing Leninism, such men can advocate a program of westernization without abandoning their hatred and fear

The doctrine of Socialism in One Country did not directly address itself to the question of whether the USSR could remain at peace with its capitalist neighbors. Its orientation was largely domestic, to give guidance to the Russian people. By implication, however, Socialism in One country abandoned the notion of a revolutionary war, a war that would have been initiated by Russia's proletariat to assist its comrades in Europe to overthrow capitalism. In this sense, it constitutes a softening of the ideological warfare between the two worlds.

Stalin, nevertheless, never totally abandoned the notion of an inevitable conflict between the Soviet Union and capitalism. During the 1920s and 1930s he developed two additional concepts as corollaries to Socialism in One Country. They were the theories of the "Two Camps" and "Capitalist Encirclement." According to the Two Camp analogy, the world had become polarized around two hostile camps with neither camp in a position to destroy the other. Objective historical conditions required both camps to endure the existence of the other. Stalin reported to the Fourteenth Party Congress in 1925 that:

The fundamental and new, the decisive feature, which has affected all the events in the sphere of foreign relations during this period, is the fact that a certain temporary equilibrium of forces has been established between our country . . . and the countries of the capitalist world: an equilibrium which has determined the present period of "peaceful coexistence."[21]

This coexistence could not be permanent, however. As Stalin reminded his colleagues at the next Party Congress, even if "we succeed in delaying the war with the capitalist countries," it is nonetheless "inevitable."[22] War was inevitable, but not imminent. In the meantime, Soviet weakness mandated that the Soviet Union maneuver carefully in the world of international diplomacy so as to avoid provoking a showdown with the capitalist powers.

What Stalin was advocating in more conventional language was a careful adherence on the part of the Soviets to the rules of the balance-of-power game. "The whole purpose of the existence of the People's Commissariat of Foreign Affairs," Stalin warned, "is to take account of these contradictions [in the non-Soviet world], to base ourselves upon them, and to maneuver among these contradictions."[23] One powerful factor that he perceived working to the Soviet advantage was the sharp divisions within the capitalist world, particularly between the victors and the vanquished of the recent world war. But Stalin, never one to rely on external circumstances for survival, also stressed the need for his country to build up its industrial-military might.

The idea of capitalist encirclement was a complement to the two-camp/inevitable war theme. It provided a justification for Stalin's harsh rule at home and aggressive posture abroad. While Stalin had proclaimed the possibility of

of the West. Their very advocacy of westernization is a proclamation of rebellion; just because they are afraid of the West they must westernize, so as to be able to proclaim their independence.[13]

Lenin himself became increasingly anti-Western in his outlook. Toward the end of his life he expressed a conviction that the victory of socialism would follow a great confrontation between "the counterrevolutionary imperialist West and the revolutionary and nationalist East," a confrontation in which the Soviet Union would be joined with China and India against Europe and the United States.[14]

SOCIALISM, WAR, AND CAPITALIST ENCIRCLEMENT

The establishment of the World's first socialist state in November, 1917 created an entirely new problem for the theorists of socialism. What was to be the nature of the relations between the only socialist and the many capitalist states of the world? (Some three decades later, that problem would be broadened to include the question of the relationship between the first socialist state and other socialist states.) At the heart of the problem was the issue of peace or war between socialism and capitalism, or more specifically, between the Soviet State and the leading capitalistic states of the day. One of the more controversial tenets of the theory of imperialism is that of the "inevitability of war." Lenin asserted that as long as capitalism existed, wars were inevitable, but it is important to remember that he was referring to wars *between capitalist powers,* not wars between capitalist and socialist states.

There is another theory of the inevitability of war not associated with the theory of imperialism: the theory of war between socialism and capitalism. There are two basic questions involved with this theory: (1) is war inevitable between the Soviet Union and one or more capitalist states, and (2) if war breaks out, who will initiate it? Even before he wrote his *Imperialism,* Lenin had proposed a program of "revolutionary war." He predicted the possibility of a socialist revolution in one country followed by the victorious proletariat of that country rising "up against the rest of the capitalist world, attracting to itself the oppressed classes of other countries, provoking among them a revolt against the capitalists, appearing if necessary with armed force against the exploiting classes and their states."[15] It is clear in this scenario that the initiative for war would come from the socialist side.

After coming to power, Lenin made infrequent reference to the idea of a "revolutionary war," but he remained convinced that a clash between the two social systems was inevitable. His statements on the coming conflict with the West, however, did not always indicate who would initiate the struggle or why.

"International Imperialism," he stated in a secret report to the Party's Seventh Congress, "could not under any circumstances, on any condition, live side by side with the Soviet Republic. . . . History suggests that peace is a respite for another war."[16] Reporting to the Eighth Party Congress in 1919, Lenin made his most famous statement on the inevitability of war:

We are living not merely in a state but in a system of states and the existence of the Soviet Republic side by side with imperialist states for a long time in unthinkable. One or the other must triumph in the end. And before that end supervenes, a series of frightful collisions between the Soviet Republic and the bourgeois states will be inevitable. That means that if the ruling class, the proletariat, wants to hold sway it must prove its capacity to do so by its military organization.[17]

Note the unclarity regarding who would attack whom first. Lenin never developed this version of the "inevitability of war" into a comprehensive doctrine as he did in *Imperialism* with the inevitability of war between capitalist states. His statements on war and peace changed as the perspectives and needs of the Soviet state changed. That he considered a military clash with the West likely at some time in the future seems abundantly clear, but his ideas were vague as to the duration of the period of peace and whether, when war did come, it would be initiated by the proletarian state as a revolutionary war or by the enemy as a counterrevolutionary attack on the Soviet state.

What we tend to think of today as Communist doctrine regarding war and peace between socialism and capitalism is largely a collection of propagandistic and programmatic statements made by Soviet leaders to serve the current needs of Soviet foreign policy. With the shifts in Soviet foreign policy objectives or changes in the international environment came modifications in the emphasis between the prospects for war or peace. Toward the end of his rule, as he became increasingly preoccupied with consolidating power and building a stable society, Lenin came to foresee a long period of peace between Soviet Russia and the West, giving rise to the notion of peaceful coexistence.[18]

Even more than Lenin, Stalin had to come to grips with a solitary socialist state accommodating itself to a world dominated by capitalist powers. Stalin was not a theorist but he felt obliged to explain and justify the policies of his government in doctrinal terms. These policies varied from defensive to aggressive, from isolationist to interventionist, from alliance with and then alliance against European fascism so that, not surprisingly, the emphasis of his doctrinal statements changed at different times. The underlying question that permeated all of his foreign policy analyses was simply this: What are the prospects of war between the Soviet Union and the leading capitalist states?

There were generally two possible answers to that question: (1) that war was inevitable, likely, or imminent, or (2) that war could be avoided. Stalin varied

his answers to this question according to circumstances. By circumstances, we mean more than just his judgment of what the objective possibilities were. For Stalin, as for Lenin, doctrine had an important instrumental function: he used the theory to achieve specific political objectives, sometimes internally as in his power struggles, and sometimes in the realm of foreign policy. Thus, for example, the doctrine of "Socialism in One Country" was a very useful polemical weapon in the struggle for power with Trotsky, Zinoviev, and Kamenev.

Socialism in One Country emerged as Stalin's major theoretical contribution to the post-Lenin debate on the relationship between the new Soviet state and the noncommunist world. As with most of Stalin's theoretical pronouncements, this concept was neither completely original with him nor a fully developed theoretical position. It addressed itself largely to one fundamental question: Could socialism be constructed in one country (the USSR) before revolution broke out in the advanced industrial countries of Europe? In the following formulation, Stalin argued that it could be:

Formerly, the victory of the revolution in one country was considered impossible on the assumption that it would require the combined action of the proletarians of all or at least of a majority of the advanced countries to achieve victory over the bourgeoisie. Now this point of view no longer fits with the facts. Now we must proceed from the possibility of such a victory, for the uneven and spasmodic character of the development of the various capitalist countries under the conditions of imperialism, the development, within imperialism, of catastrophic contradictions leading to inevitable wars, the growth of the revolutionary movement in all countries of the world—all this leads, not only to the possibility but also to the necessity of the victory of the proletariat in individual countries.[19]

Stalin juxtaposed his idea of Socialism in One Country against Trotsky's theory of Permanent Revolution. Trotsky had argued, inter alia, that the bourgeois-democratic and socialist revolutions could be made at the same time in Russia (as happened in 1917) but that Russia itself could not build a complete socialist society on its own. That would have to await the spread of revolution to industrialized Europe. Trotsky based his argument upon the traditional Marxist premise of the unity of the world economy—a unity that was more than the sum of many national parts. By 1923, just before Stalin enunciated his doctrine, revolutionary ferment in Europe had already subsided, and it had become apparent that in the foreseeable future Russia would have to go it alone. Stalin's position proved more politically efficacious than Trotsky's. It offered the Russians the hope that a new society could be built independently of what happened abroad. And it promised the people a respite from involvement in further revolution or war. Trotsky seemed to be arguing for more and more revolution before the hope of a real socialist society could be realized.[20]

building a socialist society in Russia, he denied that it would ever be fully secure as long as capitalism was rampant in the world. "To win a final victory," he declared, "it is necessary for the present capitalist encirclement to be replaced by a socialist encirclement."[24] When Stalin introduced a new constitution in 1936, he needed an ideological explanation for the inconsistency between the Marxist principle that under socialism the state withers away and the obvious fact that the Soviet state was becoming more, not less, powerful. In 1939, at the Eighteenth Party Congress, he asked rhetorically: "Is it not time we relegated the state to the museum of antiquities?" To which he answered that those who would ask such a question "do not understand present day international conditions, have overlooked the capitalist encirclement and the dangers it entails for the socialist country."[25]

During his quarter-century guidance over Soviet foreign policy, Stalin alternatively stressed the ideas of peaceful coexistence and the inevitability of war. In the late 1920s, he moved toward militancy, as illustrated by the hard line that he had the Comintern take toward the West at its Sixth Congress in 1928. Somewhat ironically, in the period prior to 1933 when the real threat to Soviet security was minimal, Stalin publically stressed the theme of the inevitability of counterrevolutionary war. But after Hitler came to power in 1933 and presented the Soviets with a really serious threat, Stalin switched his public pronouncements to the theme of the avoidability of war. This change was most dramatic at the Comintern's Seventh World Congress in 1935 when the strategy of the "united front against fascism and war" was promulgated. The reason for Stalin's new line was obvious: he desperately sought a system of collective security against the threat of German and possibly Japanese aggression and he needed to create an ideological position rationalizing a coalition with the Western democracies. The late 1930s required a policy of peace and coexistence.

Without being unduly arbitrary, one can divide Stalin's administration into two parts, the dividing point being the period just before the outbreak of war in Europe. During the first half of his rule, Stalin was preoccupied with internal problems dominated by the issues of the succession struggle and economic reconstruction in the 1920s and industrialization, collectivization, and the purges in the 1930s. From the onset of war in Europe until his death, Stalin was compelled to give his primary attention to foreign policy issues. It is somewhat ironic that Stalin's contributions to foreign policy theory, such as they are, were made in the earlier period instead of the later period when foreign policy was more important.

As World War II approached, Stalin carefully avoided dogmatic assertions about the inevitability of war, either of the imperialist (i.e., intercapitalist) or capitalist-socialist variety. In the period leading up to the Nazi-Soviet pact, it would have been counterproductive to stress Lenin's theory of the inevitability of intercapitalist wars because that theory makes no distinction between "good" or "bad" capitalist nations; they are all "imperialist bandits" and Stalin desperately needed an alliance with one or the other capitalist side in the impending conflict. Stalin's approach was cautious: "We stand for peace and the strengthening of business relations with all countries."[26] His decision to align with Nazi Germany in August 1939 was made on political and military, not ideological, grounds. The fact that the Soviet Union fought the war as an ally of the Western democracies against the European Axis powers was determined by Hitler's unwise military calculations. It was not a coalition desired by Stalin, who would have preferred being Hitler's ally, or even preferably, remaining neutral. From the moment of the German invasion of the Soviet Union, the war was described in Soviet propaganda as an "anti-Fascist" war rather than an "imperialist" conflict, as the first world war had been described. Obviously the Soviets could not put themselves in the position of abetting one group of "imperalist robbers" against another.

As the cold war emerged in the aftermath of the second World War, it was not necessary for Stalin to develop any new concepts to describe the changing relationship between the Soviet Union and its former allies. He had only to revive the old "two-camps" thesis with its message about the danger of a capitalistic attack against the Soviet Union. Andrei Zhdanov's speech at the founding conference of the Communist Information Bureau (Cominform) in September 1947 heralded a new militant phase in Soviet policy toward the West. He accused the United States of seeking world supremacy, of plotting to "hatch a new imperialist war." These accusations notwithstanding, Zhdanov continued to reaffirm the possibility of peaceful coexistence between the two systems "provided that the principle of reciprocity is observed."[27] In other words, in a typical fashion, the Soviet line incorporated two essentially contradictory messages, stressing one theme—in this case militancy—while simultaneously holding an opposing theme in reserve.

Only toward the end of his life did Stalin abandon the "leftist" hard-line characteristic of the cold war and move toward a more accommodating position with the capitalist West. This he did in his theoretical papers, *Economic Problems of Socialism in the U.S.S.R.*, written for the Nineteenth Party Congress in 1952. It was his last theoretical work and was less significant for the novelty of its argument than for the political implications of the line it sought to establish. The main thrust of his argument was the revitalization of the classic Leninist thesis that wars between capitalist states continued to be inevitable. "To eliminate the inevitability of war," he wrote, "it is necessary to abolish imperialism."[28] But what about war between the United States and the Soviet Union? This Stalin downplayed. He admitted that "theoretically" the "contradictions" between capitalism and socialism were greater than those between capitalist nations, but they were not so in fact, because "the struggle of the capitalist countries for markets and their desire to crush their competitors proved in practice to be stronger than the contradictions between the capitalist camp and the socialist camp."[29] His failure to clarify the difference between theory and practice among all these contradictions makes this work a poor piece of theoretical analysis, but the political import of his message was clear: The Soviet Union was prepared to take steps to avoid a general war with the United States. Stalin referred to the Peace Movement as an important vehicle for the preservation of peace, and to assure the capitalist world, he emphasized that the object of the Peace Movement was not to overthrow capitalism (as was the peace movement during World War I), but solely to prevent a particular war. Though not explicit, this last work of Stalin constitutes an implicit repudiation of his theory of capitalist encirclement. Along with the agreement to negotiate a truce in Korea, this article was a major step in the transformation of the cold war.[30]

Although not a theorist, Stalin was the chief ideologist among the Soviet Union's ruling leadership. His speeches and writings constituted a formal exegesis of Marxist-Leninist doctrine. None of his successors has attempted to exercise the same function. Ideological exegesis, rationalization, and explanation continue to play an important part in legitimizing Soviet authority and action but since Stalin, that function has been relegated to professional specialists in ideological matters within the ruling elite.

KHRUSHCHEV AND PEACEFUL COEXISTENCE

Khrushchev was neither the theoretician that Lenin was nor could he compare as an ideologist with Stalin. Nevertheless, his pronouncements on foreign policy significantly modified the content of Communist foreign policy doctrine. His major contribution was the theory of "peaceful coexistence" which he first elaborated in his report to the Twentieth Congress of the Soviet Communist Party on February 14, 1956. The general purpose of this new line seems abundantly clear. Recognizing the danger of a nuclear war with the United States, Khrushchev needed to establish an ideological basis for the existence of a long-term relationship between communism and capitalism that would not lead to war. Nikita Khrushchev, like his predecessor, Georgi Malenkov, recognized that nuclear weapons had fundamentally altered the character of international politics. Although the atomic bomb came into existence while he was in power, Stalin refused to see that it affected the character of the class struggle or the role of war in the relations between nations. War, Stalin insisted until his end, was governed by what he called "permanently operating factors" that included leadership, morale, good weapons, and a quantity of trained soldiers.[31] He would not acknowledge that nuclear weapons made possible the total destruction of an adversary in a surprise attack. It fell to Khrushchev to integrate the consequences of the changing technology of warfare into a new theoretical framework, just as it had fallen to Stalin thirty years earlier to explain in doctrinal terms the relationship between the new socialist state and its capitalist environment.

Nuclear weapons and missiles to deliver them had made the idea of the inevitability of war obsolete. It was clearly in the best interest of the Soviet Union to avoid a war with a nuclear-armed United States. Georgi Melenkov, Stalin's immediate successor, admitted as much in 1954 when he stated that a nuclear war could result in the "mutual destruction" of both communist and capitalist societies. Khrushchev initially criticized Malenkov's thesis, but as he himself moved toward the center of power he came around to essentially the same position. By the mid-20th century, Lenin's strictures on the inevitability of war and the role of war as a midwife of revolution had become a doctrinal liability that Khrushchev was not above jettisoning.

Khrushchev's report to the Twentieth Party Congress contained essentially two important modifications of communist doctrine: (1) a rejection of the thesis of the inevitability of war, and (2) the assertion that communism could be achieved by parliamentary or peaceful means. On the first point he stated as follows:

There is, of course, a Marxist-Leninist precept that wars are inevitable as long as imperialism exists. This precept was evolved at a time when (1) imperialism was an all-embracing world system, and (2) the social and political forces which did not want war were weak, poorly organized, and hence unable to compel the imperialist to renounce war.

People usually take only one aspect of the question and examine only the economic basis of wars under imperialism. This is not enough. War is not only an economic phenomenon. Whether there is to be war or not depends in large measure on the correlation of class, political forces, the degree of organization and the awareness and determination of the people. Moreover, in certain conditions the struggle waged by progressive social and political forces may play a decisive role. Hitherto the state of affairs was such that the forces that did not want war and opposed it were poorly organized and lacked the means to check the schemes of the war-makers. Thus it was before the First World War, when the main force opposed to the threat of war—the world proletariat—was disorganized by the treachery of the leaders of the Second International. Thus it was on the eve of the Second World War, when the Soviet Union was the only country that pursued an active peace policy, when the other great powers to all intents and purposes encouraged the aggressors, and the right-wing Social-Democratic leaders had split the labour movement in the capitalist countries.

In that period this precept was absolutely correct. At the present time, however, the situation has changed radically. Now there is a world camp of socialism, which has become a mighty force. In this camp the peace forces find not only the moral, but also the material means to prevent aggression. Moreover, there is a large group of other countries with a population running into many hundreds of millions which are actively working to avert war. The labour movement in the capitalist countries has today become a tremendous force. The movement of peace supporters has sprung up and developed into a powerful factor.

In these circumstances certainly the Leninist precept that so long as imperialism exists, the economic basis giving rise to wars will also be preserved, remains in force. That is why we must display the greatest vigilance. As long as capitalism survives in the world, the reactionary forces representing the interests of the capitalist monopolies will continue their drive towards military gambles and aggression, and may try to unleash war. But war is not fatalistically inevitable . . . .[32]

Khrushchev carefully refrained from making a distinction between intercapitalist wars and wars between capitalism and socialism but the message was clear that he meant both to be avoidable. The reference to World War I obviously alluded to the Leninist formulation of the theory of imperialism.[33] In one fell swoop, Khrushchev abandoned Stalin's theory of capitalist encirclement and the two-camp theory as well as both varieties of the theory of the inevitability of war. Admittedly, in the past utterances of Lenin, Stalin, and the Comintern, one could find statements that were precursors of Khrushchev's peaceful coexistence, but none that so comprehensively and systematically charged a new line.[34] Khrushchev was not responding to a change in the balance of power or some temporary external threat; he was charting a broad shift in communist thinking in response to a fundamental change in the technology of war.

Khrushchev's thesis on peaceful coexistence was good politics but weak theory. Beyond a vague and simplistic identification of war with imperialism (i.e., capitalism), Khrushchev offered no explanation of what the causes of war might be. "War is not only an economic phenomenon," he insisted, but he failed to clarify the relationship between economic and other factors. Presumably economic factors cause war while political factors prevent them. This interpretation would be consistent with his agreement with Lenin that so long as "imperialism" exists, "the economic basis giving rise to wars will also be preserved." But what of the possibility that a socialist state might initiate war? He asks rhetorically, "Is there a single reason why a socialist state should want to unleash aggressive war?" He answers in the negative. The Soviet Union has no classes or groups interested in war as a means of enrichment. It does not lack for territory, natural wealth, raw materials, or markets. Essentially his argument boils down to a situation of asymmetrical deterrence: capitalism threatens the peace but the power of the socialist camp will stop it from going to war. "Today there are mighty social and political forces possessing formidable means to prevent the imperialists from unleasing war."[35] Note that this theory of deterrence is not a balance one. Khrushchev does not suggest that peace might be kept by a mutual deterrent. He apparently rejects the scenario of a capitalist deterrent that would frustrate the aggressive inclinations of a socialist power. Nor does he contemplate a socialist deterrent force that might be directed against another socialist state. Though the Sino-Soviet rupture occurred during his administration, Khrushchev never formulated a theoretical justification for the military defense of one socialist state against another.

A corollary to the theory of peaceful coexistence between the two systems was the Khrushchev assertion that a communist revolution can be brought about by peaceful means. In his report to the Twentieth Party Congress he noted that "In connection with the radical changes in the world arena new prospects are also opening up as regards the transition of countries and nations to socialism.... Our enemies like to depict us Leninists as advocates of violence always and every-where . . . [but] It is not true that we regard violence and civil war as the only way to remake society." Khrushchev then raised the question of whether socialism could be achieved by parliamentary means and answered it as follows:

the present situation offers the working class in a number of capitalist countries a real opportunity to unite the overwhelming majority of the people under its leadership and to secure the transfer of the basic means of production into the hands of the people. The right-wing bourgeois parties and their governments are suffering bankruptcy with increasing frequency. In these circumstances the working class, by rallying around itself the working peasantry, the intelligentsia, all patriotic forces, and resolutely repulsing the opportunist elements who are incapable of giving up the policy of compromise with the capitalists and land-lords, is in a position to defeat the reactionary forces opposed to the interests of the people, to capture a stable majority in parliament, and transform the latter from an organ of bourgeois democracy into a genuine instrument of the people's will.[36]

This too was a clear repudiation of Lenin, if not explicitly, certainly by implication. Lenin had always looked upon war as a legitimate midwife of revolution. While never a prerequisite for social change, war hastened the revolutionary process. The first World War ostensibly justified this assumption for Lenin as did the second World War for Stalin. Now Khrushchev was arguing that communism could expand without war. He wanted to avoid the pitfall of anticipating either Armageddon or a stalemate in the class struggle.

Peaceful coexistence clearly did not mean a peaceful reconciliation of the two systems. The class struggle would go on but it need not necessarily take the form of a violent confrontation. (According to Khrushchev, whether it did or not was up to the capitalists.) In an article for the readers of *Foreign Affairs*, Khrushchev described the struggle between the two systems in its most benign form: "Peaceful coexistence can and should develop into peaceful competition for the purpose of satisfying man's needs in the best possible way."[37] In other words, whichever system could best meet the material and spiritual needs of the masses would win their hearts and minds. At the same time the Soviet leaders made it clear that there would be no relaxation in the struggle against bourgeois ideology and the remnants of capitalism in the people's minds.

The class struggle would continue but not in the form of war between states. A distinction is made between relations between states and relations between classes. Peaceful coexistence applies to the former but not the latter. Among the categories of conflict which fall under the heading of class relations are the so-called "wars of national liberation." These would continue, as would the obligation of the Soviet Union to support them. Khrushchev and his successors have attempted to reconcile peaceful coexistence (later to become "detente") with Soviet support of anti-Western political parties and revolutionary insurgencies on the grounds that each of these spheres of political relations is governed by a different set of laws.

One of the consequences of Khrushchev's revisionism was an ideological split between the Soviets and the Chinese. For a few years the Chinese appeared to go along with much of Khrushchev's formulations on peaceful coexistence. As late as November 1957, Mao Zedong was willing to endorse the thesis that war was not inevitable. But for reasons that are explored below, in the late 1950s, the Chinese and Russians began to diverge in their foreign policies and part of that divergence involved ideological differences over the nature of communist-capitalist relations and the role of force in promoting revolution.

Until the Chinese leaders came to view the Soviet Union as a threat equal to if not greater than the United States, their principal grievance against the Russians was a charge of timidity in the face of Western imperialism.[38] Khrushchev was accused of overestimating Western power and "nuclear fetishism." Chinese objections to peaceful coexistence were tactical, not strategic. They were afraid that Soviet timidity and caution would impede the world revolutionary movement. Ironically, Chinese willingness to take risks stemmed from the same condition that led the Soviets to be cautious: the growth of Soviet nuclear power. But where Khrushchev saw Soviet nuclear power as a guarantee of world peace, the Chinese saw it as the means for advancing world communism.

The doctrinal differences between the two powers were not originally sharp. The Chinese did not formally reject Khrushchev's thesis that war was avoidable. They simply insisted that as long as imperialism of any kind existed, wars of one kind or another would continue. At issue was the question of what kind of wars were likely or possible. Both sides ruled out world wars and both were in agreement that wars of national liberation would continue until imperialism disappeared. Where they differed was on the issue of local wars between states. Khrushchev recognized that local wars could escalate into a nuclear confrontation between the superpowers so they were to be avoided if at all possible. To the Chinese local wars were an important part of the revolutionary process and had to be accepted as a part of the international landscape while imperialism survived.

Another major issue between the communist giants is the role of war and violence in bringing about the transition from capitalism to socialism. Khrushchev modified Lenin at the Twentieth and Twenty-First Party Congresses by abandoning the connection between war and revolution. The Chinese have insisted that communism cannot achieve a global victory without violence of some sort. There are ample citations from Lenin to back them up, such as the dictum quoted in the document "Long Live Leninism" published on the occasion of the 90th anniversary of Lenin's birth: "Not a single great revolution in history has ever been carried out without a civil war and no serious Marxist will believe it possible to make the transition from capitalism to socialism without a civil war." Khrushchev responded to this use of Lenin by saying that "one cannot mechanically repeat now on this question what Vladimir Illyich Lenin said many decades ago on imperialism."[39]

As the conflict between the Soviet Union and China deepened, the Chinese developed a new concept—"hegemony"—to describe the behavior of the two superpowers. Hegemony, as defined by the Chinese, "means expansion of power politically and economically, and exercise of control."[40] It is a term not clearly defined either in international law or communist doctrine, though the Chinese have argued that the struggle for hegemony could lead to a world war. At the Tenth Congress of the Chinese Communist Party in August 1973, Zhou En-lai charged that "it is mainly the two nuclear superpowers—the U.S. and the U.S.S.R.—that are contending for hegemony."[41] Chinese diplomacy subsequently demonstrated that "anti-hegemonism" was directed primarily against the Soviet Union. The sources of Communist theory today are, thus, not only multiple, they have become antagonistic.

THE OPERATIONAL CODE OF LENINISM

We distinguished earlier between two components of any ideology: beliefs and values. According to our distinction, beliefs are ideas about the real world that are in some measure subject to measurement and verification, and values represent subjective judgments and attitudes, the ingredients that give the doctrine its passion and sense of moral righteousness. The above survey of communist ideology focused on those elements that purported to describe, albeit in broad generalizations, the real behavior of individuals, groups and nations, i.e., the belief component of Marxist-Leninist theory. If nothing else, this survey establishes that communist doctrine is not static. It changes with times and circumstances. Marx changed his own beliefs on many subjects during his life, so that in some areas we can distinguish between the "young Marx" and the "mature Marx." Lenin, though he never admitted it, modified a number of important Marxist concepts, as Stalin did of Lenin and Khrushchev of both Lenin and Stalin. They all changed theories to suit their politics. The basic fact is that the international environment has changed in many important ways during the century since Marx's death and those who have wielded power in his name have simply had to acknowledge the changes. This pliability would suggest that instead of dominating Soviet policymakers, ideology is itself molded to meet the requirements of policy as its leaders see them.

But how do political leaders see the requirements of policy? Quite clearly those who make foreign policy are influenced by many factors: the external environment, threats posed by potential enemies, opportunities that arise unexpectedly, the domestic condition, the political security of those in power, and economic conditions, to name but a few. In this listing we would need to include pyschological factors that influence the policymaker's perceptions. And this brings us back to ideology because ideology colors the vision of the policymaker. Of the two components of ideology—the empirical (factual) and the attitudinal (values)—it is the latter that particularly influences how the communist ideologue looks at the political universe.

There is a complex of attitudes in Marxist-Leninist theory that characterize the communist's view of the political world and his relationship to it. These attitudes are for the most part implicit in the thought of communist theoreticians, though many of the tactical prescriptions that flow from these attitudes are quite explicit, particularly in the writings and speeches of Lenin. They address themselves to such questions as: What is the nature of politics? Are political relations essentially harmonious or conflicting? How should one's opponents be viewed? How bright are the prospects of victory, in the long run and the short run? To what extent is political success the result of chance or unpredictable occurrence? What are the best tactics for achieving victory? The answers that communist leaders have consistently found for these and related questions can be summed up under the heading of the "operational code" of communism.[42] The perspective on international politics that comprises this code has been shared in varying degrees by every Soviet leader from Lenin to Brezhnev.

At the beginning of this chapter we examined the general characteristics of the international system and observed that one of them was the struggle for power. Between the "utopian" view of an essential harmony of interest between nations and the "realist" assumption of a conflict of interest, our description clearly comes closer to the latter. The first thing to note about the communist operational code is that it is fully compatible with the nature of international politics as described here. The communist perspective, however, goes much further than even political realism in rejecting moderating influences in the struggle for power. Leninism in particular is stridently *realpolitik*. It rests upon the fundamental premise that all political activity—domestic as well as international—involves conflict. Indeed Marx and Lenin both viewed politics as a bitter struggle between groups that could ultimately be resolved only by the victory of one side and the defeat of the other. The classical expression of this view is revealed in one of Lenin's most widely quoted phrases, "Who will destroy whom? Communist political literature is characteristically replete with the terminology of military combat to describe the ordinary process of politics. Words like "battle," "struggle," "front," "advance," and "retreat" are common in Party slogans, Central Committee reports, and public statements of Soviet leaders. Lenin was a great admirer of the German military strategist, Karl von Clausewitz, and often cited his famous dictum that "War is the continuation of politics by other means" as a valid insight. "Marxists," he said, "have always rightly regarded this thesis as the theoretical basis of views on the significance of any war."[43] In a world of differing social systems, war and conflict are the normal state of affairs; peace is the exception. The American assumption of international relations, by contrast, has tended to view peace as the normal state of affairs with war the exception.

Fundamental to the Soviet outlook on international politics is its image of the opponent. In communist writings, the enemy is described as thoroughly hostile, shrewd, and determined. George Kennan compared the attitudes of the Soviet regime toward the West with those that would prevail toward an enemy in time of war. "In thirty years experience with Soviet official literature," the former ambassador to the Soviet Union wrote, "I cannot recall an instance of a non Communist government being credited with a single generous or worthy impulse."[44] In traditional Western international relations theory, recognition is given to the fact that between all nations—friends and foes alike—there exists some measure of antagonism. But even among nations at war that antagonism is muted; there is an element of shared common purpose. This idea of a common set of objectives or aspirations is substantially if not totally rejected in communist theory. The enemy is considered evil. The differences between the proletariat and the bourgeosie and the states that embody these class identities is fundamental and irreconcilable. Furthermore, these differences have their roots not in the behavior of the parties involved—after all, behavior patterns can change—but in the essential character or make-up of the enemy.

Consistent with these views is the communist tendency to think in terms of an all or nothing dichotomy. They find it difficult to imagine an intermediary position between total victory and complete defeat. Until they have achieved a global victory for communism, they are faced with the everpresent prospect of being annihilated. Any position between these two extremes can only be viewed as temporary and unstable. Out of this insecurity emerges an aggressive posture. It is difficult for communists to contemplate a condition of security that does not ultimately require the destruction of all opposing political systems. Note, we are referring here not to actual Soviet behavior but to psychological moods. There are many aspects to this tendency to push political ideas to extremes. One, for example, is reflected in the antagonism of the ideology toward compromise. Compromise involves the idea of live and let live. It is based upon the premise of a harmony of interest that, as we noted above, is singularly lacking in Soviet theory. There may well be times when compromise is desirable or necessary but it becomes acceptable only as a tactic toward the achievement of final victory.[45] There can be no permanent agreement based upon compromise, only a temporary arrangement which reflects a transitory stage. Another manifestation of the either/or mentality of communist thinking was Khrushchev's strictures against political neutrality at the United Nations. He could not conceive of a Secretary-General who would be politically impartial between the interests of the Western and Communist worlds. Therefore, Khrushchev sought, unsuccessfully, to replace the Secretary-General with a three man "troika," each representing one of the three worlds into which the political universe was then divided.

Still another element of the "operational code" is the importance in communist thinking of change as a characteristic of political behavior. It is this element that gives Marxist-Leninist ideology much of its dynamism. The Soviet approach sees international affairs in a constant state of flux. Nothing is permanent. A prime responsibility for the Soviet analyst is to understand the particular period or stage in which history is moving. The rules governing one phase do not necessarily apply to another. Again in contrast, Americans tend to look for universal or general rules that can bring permanent peace and stability. To leaders in the West, it is possible to achieve progress under conditions of relative stability. Not so to the Soviets; progress means revolution, which necessitates change.

The doctrine, of course, points toward the direction the change should take—namely, the spread of communism. It is this more than anything else that gives Marxism-Leninism its aggressive character. All Soviet leaders are under an historical obligation to promote the spread of communism. This is their highest value, the principal rationale for the maintenance of Party rule. In theory, if the national interest should conflict with international obligations, it is the former that must give way. But, in fact, the Soviets could not even acknowledge the possibility of conflict between the domestic and foreign objectives of the Party. Though it might appear to outsiders that Soviet diplomacy served the interests of the nation at the expense of the movement, it would be imperative for the communist leadership to justify and explain Soviet action as furthering the worldwide spread of communism. One of the reasons why the Sino-Soviet dispute became so bitter in the 1960s was that the Chinese openly and vigorously accused the Russians of putting the interests of the USSR above those of the communist cause. The accusation obviously struck a very sensitive Soviet nerve.

The mood of communist theory is ambivalent. If the question is posed: What are the prospects for ultimate political victory, one can arrive at two rather contrasting conclusions. In a formal sense, the doctrine is optimistic, following the premise that eventually the entire world will be communist.

Marx and Engels' theory of history and their laws of capitalism in particular foresaw the inexorable progression of events that would culminate in the overthrow of bourgeois rule and the establishment of the dictatorship of the proletariat. While Marxism provides the basis for a philosophic optimism, Leninism, on the other hand, springs from a profound pessimism about the historical process. Lenin's pessimism was fundamental though not overt.[46] Quite clearly Lenin had doubts about the masses and their ability to bring off the revolution. He was aware of the everpresent possibility of failure. His writings warn of the catastrophic dangers that can follow poor theory, poor leadership, or inadequate calculations. Lenin's most basic trait—his insistence that consciousness must control history—stems from a pessimistic assessment of what would happen if one relied on chance or spontaniety. Marx and Engels believed that revolution would spring forth spontaneously when the conditions were right. Lenin was not so sure: thus, his insistence upon a party to lead the proletariat and a trained elite to guide the party.

On balance, because of the special influence of Lenin on all of Russia's leaders, the pessimistic strain of the doctrine has prevailed over the optimistic. From this mood of pessimism has sprung many of the tactical elements of the communist operational code: the emphasis on manipulation, the importance of organization and strategy, a pragmatic flexibility in tactics, and an acceptance of the idea that the ends desired justify any means, however ruthless. All of these traits transferred into Stalinism where they were carried to even greater extremes. Although quite different from Lenin in background and personality, Stalin shared with his mentor the same profound distrust of men and mankind. His policies and the manner of executing them, like those of Lenin, gave primacy to party control and the struggle for power.

The literature of communist doctrine is replete with advice and warnings on tactics and strategy. Alexander George uses the concept of "optimizing strategy" to describe the general approach advanced in communist doctrine for attaining political objectives. By that he means that when communists undertake political initiatives, they seek not one single objective but a set of graduated objectives.[47] It is a strategy that strives for a maximum payoff through the simultaneous achievement of several goals. If the situation reveals that one objective cannot be attained without paying too high a price, the Party can always settle for lesser gains. The important point is to "avoid adventures" and not get caught overextended.

Many of the tactics stressed in the theoretical literature are contradictory (suggesting perhaps the influence of the dialectic). For example, two important tactical maxims are "push to the limit" and "engage in pursuit." It is important to maintain pressure even in the face of bitter resistance, and once the opponent has weakened, perhaps by abandoning demands or offering concessions, it is imperative to keep up the pressure. At the same time, however, these injunctions are coupled with the rule, "know when to stop." Too rapid an advance may create the psychological danger of being carried away and lead to an overextension that could prove costly. During the Cuban missile crisis, President Kennedy turned to specialists on Soviet behavior for advice. One of them, Charles Bohlen, cited one of Lenin's maxims, which utilized the analogy of a bayonet drive: "If you strike steel, pull back; if you strike mush, keep going."[48] Another set of conflicting tactical rules are the admonition to resist an enemy's encroachments from the start, but at all costs to avoid enemy provocations and retreat before superior force. Communist literature warns of the dangers that may follow a failure to resist an opponents encroachments. To do so might encourage the enemy to intensify his attack. But communists must always be wary of falling into the trap of engaging in conflict when the enemy is clearly in a stronger position. Lenin warned of this in 1920 in his classic article on problems of strategy, *Left-Wing Communism—An Infantile Disorder:* "It is folly . . . to deprive ourselves in advance of any freedom of action, openly to inform an enemy who is at present better armed than we are whether we shall fight him and when. To accept battle at a time when it is obviously advantageous to the enemy, but not to us, is criminal."[49]

A central concern that permeates communist tactical thought is the problem of knowing when and how to engage in risky action. Ever sensitive to the perils that surrounds him, beseiged in a hostile global environment, the communist tactician places the highest value on the control of risks. This fear of the outside world, which at times assumes many of the dimensions of paranoia, is not entirely without some basis in the real world. From the beginning, Bolshevik revolutionaries were confronted with powerful adversaries: the Tsarist government before 1917, and the leading capitalist powers after. Yet there can be no politics without risks, in either the domestic or the international worlds. Communist theory advocates the taking of risks, even grave ones, provided the means used in their employ is limited. As long as the means are limited and each step in a progression of steps is controllable, Soviet leaders feel reasonably confident that they can take the necessary gambles required by international politics and still avoid catastrophe, if events turn out to be different from what was anticipated.

DOES IDEOLOGY MATTER?

It is widely agreed that the current group of Soviet leaders is the least ideologically inclined of all those who have exercised power since the revolution. Most of them, including Brezhnev, are pragmatic politicians far removed from the ideologues of Lenin's generation. Of course, they pay lip service to the Marxist-Leninist vision but it is difficult to imagine that the imperatives of communist theory dominate their thinking on foreign policy issues. Policy decisions in the Soviet government have become so routinized within the Party bureaucracy that one is led to suspect that ideology may, if it has not already, become irrelevant to policy formation. Does ideology matter?

Our argument is that it does, but it is difficult to establish a simple and direct connection between ideology and Soviet behavior. One cannot predict, on the basis of anything that Marx or Lenin wrote or said, what the Soviet Union will do in any given instance. From a practical point of view, much of the theory is scholastic ballast of little relevance to the actions of the USSR in the realm of foreign policy.

On the other hand, we cannot go to the opposite extreme and conclude that ideology is totally and always irrelevant to Soviet decisionmaking. There are those who argue that the key to Soviet foreign policy is "the national interest," as it is for all great powers.[50] Soviet expansion since the second World War is viewed as part of a struggle for power in which all great powers indulge. By this reasoning the United States and the Soviet Union would have become involved in a cold war after 1945 regardless of what kind of a regime controlled the Kremlin, simply because both countries were powerful and confronted each other against a relative vacuum of power.

The weakness of the national-interest argument is that it assumes an antagonism between power and ideology—an antagonism that does not in fact exist. Indeed, to a striking degree, there is a compatibility between Marxist-Leninist theory and most theories of international relations including the summary described at the beginning of this chapter. Both place a high degree of reliance upon the factor of power; both recognize the importance of economic influences motivating political behavior; and both look to the political dynamics behind formal legal structures to assess the meaning of state behavior. Admittedly there is much in communist theory that might misinform and misguide the student of international politics—notably its downgrading of nationalism—but the theory can serve equally to alert the dedicated communist to many of the realities of international politics.

There is an interacting, circular relationship between communist ideology and Soviet policy. As observed above, parts of the doctrine—the empirical beliefs—are continually modified to suit the needs of policy, but at the same time the values and attitudes implicit in the theory color the perceptions of Soviet policymakers, influencing the kinds of policies they will pursue. It is impossible to know how much of an impact communist doctrine has had on the hearts and minds of Soviet citizens or their leaders. We know that Soviet citizens are indoctrinated with communist theory from the beginning of the socialization process and bombarded throughout life with Marxist-Leninist symbols and ideas. Every public policy is explained and justified in doctrinal terms, and all of this is done to the exclusion of any competing set of ideas. The Soviet people could not possibly remain unaffected in their sentiments by the lifetime habits of thought and speech.

But what of the ruling oligarchy, those who control the propaganda machinery of the state? They have access to outside sources of information and thus are presumably in a better position to look at the world objectively. The commitment of Soviet leaders to doctrine has unquestionably varied. The commitment with Lenin was greater than it was with Stalin and with Brezhnev less so than with Khrushchev. The trend appears to be toward a declining influence on the leadership of the ideology. Still, even the oligarchs cannot help but be influenced by it in their perceptions of the outside world. It provides a framework or analytical prism through which they observe and interpret events. The doctrine assists them in distinguishing friends from adversaries. Capitalists tend to react as negatively to the symbols of Marxism-Leninism as communists react positively. The ideological conflict between the United States and the Soviet Union may not have been the cause of the cold war but it has certainly impeded the search by both sides for a *modus vivendi*. All things being equal, a communist regime or a Marxist leadership abroad is more likely than not to be supportive of Soviet goals.

Whatever doubts any Soviet leader might have about the validity of any part of the doctrine, he could not voice them publicly; to do so would undermine his own legitimacy. Of the many functions performed by ideology in the Soviet system, none is more critical than that of legitimizing the power of those who rule. Soviet theory provides the rationale for domination of Soviet society by the Communist Party. Those individuals who have acquired control over the Party bureaucracy are obliged to justify their power on the basis that they are correctly applying the principles of Marxism-Lenism to the issues of the day better than their opponents are. Ideology is the most cohesive moral force in Soviet society. Those who acquire power in the Kremlin cannot claim legitimacy on the basis of elections, adherence to constitutional or traditional procedures, or descent through blood lines. Nor are Russia's rulers prepared to hold power strictly by military means. Ultimately political stability requires the institutionalization of some kind of political philosophy acceptable to the popular masses. Without its ideology, the Soviet Union would face anarchy.

NOTES

1. Kenneth N. Waltz, *Man, the State and War* (New York: Columbia University Press, 1965), p. 238.
2. Hans J. Morgenthau. *Politics Among Nations,* 5th ed. (New York: Alfred A. Knopf, 1973), p. 167.

3. For a good analysis of the theory of the balance of power, see Inis L. Claude, Jr., *Power and International Relations* (New York: Random House, 1962), pp. 11–93.

4. See Louis Fischer, *The Soviets in World Affairs,* vols. I and II (Princeton, N.J.: Princeton University Press, 1951), pp. 340–344, 601.

5. For a probing assessment of the Nazi-Soviet Pact, see George F. Kennan, *Russia and the West Under Lenin and Stalin* (New York: Little Brown and Co., 1961), pp. 314–348.

6. Quoted in Vernon Aspaturian, *Power and Process in Soviet Foreign Policy* (New York: Little Brown and Co., 1971), p. 338.

7. Lewis S. Feuer, ed. *Marx and Engels, Basic Writings on Politics and Philosophy* (Garden City, N.J.: Doubleday Anchor Books, 1959), p. 26.

8. On the German patriotism of Marx and Engels, as well as their endorsement of war to achieve national objectives, see Bertram D. Wolfe, *Marxism, 100 Years in the Life of a Doctrine* (New York: Dial Press, 1965), chap. 1-4.

9. The distinction between right, center, and left is taken from Merle Fainsod, *International Socialism and the World War* (Garden City: N.J.: Doubleday Anchor Books, 1969), pp. 26–31. See also Wolfe, *Marxism,* pp. 270–289, and Waltz, *Man, the State and War,* pp. 124–158.

10. For the text of "Imperialism, the Highest Stage of Capitalism," see Robert C. Tucker, ed. *The Lenin Anthology* (New York: W. W. Norton, 1975), pp. 204–274. An excellent summary and analysis is contained in Alfred G. Meyer, *Leninism* (Cambridge: Harvard University Press, 1957), pp. 235–256.

11. See "The Dialectics of Backwardness" in Meyer, *Leninism,* pp. 257–273. Much of the analysis of the significance of Leninism is derived from Meyer's chapter.

12. See Wolfe, *Marxism,* pp. 83–95.

13. See Meyer, *Leninism,* pp. 259ff, 269, and 270ff.

14. "Better Fewer, but Better," *Pravda,* March 4, 1923, reproduced in V. I. Lenin, *Selected Works,* vol. II, part 2 (Moscow: Foreign Languages Publishing House, 1951), p. 750.

15. Quoted in Frederic S. Burin, "The Communist Doctrine of the Inevitability of War," *The American Political Science Review 57,* 2 (June 1963): 337.

16. "Report on War and Peace" in Tucker, *The Lenin Anthology,* pp. 542 and 549.

17. Joseph Stalin, *Problems of Leninism* (Moscow: Foreign Languages Publishing House, 1953), p. 193.

18. See Burin, "The Communist Doctrine," p. 337.

19. Stalin, p. 188. For a discussion of the intricacies of the debate between Stalin and Trotsky, see Elliot R. Goodman, *The Soviet Design for a World State* (New York: Columbia University Press, 1960), pp. 129–163.

20. Trotsky's position was more complex than as summarized here. He did advocate going ahead to build socialism, contending, however, that it could not be completed alone. Furthermore, Stalin himself admitted that the *final* victory of socialism would have to await world revolution.

21. Quoted in Aspaturian, *Power and Process,* pp. 340–341.

22. Stalin, speech to the Fifteenth Party Congress, cited in Burin, "*The Communist Doctrine,*" p. 338.

23. Goodman, *The Soviet Design,* p. 169.

24. Ibid., p. 149.

25. Stalin, *Problems of Leninism,* pp. 790–791.

26. Ibid., p. 758.

27. Alvin Z. Rubinstein, ed., *The Foreign Policy of The Soviet Union* (New York: Random House, 1960), pp. 237–238.

28. Bruce Franklin, ed., *The Essential Stalin, Major Theoretical Writings, 1905-1952* (New York: Doubleday Anchor Books 1972), p. 473.

29. Ibid., p. 472.

30. Scholars differ in their interpretation of *Economic Problems of Socialism in the U.S.S.R.* This interpretation is developed in Marshall D. Shulman, *Stalin's Foreign Policy Reappraised* (Cambridge, Mass.: Harvard University Press, 1963), pp. 240–254. For a sharply differing analysis, cf. Robert C. Tucker, *The Soviet Political Mind,* rev. ed. (New York: W. W. Norton, 1971), pp. 99–102.

31. For an analysis of the post-Stalin change in Soviet thinking on warfare produced by nuclear weapons, see Herbert S. Dinerstein, *War and the Soviet Union* (New York: Frederick A. Prager, 1959).

32. The text of Khrushchev's speech is in *The Sino-Soviet Dispute,* documented and analyzed by G. F. Hudson, Richard Lowenthal, and Roderick Mac-Farquhar (New York: Frederick A. Praeger, 1961), pp. 43–44.

33. This point is developed in Burin, "The Communist Doctrine," pp. 343–347.

34. Paul Marantz argues that Khrushchev's use of peaceful coexistence went well beyond its previous propagandistic function and provided a new conceptual framework for comprehending international politics. See "Peaceful Coexistence: From Heresy to Orthodoxy," in *The Dynamics of Soviet Politics,* ed. Paul Cocks, Robert V. Daniels, and Nancy Whittier Heer (Cambridge, Mass.: Harvard University Press, 1976), p. 303.

35. Hudson et al., *The Sino-Soviet Dispute,* pp. 42–44.

36. Ibid., pp. 45–46.

37. Nikita S. Khrushchev, "On Peaceful Coexistence," in Philip E. Mosely, ed. *The Soviet Union 1922-1962, A Foreign Affairs Reader* (New York: Frederick A. Praeger, 1963), pp. 401–402.

38. The Sino-Soviet ideological differences during the Khrushchev administration are described in Burin, "The Communist Doctrine," pp. 348–54.

39. Quotations from Hudson et al., *The Sino-Soviet Dispute,* pp. 101, 136.
40. Jaochim Glaubitz, "Anti-Hegemony Formulas in Chinese Foreign Policy," *Asian Survey 16,* 3 (March 1976):205-206.
41. Zhou En-lai, "Report to the Tenth National Congress of The Communist Party of China," *Peking Review 35-36* (September 7, 1973): 22.
42. The term "operational code" was developed by Nathan Leites in a classic work, *A Study of Bolshevism.* Subsequently he published a portion of the larger study as *The Operational Code of the Politiburo.* As used by Leites, the term operational code referred primarily to the precepts or maxims of political tactics that characterized the Bolshevik approach to politics. As used here, the term is broadened to include a wide range of attitudes and values that characterize communist thinking on foreign policy. Part of this chapter relies on the excellent analysis of the Leites work by Alexander L. George, "The 'Operational Code': A Neglected Approach to the Study of Political Leaders and Decision-Making," in *The Conduct of Soviet Foreign Policy,* ed. Erik P. Hoffman and Frederic J. Fleron, Jr. (Chicago: Aldine-Atherton, 1971), pp. 165-190.
43. See "Socialism and War," in Tucker, *The Soviet Political Mind,* p. 188.
44. See Kennan, *Russia and the West,* pp. 191, 187f.
45. See Lenin, "Left Wing Communism, An Infantile Disorder," in Tucker, *The Soviet Political Mind,* pp. 550-561.
46. See Meyer, *Leninism,* pp. 276-277.
47. George, "The 'Operational Code,'" pp. 177-185. The paragraphs that follow rely heavily on this article which in turn relies on Leites' *A Study of Bolshevism.*
48. Cited in ibid., p. 179, fn. 33.
49. Tucker, *The Soviet Political Mind,* p. 596.
50. For this position, see Samuel L. Sharp, "National Interest: Key to Soviet Politics," in Hoffman and Fleron, *The Conduct of Soviet Foreign Policy,* pp. 108-117.

Chapter 3
The Origins of the Cold War

SOVIET DIPLOMACY DURING THE SECOND WORLD WAR

From the time of Nazi Germany's surprise attack of June 22, 1941 until the conclusion of the battle at Stalingrad a year and a half later, the Soviet Union was entangled in a desperate predicament. Most of the USSR's wartime losses—at least 20 million dead by Moscow's own estimates—were suffered during this period.[1] Within the first four months, territory containing 40 percent of the country's population was captured by the Nazis and Soviet industrial production was cut in half. Such terrible wartime losses inscribed an ineradicable mark on the USSR. Few of the West's military experts expected that she could withstand Hitler's blow. From the vantage point of 1941, to expect that the Soviet Union could emerge from the war as the mightiest European power was almost unthinkable.

Stalin's initial reaction to Hitler's invasion can be characterized simply: he suffered a breakdown. He withdrew into the Kremlin in morose silence and saw nobody; the first speech concerning the attack was made by Molotov, Stalin's foreign minister and faithful lieutenant. Stalin himself did not speak to his people until July 3. He addressed his listeners on that occasion as "brothers and sisters" and repeatedly referred to Nazi "treachery."[2] From that moment until the war's tide turned, the regime unleashed a torrent of patriotic and nationalist propaganda as the basis for enlisting the support of its people. Stalin had ample reason to doubt that they would fight for him or for socialism.

Although two years earlier he had spurned alliance with the British and French when he had chosen to make common cause with Hitler instead, Stalin was now desperate for Western assistance. An agreement for military cooperation with Britain was concluded in July 1941, and Stalin immediately urged Churchill to open a second front in northern France. In the same month, he told President Roosevelt's emissary, Harry Hopkins, that American troops were welcome anywhere on the Soviet front.[3] From the man who would shortly refuse to allow even Allied observers on the Russian front, this invitation was a solid clue to Stalin's state of alarm.

But a combination of circumstances not under Stalin's control—including the early onset of winter, Hitler's bad strategy which bogged his army down in the effort to destroy Leningrad and Moscow, his failure to force Japan into the war against the USSR, the terror utilized against people in territories occupied by the Germans, and the concomitant stupidity of the Germans in failing to tap the anti-Soviet sentiment of the population—helped to stall the German drive in the autumn of 1941 at the gates of Moscow.

On November 6, speaking on the occasion of the twenty-fourth anniversary of the Bolshevik revolution, Stalin sought to rally his people for the cause of liberating their homeland and the other "enslaved nations" of Europe:

But if these aims are to be achieved, we must crush the military might of the German invaders, we must destroy, to the last man, the German forces of occupation who have intruded into our country for the purpose of enslaving it.[4]

Indeed, Stalin's brave talk would have suggested that the task was all but accomplished. He claimed that the Nazi invaders had already "lost over four and a half million men, killed, wounded and taken prisoner." Only a year earlier, sitting in a Berlin air raid shelter listening to Hitler describe the destruction of Britain, Molotov had asked his ally: "Then whose bombs are these falling overhead?" Had Stalin's audience, assembled in a Moscow subway station, known that his figure equalled the approximate size of the entire German army on the Soviet front, they might well have asked the same question.

But even during this desperate period, Stalin was seeking opportunities to advance Russia's postwar objectives. In discussions with British Foreign Minister Anthony Eden in December 1941, he suggested that there might be a secret addendum to the Anglo-Soviet treaty of alliance: "I suppose you will not object if we add a small protocol to our agreement on postwar reconstruction."[5] In essence, Stalin's "small protocol" called for British recognition of the Soviet annexations accomplished in 1939–40 under the Nazi-Soviet Pact, as well as provisions for postwar Soviet bases in Finland and Rumania and the virtual dismemberment of Germany. But the British demurred, and Stalin did not press his demands at this time, settling for an alliance which made no mention of frontier annexations.

The entry of the United States into the war in the same month brought a substantial increase in the American contribution to the Soviet war effort. The importance of this aid to the Soviet victory was belatedly conceded by Khrushchev in his memoirs. Although he alleges that the West was driven by a desire to "bleed us dry so that they could come in at the last stages and determine the fate of the world," and that Western aid was sent not out of compassion or respect but out of concern for the West's own survival, the former premier does acknowledge that no one Allied country could have won the war by itself.

Although he failed to take the opportunity while he was in power himself, from retirement he wrote that "to avoid excessive haughtiness," the people and Party should have been properly informed about the Allied contribution rather than perpetuating the illusion that the USSR singlehandedly vanquished the Germans. "Without Spam," he concedes, "we wouldn't have been able to feed our army."[6]

But the need for additional Allied cooperation and assistance was very much on the Soviet agenda when Molotov traveled to London and Washington in the spring of 1942. And the most urgent requirement from Moscow's standpoint was the rapid establishment of the second front in Europe. Stalin's pressure on this issue was probably motivated not only by the desire to relieve the German pressure on the Soviet front but also by the internal political necessity of re-establishing Soviet control over occupied territory before movements opposed to Stalin's rule and collaboration with the Germans became too deeply rooted. In his conversations with the British in May 1942, Molotov gained neither a promise for a rapid invasion of the continent nor a recognition of Moscow's claims to the territory in its possession prior to Hitler's attack. Nevertheless, the Soviets concluded a 20-year treaty of alliance with the British in which each party pledged not to interfere in the internal affairs of other states, not to sign a separate peace with the Germans, and not to participate in any pact directed against the other.

The results of Molotov's conversations in Washington were less concrete but more encouraging to the Russians. President Roosevelt's basic approach was to turn his personal charm on the Soviets in an effort to establish a close relationship. He apparently calculated that the creation of such bonds of friendship would guarantee the maintenance of cooperation, thus allowing political issues to take care of themselves. From this standpoint, the White House regarded Molotov's visit as a success; Harry Hopkins reported that it "went extremely well. He and the President got along famously and I am sure that we at least bridged one more gap between ourselves and Russia."[7] For the Russian's part, he was undoubtedly pleased that the final communique recorded "full understanding . . . with regard to the urgent task of creating a second front in Europe in 1942."[8]

But hard military realities, in terms of shortages of trained troops and the necessary supplies, overtook this optimistic prognosis. It fell to Prime Minister Churchill to journey to Moscow in the late summer to inform Stalin that the second front in Europe would have to be postponed and that the next allied operation would occur in northern Africa, not in France. Stalin's reaction was harsh, and he demanded of Churchill, "why were we so afraid of the Germans?" But Churchill persisted, mustering some of his own personal magnetism in an effort to assuage the Soviets' anger, and at the mission's end he recorded that "at least the ice was broken and a human contact established."[9]

The Allies' military fortunes began to improve in the autumn and the great Soviet victory at Stalingrad in January is widely regarded as a turning point of the war, that ensured the ultimate defeat of Hitler's armies. It also brought about a shift in the political arena, as ideological themes began to creep back into internal political communications in the USSR and Stalin began to focus more deliberately on the problem of securing his postwar foreign political objectives. A signal, perhaps deliberate and certainly misleading, that these might be limited in scope and nonrevolutionary in means was given in May 1943 when Stalin announced the dissolution of the Communist International. Ostensibly designed to put an end to the "propaganda" that international communism was simply a tool of Moscow, the termination of the Comintern may have been intended to encourage the impression in the West that the postwar Soviet regime would be more circumspect in its behavior and limited in its ambitions. In fact, the organizational machinery was no longer needed since the foreign communist parties were almost totally subservient to Soviet control and the necessary coordination could be accomplished through the Secretariat of the Communist Party of the Soviet Union (CPSU).

To say that Stalin consciously approached the wartime events from the perspective of ensuring the most favorable postwar situation for the Soviet Union is not to argue that all that ultimately transpired in Eastern Europe and the Far East was the result of a firmly preconceived "blueprint." In addressing each political issue, Stalin sought to keep his options open and to explore alternative approaches. Thus, for example, the Soviets sponsored the formation of a Free German Committee, to be held in reserve as an instrument of Soviet influence in case Hitler's regime should collapse before Soviet armies could arrive in Germany.

Perhaps the best example of Stalin's strategy is found in his maneuvers concerning the future status of Poland—the political issue that was to dominate the wartime negotiations among the "Big Three." Sensitive to British and American sentiments, the Soviets had recognized the Polish government-in-exile in London in July 1941. Although the agreement declared the Nazi-Soviet accord on Poland to be invalid, the Soviets would not agree to the legitimacy of Poland's prewar boundaries and referred only to the postwar restoration of an "ethnic Poland."

During Polish Prime Minister Sikorski's visit to Moscow in December, the beleaguered Soviets intimated that some compromise between the former boundary and the Nazi-Soviet line might be possible, but the Poles stubbornly refused to contemplate any concessions. Relations between the two governments continued to be strained, with persisting quarrels over territory and the treatment of some 1.5 million Polish citizens held in the USSR. In search of an alternative, Stalin set up a communist-dominated Union of Polish Patriots in Moscow, but he held off recognizing it as a "legitimate" government.

In the interim, Stalin found a pretext to free his hand by breaking off relations with the London Poles. The precipitating event came in April 1943 when the Germans announced the discovery of a mass grave in the Katyn Forest of several thousand Polish officers, the bulk of Poland's military leadership. The Germans charged (accurately, as the evidence later confirmed) that the Soviets had committed the atrocity during their occupation of that sector of Poland, though the Soviets claimed that the massacre had occurred only after they had been pushed back from this area following the Nazi attack. The Polish government's demand for an International Red Cross investigation was termed a "treacherous blow" by Moscow, who announced that it was severing diplomatic relations.[10]

The British and Americans were irritated and embarrassed at the behavior of the London Poles, but their feelings of guilt were deepened the following month by their announcement to Stalin that the second front would have to be postponed for yet another year. Stalin's enraged reply heightened the Western concern for the preservation of Allied cooperation and provoked new anxieties that the Russians might seek a separate peace (in the manner of Brest-Litovsk) with the Germans. Although Stalin's anger and distrust were undoubtedly genuine, he must have realized that the more he complained, the more inclined the Western allies might be to offer concessions toward his territorial demands. As Louis Fischer has aptly noted: "Stalin's genius for blackmail matched his talent for brutality."[11]

Roosevelt was eager for a personal meeting with Stalin, to "win him over" and soothe his feelings. After prolonged wrangling over a site for a Big Three meeting—Stalin never flew and refused to leave territory controlled by Soviet troops—Roosevelt and Churchill agreed to meet Stalin at Teheran in November 1943.

The Teheran Conference was significant in a number of respects, not the least of which was that it demonstrated to Stalin that his British and American allies could be played off against each other. Beginning with Roosevelt's efforts to amuse Stalin with jokes at Churchill's expense and continuing through Anglo-American differences on a number of issues, the conference hardly demonstrated (as some revisionist historians would have it) united capitalist pressure to deprive the USSR of hard-won wartime gains. There was maneuvering at Teheran over the political implications of the future conduct of the European war, but Roosevelt left most of this to Churchill and Stalin. The Americans failed to support the British argument that Overlord (the invasion of northern France) should be postponed in favor of an Anglo-American thrust into southeastern Europe designed to put additional pressure on the Germans and force neutral Turkey into the war. Such an operation might well have altered the political fate of Eastern Europe, but Roosevelt supported Stalin's insistence that Overlord must be given highest priority.

Poland's fate was essentially decided in a bilateral conversation between Churchill, Eden, and Stalin. The British plan—to move Poland westward, compensating for Soviet gains by ceding German lands to Poland—was illustrated by Churchill with the aid of three matchsticks. He observed that the idea "pleased Stalin."[12] Roosevelt later assured Stalin that he too supported the Soviet annexation of the eastern half of Poland, although, given the strength of the Polish-American voting bloc, he preferred not to participate in any decision on Polish boundaries until after the 1944 presidential election.

It was also Churchill who volunteered that Russia deserved warm-water ports. Stalin replied that it "might be well" to relax the existing regime in the Turkish straits. Stalin then asked what could be done for Russia in the Far East. He had already won American gratitude by announcing that the Soviet Union would enter the war against Japan after the defeat of Germany, and now Roosevelt suggested that the port of Dairen might be made available to the Soviets.

Stalin appeared so reasonable at Teheran that he had Roosevelt and Churchill volunteering the prizes he desired. The most grandiose instance of this was a statement of Churchill's, which can be viewed in retrospect as sanctioning Russian postwar imperialism:

It was important that the nations who would govern the world after the war should be satisfied and have no territorial or other ambitions. If that question could be settled in a manner agreeable to the great powers, he felt then that the world might indeed remain at peace. He said that hungry and ambitious nations are dangerous, and he would like to see the leading nations of the world in the position of rich, happy men. The President and Marshal Stalin agreed.[13]

The Western allies' fixation at Teheran with retaining Russian friendship represented an enormous gamble that a basic change would occur in the nature and objectives of the postwar Soviet regime. Their only alternative was to modify their military strategy in Europe, and probably also to drop their insistence on the unconditional surrender of Germany, in order to challenge directly the emerging Soviet sphere of influence in Eastern Europe. The decisions at Teheran thus represented a momentous choice, and no more so than on the issue of Poland. By agreeing to concede the Russian demands for the Molotov-Ribbentrop line in Poland, the British and Americans were ensuring that no independent Polish government could accept this arrangement and thus that a puppet government would have to be installed. At the same time, by agreeing to compensate Poland with a large amount of German territory, they were ensuring future German-Polish enmity and Poland's dependence on the USSR for security. Thus, the concession at Teheran of Russia's "security needs" by way of the cession of Polish territory sealed the fate of Poland and made moot the issue of Polish self-determination. It also predetermined the fate of Germany by making a separate German agreement with the West impossible. The subsequent Western bickering with Moscow on these issues certainly confirmed and probably strengthened (but did not create anew) Stalin's suspicions of a devious Western plot to deprive the Soviet Union of its legitimate wartime gains.

The summer of 1944, with the second front finally launched and Soviet armies marching westward, produced several excellent examples of the manner in which Stalin's military strategy was attuned to his political aspirations. The Red Army occupied all of Rumania despite that country's break from the Axis alliance. The Soviets declared war on Bulgaria just as its government was in the process of suing for peace in talks with the British and Americans. And most dramatically, in August–September 1944, the Red Army paused outside Warsaw while the nationalist Polish underground, under command of the London Poles, waged a desperate rear-guard battle against the Nazis. Only after the slaughter of the nationalists did the Soviets march in to capture the city—the administration of which was then turned over to the Polish Committee of National Liberation, the Communist-dominated successor to the Union of Polish Patriots.

As the Soviet armies penetrated deeper into Eastern Europe, Winston Churchill traveled to Moscow for the last time in October 1944. Freed of the presence of the idealistic Americans, Churchill indulged himself in a maneuver that was both cynical and simplistic—the division of Eastern Europe into Western and Soviet spheres of influence, stated in percentage terms. According to the Prime Minister's proposal, Russia was to have 90 percent predominance in Rumania, "the others," 10 percent; Britain, in accord with the United States, was to have 90 percent of the say in Greece, and Russia, 10 percent. Yugoslavia and Hungary were to be divided 50-50, while 75 percent of Bulgaria was allocated to Russia and 25 percent to the others. By Churchill's account (which admits the cynicism of the proposal but fails to explain how influence could be so divided) Stalin "took his blue pencil and made a large tick upon it, and passed it back to us. It was all settled in no more time than it takes to set down."[14] Of course, it was not to be settled in this fashion but rather, as Stalin understood clearly, through the disposition of armed forces upon the terrain of Europe.

It was the military realities in Poland that accounted for the desperation with which Churchill again sought to bring about an agreement between the London Poles and the Soviets. Polish premier Mikolajczyk was brought to the meeting and pressured by both the British and the Russians to agree to the Soviet territorial demands. Mikolajczyk resisted but Churchill washed his hands of the matter, determined not to let the Polish issue spoil Allied relations with the Russians: "Because of quarrels between Poles we are not going to wreck the peace of Europe."[15]

CONFLICT AMONG THE PEACEMAKERS

The fate of Poland was resolved by Soviet conquests well before the last conference between Roosevelt, Churchill, and Stalin convened at Yalta in February

1945. There, as the fruit of endless hours of talk about the subject, Stalin gave his Western partners a sop by agreeing to take a few London Poles into the newly established Lublin government and by promising to see that free elections were held "as soon as possible." But the Soviets did not surrender the prerogative of determining which parties were to be certified as "anti-fascist" and thus eligible to participate in the elections. It would take more than the democratic rhetoric adopted at Yalta in the Declaration on Liberated Europe to ensure that the choice given to the Polish people would be a fair one.

Not only in his assent to the Yalta Declaration but also in his willingness at the conference to alleviate American concerns about the Soviet entry into the Pacific war and about the contours of the postwar international organization, Stalin repeated his Teheran strategy. He was able, thus, to play off the divisions within the Western alliance and elicit concessions on the territorial and political issues of greatest priority to Moscow while appearing quite cooperative on issues of vague principle or lesser moment.

Determined not to repeat Woodrow Wilson's mistake, Roosevelt was anxious to win agreement on the United Nations prior to the final political settlements. On most of the organizational details, Stalin showed relatively little interest; he dropped his earlier demand for 16 seats in the General Assembly for the Soviet republics, settling for the promise of three (and offering to support the same number for the United States). Fully realizing that the USSR and its allies would be outnumbered in the United Nations and that the Security Council represented a big power's haven, he insisted on the retention of the veto principle but agreed to the American formula for limiting its use in procedural questions.

Likewise, Stalin won Roosevelt's gratitude for his reaffirmation of the Soviet willingness to enter the war against Japan three months after the German surrender. From the vantage point of early 1945, the American leaders fully expected the war in the Far East to continue for 18 months beyond the victory in Europe; the earliest possible assistance of Soviet armies was seen as essential to a tolerable conclusion of the war against Japan. Stalin's interests were served by this design, not only because it heightened Roosevelt's eagerness to dispose quickly of Hitler, but also because it entitled the Soviet Union to a voice in the division of the spoils in the Far East. That Japan would be stripped of her empire had already been decided by Roosevelt and Churchill at the Cairo conference in 1943; in such a context, it was not at all unreasonable for Stalin to ask for the recovery of territories lost by the Russians at the beginning of the century. The American government assisted in this enterprise, persuading Chiang Kai-shek to recognize the territorial rearrangement by means of a Treaty of Friendship and Alliance signed with the USSR on August 14. Stalin was thus unchallenged in his attempt to acquire Soviet security objectives in the Far East: from Japan, acquisition of southern Sakhalin and the Kuriles, and from China, recognition of the independence of Outer Mongolia, access to Dairen, a naval base in Port Arthur, and joint ownership of the Manchurian Railway.

On the vital issue of Germany's future, Stalin pressed hard to ensure against the postwar revival of the German threat to Soviet security and hegemony. The three leaders agreed at Yalta that Germany would be divided into four zones of occupation, although they postponed a decision on implementing the principle of dismemberment. Churchill, already conscious of the danger of Russian hegemony in Europe and aware of the need to maintain a German balance to Soviet power, balked at an agreement that would entirely strip Germany of her resources. Stalin was able to stake his claim to $10 billion in reparations, to be paid in kind over a ten-year period, but there was no support for his suggestion that two or three million Germans might be used as forced labor in the rebuilding of the Soviet economy.

No sooner had the ink dried on the Yalta agreements than Stalin began moving to consolidate the Soviet hold over Eastern Europe. The participation of democratic elements in Poland was seriously constricted: despite promises of immunity, 16 leaders of the underground movement were arrested by the Soviets. Western diplomatic protests were fruitless, as were British and American efforts to send observer teams to Warsaw. A communist government was forced on Rumania, and communists and their allies moved into leading positions in the new regimes in Bulgaria, Hungary, and Czechoslovakia. Tito's communist faction in Yugoslavia broke off its coalition arrangement with the representatives of noncommunist parties and moved to consolidate its hold on the reins of power. Not only were Western complaints turned aside by the Soviets, but Moscow announced, as if in retaliation to these protests, that Foreign Minister Molotov would not be able to attend the founding conference of the United Nations in San Francisco. (The decision was subsequently reversed and Molotov did lead the Soviet delegation.)

The initial American interpretation of this turn of events was that Stalin was being subjected to pressure by unreconstructed hard-liners in his Politburo. But following Roosevelt's death on April 12, the Truman Administration seemed inclined to respond to Soviet behavior with a tougher attitude, which was reflected in the suspension of Lend-Lease assistance in May.

Soviet-American tensions were temporarily eased later in the month by the visit to Moscow of presidential envoy Harry Hopkins. In return for the American's reassurance that Poland was not important in itself, and that the United States desired that not only Poland but all of the USSR's neighbors be "friendly" to her, Stalin agreed to token participation of noncommunist elements in the Warsaw government. On July 5, Washington and London granted recognition to the new Polish regime. This seeming resolution of the perennial Polish issue set the stage for the opening in Potsdam on July 16 of the last wartime summit conference.

Ironically, but not coincidentally, the nuclear age in international politics began on the same day. Just prior to his first meeting with Stalin, President Truman received word from the New Mexico desert that the first test of the atomic weapon had been a success. Although the full extent of its destructive power and military effectiveness was not yet known, the atomic bomb was perceived by at least some American leaders as an instrument of great political potential in their dealings with Stalin. Churchill was even more explicit in his awareness of its possible impact upon the process of bargaining about to begin at Potsdam: "We seemed suddenly to have become possessed of a merciful abridgment of the slaughter in the East and of a far happier prospect in Europe. I have no doubt that these thoughts were present in the minds of my American friends."[16]

A week later, Stalin was "casually" informed by Truman "that we had a new weapon of unusual destructive force." Stalin, the president's memoirs record, "showed no special interest. All he said was that he was glad to hear it and hoped we would make 'good use of it against the Japanese.'"[17] Although Truman and Churchill concluded that the significance of this development had been lost on Stalin, the Soviet leader's innocence was quite probably feigned. The Soviets' own atomic research program had by this time been underway for over two years and their intelligence agents had undoubtedly alerted them to the Americans' progress. Marshal Zhukov recorded that Stalin told Molotov of Truman's remark later that night, and that Molotov had said, "'We'll have to talk it over with Kurchatov and get him to speed things up.' I realized they were talking about research on the atomic bomb."[18] Although his own official military doctrine was to belittle the significance of atomic weapons, Stalin was clearly determined to have them himself as quickly as possible.

The main focus of discussion at Potsdam was not Truman's new weapon and its planned use against Japan, but the arrangements to be made in reorganizing and governing defeated Germany. The Big Three had no difficulty agreeing on the disarmament and de-Nazification of the country, but the delineation of its borders and disposition of its economic resources caused considerable controversy. Despite the united insistence of both the communist and noncommunist factions in the new Polish government, Britain and the United States were reluctant to agree to continued Polish control of the former German territory that had been turned over to Polish administration by the Soviet troops. Now that he contemplated the political coloration of the Polish regime and the bleak prospects for a balance of power in central Europe, Churchill in particular was no longer so enamored of his scheme for moving Poland westward. The Soviets, confident of the friendship of the Polish government and still uneasy about postwar Germany, urged recognition of the existing zones of control. In the spring, Stalin had forecast to the Yugoslav communist, Milovan Djilas, that Germany would be on its feet again in 12 to 15 years. "And this," he said, "is why the unity of the Slavs is important."[19]

To help prepare for the coming struggle, Stalin sought to implement a reparations scheme that would have given the Soviets the lion's share of the economic spoils from all of Germany, and not just from the Soviet zone of occupation. The Western leaders foresaw that this would leave them with the burden of having to give massive economic assistance to Germany so that it might survive while paying its reparations to the USSR. It was not that their hearts had melted, but rather that Truman and Churchill dreaded the prospect of a Germany weakened and drained of resources over the long term. Such a country was not only a poor trading partner and a target for revolutionary rhetoric, but it was also an inadequate barrier to the westward spread of Soviet influence.

In the end, the three leaders accepted a compromise that left the disputed territory in Polish hands pending final determination of borders at a peace conference, and that called for the Soviets to receive the bulk of their reparations from their own zone of control. Although the four occupation zones were said to be just an administrative convenience, and the Central Control Council was to ensure that Germany was treated as a unit, the decision on reparations was the first step toward determining that Germany would not in fact be governed as an economic unit.

The three powers also quarrelled over the postwar political trends in their respective spheres of influence. Churchill was discovering that 10 percent of the influence in Rumania or 25 percent of the influence in Bulgaria was amounting to nothing for the British and American representatives, and he pressed Stalin to agree to reorganization of the governments in those countries as a precondition for Western recognition. Stalin clearly resented his allies' attempt to meddle in the affairs of areas that they had earlier seemed to concede to the Soviet sphere. He and Molotov were ready with countercharges about Western suppression of "democratic" forces and tolerance of "profascist" elements in Greece, Italy, and even Spain. In the former case, Soviet diplomats and propagandists had raised no great stir when the British had used their troops to suppress procommunist forces in the civil war that had erupted in December. Evidently Stalin expected Churchill to be as tolerant of Soviet activity in Moscow's sphere as he had been of the strong-armed British influence in Greece. But nothing was resolved in this dispute and the task of drawing up the peace treaties with Hitler's former allies was left to the foreign ministers.

It is difficult to explain the diplomacy at Potsdam simply as the result of the application of a "sphere of influence" approach by the great powers. The Americans had never conceded the legitimacy of such an approach, and even Churchill and Stalin, who seemed more comfortable with it, disagreed sharply on how the respective spheres were to be defined. Thus, Stalin could hark back to the vague discussions at Teheran concerning warm-water ports and revision of the regime in the Turkish straits; he used this at Potsdam as the basis for renewing his claim to a Soviet base in the straits. But Soviet ambition did not stop at the Bosporus; the Russians also demanded a share in the trusteeship system, thereby hoping to gain a foothold in the Mediterranean itself. Moscow announced that it wished to be responsible for the administration of Tripolitania, a former Italian colony in western Libya. On neither score did the Western allies comply.

The last major item on the Potsdam agenda was the continuing war in the Pacific. Stalin discussed with his counterparts the Japanese efforts to gain Soviet mediation in bringing about peace talks. He reiterated his intention to join in the war against Japan soon although he did not associate himself with the declaration issued from the conference in the name of Britain, the United States, and China, in which the demand for an unconditional surrender by the Japanese was repeated.

Truman evidently hoped that the Japanese defeat would be accomplished prior to Russian entry into the war; the atomic bombing of Hiroshima on August 6 and of Nagasaki on August 9 should certainly be viewed in this political context as well as in terms of military strategy.[20] Nevertheless, the Soviets entered the war exactly on schedule—three months after Germany's surrender and less than a week prior to Japan's acceptance of the Potsdam terms. The Soviet contribution was certainly not militarily decisive, as their own histories have claimed, but it was politically effective. Although it cost far more in terms of men and material than was needed, Stalin's military strategy was again closely attuned to territorial objectives.[21] By the time they had finished fighting, Soviet forces had managed to occupy the northern part of Korea and to sweep through northern Manchuria, where they linked up with the army of the Chinese communists. Through the force of their own arms, the Soviets succeeded in acquiring the territories that had been conceded to them at Yalta and yet they were unsuccessful in their efforts to expand their influence through sharing in the occupation and governance of Japan itself.

Shortly after the end of the second World War, communism had spread from one country (two, counting Mongolia) to a system that held under its sway 100 million additional people in 11 more states of Europe: Latvia, Estonia, Lithuania, Poland, the eastern zone of Germany, Czechoslovakia, Hungary, Rumania, Bulgaria, Yugoslavia, and Albania. The first three were reannexed into the USSR—an act unrecognized but not strenuously protested by the West. The remaining states comprised an extremely diverse group. They contained a dozen major nationalities, most of which were Slavic (with the major exceptions of the Magyars, Rumanians, and Albanians). Even the Slavs among them were not historically noted for their close affinity. There was great religious diversity, spanning Catholic, Protestant, Orthodox, and Moslem cultures. For the most part, the area was economically underdeveloped, with great variations in economic wealth and class conflicts often reinforced by national divisions. It was also politically retarded, with only a weak tradition of national independence or of democracy.

At the beginning of the war, communist parties were nonexistent in Albania, Germany, and Poland, and almost so in Rumania and Hungary. They were stronger in Bulgaria and Yugoslavia and strongest of all in Czechoslovakia. All were under the tight control of the Comintern and thus of Stalin himself. Most of the East European party leaders (with the notable exception of the Yugoslavs and Albanians) spent the war years in Moscow.

After the war, the vacuum created by the defeat of German occupation forces was filled with Soviet military power. And yet the presence of the Red Army, though a strong factor in bringing about the ascent of communism in the region, was not a solitary or sufficient reason. Communist victories in Yugoslavia and Albania were secured primarily by the actions of native guerrilla forces who exploited nationalist sentiments and favorable terrain to defeat both the German forces and rival claimants to power. Czechoslovakia, not an Axis power, was liberated by Soviet troops, which were then withdrawn from the country. Part of Austria remained under Soviet occupation for a decade but a communist regime was never imposed. And Finland—described by Molotov in 1948 as a "peanut"[22]—was a defeated enemy state that was subjected neither to Soviet occupation nor to direct communist rule.

Clearly, then, there was no single tactical blueprint for Soviet domination of Eastern Europe. Events unfolded during the immediate postwar years according to the influence of both domestic factors and the diplomatic balance. The seeming belatedness of the Western leaders' interest in the composition of postwar governments probably stemmed from their failure to understand Stalin's own perceptions of the meaning of "secure" borders and "friendly" neighbors. For the Soviet leader, the control of these governments by communist politicians of certain loyalty to the USSR (and to Stalin personally) was not simply an ideological desideratum but was part and parcel of a minimum security guarantee. And yet Stalin was reluctant, particularly in cases such as Finland and Greece, to intervene too directly in countries where the West was capable of taking sharp counteraction.

In Poland, Hungary, and Czechoslovakia, the pace of consolidation of communist control over the government was relatively slower than in Yugoslavia or Albania. In Poland, British and American pressure brought a temporary broadening of the government coalition, though the communists held on to key positions. In Hungary and Czechoslovakia, relatively free elections produced governments containing, but not controlled by, the communists. But communist control of important ministries (usually including interior, information, education, and agriculture) and the presence of Soviet troops in the background helped ensure the success of the "salami tactics" through which genuine coalitions became sham coalitions.

The gradual tightening of political control was accompanied by a process, featuring either payments of reparations or establishment of joint-stock companies or both, by which the economies of the area were tied to that of the USSR. Politically, these countries were said not to be dictatorships of either the proletariat or the bourgeoisie; economically, they were systems characterized by neither socialism nor capitalism. A new theoretical construct—"people's democracy"—was eventually invented in an effort to encompass this very diverse set of regimes now under the jealous tutelage of the USSR. But it was in terms of power and not of theory that Stalin had described to Djilas the emerging situation in Eastern Europe at war's end: "This war is not as in the past; whoever occupies a territory also imposes on it his own social system. Everyone imposes his own system as far as his army can reach. It cannot be otherwise."[23]

It was this reality that could not be circumscribed during the lengthy negotiations of 1945 and 1946 concerning the peace treaties to be signed with Bulgaria, Rumania, Hungary, Finland, and Italy. In the succession of conferences of foreign ministers, mutual recriminations only deepened mutual suspicions. The Western representatives did not succeed in reversing the trend toward tighter Soviet control in Eastern Europe and the Soviets were likewise unable to win their colleagues' consent for a base in the Mediterranean, a role in the occupation of Japan, or other forms of participation in areas not already under the sway of Soviet arms. In the end, the *fait accompli* was conceded, and the treaties were signed in February 1947.

THE COLD WAR BEGINS

What had happened to the cooperative alliance between the Soviet Union and its wartime partners? Where was the spirit of compromise and the close relationship among the heads of state that the Western leaders had been so anxious to preserve only two years before? Were the promises and expectations generated in wartime conferences now being broken and ignored? These are issues on which American historians of the period have long been in conflict, as the "revisionists" weave a tale of betrayal of the idealism of Roosevelt and Hull by the successor administration while the "orthodox" perceive a casting away of naive illusions by politicians more realistic about the Soviet "blueprint for expansionism."[24] While we are not able here to summarize the arguments in this debate fully, it should be clear from the foregoing account that the basic premise implied in these questions is itself faulty. For the wartime alliance was in fact only a marriage of convenience, marred on both sides by continuing suspicion, misperception, and even deception. There had never been a shared vision of the postwar order among the Big Three, and many of the issues that reflected the deeper divisions in world views had simply been resolved *de facto* or postponed for later consideration.

It was certainly Stalin's conviction that the postwar conflict was neither avoidable nor reversible. This view was articulated in his speech of February 9, 1946, delivered just prior to the nationwide elections for the Supreme Soviet. An authoritative statement of the Soviet world view, the speech sets forth Stalin's interpretation of the nature and meaning of the second World War, his justification for policies pursued before and during that conflict, and prescriptions for the future. [25] If contemporary observers had failed to discern from the massive purges of the 1930s or from collectivization horrors what Stalin's true intentions and methods were, then this speech and events that would soon transpire should have cleared away any uncertainties.

If there was any doubt of his regime's continuing commitment to a Marxist-Leninist world view, it should have been dispelled in Stalin's analysis of the causes of the war. He described it as "the inevitable result of the development of world economic and political forces on the basis of modern monopoly capitalism," and in particular of the "law of uneven development" of capitalism. As such the war was an unavoidable and inevitable consequence of capitalism, and it was also not unlikely that such a struggle could again occur.

How, then, had the Soviet Union found itself enmeshed in a struggle between two hostile camps of the capitalist world? Soviet participation, Stalin said, was founded upon and enhanced "the anti-fascist and liberation character" of the war. It was on this basis and no other that the great coalition among the United States, Great Britain, and the USSR had been created. Although this argument blatantly ignores the fact that in 1939 the Soviet Union had broken away from the antifascist struggle and pursued a tactical alliance with Hitler, Stalin's concern was less to provide his listeners with a complete history than to demonstrate to them the very limited purposes for which the Soviets had made common cause with the Western allies.

Much can be learned from the manner in which Stalin adduced the reasons for and meaning of the Soviet victory in the war. First of all, it meant the triumph of the "Soviet social order"—by test of fire it had proven "its unquestionable vitality" and its superiority to any non-Soviet form of social organization. Second, victory had proven the viability of the "multinational" Soviet state system. Third, and clearly last, the Soviet triumph had shown the heroic character of the Red Army.

This statement represented a kind of consummation of the revival of ideological militancy that had taken place in the Soviet Union since the victory at Stalingrad. The earlier stress on purely nationalist traditions and symbols and the patriotic pride in the exploits of the army and its heroes had given way to a reassertion of pre-war socialist orthodoxy. A new generation of recruits had been absorbed into the Communist Party and it needed no illusions about the superiority of the socialist order. In the next few years, this chauvinistic stance—which represented a fusion of Russian nationalism with Stalinist-style socialism—was to lead to the absurd extremes of altogether denying the accomplishments of Western science and culture. It was as though Stalin was seeking to counter-act the ideological contamination of that large portion of the Soviet population that had lived under Nazi occupation or ventured with the Soviet army into the land of the bourgeoisie.

Ironically, in light of Stalin's bow to the multinational character of his state, his suspicion of infection and even betrayal fell most heavily on some of the minority nationalities. As Khrushchev was to document a decade later, during and immediately after the war Stalin engaged in the mass deportation of whole nations, including the party members among them: not only the Volga Germans and Crimean Tatars (unmentioned by Khrushchev), but also the Karachai, Kalmyks, Chechen-Ingush, and Balkars. Indeed, Stalin's successor claimed, "the Ukrainians avoided meeting this fate only because there were too many of them and there was no place to which to deport them. Otherwise, he would have deported them also."[26]

The isolation imposed upon the Soviet Union after the war was a result not only of ideological antipathy toward the West but of Stalin's own perception of insecurity. As Solzhenitzyn has documented, Soviet prisoners of war returned home not as heroes but as suspected collaborationists, and hundreds of thou-sands of them were routed directly to the labor camps of the Gulag Archipelago. No potentially discordant voices were to be left free to dispute the claims of the rottenness of the capitalist system or the perniciousness of bourgeois ideas.

Stalin's insecurity is evident also in the assertions he put forth in his speech regarding the state of the country's preparation for the war. Knowing full well that there must have been grave doubts, he repeatedly insisted that "it would be a mistake" to think that the country could have been prepared in only a short time or "that we won only owing to the gallantry of our troops." Rather, it was by its farsighted policies of industrialization and collectivization that the party had prepared the way for victory. Nor had this been accomplished without resistance:

many prominent members of the Party . . . systematically dragged the Party backward and tried by hook or by crook to divert it to the "usual" capitalist path of development. All the anti-Party machinations of the Trotskyites and the Rightists, all their "activities" in sabotaging the measures of our government, pursued the single aim of frustrating the Party's policy.

Thus, not only the Five Year Plans and collectivization but the Great Purge itself could be seen as wise and justified policies enabling the Party (and appar-ently it alone) to supply the resources and weapons needed for victory over the fascists.

Even in triumph Stalin was not able to rest from his suspicions of even his closest comrades. As Khrushchev tell us, "Stalin was a very distrustful man, sickly suspicious. . . . Everywhere and in everything he saw 'enemies,' 'twofacers,' and 'spies.'"[27] This was amply confirmed in his later years not only by the wide-ranging purge of the Leningrad party apparatus just prior to his death, but also in the demented "Doctor's Plot," through which Stalin was apparently planning to eliminate many of his closest associates.

Was Stalin's personal dementia capable of shaping the foreign policy of an entire mighty state? That this one man was fully in command of the Soviet decision-making apparatus to the extent that he used it as his personal instrument is fairly well documented. Djilas graphically describes the manner in which his associates fearfully deferred to him, even to the point of not daring to contradict his assertion that the Netherlands was not a part of the Benelux customs union.[28] Khrushchev's memoirs confirm the point:

He jealously guarded foreign policy in general and our policy toward other socialist countries in particular as his own special province. Stalin had never gone out of his way to take other people's advice into account, but this was especially true after the war. The rest of us were just errand boys.[29]

The result, Khrushchev concluded in his secret speech of 1956, was that Stalin's personality was deeply imprinted on postwar Soviet foreign policy: "He had completely lost consciousness of reality; he demonstrated his suspiciousness and haughtiness not only in relation to individuals in the USSR, but in relation to whole parties and nations."[30] No account of Soviet foreign policy in the postwar years and no explanation of the origins of the cold war can be complete without an awareness of the extent to which Stalin's policies and personality *required* isolationism, an atmosphere of hostility, and an omnipresent enemy.

But what, from the standpoint of 1946, were Stalin's own expectations for the future? His speech makes it clear that there was to be no period of relaxation, no easing of the forced-pace drive to "organize a new mighty upsurge in the national economy." And the reason for this continued sacrifice, he implied, was the external threat:

Only under such conditions can we consider that our homeland will be guaranteed against all possible accidents. That will take three more Five-Year Plans, I should think, if not more. But it can be done and we will do it.

It is strange that a speech that began with a reference to the inevitability of war should end by alluding to "accident." Perhaps Stalin wished to leave his listeners with the hope that their labors and sacrifices might indeed be sufficient to stave off another war. He had expressed his own view to Djilas only a month before the last war had ended: "The war shall soon be over. We shall recover in fifteen or twenty years [three more Five-Year Plans!] and then we'll have another go at it."[31]

But this evidence does suggest that Stalin expected at least some years of respite, that he did not anticipate in the intermediate term a Western effort to pry away the fruits of Soviet victory by force of arms. Stalin had reason to expect that his actions in Eastern Europe would not be challenged by American arms, if only in Roosevelt's statement at Yalta that American troops would be withdrawn from Europe within two years after the war's end. Moreover, Stalin fully expected that while he was rebuilding his own economy the United States would be plunged into another economic depression in the postwar period, and he hastily silenced the one Soviet economist, Yevgenii Varga, who dared to assert otherwise. Certainly a leader who expected imminent armed conflict would not have taken steps to demobilize the largest portion of his own army; by Khrushchev's calculations, the Soviet armed forces were reduced from a wartime peak of over 11 million to a level in 1948 of 2,874,000.[32]

From this perspective we can more easily understand Stalin's postwar political strategy in Europe. He did not expect an aggressive military challenge from the West, despite the ideology's assumption of inherent capitalist hostility and the American atomic monopoly and advantage in strategic delivery forces. Never having been one to take undue risks, however, Stalin sought to deter Washington from employing its military forces (while making it possible for the USSR to probe for opportunities to expand its influence) through a combination of military and political measures.

Stalin's chief tactic toward this end was to capitalize on the Soviets' own substantial lead in conventional arms and to exploit the image of a Western Europe that lay hostage to the Red Army. For despite the postwar reduction in Soviet force levels, the American demobilization had reduced the U.S. armed forces to a figure one-half that of the Soviet troop strength. The imbalance in postwar conventional strength was most striking on the European front. Stalin maintained about 30 Soviet divisions (a half million men) in a forward deployment in Germany and Eastern Europe, backed up by substantial forces stationed in the western USSR (together with a large trained reserve force, capable of rapid mobilization). In addition, by the time of Stalin's death the East European armies had been reequipped and numbered about one and one-half million men (in varying stages of combat readiness). Prior to the formation of NATO in 1949, the West maintained only about ten loosely coordinated divisions in the European theatre. Although the large Soviet troop concentration was designed to serve the need to maintain political control in Eastern Europe as well as to confront the forces of the West, it is little wonder that the effect of the disparity in conventional armaments was to arouse deep concern in the West.

Stalin did not intend to rely indefinitely on superior land forces to meet his military needs. An active program of atomic research was intended to break the American nuclear monopoly at the earliest possible date. Medium-range bombers were being developed to serve as the delivery system for the anticipated nuclear arsenal. Soviet naval forces were also being expanded by means of construction of both surface vessels (cruisers and destroyers rather than aircraft carriers) and submarines.

In addition to military deterrence, the Soviets sought to ensure the nonuse of American atomic weapons by erecting political restraints. As we shall see below, an elaborate "peace movement" was developed to enlist public pressure against the "imperialist warmongers"; the centerpiece of this campaign was a "ban-the-bomb" appeal. Postwar discussions on disarmament were also utilized by the Soviet Union to build restraints against the possible American use of its atomic monopoly. The chief American proposal, the Baruch Plan, called for the creation of an international authority that would own all uranium mines and plants capable of producing atomic weapons; its powers of inspection and control would not be subject to great-power veto in the U.N. Security Council. The Soviets rejected this idea, depicting it as a capitalist plot to interfere with Soviet industrial production, and they proposed instead that the atomic bomb be prohibited and all existing stocks destroyed.

Not surprisingly, under the circumstances, Stalinist military doctrine downgraded the significance of nuclear weapons and stressed the importance of conventional forces and superior morale. Stalin had publicly denigrated the importance of nuclear weapons as early as in 1946: "I do not believe the atomic bomb to be as serious a force as some politicians seem to regard it. Atomic bombs are intended to intimidate the weak-nerved, but they cannot decide the outcome of a war.[33] Having thus denied (as the Chinese would later) the strategic significance of nuclear forces, Stalin in effect put a straitjacket on public Soviet discussion of the issue. Rather than seek to adjust its doctrine and planning to the new military realities, Stalin ordered the Soviet military in 1946 to prepare the army and develop "Soviet military science" solely "on the basis of a skillful mastering of the experience of the recent war."[34]

In studying that experience, Soviet military planners were to be guided by Stalin's thesis that a war's outcome is decided not by transitory factors such as surprise but by "permanently operating factors" in which the USSR had a seemingly lasting advantage. As promulgated in 1942, these factors were five in number: stability of the rear, morale of the army, quantity and quality of divisions, armaments, and organizational ability of commanders. The Soviet generals themselves were later to complain that this dogmatic stance would seriously retard the development of Soviet military thought for almost a decade. But despite this complacent doctrine and Soviet conventional superiority, Stalin remained a realist; he seemed determined not to risk a reversal of the relatively favorable postwar situation by actions so bold as to provoke the West into military expansion and confrontation.

The first major postwar crisis well illustrated both Stalin's opportunistic probing and his unwillingness to court great risks in the quest for expanded influence. The crisis occurred in Iran, a strategic border state and a pathway to the Middle East of long-standing interest to the rulers in Moscow. Iran had been jointly occupied by British and Soviet troops in August 1941 in an effort to ensure the security of supply lines to the USSR. At the Teheran Conference, Stalin agreed to liquidate the occupation shortly after the end of the war, but when the scheduled time arrived and British troops began to leave southern Iran, the Soviets found excuses to keep their 30,000-man force in the northern provinces. Under Soviet patronage, a former Comintern functionary declared in December 1945 the establishment of the Autonomous Republic of Azerbaijan; shortly thereafter, a Kurdish Peoples Republic was announced in the neighboring territory.

An effort by the Iranian central government to reincorporate the secessionist areas by force was blocked by Soviet troops. Under strong pressure from the communist-controlled Tudeh party, a new government entered into negotiations with the Soviets at the beginning of 1946. Moscow's demands included the recognition of an autonomous status for the two northern provinces and formation of a joint Soviet-Iranian oil company in the region (similar to an Anglo-Iranian arrangement that already existed in the south).

Clearly the Soviets were staking a claim to a "sphere of influence" in northern Iran and were again using the presence of the Red Army as their primary instrument of pressure. Early in March, both Britain and the United States lodged formal protests with the Soviets over their failure to honor the agreement for troop withdrawal. These tough statements raised an implicit threat that Washington and London were prepared to use force to dislodge Moscow from Iran. At the end of the month, the Iranian government brought the dispute to the Security Council as the first major crisis ever presented to the United Nations. There, under strong Anglo-American pressure, the Soviet delegate (Andrei Gromyko) pledged, on March 26, that Soviet troops would be withdrawn from Iran within six weeks.

From all appearances, the Soviets had accomplished their objectives through their pressure-laden negotiations with the Iranians. An agreement conceding the major Soviet demands was concluded in April and Soviet troops departed within the promised time frame. But the seeming Russian triumph fell prey—and not for the last time—to the vagaries of Middle Eastern policies. At the end of the year, the Iranian government liquidated the separatist movements and expelled the Tudeh party from the ruling coalition in Teheran; the following year the Iranian parliament refused to ratify the concession for a joint stock company. Thus, scarcely two years after the end of the war, the Soviets were left with virtually no influence with their southern neighbor.

The effect of the crisis was far-reaching for it accelerated the West's change of perceptions of its former ally. In the midst of the crisis on March 5, 1946, Winston Churchill delivered his celebrated speech at Fulton, Missouri, in which he declared that from the Baltic to the Adriatic, an "Iron Curtain" had descended across the Continent. Although the American administration did not immediately and publicly associate itself with Churchill's gloomy assessment, it had in fact recently received from George F. Kennan, its counselor at the Moscow embassy, a lengthy cable putting forward a similarly pessimistic view of Russian intentions. But the crises of 1946 were met singly; negotiations on the peace treaties continued and there was as yet no concerted Western strategy in response to the Soviet challenge.

This situation was altered in the first half of 1947, when the words "cold war" and "containment" entered the American vocabulary and the bipolar nature of the postwar conflict became abundantly clear. The process began in February, with the delivery by a British emissary to the State Department of two notes regarding the increasingly difficult situation in Greece and Turkey. In the former country, communist-led guerrillas had renewed the civil war in mid-1946. Using the territory of Bulgaria and Yugoslavia (their primary sponsors) as a sanctuary, the guerrillas were posing a serious threat to the Greek government. Turkey had been in a state of mobilization for months in response to continuing pressures from the Soviet Union aimed at acquiring several frontier districts and obtaining a base in the straits. In addition to its diplomatic and propaganda campaigns, Moscow had massed troops at the border. A Soviet demand of the United States and Britain that the regime in the Turkish straits be changed was rejected; Washington's reply was accompanied by the dispatch of a naval task force into the Mediterranean.

In both cases the British had sought to play their traditional role as guarantors of Western security interests in the eastern Mediterranean, but they were struggling through a severe financial crisis of their own, which was indicative of the rapid erosion of Britain's ability to support her overseas commitments. The British notes told the United States government that London's role as patron and protector of the Greek and Turkish regimes would have to be surrendered by the end of March. By American estimates, the Greek government would only be able to carry on alone in its efforts to withstand the civil conflict for a few weeks. The collapse of Greece seemed sure to doom Iran's and Turkey's efforts to resist Soviet demands.

With a pronounced sense of crisis and a consciousness that an historic shift was in the making, the Truman Administration entered a period of strategic planning. The previous American policy had been limited to an effort to deny further concessions to the Soviets at the conference table. Now the approach was to take active steps to prevent the Russians from taking by subversion,

pressure or use of force the objectives that had been refused them in negotiations. The first fruit of the new strategy was the enunciation by the president—in a speech to Congress on March 12—of the "Truman Doctrine." He
specifically proposed that the United States appropriate $400 million in
assistance to Greece and Turkey. Although there was no explicit mention
in the speech of the threat from the Soviet Union, it did employ language
that committed the United States to the vanguard role in responding to the
broader Soviet challenge:

I believe that it must be the policy of the United States to support free peoples
who are resisting attempted subjugation by armed minorities or by outside
pressure. . . . At the present moment in world history, nearly every nation must
choose between alternative ways of life. The choice is too often not a free
one.[35]

The public debate following Truman's speech immediately focused on an
issue the President had not addressed: Why should the Greek and Turkish
issues not be referred to the United Nations? The response of Senator Tom
Connally was blunt but symptomatic of the government's evolving attitude
toward the United Nations: it "could not handle it if it had it, and it would
be a buck-passing arrangement, just a dodging and trimming and flim-flamming
around."[36] In official American quarters at least, the high wartime expectations
for the international organization had been dashed by the experience of its
first years.

The Soviets, of course, had never expected as much from the United Nations.
At Yalta, Stalin had made it clear that he regarded the USSR's national sovereignty and Great Power status as beyond the reach of whatever restraints the
United Nations might seek to impose on lesser states. Stalin said, according
to Secretary Stettinius, that "[h] e would never agree to having any action of any
of the Great Powers submitted to the judgment of the small powers."[37] The
Soviet Union and its allies were in a seemingly permanent minority in the
General Assembly; Moscow looked to the Security Council—where its interests
were protected by the veto—as an organ that could and should be effective
only if the wartime Great Powers cooperated. The Soviet Union had participated
in the formation of the United Nations not expecting to create a supranational
authority but for more limited and essentially defensive purposes. As Alexander
Dallin has put it, the USSR preferred "joining to avoid the stigma of nonpartici-
pation and to prevent the body from becoming a hostile instrument. Armed
with the veto, the Soviet Union was confident that it could prevent action
against itself by the U.N. . . . So long as 'Great Power unanimity' was accepted,
it had nothing to lose and perhaps something to gain."[38]

Once it came to a realization of this fact, the Truman Administration was
persuaded that only a direct American response to the crisis in the eastern

Mediterranean could be effective, yet it also understood that the situation in Greece and Turkey was only a limited part of a much broader threat to the stability of Europe. Despite United Nations relief and rehabilitation assistance and loans from the United States, Europe's economy following the unusually bitter winter of 1946-47 was in a dangerous condition and the morale of the people was extremely low. The communist parties in France and Italy were demonstrating increasing electoral appeal. In Washington's view, the key to reversing this trend and achieving political stability was the recovery of the European economy, which could come only through a massive and coordinated injection of dollars. On April 29, Secretary of State George Marshall directed George Kennan and the new Policy Planning Staff to make a thorough but urgent survey of Europe's needs for reconstruction.

It was on the basis of this study, which recommended that the American response to the problem rely on nonmilitary instruments and assume a non-ideological tone, that Secretary Marshall presented his "plan for a plan" at the Harvard commencement in June. Stating the administration's determination to assist in the restoration of economic health, "without which there can be no political stability or assured peace," the Secretary declared:

Our policy is directed not against any country or doctrine but against hunger, poverty, desperation and chaos . . . governments, political parties or groups which seek to perpetuate human misery in order to profit . . . politically will encounter the opposition of the United States.[39]

Following up on Marshall's open and inclusive invitation to the European governments to formulate a response to this plan, representatives of the European "big three" convened in Paris on June 27. The British and French delegations were joined by Foreign Minister Molotov, accompanied by a retinue of over 80 economic and technical specialists. While Molotov's opening speech questioned the American motives, it did seem to presage Soviet participation. It was soon clear that the Soviet preference was for a series of bilateral agreements between the United States and individual European states, rather than a coordinated European effort to receive and disburse the aid.

Less than a week of negotiations had passed, however, when the Soviet delegation apparently received fresh instructions from Moscow. On July 2, Molotov, denouncing the Marshall Plan as an attack on the sovereignty of the states of Europe, declared that the Soviet Union would not participate after all. Shortly thereafter, the Czech and Polish governments, who had indicated an interest in attending the follow-up conference, announced that they too would spurn Marshall aid.

Stalin's decision that the USSR and its allies would not take part in the European Recovery Program was a blunder of major proportions that had a profound effect on the future course of European politics. In the form it eventually assumed, the Marshall Plan was to stimulate an "economic miracle" in Western Europe that undoubtedly contributed to the region's political stability and thus helped lessen communist prospects. Had the Soviet Union decided to participate, the consequences might have been more favorable for Moscow. Had the Soviet Union and its East European neighbors shared in American aid, their own recovery might have been stimulated and the later stark contrast between the prosperity of the West and the stagnation of the East might have been eased. Or, more likely, Soviet participation might have altered the nature and political effect of the Marshall aid—even to the point of making it far more difficult for the American Congress to support. Second-guessing aside, however, what Stalin's decision clearly did accomplish was the political and economic division of Europe, only two years after the war's end.

THE IRON CURTAIN DESCENDS

Simultaneous with Stalin's decision that the USSR and its allies would not take part in the European Recovery Program, the American strategy of "containment" of the Soviet Union was publicly articulated for the first time. In an anonymously published article on "The Sources of Soviet Conduct," George Kennan called for the United States to respond to Soviet behavior with a policy aimed at "long-term, patient but firm and vigilant containment of Russian expansive tendencies" without resorting to "outward histrionics" or "superfluous gestures of outward 'toughness'." The characteristic approach of this policy would be "the adroit and vigilant application of counterforce at a series of constantly shifting geographical and political points, corresponding to the shifts and maneuvers of Soviet policy."[40]

Kennan's pronouncement had a semiofficial ring to it and seemed to signal a determination on the part of the United States to settle in for a protracted across-the-board struggle with the Soviet Union. For Moscow's part, a similar function was served by a speech delivered by Andrei Zhdanov, Stalin's chief lieutenant, at the founding conference of the Communist Information Bureau (Cominform) in Poland in September 1947. The master image of Zhdanov's speech—a massive struggle between "two camps"—acknowledged the starkly bipolar nature of postwar politics and prescribed a rigid and dogmatic approach to the struggle against "imperialism."[41]

Zhdanov's speech began with an analysis of the "nature of the present epoch." The decisive role played by the Soviet Union in the victory over fascism, he said, "sharply altered the alignment of forces between the two systems— the socialist and the capitalist—in favor of socialism." As a result of the war, a number of countries had dropped out of the imperialist system and were now "paving the way for entry onto the path of socialist development." Only two great imperialist powers remained, and one of them—Britain—had been seriously weakened, in part by the "crisis of the colonial system." The other power, the United States, seeking to consolidate its monopoly position and reduce its capitalist partners to a state of dependency, had "proclaimed a new frankly predatory and expansionist course." The main obstacle to the American aspiration to world supremacy was the USSR, and thus Washington, "literally on the day following the conclusion of World War II," had set up a reactionary anti-Soviet front and proclaimed itself as the savior of the capitalist system from the communist threat.

The world was now divided into "two major camps: the imperialist and anti-democratic camp, on the one hand, and the antiimperialist and democratic camp, on the other." The former camp was led by the United States and supported not only by the major capitalist and colony-owning countries but also by "reactionary anti-democratic regimes" such as Turkey and Greece and by countries "politically and economically dependent" on the United States, "such as the Near-Eastern and South-American countries and China." Its purpose was "to strengthen imperialism, to hatch a new imperialist war, to combat socialism and democracy, and to support reactionary and anti-democratic pro-fascist regimes and movements everywhere." Zhdanov's very cadences were mockingly reminiscent of the sweeping language employed by Truman in his address to Congress a few months before.

The second camp was based on but not limited to the USSR and its East European allies: "Indonesia and Viet Nam are associated with it; it has the sympathy of India, Egypt and Syria." Backed by the "fraternal communist parties in all countries" and by "all progressive and democratic forces," its purpose was to "resist the threat of new wars and imperialist expansion, to strengthen democracy and to extirpate the vestiges of fascism." External peace was one of the most favorable conditions for the building of communism; thus, the Soviet Union had no desire for war and, moreover, sought to reduce armaments and outlaw "the most destructive of them—the atomic bomb." In essence, Soviet policy

proceeds from the fact of the co-existence for a long period of the two systems—capitalism and socialism. From this it follows that cooperation between the USSR and countries with other systems is possible, provided that the principle of reciprocity is observed and that obligations once assumed are honored. Everyone knows that the USSR has always honored the obligations it has assumed. The Soviet Union has demonstrated its will and desire for cooperation.[42]

Unfortunately, he said, the United States had spurned such cooperation and was preparing new military adventures. The U.S. government was militarizing the country, stockpiling new and dangerous weapons, and establishing far-flung foreign bases. But ideological struggle and economic expansionism were also important weapons in the American arsenal. It is in such a context, Zhdanov asserted, that the Marshall Plan should be understood. The invitation for Soviet and East European participation had been a trap aimed at severing the close economic and political ties that Moscow had built with the countries of Eastern Europe, but the Soviet Union had exposed this plan, demonstrating that American credits, far from being an act of generosity, were in fact designed to undermine the independence of the European countries while staving off economic collapse in the United States itself.

What is evident from both the Zhdanov and Truman speeches is that by 1947 the Soviet Union and the United States were both perceiving the world in terms of tight bipolarity. Each state saw itself at the head of a coalition defending the interests of world peace and human amelioration against the determined assaults of a rival coalition. The leaders of both states described this struggle in ideological terms that allowed no room for bargaining and compromise and acknowledged no legitimate noninvolvement and no viable third alternative. Each side spoke to its people of the need for vigilance and persistence in the conduct of a protracted struggle, and yet each side seemed anxious to avoid provoking the other into the use of force; a note of caution underlay the tough rhetoric in both camps.

In such an atmosphere and within the limits noted, there was little further need for Stalin to exercise care not to offend Western sensibilities in his dealings with Eastern Europe. In fact, in light of the stepped-up American involvement in Europe, he may have perceived a new urgency to the task of consolidating the Soviet position and insulating the East Europeans against the enticements of American aid or propaganda. The establishment of the Cominform was clearly one step in this process. As Zhdanov had admitted at the founding conference, "the need for mutual consultation and voluntary coordination of action between individual parties has become particularly urgent at the present juncture when continued isolation may lead to a slackening of mutual understanding, and at times, even to serious blunders." What the Cominform was designed to do in the way of enforcing uniformity in the "informational" sphere, the Council for Mutual Economic Assistance (COMECON) was intended to accomplish in the economic arena. A crude imitation of the European Recovery Program, it helped to ensure Soviet access to East European resources and to bind the economies of these countries more closely to that of the USSR.

The growing political uniformity of the East European regimes was dramatically underscored in February 1948 with the communist "coup" in Czechoslovakia. The resignation of 12 noncommunist ministers from the coalition government that month led to the demand, backed up by intense Soviet diplomatic pressure combined with veiled threats of armed interference, for the formation of a new government more overtly under communist control. Sensing his country's isolation, President Eduard Beneš complied with the demands, and the last vestige of popular accountability disappeared from the East European political landscape.

Ironically, this extension of monolithic control to Czechoslovakia was occurring just as the solidarity of relations between the Soviet Union and Yugoslavia was being called into question. Although there was little doubt of Tito's orthodoxy and loyalty to the Soviet Union, his ability to operate in Yugoslavia from an army and party base under his own rather than Stalin's control was proving unacceptable to the Soviet dictator. In January 1948, Stalin sought to assert his authority by ordering the Yugoslavs to "fold up" the communist uprising in Greece, by undercutting Tito's plans for a South Slav Federation, and by attempting to insert his own agents into Tito's apparatus. Although we shall consider the details of the Stalin-Tito split in a later chapter, our purpose here is to note that Stalin's insistence on absolute authority in "his" sphere of influence left Tito and his followers no choice but to capitulate entirely or break away from the socialist "camp." Choosing to resist, the Yugoslavs were expelled from the Cominform and subjected not only to a torrent of invective but also to a sustained campaign of diplomatic, economic, and military pressures. Although Stalin was said (by Khrushchev) to have boasted, "I will shake my little finger—and there will be no more Tito," the solidity of the Yugoslav leader's internal support, together with timely assistance from the West, enabled the Yugoslavs to withstand the Soviet pressures.

Apparently unwilling to risk war to destroy Tito, Stalin set about ensuring that any potential imitators in Eastern Europe were purged from the leadership ranks. Simultaneously, "domesticist" deviations of policy from the orthodox Soviet pattern of development were ended. As the region underwent purge and forced Sovietization, the main functions of the Cominform came to be the enforcement of uniformity and the conduct of the struggle against "Titoism."

With Tito thus excluded from the fold, the one remaining chink in the "Iron Curtain" was Germany—and particularly as this was symbolized in the continuation of Western occupation forces in Berlin, 100 miles within the Soviet zone of control. The Yalta image of occupied Germany as a single administrative and economic unit, partially undermined by the Potsdam decisions, had been further eroded in the spring of 1946, when the Western powers ceased their reparations deliveries to the Soviet zone in protest of Moscow's failure to reveal the magnitude of resources taken as reparations from its own zone. And yet the Soviets did not seem ready to opt finally for a divided Germany; they were still both attracted by the possibility of a unified and demilitarized Germany under procommunist rule, and haunted by fears of the threat that might emanate from a rebuilt and rearmed Western Germany tied in to the American sphere of influence. This concern was evident in the stance assumed by the Soviets at the Moscow foreign ministers' conference in March–April 1947, although they were not sufficiently precise in proposing an acceptable alternative.

Zhdanov's characterization in September of the two sides' positions on Germany suggested no remaining possibility for compromise, but it did renew Moscow's claim to support a unified Germany: "It is known that the USSR is in favor of a united, peace-loving, demilitarized and democratic Germany." The West, on the other hand, was pictured as opposing this objective and seeking "not only to prevent the democratic reconstruction and demilitarization of Germany, but even to liquidate her as an integral state, to dismember her, and to settle the question of peace separately."

The Western Allies' decision in February, 1948 to carry out a desperately needed currency reform in the three western zones signaled a resolve not only to deal with the problems of the economy without Soviet participation, but also to move toward organization of a German federal republic, which would be included in the European Recovery Program. The Soviets apparently read these plans as a mere prelude to the remilitarization of western Germany and to its transformation into the armed instrument of America's anti-Soviet coalition. If the Western Allies could be made to retreat from their strategy, Moscow might not only save itself from the spectre of a rearmed and hostile German state, it might also be able to demonstrate to the West German public that it could not entrust its security to its unreliable capitalist patrons.

By a series of moves beginning in the spring, Moscow began to exert pressure on the Western powers designed to force them to surrender the control of currency in all of Berlin to the Soviets and to retreat from the plan to create a West German state. This campaign culminated in June with the blockade of all land and sea routes into Berlin. Stalin apparently felt that the risks of such a step were tolerable, given the local military superiority of the Soviets and the unlikelihood that the Western powers would take on the onus of initiating the use of force to break the blockade.

The American response, however, succeeded in shifting this responsibility back to the Soviets. Calling on its own substantial airlift capabilities, the United States mounted a continuous airborne supply shuttle, totaling over a quarter of a million flights over the next 12 months.[43]

The Berlin blockade's effect upon the American and European publics and governments was just the opposite of what Stalin had expected. With increased support from the Germans, the West proceeded with its plans to create a unified state in its zones of occupation, and the Federal Republic of Germany came into being in May 1949. More important, the blockade helped spark the decision of the United States government to commit itself in peacetime to the defense of Europe. The North Atlantic Treaty Organization was created on April 4, 1949;

shortly thereafter General Eisenhower was named supreme commander of allied forces in Europe.

Acknowledging defeat, the Soviet Union ended the blockade of Berlin on May 12, and five months later it sponsored the formation of the communist-ruled German Democratic Republic in its own zone of occupation. Although the Soviets were by no means reconciled to the continuing anomalous situation in Berlin, the territorial division of Europe now seemed complete and a competitive stalemate had settled in over the continent.

THE TURN TO ASIA

It is, on the surface, surprising that the Soviet Union paid so little attention to Asia in the period from the end of the war until 1948-49. Not only was a communist army challenging the ruling elite of the world's largest country, but the great European colonial empires in South and Southeast Asia were in the process of collapse, leaving enormous anti-Western sentiment and political instability in their wake. The Soviets were certainly busy protecting vital security interests and probing for opportunities to expand their sphere of influence in Europe, but this is not a complete explanation for Stalin's seeming unconcern for revolutionary possibilities in Asia.

Another salient factor helping to shape Stalin's sense of priorities was the memory of his earlier, unsuccessful involvement in an effort to ride the tide of Asian nationalism and revolution. The Soviet and Comintern failure in China in 1927 had not only squandered communist influence and strength in China but had also colored Stalin's future perceptions to the point that he had simply precluded future defeats by refusing to reinvest Soviet energies and resources in an Asian revolution. Frustrated by his inability to achieve his objectives by cooperating with forces that eluded his total direct control, Stalin had chosen not to attempt again a similar exercise in conjunction with unreliable Asian nationalists and communists.

Thus, Mao Zedong's ascent to leadership of the Chinese Communist Party in 1935 had occurred without Soviet participation or endorsement, and Mao's peasant-based struggle against the Nationalist regime of Chiang Kai-shek had grown and endured without Soviet support. Indeed, in their anxiety to avoid a wartime Soviet-American confrontation over the internal struggle in China, the Soviets had sought to encourage the United States to aid the Chinese "in unifying their country, improving their military and economic conditions." In this same conversation with Ambassador Patrick Hurley, Molotov went so far as to assert that Mao's forces "were related to Communism in no way at all. It was merely a way of expressing dissatisfaction with their economic condition and they would forget this inclination when their economic condition improved."[44] Not only were the Soviets encouraging the United States to forge a coalition between the contending Chinese forces, but they were at the same time—out of fear that the Americans might intervene militarily—seeking to discourage the Chinese Communists from undertaking a full-scale civil war.

As we have already seen, Stalin was able to secure his major territorial ambitions in Asia through agreement with the United States and Kuomintang regime—without the expense or bother of revolution. The Chinese communists cannot have been happy about the August 1945 Sino-Soviet treaty, for it not only sacrificed certain Chinese interests, it also signaled a Soviet expectation that the Kuomintang would continue to rule in China for the foreseeable future. While the Soviets did turn over to Mao in March 1946 the portion of Manchuria under their occupation (and the arms captured from the Japanese), thus forcing Chiang to dissipate enormous resources in recapturing it from the communists, they did so only after removing approximately two billion dollars' worth of industrial equipment to the USSR.

A direct confirmation of the Soviets' nonsupportive postwar attitude toward Mao's revolution can be found in a remark Stalin made to Djilas in the quite different context of January 1948:

We, too, can make a mistake. Here, when the war with Japan ended, we invited the Chinese comrades to reach an agreement with us as to how a *modus vivendi* with Chiang Kai-shek might be found. They agreed with us in word, but in deed they did it their own way when they got home: they mustered their forces and struck. It has been shown that they were right, and not we.[45]

If even Stalin could acknowledge the mistake in the Soviet position, how bitterly it must have sat with Mao Zedong!

As late as 1947, following the failure of the American effort to mediate the civil conflict and the turning of the tide of battle in Mao's favor, the Soviets continued to play down the Chinese communists' successes, virtually ignoring them in their media and failing to invite them to the founding conference of the Cominform. Given the Truman Administration's reaction to communist fishing expeditions in Iran and Greece, Stalin must have been expecting more active U.S. support of Chiang. The ineptitude of the Nationalist forces hastened their collapse but Moscow still hesitated to cut its ties to Chiang, directing its ambassador to accompany the Kuomintang government when it fled from Nanking to Canton in the spring of 1949. The United States seemed to wash its hands of the China debacle with the publication in August of the State Department White Paper, which both blasted the corruption and inefficiency of Chiang's forces and attacked Mao as a Soviet agent. But the Soviets still held back their recognition of the changed situation—and Mao postponed his proclamation of the People's Republic—until the beginning of October when the military victory of the communists was all but complete.

A similar kind of ambivalence marked the Soviet stance toward the growing revolutionary turbulence elsewhere in Asia. Zhdanov's speech to the Cominform had alluded to the "sharpening of the crisis of the colonial system" and to "increasing armed resistance" to imperialism by colonial peoples, and yet it had neither directly prescribed a strategy of armed revolution to Asian communists nor pledged Soviet material support for such activity. Not only did the Soviets hold back at first from directly exploiting nationalist and antiimperialist sentiment in South and Southeast Asia, they also evidenced initial ambiguity in their assessment of the stance that should be taken by Asian communists toward the nationalist movements in the area. In India, for example, the communist party shifted early in 1948 to a more militant stance on a signal from the Yugoslav rather than the Soviet party and its decision was pointedly ignored in the Soviet press. A communist-sponsored conference of Asian youth and students, which met in Calcutta in February 1948, is thought by some observers to have "given the orders" for the subsequent militant uprisings in Southeast Asia. But even this meeting in fact gave no general endorsement to armed struggle and failed unambiguously to condemn "bourgeois nationalist" Asian governments.[46]

Only in mid-1949 did the Soviets publicly endorse the path of armed struggle already being pursued by the communist parties in Indochina, Indonesia, India, Burma, Malaya, and the Philippines. The endorsement took the form of publication in *Pravda* of a long article by one of the foremost leaders of the Chinese revolution. Liu Shaoqi—although the article had actually been written six months earlier. Liu's message stressed the necessity for communist parties to form alliances with bourgeois nationalism in the antiimperialist struggle.

By the end of the year, the Soviet press was explicitly commending to its Asian comrades the "Chinese path" to revolution and was unambiguously endorsing armed struggle as the primary tactic in this struggle.[47] In so doing, Moscow seemed to be both overestimating the strength and appeal of the communist parties and underestimating the value of forging ties with the noncommunist leaders of independence movements in these countries. But in fact Stalin's purposes in giving his assent to the Asian revolutions may well have been less directed to the well-being of the local communists and more to the prospect that such uprisings might absorb the energies and tie down the armies of his NATO adversaries.

A revealing indication of the extent of Stalin's generosity was that the Soviet press, even as it hailed the victory of the Chinese communists and commended the Chinese path to other Asian parties, took pains to deny Mao Zedong's authorship of the Chinese strategy. The Chinese had in fact claimed that Mao's theory was of universal significance and a signal contribution to the treasure house of Marxism-Leninism. Soviet theorists responded by demonstrating the dependence of the entire Chinese movement on Leninist-Stalinist teachings. One writer claimed that a 1925 speech by Stalin "brilliantly foresaw" the entire course of development in China; moreover, it had been the Soviet victory over the German and Japanese aggressors (directed, of course, by comrade Stalin) that had been decisive in changing the correlation of forces in China and making Mao's victory there possible.[48]

But Mao was to discover at first hand the state in which he was regarded by Stalin. When, on December 19, 1949, he arrived at the train station in Moscow leading a delegation to negotiate a treaty with the Soviet Union, he was greeted by Molotov, not by Stalin. Mao was to stay in Moscow for nine weeks, during which he found himself engaged in extremely hard bargaining. At the end of the process, following the conclusion of the Treaty of Alliance, Friendship and Mutual Assistance on February 14, 1950, *Pravda* carried a picture of the two leadership teams. In it, Stalin and Mao are shown unsmiling, and the caption identifies the Soviet dictator and his Politburo colleagues as *Comrade* Stalin, *Comrade* Malenkov, etc., while it refers to their new allies as *Mister* Mao and *Mister* Zhou.

This uncomradely display well reflected the very mixed feelings with which the Soviets must have regarded the Chinese communist victory. True, the Chinese triumph represented the first genuinely revolutionary communist victory since the Bolshevik revolution itself, and as such, it significantly advanced the cause of world revolution. In so doing, it provided a new model and fresh inspiration and support for the cause of revolutionaries elsewhere in Asia. But to the extent that the Chinese path represented an alternative to the Soviet model and guidance, it was a mixed blessing for Moscow. Moreover, the Soviets had already discovered with Tito the difficulties they could have with a communist neighbor who had largely forged his own victory and ruled without Soviet tutelage or control.

Even apart from the implications of possible new difficulties in managing the international communist movement, Mao's victory could be disadvantageous at the level of state-to-state relations as well. Moscow had already had a quite satisfactory treaty relationship with Chiang's regime—one that had brought certain benefits no longer present in the new treaty. Under its terms, the Soviets were to return control of the Manchurian railway and the base at Port Arthur by no later than the end of 1952, and although the determination of the final status of Dairen was postponed, it also was to pass to Chinese administration. In the 1950 treaty, China acquiesced to the status of Outer Mongolia, but Chiang had done the same in the 1945 pact. And in the new treaty the Soviet Union incurred some defense obligations that were also of mixed value. Moscow had acquired an ally 500-million strong, but it had promised to render assistance to China against aggression by Japan or "any other state which should unite with Japan, directly or indirectly, in acts of aggression."[49] Although the wording was carefully hedged, this seemed to obligate the USSR in a far more precise way than before to the protection of Chinese interests against possible American incursions. Finally, the Soviets agreed in the 1950 treaty to provide a loan of $300 million to China. While this was a miserly sum indeed, and the Soviets were to gain the right to establish joint stock companies in China, this provision raised the prospect that Moscow would now be assuming a possibly costly obligation of fraternal economic assistance to China in its efforts to build socialism from a very backward economic base.

If the Sino-Soviet Treaty gave little cause for Mao to remember Stalin well, events later in 1950 were to raise even more questions about the balance of costs and benefits in the new relationship. By the end of the year, the Chinese found themselves diverted from their own priorities and engaged, with arms *purchased* from the USSR, in a military conflict with the United States that was provoked by a Soviet miscalculation. Whereas they might otherwise have been able to concentrate on finishing off Chiang Kai-shek and incorporating Formosa under their rule—with little prospect that the United States would have intervened in such a situation—they were instead not only fighting against the United States in Korea but also facing the American Seventh Fleet interposed between themselves and Formosa.

The evidence suggests that the Chinese had little role in the decisions that precipitated the war in Korea. The regime in North Korea had been established by Soviet-trained communists following the withdrawal of Soviet occupation forces in 1949. The state that had succeeded the American occupation in the southern half of the peninsula was militarily and politically weaker and seemed ripe for conquest. Particularly in light of its failure to ward off the communist victory in China, the United States seemed unlikely to come to the defense of its client in Korea. American statements seemed to confirm this, particularly the pronouncement of Secretary of State Acheson in January, which failed to include South Korea within the American "defense perimeter."

Moscow's interest in this situation went beyond the prospect of unifying the Korean peninsula under a single communist regime. The more important target was Japan, whose future political and security orientation was still in question. Despite the growing strength of the Japanese communist party, the USSR feared that it might soon be more decisively excluded from an influential role in Japan by virtue of American attempts to conclude a separate peace treaty and incorporate Japan into a security alliance with the United States. Just as the Berlin blockade had been calculated to arouse doubts among the German public about their growing ties to the American sphere, the North Korean attack was apparently designed to forestall Japan's movement into Washington's sphere in Asia.

The North Korean invasion on June 25, 1950, was followed two days later by a Security Council decision to condemn the aggression and call on member states to assist South Korea. The Soviets, who had been boycotting the United Nations since January in protest of the continued presence of Chiang's delegation as the Chinese representatives, were caught by surprise; they were probably even more startled when President Truman ordered U.S. land, sea, and air forces to Korea.

The United States eased the threat somewhat by taking pains to reassure Moscow that it sought no direct conflict in Korea with the USSR—which had in 1949 broken the American monopoly and become an atomic power. The Americans asked the Soviets to disavow any responsibility for the North Korean attack, which the Soviets promptly did, claiming that indeed South Korea had attacked the north. Thus aware that the United States was not seeking a broader conflict, the Soviet Union couched its response in a way that carried no threat of intervention in Korea. At any rate, this appeared totally unnecessary, given the spectacular initial success of the North Korean armies.

By October, however, the tide of battle had turned, and the United Nations forces under General MacArthur had driven the North Koreans back across the 38th parallel and were pursuing them toward the Yalu River border with Manchuria. Suddenly the situation grew more uncomfortable for Stalin as the United Nations forces seemed on the verge of forging a unified Korea under noncommunist control and American influence. The Soviets faced not only a loss of their initial objectives but also the humiliating and dangerous prospect that a communist government might be defeated by American arms. But the Chinese faced an even more unacceptable loss for this new hostile state would be lodged at a vital section of their border; moreover, some Americans were already beginning to talk of carrying the war beyond the Yalu to China itself.

China had not brought this dilemma upon itself, and it appeared very reluctant to use military force to resolve it. Only after several fruitless warnings to the United States (delivered through the Indians), and then after having apparently extricated an agreement from Moscow that it would provide aid for the venture, did Chinese "volunteer" forces enter the fighting at the side of the North Koreans.

After months of bitter fighting and movement back and forth across the 38th parallel, the war settled into a bloody stalemate at this line. On June 23, 1951, the Soviet Ambassador to the United Nations spoke to suggest that an armistice might be possible in Korea even without satisfaction of the prior preconditions of political settlement and U.S. troop withdrawal. Although the armistice talks were to begin the following month, the Soviets found a number of advantages in allowing them to drag on without conclusion for two more years. Stalin did not find it unacceptable to have the forces of his major adversary tied down in a protracted conflict with a Soviet proxy, which was itself thereby becoming even more dependent on the USSR. Moreover, the lengthy war was provoking intense political controversy both within the United States and between

Washington and its European allies, who agreed with the American critics that the administration was fighting "the wrong war at the wrong place at the wrong time."

But the Soviets did not find the outcome in Korea wholly to their liking. The original Soviet objectives had been lost, and Japan—now firmly oriented in an anticommunist direction—had not only concluded a separate peace treaty with the United States but had also entered into a security alliance with Washington. Moscow had had to bear a large part of the costs of arming its Chinese ally, but the much costlier burden assumed by Beijing, as a result of Moscow's blunder, meant that the USSR had incurred a certain obligation to its ally that had altered the earlier, more one-sided nature of their relationship. Finally, the war had occasioned a large increase in American defense expenditures and troop strength and had aroused renewed American interest in spreading the defense burden—particularly through the rearmament of Germany. On the whole, Moscow was concluding, both from the increased American willingness to intervene to contain communist expansion in Asia and from the inability of other Asian revolutionary movements to match the Chinese success, that the new conditions in Asia were far less favorable to armed struggle. Once this decision had been reached, Stalin was again altering his tactics and priorities in preparation for one last attempt to alter the unfavorable situation in Europe.

ENDURING STALEMATE

As discussed above, the Berlin blockade had backfired on the Soviets; it both failed in achieving its immediate objectives and helped to stimulate the military mobilization of the West. The militant Soviet tactics associated with the Zhdanov line had not succeeded in Europe and were also in the process of miscarrying in Asia. One legacy of this failure was the weakened condition of the nonruling communist parties on both continents. Urged by Zhdanov in 1947 to intensify the class struggle and step up the campaign against noncommunist governments, the communists had consequently found themselves generally isolated and discredited. No clearer example can be found than that of the French Communist Party. In February 1949, its leader, Maurice Thorez, had gone so far as to declare his party's unconditional support for the Soviet Union and its army, even should that army enter upon the territory of France itself. Needless to say, the storm of protest unleashed by this unpatriotic remark hardly strengthened the popular appeal of the French Communist Party, though it may have assured Stalin that no potential Titoists lurked within that organization.

Zhdanov's sudden death in August 1948 was followed by a bloody purge of his Leningrad party organization and a period of jockeying for advantage among Stalin's other lieutenants. The ascension of Georgi Malenkov as the new apparent second-in-command seemed to coincide with a new effort in Moscow to break out of isolation and broaden Soviet and communist appeal while weakening Western solidarity.

A noteworthy manifestation of this altered approach was the Peace Movement of 1948–1952, the primary objective of which was to enlist neutralist, nationalist, and anti-American sentiment in order to pressure Western governments to soften their resistance to Soviet objectives. As summarized by Marshall Shulman, the strategic functions of the Peace Movement were:

to reduce the danger of war during a period of maximum Soviet vulnerability; to neutralize the superior atomic capability of the West by building up popular feeling against the use of the atomic bomb; to reduce the political advantages to the West of its atomic monopoly; and to weaken the West's aircraft delivery system by rendering the overseas airbases politically insecure.[50]

The campaign originated early in 1948 in France, where the sentiments against an integrated Western defense system and a rearmed Germany were particularly strong. Working through ostensibly noncommunist front organizations, the Soviets and their allies began to exploit the movement for their own purposes. In August, a World Congress of Intellectuals for Peace was held in Poland. A few months later, Stalin spurred the campaign with an interview in *Pravda* in which he called upon the forces working for peace to step up their political efforts to unseat war-mongering leaders in the United States and Britain. The movement took on organizational form in April 1949 when the World Congress of Partisans of Peace ended its meeting in Paris by setting up a permanent World Peace Council. By the end of 1949, the Peace Movement had become such a prominent and successful tactic that communist parties were urged by the Cominform to make it the "pivot" of their activities. The movement climaxed the following year with the Stockholm Peace Appeal, a "ban-the-bomb" petition that eventually gained millions of signatories.

It is difficult to gauge the actual effects of this activity upon the policies of the Western governments. Certainly, war-weariness and alarm at the dangers posed by the cold war were widespread enough sentiments that Soviet propagandists during this period were able to broaden the audience for their message. But Moscow did not rely upon the arousal of public opinion as the sole tactic in its effort to weaken the Western alliance. Formal diplomatic contacts were also employed by the Soviet Union in its campaign to prevent the rearmament of West Germany and its incorporation into the NATO alliance. A number of proposals were made by the Soviets with an eye toward exacerbating the "contradictions" with the Western camp. The considerable French nervousness at the prospect of a German army being revived only half a decade after the end of the war had led Western statesmen to search for a formula whereby

German manpower and resources might be utilized for Western defense without the creation of a separate West German army.

As these efforts seemed to near fruition, the Soviet Union proposed in November 1950 that a meeting of foreign ministers be assembled to resume negotiations on a German peace treaty that would be accompanied by the creation of a united and demilitarized German state. The West allowed the proposal to sink into the diplomatic morass, and it soon disappeared altogether in the wake of the Chinese intervention in Korea and the slowed pace of the effort to rearm Germany.

By the end of the following year, however, the West again seemed to be making progress toward obtaining a German contribution to the allied defense effort. It was in this context that Moscow made its most intriguing—and possibly its most serious—proposal to alter the status of Germany. The Soviet note of March 10, 1952, differed from the earlier proposal in one significant respect: it held out the prospect that a reunited Germany might have her own army if she were pledged to permanent neutrality.

Some analysts argue that Stalin was making a serious and last-ditch effort to reach a compromise on the worrisome problem of Germany, and that he was actually prepared to sacrifice communist East Germany for the larger objective of preventing Germany's rearmament as part of the Western defense network. Others argue that the United States and the Adenauer government in Bonn were right in spurning this proposal as a flagrant effort to derail the Western defense plans; they point out that Stalin of all people would never have felt secure had the only restraint on a rearmed and reunified Germany been a mere neutrality treaty.[51] The controversy cannot be definitively settled, but either interpretation suggests both the degree of Stalin's alarm at the prospects in Germany and his continuing ability to shift his tactics in order to take advantage of perceived diplomatic openings.

We have already noted in the previous chapter that Stalin's last theoretical pronouncement—on "Economic Problems of Socialism in the USSR"—decreed war between the socialist and imperialist camps was less likely than war among the capitalist nations themselves. The implied message—that a reduction of tensions between the USSR and the United States was possible—was reiterated a month later in Malenkov's report to the Nineteenth Party Congress. Soviet policy, he asserted, was based on the premise that

the peaceful coexistence of capitalism and communism and cooperation are quite possible, given a mutual desire to cooperate, readiness to carry out commitments undertaken, and observance of the principle of equality and non-interference in the internal affairs of other states.[52]

Thus, in Stalin's last years the militant tactics of class struggle and confrontation were being replaced by an approach that sought to employ political pressure against the West in order to weaken its unity and alter its policies. Stalin's closing address to the Nineteenth Congress urged the "representatives of the Communist and democratic parties" to lift the banners of "bourgeois democratic freedoms" and of "national independence and national sovereignty" in order to increase their popular support in this struggle. The message was applicable not only to the European parties, for the Asian comrades were simultaneously being urged by Moscow to drop their uncompromising hostility toward the new "bourgeois nationalist" leaders of the region in order more effectively to influence their countries' policies in an antiimperialist direction.

These tactical changes during Stalin's later life were not sufficient to bring about a major reorientation of the Soviet approach to the world. What was needed was a more thoroughgoing reassessment of the international situation, which in turn necessitated a disavowal of some of Stalin's own fundamental theses on foreign policy. In a very real sense, the aging dictator had outlived his usefulness to his country, and only with his death in March 1953 would a more venturesome strategy to attempt to break the stalemate of cold war emerge.

Ironically, the years we have surveyed in this chapter were at one and the same time a period of great weakness and vulnerability and an era in which the Soviet Union achieved major successes and became one of the world's two nuclear superpowers. Yet the dangers had multiplied with the achievements. The cold war divisions between East and West seemed to have hardened and even within the Soviet sphere great stresses and tensions were barely concealed below the surface. Stalin's legacy in international affairs was surely a mixed one even by Soviet standards. His own immediate successors criticized him bitterly for the inflexibility of his assessments, which led to policies divorced from reality. Among his greatest mistakes, they pointed out his treatment of Yugoslavia, his insensitivity to opportunities for the expansion of Soviet influence among the newly emerging nations, and his sterile and antiquated military doctrine. The heirs of his heirs, on the other hand, having seen the risks entailed in bold experimentation, have been more tolerant in their assessment of Stalin's legacy. Thus, even in death, the "genius leader of all mankind" continues to be a dominant, controversial, and unsettling figure for both his own people and the entire communist world.

NOTES

1. Louis Fischer, *The Road to Yalta: Soviet Foreign Relations 1941-1945* (New York: Harper and Row, 1972), p. 1.
2. J. V. Stalin, *The Great Patriotic War of the Soviet Union,* 5th ed. (Moscow, 1950), p. 15.

3. Robert E. Sherwood, *Roosevelt and Hopkins: An Intimate History,* rev. ed. (New York: Harper and Brothers, 1948), pp. 323-347.

4. Excerpts from the speech are found in Myron Rush, ed., *The International Situation and Soviet Foreign Policy* (Columbus, Ohio: Charles E. Merrill, 1970), pp. 117-123.

5. Quoted in Ivan Maisky, *Memoirs of a Soviet Ambassador: The War 1939-1943,* trans., Andrew Rothstein (London: Hutchison, 1967), p. 231.

6. *Khrushchev Remembers,* with an introduction, commentary, and notes by Edward Crankshaw, trans. and ed., Strobe Talbott (Boston: Little, Brown and Company, 1970), pp. 223-226.

7. Sherwood, *Roosevelt and Hopkins,* pp. 556-557.

8. Herbert Feis, *Churchill, Roosevelt, Stalin* (Princeton, N.J.: Princeton University Press, 1957), p. 67.

9. Winston S. Churchill, *The Second World War: The Hinge of Fate* (Boston: Houghton Mifflin Co., 1950), p. 483.

10. For a full discussion of the circumstances and the evidence, see Fischer, *The Road to Yalta,* pp. 75-90.

11. Ibid., p. 100.

12. Winston S. Churchill, *The Second World War: Closing the Ring* (Boston: Houghton Mifflin Co., 1951), pp. 359-362.

13. U.S. Department of State, *Foreign Relations of the United States: Diplomatic Papers: The Conferences at Cairo and Teheran 1943* (Washington: U.S. Government Printing Office, 1961), p. 567-568.

14. Winston S. Churchill, *The Second World War: Triumph and Tragedy* (Boston: Houghton Mifflin Co., 1953), p. 227.

15. Quoted in Fischer, *The Road to Yalta,* p. 186.

16. Churchill, *The Second World War: Triumph and Tragedy,* p. 639.

17. Harry S. Truman, *Memoirs,* vol. I (Garden City, N.Y.: Doubleday, 1955), p. 416.

18. Zhukov, G. K., *The Memoirs of Marshal Zhukov,* (New York: Delacorte Press, 1973), pp. 674-675.

19. Milovan Djilas, *Conversations with Stalin,* (New York: Harcourt, Brace and World, 1962), p. 114.

20. For a persuasive argument that the bombings were known by the American government not to be militarily necessary, see Charles L. Mee, Jr., *Meeting at Potsdam* (New York: Dell, 1975), especially chap. 17.

21. For details of the strategy and its cost, see Adam B. Ulam, *Expansion and Coexistence: Soviet Foreign Policy 1917-1973,* second ed. (New York: Praeger, 1974), pp. 395-398, 477.

22. Djilas, *Conversations with Stalin,* p. 155.

23. Ibid., p. 114.

24. For a fuller documentation of the contending viewpoints in this debate, see Robert James Maddox, *The New Left and the Origins of the Cold War*

(Princeton, N.J.: Princeton University Press, 1973); Thomas G. Paterson, *The Origins of the Cold War* (Lexington, Mass.: D.C. Heath, 1970); William Appleman Williams, *The Tragedy of American Diplomacy*, rev. ed. (New York: Dell, 1962); Christopher Lasch, "The Cold War, Revisited and Re-Visioned," *New York Times Magazine*, January 14, 1968; Lloyd C. Gardner, Arthur Schlesinger, Jr., Hans Morgenthau, *Origins of the Cold War*, (Waltham: Ginn & Co., 1970); Norman A. Graebner, "Cold War Origins and the Continuing Debate: A Review of Recent Literature," *Journal of Conflict Resolution 13* (March 1969): 123-132.

25. Excerpts in Rush, *The International Situation*, pp. 117-123.
26. *The Anti-Stalin Campaign and International Communism*, A Selection of documents edited by the Russian Institute, Columbia University (New York: Columbia University Press, 1956), p. 57.
27. Ibid., p. 40.
28. Djilas, *Conversations with Stalin*, p. 181.
29. *Khrushchev Remembers*, p. 361.
30. *The Anti-Stalin Campaign*, p. 60.
31. Djilas, *Conversations with Stalin*, p. 115.
32. N. S. Khrushchev, "Disarmament is the Path toward Strengthening Peace and Ensuring Friendship among Peoples," *Pravda*, January 15, 1960.
33. Quoted in Thomas W. Wolfe, *Soviet Power and Europe 1945-1970* (Baltimore: Johns Hopkins University Press, 1970), pp. 62-63.
34. Quoted in Raymond L. Garthoff, *Soviet Strategy in the Nuclear Age* (New York: Praeger, 1958), p. 62.
35. Quoted in Joseph M. Jones, *The Fifteen Weeks* (New York: The Viking Press, 1955), p. 22.
36. U.S. Senate Committee on Foreign Relations, 80th Congress, 1st Session, *Hearings on a Bill to Provide for Assistance to Greece and Turkey*, p. 152.
37. Quoted in Alexander Dallin, *The Soviet Union at the United Nations* (New York: Praeger, 1962), p. 22.
38. Ibid., p. 25.
39. Quoted in Jones, *The Fifteen Weeks*, pp. 34-35.
40. George Kennan, "The Sources of Soviet Conduct," in *American Diplomacy 1900-1950* (New York: Mentor, 1952), p. 99.
41. Excerpts in Rush, *The International Situation*, pp. 125-139.
42. Ibid., p. 132.
43. At the peak of the airlift, Anglo-American flights were landing in Berlin at the rate of one every 45 seconds. See U.S. Department of State, *Background: Berlin–1961* (Washington: U.S. Government Printing Office, 1961), p. 11.
44. U.S. Department of State. *U.S. Relations with China, with Special Reference to the Period 1944-1949*, (Washington: U.S. Government Printing Office, 1949), p. 72.

45. Djilas, *Conversations with Stalin,* p. 182.
46. For a fuller explication of this point, see Robert H. Donaldson, *Soviet Policy toward India: Ideology and Strategy* (Cambridge, Mass.: Harvard University Press, 1974), pp. 74-78.
47. Ibid., pp. 85-93.
48. G. V. Astaf'iev, "Ot polukolonii k narodnoi demokratii" ["From Semi-Colony to People's Democracy"] in E. M. Zhukov, ed., *Krisis kolonial-'noi sistemy: natsional'no svoboditel'naia bor'ba narodov Vostochnoi Azii* [Crisis of the Colonial System: The National-Liberation Struggle of the Peoples of East Asia] (Moscow, 1949), p. 82.
49. Royal Institute of International Affairs, *Documents on International Affairs, 1949-1950* (London: RIIA, 1950), p. 543.
50. Marshall D. Shulman, *Stalin's Foreign Policy Reappraised* (New York: Atheneum, 1965), pp. 80-81.
51. For a fuller account, see Ulam, *Expansion and Coexistence,* pp. 534-537; Shulman, ibid., pp. 191-194; and Thomas W. Wolfe, *Soviet Power and Europe 1945-1970,* (Baltimore: Johns Hopkins University Press, 1970), pp. 27-31.
52. G. M. Malenkov, "Report to the XIX Party Congress, October 5, 1952," in Rush, *The International Situation,* p. 152.

Chapter 4
The Perilous Path to Peaceful Coexistence

STALIN'S SUCCESSORS TAKE STOCK

The official communique announcing Stalin's death to the Soviet population stressed the necessity of "prevention of any kind of disorder and panic." This declaration provides a revealing insight to the disarray into which the leader's death had temporarily plunged his lieutenants, and to the lack of confidence with which they viewed their future. Khrushchev's memoirs record that in the realm of foreign policy the old dictator had expressed his own doubts as to the prospects of his heirs:

Right up until his death Stalin used to tell us, "You'll see, when I'm gone the imperialistic powers will wring your necks like chickens." We never tried to reassure him that we would be able to manage. We knew it wouldn't do any good.[1]

Coping with Stalin's legacy in foreign policy, Khrushchev adds, was to be "an interesting challenge for us."

Stalin had deliberately fostered insecurity and competition among his subordinates, retaining for himself the role of final and infallible resolver of conflicts. His efforts had been directed toward the relentless mobilization of human and material resources and the forging of a heavy industrial base and superior military strength, to the neglect of consumer goods and agricultural production. The inevitable hardships and sacrifices had been blamed on scapegoats—either traitors within or the enemy without. This policy achieved a great deal but exacted a heavy toll not only in human lives but in unmet needs and in personal insecurity for the privileged and the underprivileged alike.

Stalin's successors recognized the dangers inherent in an attempt to continue along this road, and they worked to rationalize the rule of the party without weakening its monopoly of power or abandoning its goals. Reliance on terror

84

had undermined both initiative and morale; the new regime lessened the role of the police and attempted to place greater reliance on material incentives and persuasion. An effort to improve the standard of living was a corollary of this policy of domestic reorientation, and yet the achievement of domestic stability and amelioration of living standards—including the strengthening of Soviet agriculture—served as an important base for a successful foreign policy as well.

In the international arena, several trouble spots threatened to divert the energy and resources needed for this heavy domestic agenda. Prominent among these were the continuing conflict in Korea, the unproductive quarrel with Yugoslavia, and the quickening approach of West German rearmament. Foreign policy issues could not be ignored by the new leaders, but they could not be allowed to boil over into active confrontation between Moscow and its adversaries.

Within hours of Stalin's death, his lieutenants had agreed to restrict participation in the new collective leadership to a smaller group than had been named to the expanded Party Presidium (the successor to the Politburo) at the Nineteenth Party Congress the previous fall. Within this collective, Georgi Malenkov initially acted as head of both the Soviet government (Chairman of the Council of Ministers) and the Party Secretariat, but by March 14 he was apparently obliged by his colleagues (who relished no continuation of one-man rule) to choose between the two posts. That he chose to remain in the former position is a revealing indication of the relatively low state to which the Party apparatus had fallen in Stalin's last years. Joining Malenkov in taking high government posts were Lavrenti Beria, head of the secret police, Lazar Kaganovich, a deputy premier, Nikolai Bulganin, the defense minister, and Vyacheslav Molotov, who resumed his former role as foreign minister. Nikita Khrushchev, relatively junior to his colleagues (though he had served as head of both the Ukrainian and Moscow party bureaucracies), was given a post in the Party Secretariat.

This new coalition quickly proved unstable, however, as Beria showed signs of attempting to use his control of the organs of repression as a lever for expanding his own role in the leadership. Wisely afraid of the potential threat from the secret police chief, in July 1953, his colleagues arranged (with the assistance, Khrushchev says, of 11 generals and marshals) to have him arrested. Charged with a whole catalogue of crimes, Beria and his top subordinates were executed before the end of the year. Significantly, he was the last Soviet leader to suffer the ultimate penalty for defeat in the struggle for power. With Beria's removal, the state security apparatus was bifurcated and again placed under the firm control of the Communist Party. In September, Khrushchev in turn took a large step toward exercising control of the Party, as he assumed the new title of First Secretary of the Communist Party of the Soviet Union (CPSU).

No individual in the new leadership possessed the stature and authority of a Stalin, however, and this was soon manifested in the sphere of bloc relations. Stalin's personal influence and style of rule had provided much of the cement that held the bloc together; even in the strikingly exceptional case of Yugoslavia, the defection of Tito was largely a result of Stalin's personal interventions.

The specter of the bloc's disintegration was raised only three months after Stalin's death when workers' demonstrations and strikes in East Berlin and other cities in the East German state had to be quelled with Soviet tanks. The particular location of this disturbance had implications beyond the bloc and the demonstration of the fragility of communist rule in East Germany probably ended whatever chances still existed that Moscow would be willing to bargain with the West for German reunification. The lessons of the Berlin uprising for Soviet relations with Eastern Europe were more immediately apparent: the subject populations of these countries might no longer tolerate the policies of naked police terror and harsh economic sacrifice that were being practiced by the "little Stalins" of the bloc. Thus, the new Soviet leadership nudged its East European allies along a "New Course" that followed the Soviet example in easing some of the more draconian trappings of Stalinist rule. At the same time that it began encouraging these prophylactic measures against revolt in the bloc, Moscow embarked on the course of seeking to reintegrate the stray member of the fold. In the month of the East German unrest, the Soviets proposed to the Yugoslav government that diplomatic relations between the two states be restored.

In the case of its relationship with Eastern Europe, as well as in other priority arenas, what the Soviet leadership sought in the immediate post-Stalin period did not amount to a change in basic objectives. The near-term goals of Soviet foreign policy remained much the same as they had been in Stalin's last year: a strengthening of the economic and military capability of the USSR, consolidation of the Communist bloc under Soviet leadership, and a reduction of the perceived threat to Soviet security in Europe posed by American influence and German military potential. What did change were the tactics and diplomatic style adopted by Moscow in these years.

New leadership brought to Soviet foreign policy a capacity to adapt to new opportunities and a flexibility such as had not been seen in Moscow for some time. As we have seen in the previous chapter, by 1953, Stalin's policies had resulted in diplomatic stalemate and near isolation for the USSR. The world's diplomatic agenda was littered with deadlocked conflicts. In certain of these situations, Moscow had limited its ability to produce movement by severing relations with an adversary.

Yugoslavia is one instance in which the new Soviet leaders sought to restore contacts in an effort to regain the initiative, but there were several others in

1953. Also, in the Balkan area, the Soviets resumed diplomatic relations with Greece, broken since the days of the civil war, and improved their standing with Turkey by withdrawing, on May 30, the territorial claims that had been made against her in the immediate postwar period. In the Middle East, the Soviet Union had been the first state to extend *de jure* recognition to Israel in 1948, but these ties had been severed by Moscow in 1953, following the explosion of a bomb in the Soviet legation. The break occurred in conjunction with the anti-Semitic campaign prompted by the spurious "Jewish Doctors' Plot." After Stalin's death and the exposure of the bogus conspiracy, relations between the USSR and Israel were restored. In central Europe, the Soviets were soon engaged in renewed negotiations over the status of occupied Germany and Austria; in both cases, a feature of Moscow's posture was the effort to persuade the peoples of those states of the benefits of neutrality and the peaceful intentions of the USSR. In Korea too, where a cold war conflict had been at the boiling point for several years, the new regime took steps to break the stalemate that had prevented conclusion of an armistice. And, finally, the new Soviet tactics were evidenced in the United Nations; within a month after Stalin's death, the Soviets had taken action that broke the long stalemate in the search for a successor to Secretary-General Trygve Lie. After agreeing to the election of Dag Hammarskjöld to that post, the Soviet delegation was soon engaged in the promotion of several new initiatives in the world organization.

The shift in Soviet foreign policy was evidenced not only by new tactics but by a new diplomatic style. Although the dour Molotov was hardly a diplomatic charmer, his replacement of Andrei Vyshinskii did produce a relative improvement in Soviet diplomatic manners. Able to draw on the talent for sustained venom that he gained from his experience as the chief prosecutor in the purge trials of the 1930s, Vyshinskii adopted a style of negotiation-by-diatribe that had helped ensure Moscow's continued alienation on the diplomatic stage. A new generation of ambassadors—including the man dubbed "smilin' Mike" Menshikov during his stay in the Soviet Embassy in Washington—helped bring new credibility to Moscow's preferred image as a peace-loving and reasonable member of the community of nations. A willingness to make contact with the "sober bourgeoisie" and a surprising penchant for foreign travel were soon to be evidenced even at the very top ranks of the Soviet diplomatic hierarchy.

But the newly flexible tactics and more civil style of Moscow's diplomacy were to prove insufficient to bring success to the more ambitious Soviet foreign policy of the 1950s and 1960s. As the vision of the Soviet leaders became more global in scope and their willingness to exploit opportunities for expanded influence increased, so the domestic constraints of limited resources, intellectual ferment, and continued high-level political intrigue proved more bothersome. Ultimately the Soviet aspiration for superpower status, strategic superiority over the West, and undisputed leadership in the bloc would tempt its leadership to court greater risks than had the more dogmatic but also more cautious Stalinist regime.

THE MALENKOV INTERREGNUM

The first decision to move toward reduction of external conflict was apparently taken just after Stalin's funeral. The delegate of the People's Republic of China, Zhou Enlai, on his return to Peking from the Moscow solemnities and meetings with the new leaders, announced that his government was willing to compromise on a major issue that was stalemating the Korean armistice negotiations. The Chinese concession on the question of forced repatriation of prisoners of war broke the deadlock and an exchange of prisoners was followed on July 27, 1953 by the conclusion of an armistice in Korea.[2] Included among the terms of the agreement was a proposal to convene a conference on the political reunification of the Korean peninsula.

Malenkov saluted the "great victory" of the communist forces on behalf of the Soviet government. The prolonged, bloody conflict had tied down American forces without engaging Soviet troops, but it had failed to achieve Moscow's original objective of reunifying Korea under communist rule or reorienting the alignment of Japan. As a spur to American rearmament and a source of Soviet-American tension, the Korean conflict had proved counterproductive to Soviet purposes and Moscow evidently perceived no further gains to be made from prolongation of the war.

Malenkov reiterated his claim of a victory "for the camp of peace and democracy" in Korea and announced a billion ruble loan for the rehabilitation of the North Korean economy in a major speech before the Supreme Soviet on August 8, 1953. The speech is notable for its *tour d'horizon* of cases in which the Soviet Union had recently acted to bring about reduction of tensions or was actively seeking normalization of trade and diplomatic relations. After this survey and a salute to the "friendly ties and brotherly cooperation between the countries of the democratic camp," including the "strong and unbreakable ties of friendship" in Sino-Soviet relations, Malenkov observed:

The active struggle for peace conducted with fixity of purpose by the Soviet Union and the entire democratic camp has yielded definite results. A change in the international atmosphere is to be observed. After a long period of mounting tension, one feels for the first time since the war a certain easing of the international situation.[3]

Yet, he warned, there were aggressive forces working against this relaxation of international tension. Some of them had sought to portray the Soviet policy as a sign of weakness. To counteract such talk, Malenkov reminded his hearers of "our sacred duty constantly to strengthen and perfect the defense of the great Soviet Union," and informed them that the United States "has no monopoly of the hydrogen bomb."

Surveying the unfinished business on the diplomatic agenda, the Soviet premier called for an end to "the policy of ignoring China" and violating the People's Republic's rights in the United Nations. He declared that settlement of the German question was of "cardinal importance" and warned against the effort to revive German militarism. Proper settlement of this issue would assist in the settlement of the Austrian question as well. Addressing the United States in particular, Malenkov declared the willingness of the Soviet Union to engage in negotiations (after creation of "appropriate prerequisites") for further relaxation of tensions, in accord with the policy of peaceful coexistence of the socialist and capitalist camps:

We firmly stand by the belief that there are no disputed or outstanding issues today which cannot be settled peacefully by mutual agreement between the parties concerned. This also relates to disputed issues between the United States of America and the Soviet Union. We stand, as we have stood in the past, for the peaceful coexistence of the two systems. We hold that there are no objective reasons for clashes between the United States of America and the Soviet Union.[4]

As early as April 1953, British Prime Minister Winston Churchill had expressed a desire to meet with the new Soviet leaders at a "Big Four Summit" to be held without an express agenda. But Malenkov's statement, with its mention of "appropriate prerequisites," revealed a certain caution (perhaps reflecting genuine nervousness) about proceeding to such a meeting. According to Khrushchev's own postretirement account, the Soviets suspected that the Western leaders perceived the new regime as vulnerable to pressure. He follows this observation with an indirect and self-serving confirmation of the point: Malenkov, he charged, was so completely without initiative and so unpredictable, so susceptible to the pressure and influence of others, that he was "unstable to the point of being dangerous." Not until his removal could the Soviet Union come to the summit.[5]

Whatever the reason, the Soviets proceeded to a top-level meeting only by stages, with the first phases being meetings of the foreign ministers on outstanding issues. The British, French, American, and Soviet foreign ministers assembled first in Berlin from January 25 to February 18, 1954, for a conference on the perennial issue of Germany. Here, in response to the Western plan for free German elections, Molotov proposed that the two German regimes participate equally in a provisional unity government, which would in turn agree on an election law and supervise all-German elections leading to the formation of a neutralized and reunified German state. The Soviet foreign minister went further, however, calling for the abandonment of NATO and the conclusion of a treaty on European security between the West and East European states. This latter idea, offering a security pact that excluded the United States and left the entire continent open to Soviet hegemony, appeared (by John Foster Dulles' account) "so preposterous that when Molotov read it, laughter rippled around the Western sides of the table to the dismay of the Communist delegation."[6]

In the face of the recent demonstration of the lack of support enjoyed by the Communist government in East Germany, the new Soviet regime was clearly unwilling to accept a plan for reunification based on the free choice of the German people. Nor was it prepared to offer a realistic alternative to the impending integration of West Germany into the Western defense system. Thus deadlocked on the German question, and similarly stalemated on the Austrian question by the Soviet insistence that withdrawal of occupation troops from that country must follow the conclusion of a German treaty, the first Big Four conference in five years broke up without agreement. To recoup some of its credibility on the issue of European security, the Soviet government amended its proposal in a note issued on March 31, conceding that the United States could participate in a European security treaty. But the seriousness of even this concession was eroded by the further suggestion in the note that the Soviet Union was willing to become a member of NATO.

As Malenkov's speech of August had made clear, Moscow was trusting that West German rearmament could be halted not by its own proposed alternatives alone but also through disunity in the Western camp. The hopes for this rested primarily on the French, with their traditional fear of German armed might, and it appeared briefly in the late summer of 1954 that these hopes might be fulfilled. On August 30, the French Assembly rejected the plan for a European Defense Community (EDC) that would include German military units merged at the lowest level into a single integrated European army.

But Soviet pleasure was short-lived; in October an agreement was initialed in Paris calling for the Federal Republic of Germany to enter the North Atlantic Treaty Organization, contributing an army that would eventually number half a million men. Unlike the EDC, under which Germany would have had no national army of its own, the Paris agreements contemplated a revived German national force under unified NATO command. Angered by this development, Moscow sought to stave off its ratification by threatening to renounce its wartime treaties of alliance with Britain and France and by briefly holding forth the prospect of free German elections.

Again insisting on the need for an all-European collective security arrangement, on November 11, Molotov invited the governments of Europe to a conference on European security to be held in Moscow. The conference was indeed convened on November 29, but it had not succeeded in luring France or the other Western governments away from the Paris agreements, and it was attended only by the East European states (excluding Yugoslavia but including China as an "observer"). The parties to the conference declared their determination, "if the Paris agreements are ratified, to reexamine the situation with a view to taking reliable measures for the safeguarding of their security and for the maintenance of peace in Europe."[7]

True to their word, the Soviet bloc states reconvened in Warsaw on May 11–14, 1955, following the ratification of the Paris Agreements and the entry of the Federal Republic of Germany into NATO, to adopt a "Pact of Mutual Assistance and Unified Command." Article Five of the Warsaw Pact established a joint command of the armed forces assigned to the alliance, and Article Six established a Political Consultative Committee to coordinate the foreign policies of the allies. In these respects, the Warsaw Pact (not unintentionally) mirrored the NATO alliance and provided a symbolic symmetry to the European defense arrangements. The agreement was primarily a formalization of an arrangement that had already evolved under Soviet aegis, although it did provide a new basis for the stationing of Soviet troops in Eastern Europe, and especially in Hungary and Rumania, where Moscow's previous rights had been tied to the occupation of Austria.

In contrast to the barren record of achievement of the Berlin conference on Germany and Austria, the Geneva Conference of April-June 1954 did produce some results favorable to the Soviet interests. Actually, the Geneva sessions consisted of two arenas: a meeting on Korea, in which 19 states participated, including the two Koreas and China, and a meeting on Indochina, attended by the Big Four, together with China, Vietnam, Laos, Cambodia, and Ho Chi Minh's Vietminh government.

The Korean phase of the conference ended in deadlock for much the same reasons as had the Berlin Conference: the Communist delegations rejected the idea of free elections for a unified government without advance "preparation" by a body having equal representation from the two existing regimes. In another parallel with the Berlin meeting, Molotov proposed at Geneva that an arrangement for "collective security" in Asia replace military alliances binding the Korean regimes to foreign powers.[8] There was little discussion of this scheme, which was clearly aimed at limiting American influence in Asia.

It is for the negotiations on Indochina that the Geneva Conference is most remembered. The Vietminh National Liberation Committee, led by Ho Chi Minh and a nucleus of communists, had proclaimed the existence of the Democratic Republic of Vietnam after the Japanese surrender in 1945 and had been fighting French colonial forces since December 1946. With the Vietminh forces armed and supported by the Soviet Union and China, the French army had become mired in an increasingly desperate and unpopular struggle. The achievement of a complete communist victory, however, appeared to require that Ho's patrons devote even more of their resources in support, and this both Moscow and Beijing seemed unwilling to do. Moreover, the prospect of a communist takeover of the entire area might well have brought Britain and the United States to France's aid, thereby converting a "national-liberation" conflict into a full-scale East-West struggle.

In this context, the Soviet government proposed in February 1954 that a conference be held in Geneva to consider both the Korean and Indochinese situations. But by the time the Indochina phase of the discussions began, the military situation in Indochina had changed significantly. Dien Bien Phu, the last remaining French outpost in the northern part of Vietnam, had fallen on May 7. On the other hand, throughout the spring there had been mounting discussion in Washington of American military assistance to the French. If the communist side had been tempted to press ahead for full victory on the battlefield, the Soviets at least were probably discouraged in some part by the statements of Dulles, but even more so by the turn of events in France itself. The French government of Bidault fell in June and the new premier, Pierre Mendes-France, pledged to resign if he did not achieve a truce in Indochina by July 20. For the Soviets, the broader significance of this development lay in the fact that Mendes-France was a bitter opponent of the proposed European Defense Community, and his continuance in power would diminish the chances of French ratification of EDC.[9]

The Soviet priorities in this situation were fairly clear: the opportunity to derail the movement for German rearmament was more precious to Moscow than the prospect of a continuing war in Indochina that just *might* result in total communist victory. As the Geneva Conference began to explore the outlines of a compromise settlement, Mendes-France's expressed willingness to partition Vietnam at the 17th parallel caused the Soviets, in Khrushchev's words, to "gasp with surprise and pleasure."[10] A truce agreement was quickly hammered out and signed on July 20 and 21, calling for the partition of Vietnam, the neutrality of the two successor states, elections in both by July 1956, French withdrawal of troops, and French recognition of the sovereignty of Vietnam, Laos, and Cambodia.

On the communist side, the agreement was hailed as a victory. A new "people's democracy" had been legally created in Asia, extending the scope of the "Sino-Soviet bloc," and French colonialism had been driven out in defeat. The triumph was especially sweet for the People's Republic of China, which had emerged with heightened influence and prestige from its first major international conference. Zhou Enlai's return to Beijing from Geneva was by way of Eastern Europe, India, and Burma, and his activities in those places underscored the gradual emergence of an independent Chinese line in international affairs. The United States refused to sign the Geneva accords and set about in an attempt to counteract the expansion of Communist influence in Asia through the establishment of the Southeast Asia Treaty Organization. Although, at the time, its results seemed to represent a genuine compromise between East and West, like many other postwar "settlements," the Geneva Conference came to be regarded by both East and West not as a final solution but merely as a springboard to further struggle. By no means would it bring a lasting peace to Indochina.

China's emergence at Geneva as a major world actor was followed later in 1954 by a significant readjustment in the Sino-Soviet relationship. A Soviet delegation headed by Bulganin, Khrushchev, Molotov, and foreign trade specialist Anastas Mikoyan, traveled to Beijing in September to conclude a new agreement which freed China from some of the more rankling features of a Stalinist satrapy. The Soviets consented to evacuate Port Arthur, the joint stock companies set up in 1950 were dissolved, and a new loan was extended by Moscow together with increased technical assistance to Chinese industry.

In May of the following year, Bulganin and Khrushchev embarked on another journey designed to readjust the relationships among the socialist countries. This one was in the form of a "journey to Canossa," for the Soviet leaders' destination was Belgrade and their purpose was to mend the Soviet-Yugoslav rift. But Khrushchev's effort to explain that the Soviet share of the blame for the quarrel was attributable to Beria was not satisfactory to Tito, and the Yugoslavs did not allow the rapprochement in state-to-state relations to extend to the party sphere.

The issue of Soviet-Yugoslav relations was one of several that was embroiling the Soviet collective leadership in major policy and power struggles. Chief among these was a quarrel between coalitions headed by Khrushchev and Malenkov and centering on the twin issues of budgetary priorities and military strategy. Malenkov was apparently the "reformer" in this debate, expressing a willingness to devote a greater share of resources that had been allotted in the past to needs (such as agriculture and consumer goods) outside the traditionally favored heavy industry and defense sectors, and arguing in support of this the view that global war was increasingly unlikely.

A special feature of this important debate concerned the impact of nuclear weapons both on the nature and likelihood of war and on the conduct of Soviet foreign policy. Discussion of this issue was suppressed by Stalin, but it posed for the Soviet Union the question of whether its doctrine and purposes, formulated in a prenuclear age and ascribing a special role to violence in the accomplishment of social change, required revision in the light of the new technology. Malenkov seemed to say that it did; in March 1954, he voiced to the Supreme Soviet the theretofore heretical view that war between imperialism and communism, "given modern methods of warfare, means the destruction of world civilization."[11] Not only did this assertion cast doubt on the confident assumption that communism would inevitably triumph in the struggle against capitalism, but it also flew in the face of the Stalinist thesis on the decisiveness of the five "permanently operating factors" in warfare.

The strategy that Malenkov deduced from this premise had far-reaching implications for both budgetary priorities and policy toward the West. It posited a reliance on "minimum deterrence"—that is, maintenance by the Soviet Union of a nuclear weapons capability sufficient to deter the United States from launching an attack. Other weapons systems were largely superfluous because if deterrence were to fail there would be nothing left to fight over. From this standpoint, then, Malenkov could assert in his March speech that the Soviet armed forces had everything they needed in order to carry out their mission, and he could advocate a shifting of budgetary priorities away from the long-standing concentration on defense. On the other hand, Soviet foreign policy would need to ensure that the all destructive war would not be launched; this presumably dictated a policy of relaxation of tensions and avoidance of crisis.

While Malenkov was asserting these views, it was evident that not all of his colleagues shared them. Presidium members Khrushchev, Molotov, Kaganovich, Bulganin, and Voroshilov, in their own speeches to the Supreme Soviet, called for the further strengthening of the Soviet armed forces. The weight of this group, undoubtedly supported by the professional military establishment, was sufficient to force Malenkov to retreat. In April, he conceded that only capitalism would be annihilated by nuclear war, and he added that the Soviet armed forces "have at their disposal or will have at their disposal" everything necessary to carry out their tasks.[12]

These issues undoubtedly contributed to Malenkov's fall from power. While he was not formally ousted from the premiership until February 8, 1955, and even then remained in the Party Presidium, Malenkov in fact made no important speeches after this April recantation. After his removal as premier, traditionalists in the Soviet military, supported by their patrons in the political leadership, publicly asserted the view that the existence of nuclear weapons was not in itself sufficient to ensure the deterrence of war, and that Soviet capabilities and military doctrine would have to be adjusted to prepare for the eventuality of waging war (and achieving ultimate victory) after the initial nuclear exchange. In an open slap at Malenkov, Marshal Voroshilov declared in March 1955: "We cannot be intimidated by fables that in the event of a new world war civilization will perish."[13] Moreover, he and several of his colleagues, warning of the increased danger of surprise attack, implied that war was not as unlikely as Malenkov had assumed. A leading Soviet strategist, Major-General Talenskii, went so far as to suggest that the surprise factor (contrary to Stalin's doctrine) could be extremely important—perhaps even necessitating that, once warned of an impending "surprise aggression by an enemy," the Soviets would have to respond by "dealing him pre-emptive blows at all levels—strategic, operational, and tactical."[14]

The Soviet debate on military doctrine illustrates the effect of a changing political system upon the conduct of Soviet foreign policy. No longer a one-man dictatorship, the system was now under the control of an oligarchy representing a divergent range of interests. In such a setting, policy was less likely to be calculated from a uniform set of goals but was increasingly the result of a process of consensus building and compromise. This is not to say, however, that there was not to be one leader who stood somewhat above the rest and exercised a larger say than his colleagues in the formulation of policy.

In the period after Malenkov's resignation and replacement by Bulganin, it was Khrushchev who, from his base in the Party Secretariat, was beginning to play this dominant role in the decision and execution of foreign policy questions. Once Khrushchev had achieved (with the apparent support of the military traditionalists) the removal of Malenkov's prerogatives in this realm, he engaged in debate with the regime's "expert" in foreign affairs, Molotov. Policy toward Yugoslavia was apparently a central issue in this clash, although it also involved the allied and larger issue of the treatment of Stalin's legacy. In a showdown between the two in mid-1955, Molotov emerged the loser although he was not formally removed from the Foreign Ministry until the summer of 1956.[15] The debates, however, were to continue, and on military issues it is ironic that Khrushchev was himself eventually to assert many of the positions taken by Malenkov during the brief interval of 1954.

THE "SPIRIT OF GENEVA"

It was neither Malenkov nor Molotov but Nikita Sergeyevich Khrushchev who brought a fresh spirit and bold ideas to Soviet foreign policy in the mid-1950s, and the imprint of his personality is evident on a whole decade of international relations. One of the first signs of his ascendancy in foreign affairs was in the Soviet approach to the issue of an Austrian treaty, on which Khrushchev's adversaries had shown marked caution. The Austrian Chancellor was summoned to Moscow in mid-April, 1955 for negotiations, and a month later the Austrian State Treaty was signed in the Belvedere Palace in Vienna. The treaty called for the withdrawal of Western and Soviet troops from their respective zones of occupation and the permanent neutralization of the Austrian state.

Although the treaty brought about a rare withdrawal of Soviet military power, its effect on the overall Soviet strategic and political position in Europe was not particularly detrimental. The Soviet abandonment of eastern Austria did not amount to a decline for "communism," since no "people's democracy" had been established there; the Austrian population, in fact, was more notice-ably anticommunist during the Soviet occupation than afterward. From a conventional military point of view, the Western pullback of forces may have had more effect than the Soviet withdrawal; after the treaty came into effect,

Austria served as a neutralized wedge of territory interposed between the NATO states of West Germany and Italy. For propaganda purposes, indeed, the neutralization of Austria may have been intended by Moscow as a demonstration to the Germans of the advantages of nonalignment. It may also have served to lessen the sense of threat from Soviet forces felt by Tito. On balance, then, from the standpoint of its public relations and its effort to promote an atmosphere of relaxation of tensions in Europe, the Soviet Union achieved a net gain from its decision to agree to the Austrian treaty.

The settlement of the Austrian issue, together with the decline in the debate over German rearmament following ratification of the Paris Agreements, helped clear the way for the first meeting of major-power heads of government since the Potsdam Conference of 1945. Khrushchev apparently felt that the Geneva Summit of 1955 presented major opportunities for the Soviet regime, but he also regarded it as a major test. He noted in his memoirs that the meeting gave the "bourgeois" heads of state their first chance to look over the new Soviet leadership, and described it as a "crucial test" of the regime's ability to represent its country competently:

Would we approach the meeting soberly, without unrealistic hopes, and would we be able to keep the other side from intimidating us? All things considered, I would say we passed the test.[16]

This comment reveals not only the nervousness felt by the Soviet leaders, but hints at the inferiority complex with which the once-outcast Soviet regime approached the Western great powers. Khrushchev confesses this sense of inferiority more directly when he observes that the Soviet delegation was "at a disadvantage" at Geneva from the very start; it had arrived in a two-engine plane, in contrast to the four-engine airplanes that transported its Western counterparts.[17]

The Soviet delegation, ostensibly under the leadership of Bulganin, included not only Khrushchev but also Molotov and the new Minister of Defense, Marshal Zhukov. The latter was included in the Soviet party for the avowed purpose of helping provide a basis for conversations with his wartime counterpart, President Eisenhower. This ploy apparently did not succeed—a fact that Khrushchev blames on the "prowling" of the "vicious cur" Dulles, who, he argues, determined foreign policy for the "good" but "soft" American president. Despite these harsh words, Khrushchev's memoirs record a grudging admiration for the secretary of state, calling him "our number one ideological enemy," "a worthy adversary," and a man who "knew how far he could push us" but who "never pushed us too far."[18] Khrushchev's comments on the leaders of the other delegations are also revealing. The Soviets had their best relations, he says, with the French, whose leader, Edgar Faure, he delighted in calling

"Edgar Fyodorovich." But, he adds, there was no point in paying serious attention to this delegation, since French governments turned over so rapidly. He also notes the warm atmosphere of his conversations with British Prime Minister Anthony Eden, from whom he received an invitation to visit London.

With respect to the issues at the conference, Khrushchev's retrospective (and probably correct) comment was that "it was probably doomed before it began." Certain questions of importance to each side was excluded by the other from the conference agenda at the very beginning. Thus, the USSR declined to discuss the status of Eastern Europe or the matter of "international Communism," while the West refused to include on the agenda questions pertaining to the Far East (out of fear the Soviets would insist upon inviting China to the summit). The items remaining for the agenda were no less intractable than those excluded; they were German reunification, European security, disarmament, and the improvement of East-West contacts.

The major Soviet proposal demonstrated the symbolic usefulness of the new symmetry of alliances in Europe; they called for the mutual disbandment of NATO and the new Warsaw Treaty Organization and the withdrawal of all "foreign" troops from the European continent, to be followed by the conclusion of a European security treaty. As in its earlier manifestations, the one-sided nature of this proposal hardly enhanced its appeal to the Western governments.

It was in the realm of disarmament that the major Western initiative came; with the discussions foundering again on the question of inspection, President Eisenhower introduced his "open skies" proposal, calling for an exchange of blueprints of military installations; it would have laid open the defense installations of each side to the aerial surveillance of the other. The Soviets did not even bother to make a formal reply to the suggestion. When, after several days of discussion, it was evident that no progress was being made on the various issues under consideration, the four delegations decided to avoid the appearance of total failure by issuing a directive to their respective foreign ministers to study the issues prior to further discussion in the fall.

Despite its meager substantive results, the Geneva Summit was important for its marked improvement in atmospherics as compared with previous East-West encounters, as the lingering popularity of the phrase "spirit of Geneva" attests. In a real sense, the meeting marked an end to the isolationism of the Soviet leaders, and even though they proved naturally unwilling to abandon the key points of their policies, they began to cultivate the image of reasonable leaders with whom it was possible to deal.

Khrushchev himself assessed the meeting (from the vantage point of his retirement) as an "important breakthrough," citing as warrant the Western leaders' realization that they would have to build the East-West relationship on new assumptions if they sought to achieve peace. If Geneva was a "test" for the Soviet leadership, Khrushchev had no doubt as to its outcome:

As a result of our showing in Geneva, our enemies now realized that we were able to resist their pressure and see through their tricks. . . . We had established ourselves as able to hold our own in the international arena.[19]

A reference to "free elections" in Germany had been included in the Geneva communique at the insistence of the American delegation (who threatened not to sign without an "unequivocal pledge" to hold elections). The exact wording, however, left ample room for interpretation:

The heads of government have agreed the settlement of the German question and the reunification of Germany by free elections shall be carried out in conformity with the national interests of the German people and the interests of European security.[20]

It soon became clear that the Soviets doubted that the risk of loss of communist power in East Germany through free elections was in the interests of Germany's people or of European security. Khrushchev had said as much during a stopover in East Berlin immediately after the summit conference: "Could the working class of the GDR agree to the elimination of all their political and social achievements, to the elimination of all their democratic reforms? We are convinced that [they] will never agree to enter such a path."[21]

Despite this warning, it appeared to come as a rude shock to the Western delegations when, at the postsummit foreign ministers' conference convened in October, Molotov confirmed that indeed the conditions for all-German elections had not yet matured. Dulles' reaction was one of anger; he cabled Eisenhower that "the clear breach of Summit directive creates a condition where no confidence can be placed on agreements with the Soviet Government and that we shall have to conduct our relations accordingly."[22]

But Moscow cared little about Washington's reaction to its "broken promises." Having achieved a propaganda breakthrough at Geneva, the Soviet Union was prepared to mark time on the substantive questions while it built up its own strength and endeavored to undermine the unity and strength of the Western position. One part of this strategy involved a diplomatic plunge into the "Third World," where the Soviets sought to weaken the underpinnings of "imperialism" by wooing the friendship of such leaders as Nasser and Nehru. We shall examine that part of Khrushchev's strategy in the next chapter. For the present, our purpose is to call attention to the Soviet campaign, which took place during the year following the Geneva conference, to "exploit the contradictions" in the Western camp by splitting its West European allies off from the United States.

Significantly, the first step in this process consisted of a bold Soviet effort to lure West Germany itself out of the American clutches. Counting on the greed of the West German capitalists to help forge a new diplomatic and commercial partnership, the Soviets hoped to gain Bonn's acquiescence to the principle of two German states while at the same time breaking the "commercial blockade" that restricted Moscow's economic dealings with the West. But when Chancellor Adenauer visited Moscow in September 1955 for talks on the establishment of diplomatic relations and commercial ties, he had his own initiative to pursue: an offer of German financial assistance in return for reunification. As the Soviets saw it, Adenauer's terms amounted to an effort to buy the GDR from Moscow in return for West German credits and reparations. Though the temptation must have been great, the Soviets proved unwilling (or unable) to deal away "their" part of Germany. Khrushchev saw it later in terms similar to the Western "domino theory"—the abandonment of socialism in the GDR would have only encouraged more Western pressure and set off a chain reaction. "Once you start retreating, it's difficult to stop."[23]

The German-Soviet talks almost foundered on the issue of the repatriation of German prisoners of war from the USSR. The Soviets, however, agreed to make concessions rather than lose out on the opportunity to establish trade and diplomatic ties with Bonn. An agreement to set up diplomatic relations was signed (though only with the Bonn government's "reservations" regarding frontiers and claiming the right to speak for all the German nation) and, by agreement, the Soviets announced a week after Adenauer's visit that the German prisoners would be released. Moscow sought to disguise the concession and to reiterate its loyalty to the East German regime, however, by declaring that the decision on prisoners had been reached only at the urging of the GDR.[24]

In the spring of 1956, Bulganin and Khrushchev traveled to London in response to Prime Minister Eden's invitation. (Their decision to take along as a traveling companion General Serov, then head of the Soviet secret police, created a furor in the British press and got their visit off to a very bad start.) The Soviet leaders' talks with the British government produced few concrete results. The chief Soviet proposal, that Britain agree to large Soviet purchases of British goods that were embargoed as strategic, was spurned by the British who saw it not only as a potential economic boon for Moscow but also as an effort to create friction between London and Washington.

During their London visit, the Soviet leaders made contacts with leaders of the Labour Party, with the hope of forging a new leftist "popular front" against NATO and American influence. The talks went badly, as Khrushchev boasted of Moscow's hydrogen bomb arsenal and hinted of a Moscow-Bonn alliance against the other Western powers, and Hugh Gaitskell replied with a demand for the release of political prisoners in the USSR and Eastern Europe. The next day the Soviet leader was said to have complained that "if this was British socialism, he preferred to be a Tory."[25]

Soviet talks with a delegation of the French Socialist Party in Moscow a few days later were almost as fruitless as the conversations with the British Laborites. Right on the heels of the party delegation came a visit of a French government team, headed by Socialist premier Guy Mollet. If the Soviets had hoped through these talks to encourage neutralist and anti-American sentiments in French ruling circles, they were singularly unsuccessful. Mollet adhered to the common Western positions concerning German reunification, European security, and disarmament, and like Eden, he refused to break the Western embargo on trade of strategic goods with the USSR.

As a prelude to this campaign to encourage neutralism in the noncommunist states of Europe, the Soviets had acted in the summer and fall of 1955 to improve their relations with Finland. As an example to the West of its sincerity in the campaign for liquidation of foreign military bases, Moscow agreed on June 1955 for the return to Finland of the Porkkala naval base that it had taken at the close of the war. In fact the base had lost much of its strategic importance, and the decision to return it and later to extend the Finno-Soviet treaty of mutual assistance clearly served propaganda purposes, demonstrating Moscow's peaceful intentions and the advantages of neutrality to Scandinavia in particular and Western Europe in general.

Although the Soviet initiatives for relaxation of tensions were well launched by February 1956 when the Twentieth Congress of the Communist Party of the Soviet Union convened, that gathering served an important function by formalizing and legitimizing the doctrinal justifications for Khrushchev's emerging foreign policy. Lenin had once written that "without revolutionary theory there can be no revolutionary policy," and for Lenin's pupils this necessitated the working out of a new doctrine to match the new policy. Such a doctrinal retooling was not meant as a mere pretext to mask the calculations made in the Soviet national interest. Doctrinal pronouncements may in fact do precisely that, but they also serve to express the more strictly Marxist-Leninist goals of which the Soviet leaders are the guardians—and in the implementation of which their very rule is justified.

As we have shown above in the second chapter, the Twentieth Party Congress performed this function, along with its necessary concomitant—the freeing of Marxist-Leninist theory from the dead hand of Stalin. Stalin's image of a "two-camp" world had denied the possibility of neutrality, temporary or otherwise. It had carried the "he who is not with us is against us" formulation to the extreme, thereby precluding effective Soviet action in conjunction with non-communist but "antiimperialist" forces. Khrushchev's interpretation in 1956, on the other hand, revived the Leninist perception that held that a temporary alliance against the common imperialist enemy was possible. But the doctrine was to be kept flexible in preparation for the inevitable moment when capitalist strength had finally been undermined and the neutralist and democratic-socialist forces began to assert the reactionary side of their nature. Then the working classes and communist cadres would be ready and able to take power, by parliamentary means or otherwise.

The principal doctrinal assertions in Khrushchev's report to the Twentieth Congress stemmed, as we have seen, from an assertion that the "main feature" of the present era was the emergence of socialism into a world system. Given the growing strength of the socialist camp and the practice of "peaceful coexistence" by the USSR as the general line of its foreign policy, it was possible for the socialist system to triumph worldwide through peaceful competition. Wars between the two systems were no longer "fatalistically inevitable," and it was even possible to avoid violence in the process of transition to socialism.

The "peace initiative" that the Soviet Union had recently pursued as the main feature of its foreign policy was summarized by Khrushchev as consisting of six features: (1) improvement of relations between the "great powers"; (2) elimination of the "breeding grounds of war" and prevention of the development of new sources of conflict; (3) adjustment of relations with a number of European countries; (4) exploration of new ways to settle issues such as European security, disarmament, and the German problem; (5) "rapprochement with all countries to preserve peace"; and (6) expansion of international contacts, including personal contacts between leaders as well as exchange of delegations.

Khrushchev seemed to dwell on fissiparous tendencies in the Western camp by noting the increasingly "fierce struggle" among the capitalist countries and predicting that it would become even sharper. He appealed especially to leaders of the labor movement and of democratic socialism to join with the communists in the struggle against war and reaction. But he also noted the special significance of the task of improving Soviet-American relations and cited the Soviet proposal for a Treaty of Friendship and Cooperation with the United States, based on the "five principles of peaceful coexistence."

As for the future tasks of Soviet foreign policy, Khrushchev outlined them as follows: (1) pursuit of the policy of peaceful coexistence; (2) strengthening of fraternal relations with the countries of the socialist camp and building better ties with Yugoslavia; (3) consolidation of the bonds of friendship and cooperation with peace-loving countries in the "Third World" and with European neutrals; (4) vigorous pursuit of a policy of further improving relations with the United States and its allies; and (5) exposure of the subversive activities of the enemies of peace and further strengthening of the defense potential of the Soviet Union.[26]

Although Khrushchev's public pronouncements at the party congress had great significance and represented a departure from the previous Soviet line, his lengthy secret speech attacking Stalin was to have even greater impact, particularly within the socialist camp itself. The very decision to go beyond the public attack on the "cult of personality" and to detail the crimes of the Stalin era was an object of intense political struggle within the top leadership.

The scope of the task of uncovering and revealing all the misdeeds of the late dictator was immense, as is suggested in the fact that in 1956–57 alone, between seven and eight million political prisoners were released and another five to six million "posthumously rehabilitated."[27] And yet by Khrushchev's own later admission, the first round of de-Stalinization left certain whole arenas of possible inquiry unexplored. In the realm of foreign policy, Khrushchev had very little of an explicit nature to say. He limited his criticism of Stalin's actions in this area to only a few issues: Stalin's lack of preparation for the German attack in 1941; his "lack of faith in the Chinese comrades," which helped retard the establishment of the communist regime in Beijing; his "shameful role" in dealings with Tito; his failure to understand the significance of the liberation of India; and his "unrealistic" assessment of the situation in Korea, leading to the creation of a "risky situation" there.[28]

As some of Khrushchev's domestic adversaries no doubt predicted, the impact of the process of de-Stalinization was simply devastating not only in the USSR itself but throughout the entire socialist world. If ever there were a real-life example of the dangers of opening "Pandora's box," surely this was it; the effects on both domestic and foreign policy were to be felt in the Soviet Union for years to come.

FROM CONFIDENCE TO CRISIS

The most serious and direct consequences of de-Stalinization outside the Soviet Union were felt in Eastern Europe in 1956. Khrushchev had actually intended his secret speech to have an impact on bloc relationships, but he hardly expected an impact of the sort that in fact developed. There is little doubt that the denunciation of Stalin and particularly of his handling of the relationship with Yugoslavia, together with enunciation in the public speech at the Twentieth Congress of the permissibility of "many roads to socialism," had been part of the price Khrushchev was paying in order to entice Tito back into the socialist camp. Other items on Tito's list of demands, including the dissolution of the Cominform and the imposition of changes in the line and leadership of the most virulently anti-Tito satellites (Hungary, Rumania, and Bulgaria) were accomplished by Moscow during the first half of 1956. The way was thus cleared for Tito to pay a "fraternal" visit to Moscow in June, during which ties between the Soviet and Yugoslav parties were reestablished.

Only a week after Tito departed from Moscow, strikes and street fighting broke out among the workers in Poznan, Poland. A series of developments opened in Poland which concluded in October with the election of a new party leadership headed by a one-time suspected "Titoist," Wladyslaw Gomulka, and with Poland's declaration of its determination to follow its own national road to communism. This challenge was followed the same month with an even more serious rebellion on the part of the Hungarian population, which led to a decision by the new premier, Imre Nagy, to dismantle one-party rule in Hungary and remove the country from the Warsaw Pact. This crisis climaxed with the bloody suppression of the Hungarian Revolution by Soviet tanks in the early days of November 1956.

A more detailed analysis of these events is reserved for chapter six; our purpose here is to comment on their significance for Khrushchev's political position and for the Soviet policy toward the West. On the former point, there is no doubt that Khrushchev's position was seriously weakened by the revolts in Eastern Europe. His adversaries had no trouble linking the uprisings there to Khrushchev's injudicious revelations concerning Stalin, which had called into question the whole foundation of Soviet authority in the bloc, and to his concessions to Yugoslavia and "Titoism." A sure sign that Khrushchev was in trouble even before the events in Hungary was the peculiar balance of the four-man Soviet leadership delegation that traveled to Warsaw in mid-October— Khrushchev and his ally Mikoyan were accompanied by the resurgent "hard-liners," Molotov and Kaganovich. In the wake of the Hungarian uprising, Khrushchev's influence sank even lower, and he did not even deliver a speech at the December plenum of the CPSU Central Committee.

The effect of the events in Eastern Europe on Khrushchev's "peace program" and Soviet relations with the West was also striking. The Soviet's brutal use of force in putting down the Hungarian uprising left no doubt as to the high priority placed by the Soviet leadership on the preservation of its East European sphere. To the extent that Moscow believed that Western blandishments and propaganda had encouraged the Poles and Hungarians, it would now be even more hostile in its response to such overtures and perhaps even more forceful in its own efforts to undermine in its turn the solidarity and strength of the West. A more obvious effect of the Soviet actions in Eastern Europe was to belie for many observers in the West, both pro-American and potentially neutral, the messages of peace, political tolerance, and noninterference that had recently been emanating from the Soviet capital.

By an accident of timing, the impact on some sectors of world opinion of the Soviet suppression of the Hungarian revolt was reduced by the coincidence of this crisis with an act of "imperialist aggression" against a nationalist regime in the Third World. For the national elites in many countries of Africa, Asia, and Latin America, the Soviet action to enforce conformity in its "own" sphere of influence was far less outrageous and threatening than the simultaneous military attack by Britain, France, and Israel on Egypt following Colonel Nasser's nationalization of the Suez Canal.

The Soviet regime adroitly managed to identify itself with this antiimperialist sentiment and indeed to claim credit for the defeat of the aggression, without in the process becoming embroiled in an actual military confrontation with the Western powers. In fact, the Soviet courtship of Nasser's Egypt had begun in 1955 (see the next chapter for our analysis of some aspects of the involvement). Among the objectives pursued by Moscow in its Middle Eastern involvement were both a desire to hasten the decline of "imperialist" (primarily British and French) influence in the area, and an effort to forestall or combat the erection of Western-sponsored anticommunist alliances—in particular, the Baghdad Pact of Britain, Turkey, Iran, Iraq, and Pakistan. The support of Nasser, as the premier nationalist and antiimperialist of the Arab world, was an important means to that objective. As Khrushchev himself was to put it, the support of Nasser's "bourgeois" regime in 1956 promised to weaken the influence of British colonialism in the Middle East "and that was in the interests of the Soviet Union."[29]

Although the United States was not a party to the Suez intervention, its action in the summer of 1956 in withdrawing its offer to finance the Aswan Dam had helped drive Nasser to the nationalization of the canal, thus precipitating the crisis. But the British and French were far more directly affected by Nasser's action; not only had they controlled the Suez Canal Company, but their trade—particularly their supplies of oil—were vitally dependent on the Canal. The Israelis, who had beem alarmed by Nasser's bellicose statements and his policy of acquiring arms from the communist world, joined with the British and French in planning a joint military action to regain control of the canal and, in the process, to topple Nasser's regime. The operation began with an attack on Egypt on October 29 by the Israeli armed forces; they quickly gained control of the Sinai Peninsula and Gaza Strip. This was followed by an ultimatum from Britain and France calling for the removal of troops to a distance of ten miles from the canal. Israel, as a party to the plot, complied but Egypt refused and the British and French sent an expeditionary force to capture Port Said and gain control of the canal.

The unexpected development in this scenario was the harsh reaction from Washington, which sternly condemned the use of force and put great pressure on its allies to withdraw. The Soviets limited themselves to protests and propaganda blasts at the aggressors until November 5, at which point the will and ability of Britain and France to continue the operation had already been seriously eroded, and by that time (not coincidentally) the November 4 Hungarian invasion was assured of success.

On November 5, the Soviet Foreign Minister sent notes signed by Bulganin to the three "aggressors" and to the United States. The letter to the British government was typical in its abusive and threatening tone:

If rocket weapons were used against Britain and France, you would doubtless call that a barbarous act. But how does this differ from the inhuman attack carried out by the armed forces of Britain and France against practically unarmed Egypt? . . . We are fully resolved to use force to crush the aggressors and to restore peace in the East.[30]

The note to the United States proposed the joint use of Soviet-American naval and air forces, "in accord with the United Nations decision," to bring a halt to the aggression against Egypt. The stern American rejection of this offer to join in military action against its NATO allies, accompanied by an alert of the Strategic Air Command, caused the Soviets to downgrade (to the provision of "volunteers") their own offer of military assistance to the Egyptian cause.

The British and French agreed to a ceasefire on November 6, and their troops were soon withdrawn and replaced by a United Nations peacekeeping contingent. The Soviets, noting that the aggression had been halted within 24 hours of their own stern warnings, claimed exclusive credit for the outcome. A more objective analysis would probably rank American pressure and the storm of protest among the British public as more salient factors in the ultimate Anglo-French capitulation. Apart from the boost to its prestige in the Third World, the Soviet gains from the crisis included the sharp blow rendered to Western unity and the drastic negative effect on British and French prestige and on the two countries' ability to halt the decline of their political and economic strength in the world. Khrushchev, terming the Suez crisis a "historic turning point," wrote that it marked the end to the notion, long shared in Russia as elsewhere, that the Middle East was an Anglo-French preserve.[31]

Despite the benefits the Suez crisis brought them, it can be argued that the style in which the Soviets managed their participation in it left much to be desired. The threats conveyed by the Soviet notes to the British and French were so blatant and crudely worded as to negate the possibility that Anglo-French alienation from Washington might make them any more disposed toward cooperation with Moscow. Moreover, the American rejection of the ill-conceived Soviet appeal for joint military action had left the Soviets in such an exposed position that they had been forced into an undignified retreat. That these features were not lost on the Soviet leadership is suggested by the fact that Foreign Minister Dimitri Shepilov, who had succeeded Molotov in the job only in June, was dismissed from his post in January 1957.[32]

Shepilov's position was by no means the only one under challenge at the end of 1956. Khrushchev, who had started the year with such apparent political strength and confidence, was now scrambling for his political life. While Khrushchev sat in silence, the December plenum of the CPSU Central Committee approved a reorganization of the administrative machinery that strengthened

Khrushchev's adversaries in the central government. By February, with the sting of his foreign policy defeats in Eastern Europe fading and having back-tracked somewhat on the de-Stalinization campaign, Khrushchev was able to organize a counterattack in the form of an even more sweeping reorganization that deprived his opponents of their base in the central ministries and greatly enhanced the supervisory authority of the regional party apparatus. After the final approval of this reform in May, his opponents apparently resolved to make their move against him. The attempted coup occurred in June, when Khrushchev found himself confronted with a "so-called arithmetical majority" in the Party Presidium demanding his resignation as First Secretary. To the evident surprise of the conspirators, Khrushchev refused to resign; with the assistance of key supporters (including, most significantly, Marshal Zhukov), he succeeded in summoning the Central Committee and gaining a reversal of the Presidium decision.

His own job saved, Khrushchev managed to deprive the chief conspirators—Malenkov, Molotov, Kaganovich, and Shepilov—of theirs, but the true extent of the "anti-Party group" (as it became known) was not immediately revealed. In March 1958, Bulganin was linked with the group and lost his position (to Khrushchev) as Chairman of the Council of Ministers, and in October 1961 Marshal Kliment Vorshilov (who had "retired" as head of state in 1960) was revealed to have been one of the conspirators against Khrushchev.

In the course of the Central Committee debate in June–July 1957, Khrush-chev's supporters accused members of the opposition of opposing the First Secretary on a number of his foreign policy initiatives. Among these issues were the doctrinal innovations on the noninevitability of war and the peaceful transition to socialism, the proposed alliance with the social democrats, the party rapprochement with Tito, the Austrian agreement, the opening of nego-tiations with Japan, the courtship of neutrals, the provision of aid to non-communist regimes in the Third World, and the new practice of foreign travel by the Soviet leadership.[33]

Khrushchev's triumph over his principal rivals in the party was quickly followed by a preventive move against a potential challenger in the military, Marshal Zhukov. After his ouster from the Party Presidium and Defense Ministry in October 1957, Zhukov was charged with having sought both to remove the professional military establishment from firm party control and to build up a "Bonapartist" cult of his own personality. Zhukov was replaced as Minister of Defense by an associate of Khrushchev's from his Stalingrad days, Marshal Rodion Malinovsky, and steps were taken to reassert party control and discipline over the military.

As he set about repairing the damage to his own position, Khrushchev was also engaged in an effort to reconstruct the socialist bloc, culminating in a meeting in Moscow in November 1957 of the leaders of 12 ruling communist parties. Although the details of this process will be considered later, two trends bear mention at this point. The first is the alienation in Soviet-Yugoslav relations that set in following the events in Hungary and resulted in a blast emanating from the Moscow meeting (which Tito boycotted) at "revisionism" in the communist movement. The second and more significant development in bloc relations in this period was the growing and more autonomous role of China. Zhou Enlai took a significant trip at the beginning of 1957 to Moscow, Warsaw, and Budapest, and his behavior during this journey was apparently interpreted by the Soviets as a presumptuous attempt to give advice to the Soviet Union on how to manage the affairs of its "own" sphere, although he openly praised the Soviet intervention in Hungary. Although Khrushchev was soon to chafe at the Chinese assertiveness, he badly needed their support at this period, not only in the search for a compromise formula for rebuilding the socialist camp but also in his mounting campaign to regain the initiative in relations with the West.[34]

By the time the Soviet Union approached its 40th anniversary, Khrushchev had made a remarkable recovery from a period of great crisis. Although he had emerged from an internal political struggle in the preeminent leadership role, his position was by no means secure. At home, de-Stalinization had been halted midstream and the economy was in need of a transfusion of resources. The foreign policy agenda he had presented to the Twentieth Party Congress had fallen far short of success. Faced with a burgeoning challenge from China, he needed to demonstrate the superiority of his version of Marxist-Leninist ideology and of his personal leadership of the socialist bloc by breaking the stalemate in Europe and achieving dramatic progress in the struggle with the United States. Khrushchev was not the kind of man who easily loses his confidence; he emerged from the crises of 1956-57 with a bold new strategy for asserting Soviet leadership on the international stage.

MISSILE DECEPTION AND THE BERLIN CRISIS

The key ingredient in Khrushchev's strategy was a sphere, not much larger than a basketball, called Sputnik and the intercontinental ballistic missile that launched it into orbit around the earth on October 4, 1957. As a scientific achievement, the launching of the artificial earth satellite was a spectacular demonstration of just how far Soviet science and technology had progressed. But Sputnik's military and political importance was equally great. Khrushchev was able to parlay this accomplishment into an assertion of Soviet strategic superiority. The world's media quickly turned the Soviet space shot into the beginning of a American-Soviet "space race" and with the first U.S. space shot coming only months later and failing, the impression of a vast Soviet lead in missile technology became established. Khrushchev himself helped create this impression; just days after the Sputnik was launched, he told James Reston of the *New York Times:* "We now have all the rockets we need: long-range rockets, intermediate-range rockets and short-range rockets." Similar statements were made to three other Western correspondents during the fall of 1957.[35]

At this time, the United States was developing plans to increase the military capability of NATO by earmarking nuclear warheads for use by allied artillery in the event of war and by establishing bases for intermediate-range ballistic missiles on the territory of its NATO partners. Immediately prior to the December 1957 Paris meetings of NATO at which this plan was to be adopted, the Soviet Union began a campaign both to pressure European members of the alliance to refuse these weapons and bases and to demand again that Bonn withdraw from NATO. In the 1954 Paris Agreements, the German government agreed not to develop or possess atomic weapons, missiles, or long-range bombers, but the Soviets doubted the reliability of the pledge and desperately sought to ensure that the Federal Republic would not become nuclear-capable. Notes were sent by Premier Bulganin to the heads of NATO governments, and though the content varied from case to case, the message was unmistakable. The note to Britain read in part:

I say frankly that we find it difficult to understand what, in taking part in such a policy, guides the government of such a country as Great Britain, which is not only in an extremely vulnerable position by force of its geographical situation but which according to the admission of its official representatives has no effective means of defense against the effects of modern weapons. Nor can there, it is true, be such defense.[36]

The Soviet campaign included not only veiled threats but also proposals for arms control and military disengagement. One such plan, first enunciated by Polish Foreign Minister Adam Rapacki in October 1957, was soon openly sponsored by the Soviet Union. The plan called for the creation of a denuclearized zone in central Europe—that is, for an undertaking by Poland, Czechoslovakia, and the two Germanies not to allow the manufacture or stockpiling of nuclear weapons on their territory. The West attacked the proposal for its asymmetry and summarily rejected it. A few months later, the Soviet government proposed a moratorium on further atomic testing; since the proposal immediately preceded scheduled series of tests by both the United States and Britain, it too was rebuffed.

The atmosphere of East-West relations remained heated during 1958, but the Soviets proved anxious not to let the level of tension boil over into open conflict. This was especially so since the unfolding Soviet campaign to use strategic threats against the West in the search for political gains was, according to the best evidence, based upon an elaborate deception concerning the extent of Soviet missile capability.[37]

In effect, the postwar bipolar competition was being waged not by means of war but through confrontation and crises. As war became mutually suicidal for states whose "super" power was based on nuclear arsenals, each state tested the other's resolve in defending its interests through crisis as a functional equivalent of war. It was not that military capabilities no longer matter, however. On the contrary, each state's *perception* of the strategic military balance could be critical in the way it defined commitments, made threats, or accepted risks.

The strategic balance was actually quite unfavorable to the USSR; the Soviets had not yet matched the extensive strategic modernization and expansion program that the United States had carried out in the early 1950s. By the middle of the decade, America's Strategic Air Command possessed approximately 1,300 aircraft capable of nuclear-strike missions against the Soviet Union; these included long-range B-47s, many of which were based overseas, as well as the new "superfortress" B-52s, capable of carrying four H-bombs 5,000 miles and returning to base in the United States without refueling. The USSR lacked bombers of this capability. The mainstay of the Soviet strategic bomber force in the 1950s was the medium-range Badger (Tu-16), useful primarily for strikes against European targets. The longer-range Bear (Tu-20) and Bison (Mya-4) lacked the speed of the American bombers and were never deployed in great numbers.

Foreshadowing the later "missile gap," was a Soviet maneuver to deceive the West about their actual strategic bomber capabilities. On Aviation Day in July 1955, the Soviets made an ostentatious display of their new Bear and Bison heavy bombers, provoking the West into greatly overestimating the extent of Soviet capabilties and intentions. Only later did American intelligence sources discover that the air show fly-by was deliberately misleading: "the same squadron of Bisons had been flying around in circles, reappearing every few minutes."[38]

In like manner, choosing not to make the considerable investment of resources required for massive first-generation ICBM production but to wait instead for the development of the next and more reliable generation, Khrushchev nevertheless sought to exploit the political and psychological advantages produced by the West's assumption that the Soviets *were* rushing ahead with actual production. This impression was carefully cultivated by the Soviets through a series of exaggerated claims regarding their rocket development program (such as the Khrushchev interviews with Western correspondents mentioned above). In his memoirs, Khrushchev was candidly to admit that such claims (for example, as to the capability of Soviet anti-missile missiles to hit a fly) were "just rhetoric to make our adversaries think twice."[39] The result of this campaign was a widespead public impression, usually confirmed by "informed sources," of a substantial and growing "missile gap" in favor of the USSR.[40]

Khrushchev assiduously exploited this missile deception (and the accompanying impression that the Soviets were sufficiently confident of their superiority to take the risk of war) in an effort to extract political concessions from the West. Although he retained a healthy respect for Western military strength and was careful not to approach the brink of war too closely, Khrushchev's willingness to take the risks entailed in this strategy could only have been founded upon a conviction that the United States would not itself initiate a war without ample cause. Despite his rhetoric about the "war-mongers" in the "imperialist camp," Khrushchev had probably concluded, on the basis of his meeting with Eisenhower and Dulles at Geneva and his experience with American crisis diplomacy (in the Hungarian, Middle Eastern, and offshore islands conflicts), that his adversaries were also determined not to step over the brink. In these circumstances he could conclude that the keys to success lay in his ability to retain the political offensive while perpetuating the West's perception of Soviet missile superiority. Thus, the heavy burden would be on the West to choose either to accept change in the political status quo or to bear the responsibility of plunging the world into war. To describe Khrushchev's thinking in another way, we may cite the "game theory" version offered by Stanley Hoffmann:

It is important for *me* to be able to throw on *you* the responsibility of forcing *me* to escalate dangerously; I must seize the ominous initiative that puts on you the onus of making the fateful move that will oblige me to resort to a perhaps fatal response.

Hoffmann notes in conclusion that it is often easier for a defensive power to play this game, though "a skillful offensive player can play it too, through the technique of *faits accomplis* in particular."[41]

Although Khrushchev was far from an amateur in his playing of the game, his later difficulties may have resulted, ironically enough, from his having succeeded *too well* in his missile deception. Persuaded of the reality of the missile gap, the United States was to engage in a massive arms buildup of its own that resulted four years later in an actual missile gap in the other direction. The Chinese, on the other hand, persuaded by Sputnik that "the East Wind prevails over the West Wind," could never understand why Khrushchev failed to press his alleged military advantage; on balance, the Sino-Soviet conflict was exacerbated by the fact that the Chinese took Soviet claims of superiority at face value and began to look for other reasons for the ostensible Soviet "softness" toward imperialism.

The quintessential use of Khrushchev's strategy was in the crisis that centered, with variable intensity over a period of four years, on Berlin. By the late 1950s, the divided former German capital provided a dramatic illustration of the contrast between East and West. The western half, under British, French, and American occupation and loosely tied to the Federal Republic, had a booming economy that reflected the West German "economic miracle." The eastern half, under Soviet occupation, was a dreary and depressing open sore. An enclave 100 miles within East German territory, Berlin served as an escape valve for the East German population; by 1961, about 3 million people had crossed from the eastern to the western half of the city and thence had escaped to the Federal Republic. The openly visible economic contrast and the steady flow of refugees helped to undermine the stability of the German Democratic Republic and, together with the country's general status of nonrecognition, to perpetuate the appearance of illegitimacy and impermanence. The future health of the GDR and its status in the Soviet sphere of influence in Eastern Europe seemed to be dependent on a change in the status of Berlin.

Berlin represented more than a localized problem. In Khrushchev's own words, it was "a sort of barometer. The slightest fluctuation in the pressure of the world political atmosphere naturally registered at that point where the forces of the two sides were squared off against one another."[42] Resolved to end this festering issue and persuaded for a number of reasons that it was too late to accomplish a satisfactory reunification of Germany, Khrushchev was determined to achieve a recognition by treaty of the division of Germany.

He was not content to allow the western half of Germany to continue its evolution as a fullfledged (and ominously threatening) member of the Western alliance. The larger objective pursued by the Soviets in the negotiations over Berlin was a change in the orientation of the Federal Republic and a solid guarantee that Bonn would not gain access to nuclear weapons. If Moscow could not accomplish this purpose through agreement with the West, it would try to achieve it by undermining the confidence of the West German people in their NATO partners. Thus, if the West could be made to agree that the status of Berlin was negotiable, then a resolution was in sight not only of the immediate issue but also of the larger one. The strategy that Khrushchev was to employ in pursuit of this aim was based on the missile deception and depended for its success on a careful alternation in the East-West atmosphere between crisis and detente.

The new Berlin crisis opened in November 1958 with a Soviet proclamation that the situation in the city was "abnormal" and that a continuation of the status quo was no longer acceptable. Khrushchev demanded that the Western occupation of West Berlin be terminated and that the western sectors be transformed into a "free city" within the territory of a sovereign GDR, to which the Soviets would in turn hand over their own rights in Berlin. Access to Berlin would then be under the control of the East Germans. The Soviet demand was in the form of an ultimatum; it stated that if the West failed to agree to a treaty embodying these terms, then after six months (on May 27, 1959), the USSR would sign a separate agreement with the GDR. The Western powers would thenceforth have to deal directly with that regime; a challenge to its prerogatives on access to Berlin would presumably embroil the West in a clash with the entire Warsaw Pact.

The proposed Soviet solution to the German problem was in the form of a draft peace treaty between the Big Four and the two German states. By the terms of this treaty, reunification would be left for agreement between the two separate and equal German regimes. These two states would be neutral, the size of their armed forces would be limited to a level necessary for the maintenance of order and protection of frontiers, access to nuclear weapons, missiles, bombers, or submarines would be proscribed and unhampered political activity would be guaranteed to the communists and their allies but denied to "revanchist and revisionist" groups.

The Western reaction was to reject the Soviet proposal and the conditions attached to it but to agree to negotiate the issue in the larger context of Germany and European security. After a winter of frenetic diplomacy, including a visit to Moscow by British Prime Minister MacMillan, the four powers agreed to convene a Foreign Ministers' Conference in Geneva in May. The Soviets agreed to postpone their deadline for agreement, and the conference assembled for inconclusive negotiations that proceeded into July.

In the midst of this first round of the crisis, the Twenty-First Congress of the CPSU assembled in January 1959. The "Congress of the Builders of Communism" (as it was called in the USSR) gathered to adopt an ambitious Seven-Year Plan designed to propel the Soviet economy to a level past that of the United States. The delegates heard Khrushchev proclaim that the triumph of socialism in the USSR had become irreversible and that a favorable shift had definitely taken place in the world balance of power in favor of socialism.

For Khrushchev, the lofty status of the USSR was confirmed when he received an invitation later in the year to pay a visit to the United States in September. The Soviet premier's highly publicized visit lasted from September 15 to 28, during which time he toured the country making numerous public statements emphasizing the danger of nuclear war and appealing for peaceful coexistence and disarmament. Khrushchev spent the last three days of the visit in private conversations with Eisenhower at the presidential retreat; from these talks emerged the phrase "spirit of Camp David."

The talks were generally unproductive in substance. The discussions of disarmament again foundered on the issue of international controls and inspection. (Khrushchev was later to say that it was impossible for the USSR to submit to these controls as long as the United States retained its military superiority, though of course his public stance at the time was quite to the contrary.)[43] Nor was there real progress on the German question, though President Eisenhower did agree to summit-level negotiations on the issue, in return for which Khrushchev again lifted his deadline for settlement.

From a public relations standpoint, the talks were a great success. Khrushchev himself commented that his conversations with the American president "broke the ice," and that it was now up to the diplomats to remove the chunks. Upon his return to Moscow, he paid a high personal tribute to Eisenhower as a man who "sincerely wants to liquidate the cold war and improve relations between our two great countries."[44]

Still confident that this "missile deception" strategy was succeeding, Khrushchev proposed in a speech delivered in January 1960 to the Supreme Soviet that the Soviet armed forces be reduced in size by about one-third (a cut of 1.2 million men including a quarter-million officers). His plan was couched in the context of a favorable report on the relaxation of international tensions, bolstered by optimistic expectations concerning the forthcoming summit meeting in Paris in May. He exuded confidence in the strength of the socialist camp and the adequacy of the Soviet strategic arsenal and, admitting for the first time that nuclear war would be mutually destructive for both capitalism and communism, Khrushchev spoke eloquently on the need for the elimination of the instruments of destruction in the context of general and complete disarmament.[45]

And yet, despite Khrushchev's assertions to the contrary, the primary motivation for the proposed military manpower reduction was probably economic. Fulfillment of the ambitious Seven-Year Plan required that resources be diverted from "guns to butter"; in particular, the postwar demographic profile of the USSR revealed a need for additional manpower in the civilian economy.

In a way, Khrushchev's military strategy represented a return to the ideas expounded by Malenkov in 1954. Confident in the mutual destructiveness of nuclear war and the sobriety of his opponents, Khrushchev was gambling on "minimum deterrence" and turning away from the earlier notion that Soviet forces needed to be large and diverse enough to wage a traditional war following the initial nuclear exchange. The doctrine he was announcing in 1960 was also similar to the American strategy of "massive retaliation" in that it assumed that any local or limited incursion would rapidly escalate into full-scale nuclear exchange, and thus downgraded the importance of large conventional forces. The United States, ironically, had already discarded this doctrine and was engaged in reshaping its own force structure to make possible first "tactical nuclear warfare" and later "flexible response"—both of which were aimed at raising the strategic nuclear threshold.

With his relative confidence that war was unlikely, Khrushchev was willing to place more emphasis on strategic deterrence; thus he raised the role of the strategic rocket forces to primacy, seeking to conserve resources by trading nuclear firepower for manpower. The size of the Soviet armed forces had already been cut from its 1955 level (said by Khrushchev to have been 5,763,000) to an announced size of 3.6 million (though these reductions had not been accompanied by significant Soviet withdrawals from Europe). A further reduction of the magnitude Khrushchev was proposing would not be achieved easily; that it was met with resistance in the Soviet military establishment is suggested by the fact that the Soviet high command was reshuffled during the spring to remove some of the more adamant opponents of Khrushchev's proposal.

Ultimately, a compromise between modernists and traditionalists in the military was reached; theater forces were trimmed somewhat, but in the process they were "nuclearized," with stress on battlefield mobility and firepower. The result, according to a leading Western authority, was that:

Khrushchev's military policy, rather than replacing Stalin's, in effect overlapped it, so that the old threat geared predominantly to land warfare continued alongside the nuclear threat, most graphically embodied in the large medium-range missile force targeted on Western Europe.[46]

Khrushchev's political career was punctuated with sharp reversals but none more precipitous than the turn in his fortunes that occurred in May 1960. After, the optimism surrounding the Camp David summit and the January speech, the month of the Paris summit should have brought great achievements for Soviet foreign policy. Instead, it saw the discrediting of much for which Khrushchev had worked. With all this, it brought a demonstration that the Soviet leader was still not immune from political challenge.

Early on May 1, the Soviet premier was informed that an American U-2 high altitude plane had penetrated Soviet air space. By his account, his foreign minister advised a diplomatic protest, but instead he ordered that it be shot down. He was aware that this was by no means the first violation of Soviet territory by a U-2, and in fact he recalled that an opportunity to down one had been missed the previous month because the antiaircraft batteries had not fired soon enough. Later in the day, while on the reviewing stand watching the May Day parade in Red Square, he was told that the plane had been successfully brought down and that the pilot had been captured alive.[47]

The Soviet interrogators had little difficulty learning from the plane's pilot, Francis Gary Powers, that its mission was photographic espionage. Over the next few days, the Soviets only gradually revealed the extent of their knowledge; they deliberately allowed the United States to release a cover story and then they proceeded to take it apart line by line. Although Khrushchev was clearly angry at this American intrusion and sought to embarrass his adversary in grand style, he apparently did not expect that President Eisenhower—the man whom he had so recently praised as a peace-loving statesman—would claim foreknowledge of the flight, defend it, and take personal responsibility for it.

Khrushchev had staked a great deal on his relationship with the American president and on his ability to extract concessions from the West at the forthcoming summit; not only his strategy for a change in the situation in Berlin but also his recently announced strategy for a defense cutback depended on it. As he watched his plans fall into disarray, a dissatisfied opposition faction composed of "steel-eaters," defense lobbyists, and hard-line ideologists took advantage of his setback to bring about, at a Central Committee plenum on May 4, a realignment in the party leadership.[48] From our hindsight concerning Khrushchev's strategy, we can understand that the U-2 incident produced not only personal anger at Eisenhower for defending an "outrageous, inadmissible action," and not merely a just and principled response to an act of espionage. (In Khrushchev's words, "If we hadn't stood up to the Americans, they would have continued to send spies into our country.")[49] What the U-2 flights had been engaged in (for several years, as it turned out) was systematic photographing of Soviet territory, looking for the famous and multitudinous missile sites that were not in fact there. What Khrushchev (and his opponents) must have realized was that his whole strategy of missile deception was in a shambles; he had no way of knowing what the Americans had learned from the flights, but even such uncertainty undermined his bluffing game.

Khrushchev proceeded to Paris in mid-May for the summit; he was accompanied by (indeed, his steps appeared to be dogged by) his Minister of Defense, Marshal Malinovskii. The Soviet leadership's decision (Khrushchev claims it was his own, arrived at on the plane to Paris) was to torpedo the summit conference by refusing to participate without an apology from Eisenhower. This decision was based not simply (as Khrushchev claims) on a determination to protect Soviet pride and prestige in the face of an outrageous action, but more likely on the foreknowledge that the summit would not produce the desired Western concessions on Berlin and Germany. And yet, with their strategy in shambles, the Soviets could not reinstate the Berlin ultimatum. Having made his angry speech attacking Eisenhower and rescinding the invitation for him to visit the USSR, thus breaking up the summit, Khrushchev also pledged that the Soviet Union would take no precipitous unilateral action on Berlin.

The summer of 1960 was a difficult one for the Soviets. They had declared that no further negotiations could be held with the West while Eisenhower remained in office. The Chinese leaders had been criticizing Moscow for excessive "softness" toward imperialism, and the Soviet stance provided a convenient demonstration of firmness. Nevertheless, their quarrel with China continued to heat up. Meanwhile, they were engaged in a messy and ultimately unsuccessful operation in the Congo. By September, Khrushchev was in an ugly mood as he traveled to the United States (on a ship, with the leaders of the East European socialist countries) to address the United Nations General Assembly. His ostensible purpose was to present to the delegates a Soviet-authored declaration condemning colonialism. But, after quarreling with Secretary-General Hammarskjöld over his handling of the United Nations operation in the Congo, Khrushchev also presented a demand for a restructuring of the U.N. Secretariat (substituting a "troika" for the "hopelessly biased" Secretary-General). It was on this occasion that Khrushchev displayed his worst diplomatic manners, including banging his shoe on his desk to show his disapproval of one of the speeches. His second trip to the United States was hardly a triumphant visit, and it stood in stark contrast to the "spirit of Camp David" of the year before.

KHRUSHCHEV AND KENNEDY: A WAR OF NERVES

The Soviets made no secret of their delight that, when President Eisenhower left office in 1961, he was succeeded not by Richard M. Nixon but by John F. Kennedy. In retrospect, they may have questioned their judgment. Nixon and Kennedy had seemed to vie with one another during the campaign for the honor of being "tougher" with the Russians. One of Kennedy's major issues had been the alleged worldwide decline in American influence and prestige; he pledged to reverse that decline and also to close the infamous "missile gap." The new administration came into office determined to pursue an activist policy and to meet the Soviet challenge in both Europe and the Third World head on.

The ill-fated invasion at the Bay of Pigs was the Kennedy Administration's first foreign policy crisis; it resulted in an American defeat that raised serious questions about just how "tough" the new president could be. The Soviet involvement in the crisis was mainly at the sidelines. Moscow's first major contact with Fidel Castro had occurred barely a year before, in February 1960, when Mikoyan had visited Cuba to establish diplomatic relations and sign an aid agreement. As Khrushchev's account confirms, the Soviets did not then regard Castro as a communist, though they knew that some of his key advisors (including his brother, Raul, and Ché Guevara) were.[50] But they had been delighted at the developing Cuban-American quarrel and only too happy at first to provide the assistance (including arms) that Castro needed in his confrontation with the United States. Khrushchev had given Castro a warm embrace during his visit to the United Nations in September, much to the consternation of American officials.

President Kennedy inherited from his predecessor a secret training base and plans for supporting an invasion, led by Cuban exiles, at the Bay of Pigs. The Administration decided to proceed with the operation, which was launched in April 1961. But faulty intelligence estimates of Castro's internal strength, combined with a decision to withhold U.S. air support for the beleaguered invaders, helped produce a disaster. As in the Suez crisis, the Soviet Union aimed noisy propaganda blasts at the invasion from the beginning but did not issue threats until the defeat of the operation was already assured. After the crisis had passed, the Soviet premier sent Kennedy a gratuitously insulting message that served to rub salt in the American wounds.

Despite this bad beginning in their relationship, the two leaders agreed in May to a meeting in Vienna the following month. Kennedy was aware that Khrushchev might have read his behavior during the Bay of Pigs crisis as indicative of a failure of nerve, and he may have been tempted to overcompensate when he met with Khrushchev. At any rate, save for an agreement that the conflict in Laos should be resolved by neutralizing the country, the meeting was unproductive. Khrushchev regarded Kennedy's position on the German issue as virtually identical with Eisenhower's, and he interpreted Kennedy's overall posture as the equivalent of a demand for a freeze in the international status quo.[51] Kennedy, for his part, found Khrushchev's behavior at the summit "sobering"; he characterized the atmosphere as "somber," and parted from the Russian leader with the comment, "It will be a cold winter."[52]

In his televised report to the Soviet people on the Vienna Meeting on June 15, Khrushchev seemed to confirm Kennedy's prognosis by reinstating the deadline for a settlement of the Berlin crisis; a peace treaty with East Germany must, he said, "be attained this year." A few days later, in a speech before a military audience, he reiterated the deadline and reaffirmed his intention to sign a separate treaty with the GDR if the West should refuse to negotiate a general one.

Khrushchev's tactics during this new phase of the crisis had none of the peace-loving aura of the "spirit of Camp David"; rather, they called to mind the rocket-rattling conduct of 1958.[53] On July 2, the Soviet premier approached the British ambassador at a reception and reminded him that it would take only six hydrogen bombs to demolish his country (and only nine to destroy France). Within the week, Khrushchev was making another Berlin-related speech; this time, he announced a one-third increase in the Soviet defense budget and a suspension of the planned reduction in the size of the Soviet armed forces.

The American administration was correctly interpreting the Soviet behavior as a test of wills, and Kennedy decided to answer Khrushchev in kind. He made a television speech on July 25 that announced an increase in the American defense budget and military manpower. As he had at Vienna, he put the burden of initiating a change in the situation squarely on Khrushchev, thereby seizing for himself what Hoffmann terms the "ominous initiative."

Khrushchev's reaction to the president's speech was harsh and included allusions to the possibility that the Soviets might resume atomic testing (including the detonation of a 100-megaton bomb). But the Soviet leader chose not (or was unable) to match the American military escalation. He apparently concluded that he would not succeed in bullying the West into negotiating a German peace treaty; nor, given the now even more unfavorable strategic balance, did he wish to turn the test of wills into a test of force. But he could not choose inaction; not only was his prestige on the line, but the problem of the Berlin escape route was daily becoming more acute. Faced with this dilemma, he apparently decided to scale down his objective and to deal with the problem of "border control" without waiting for the prior conclusion of a peace treaty.

New Soviet notes were sent to the United States, Britain, France, and West Germany, but only the latter now mentioned the year-end deadline for a solution. The notes suggested that a German peace treaty be signed, to be followed by separate negotiations concerning access and the status of West Berlin. On August 7, the Soviet premier delivered a speech that continued to focus on the peace treaty, complaining (in a Khrushchevian version of the "domino theory") that if the USSR were to abandon its objective of a peace treaty, the West would then demand the abandonment of the socialist system itself.

This continuing emphasis on the treaty was probably calculated to divert the attention from Khrushchev's new immediate objective—the closing off of the East Berlin escape route. His tactic succeeded, and the Soviet construction of the Berlin Wall (actually only barbed wire at first) on August 13 caught the West by surprise. With this *fait accompli*, Khrushchev showed that he was a "skillful offensive player," for he had in effect regained the "ominous initiative" and shifted the burden of escalation onto the West. For the next several weeks, Khrushchev kept up his insistence on treaty negotiations while his forces worked to strengthen the wall. The American response was limited to strong diplomatic protests and the dispatch to Berlin of Vice President Johnson and General Lucius Clay, and the commitment of 1500 additional U.S. troops.

Khrushchev's memoirs assert that, although it was not the same sort of "moral victory" that a peace treaty would have been, the establishment of "border control" in Berlin stabilized the situation there and produced more in the way of "material gains." The wall, he argues,

restored order and discipline in the East Germans' lives (and Germans have always appreciated discipline). Seeing that their government had reasserted control over its own frontiers, the East Germans were heartened by the solidification and fortification of their state.

With regret for the necessity to "guard the gates of the Socialist paradise," he concludes with this candid admission: "Unfortunately, the GDR—and not only the GDR—has yet to reach a level of moral and material development where competition with the West is possible."[54]

Although the construction of the wall was to solve Khrushchev's immediate problem in Berlin, neither the crisis nor his own political difficulties were resolved. In fact, a close analysis of the events in the late summer and autumn of 1961 suggests that Khrushchev faced another challenge in this period from the "hard-line" faction that confronted him the previous year, and that he was not wholly in control of Soviet policymaking during these months.

One of the decisions for which Khrushchev may not have been responsible was the Soviet Union's resumption of the atmospheric testing of nuclear weapons on August 30.[55] Indeed, in his January 1960 speech the Soviet premier had warned that stern condemnation would and should greet any country that broke the testing moratorium. But if this decision was indeed the result of the ascendancy of a rival faction (headed, it appeared, by Frol Kozlov), Khrushchev was not long in regaining the initiative. The premier held a long interview in early September 1961 with *New York Times* correspondent C. L. Sulzberger, at the end of which he delivered a secret message for President Kennedy. The message was couched in a friendly tone and suggested that the two powers negotiate an agreement on Laos, to be followed by a settlement of the Berlin issue and then by a visit by Kennedy to the Soviet Union. "I am hopeful," Khrushchev told Sulzberger, "that I shall be the one to welcome him."[56]

By mid-September, Khrushchev appeared to have persuaded the party leadership of the wisdom of moderating its demands on Berlin and cooling off the tensions with the United States. Ironically, it was Kozlov's task to suggest, in a speech in North Korea, that the Soviets were prepared to discuss "reasonable amendments to our draft treaty" on Germany. At about the same time, a Soviet newsman told Kennedy's press secretary that "the storm in Berlin is over." In early October, the two leaders exchanged encouraging letters on the international situation. In another conciliatory gesture, the USSR dropped its demand for a "troika" in the U.N. Secretariat and acceded to the selection of U Thant as successor to Hammarskjöld (who had been killed in a plane crash in the Congo in September).

The tense final fact in the Berlin crisis of 1961 was played out in the midst of the Twenty-Second Congress of the CPSU in late October. The Congress was intended as a routine affair, featuring approval of the new party program and rules, but it turned into an arena for struggles within the CPSU as well as between the Soviet party and its Chinese and Albanian challengers. Khrushchev's supporters launched a new round of de-Stalinization and a new attack on the "anti-party group," both of which provided an esoteric medium for the expression of contemporary factional struggles. According to Robert Slusser's persuasive account, the Berlin crisis itself, including an ominous confrontation between Soviet and American tanks at the border of their respective sectors on October 27-28, may have been the object of manipulation by the Kozlov "hard-line" faction challenging Khrushchev for the leadership.[57]

At the Congress, Khrushchev's opening speech was most notable for its withdrawal of the ultimatum for a Berlin settlement. The party leader also announced, as a macabre "concession," that the 100-megaton bomb would not be exploded during the current test series, but rather that the super-bomb testing would be limited to one of 50 megatons. (The storm of world protest that greeted this announcement may have been welcomed by Khrushchev, Slusser suggests, as a means of forcing his hard-line rivals to back away from even the 50-megaton test.) Khrushchev also seemed to signal a moderation of the pace of Soviet rearmament by declaring that "the rearming of the Soviet Army with nuclear and rocket weapons has been fully completed."

Khrushchev's withdrawal of the Berlin ultimatum did not seem to win universal approval at the Congress. The speech of Walter Ulbricht, the GDR party leader, was thoroughly defiant in asserting the continued urgency of a peace treaty. Even the speech of Foreign Minister Gromyko seemed to diverge from Khrushchev's by omitting any reference to the withdrawal of the deadline (as well as by failing to mention the evil deeds of the Albanians and by reaffirming the close Soviet ties with China). Thus, Khrushchev found it necessary to reassert, in his closing speech, that "what counts most is not the particular date [of a German peace treaty] but a business-like and honest settlement of the question."

On the whole, the Twenty-Second Party Congress was inconclusive for Khrushchev. It did place the Soviet charges against Albania (and indirectly, against China) on the public record, as well as the new revelations about the crimes of Stalin and the foul deeds of the "anti-party group." But it failed to follow up on the suggestion that the leading members of the "anti-party group" be ousted from the party; it did not go as far as Khrushchev would have liked in reorienting Soviet economic priorities; and—as a final signal that Khrushchev would continue to lack supreme authority in the party—it confirmed the status of his main challenger, Frol Kozlov, as the number-two ranking member of the leadership.

THE CUBAN MISSILE CRISIS AND ITS AFTERMATH

In the midst of the proceedings of the Twenty-Second Congress, an American defense official had made a significant speech challenging the Soviet claim of military superiority over the United States. Although Marshal Malinovskii had been called to the rostrum of the Congress to rebut this speech and to reassert the Soviet claims, it should have been clear to the Soviet leadership that the strategy of missile deception had been exploded. Not only had the Americans discovered that the "missile gap" in favor of the Soviets was a myth, they had also been engaged in a strategic buildup of their own that was resulting in a rapidly growing American lead in the strategic missile race.

Khrushchev's dilemma was becoming more acute. He had failed to dislodge the West from Berlin or to achieve a realignment in Germany, and Soviet prestige had suffered as a result. His worries about West German access to nuclear weapons were now compounded by a fear that an increasingly hostile China would develop an independent nuclear capability. His own country's relative strategic position was worsening and yet the internal pressures on limited Soviet resources were growing (as was the challenge to his own political primacy). He was badly in need of a spectacular victory.

Khrushchev was a great believer in the political and psychological importance of *perceived and acknowledged* power. His memoirs record the "pleasure and pride" he had felt during conversations with MacMillan and de Gaulle at the 1960 Paris Summit when those leaders acknowledged that the USSR had surpassed their own countries and ranked with the United States as one of the world's two mightiest powers.[58] At the beginning of 1962, he must have felt that if he could achieve a demonstration of Soviet military capability that was sufficiently impressive in both Washington and Beijing, then he could at last hope to proceed with the negotiated resolution of the outstanding issues between Moscow and its two rivals.

The idea Khrushchev seized upon for resolving his dilemma was typically bold. The account in his memoirs is particularly instructive:

It was during my visit to Bulgaria [May 14–20] that I had the idea of installing missiles with nuclear warheads in Cuba without letting the United States find out they were there until it was too late to do anything about them. . . . My thinking went like this: if we installed the missiles secretly and then if the United States discovered the missiles were there after they were already poised and ready to strike, the Americans would think twice before trying to liquidate our installations by military means. . . . In addition to protecting Cuba, our missiles would have equalized what the West likes to call the "balance of power." The Americans had surrounded our country with military bases and threatened us with nuclear weapons, and now they would learn just what it feels like to have enemy missiles pointing at you; we'd be doing nothing more than giving them a little of their own medicine. And it was high time America learned what it feels like to have her own land and her own people threatened. . . .

All these thoughts kept churning in my head the whole time I was in Bulgaria. I paced back and forth, brooding over what to do. I didn't tell anyone what I was thinking. I kept my mental agony to myself. But all the while the idea of putting missiles in Cuba was ripening inside my mind.[59]

Khrushchev's account here is not entirely trustworthy but it is more credible than his public postcrisis explanation to the Supreme Soviet in December 1962, in which he claimed that the Soviet missiles were placed in Cuba at Castro's request, solely to save Cuba from invasion. Castro himself denied having made the request, and Khrushchev's memoirs now acknowledge that they had "heated arguments" before Castro agreed to accept the missiles. Moreover, there were more direct and less risky ways of protecting Cuba from invasion, if that were indeed Khrushchev's main concern. Long-range missiles of the type placed in Cuba were less appropriate against invasion than weapons of other types; in fact, Khrushchev could simply have extended a guarantee (or membership in the Warsaw Pact) to Cuba, *had he not also been worried about the strategic imbalance.*

The account in his memoirs still places primary emphasis on Khrushchev's desire to save Cuba from another American-sponsored invasion, yet he cites no evidence that such an attack was being contemplated (other than the charge of "class blindness" among American ruling circles). More credible are the other reasons he cites. "Equalizing the balance of power" and "giving the Americans a taste of their own medicine" are ends for which the placement of missiles in Cuba was a more appropriate means. The military threat to the United States would have been increased, largely by virtue of the shorter distance involved in an attack from Cuba; intermediate-range missiles, once operational in Cuba, became "ersatz ICBMs." But the political and psychological impact of Soviet missiles just 90 miles off the American shores would have been even more significant. In another passage, Khrushchev also notes his desire to maintain Soviet prestige; the "loss" of Cuba would have diminished Soviet stature in Latin America, whereas the missiles would have served as a tangible demonstration of the Soviet deterrent to U.S. "imperialism" in the Third World.

The emphasis on considerations of prestige and psychological effect suggests that Khrushchev may well have been planning to use the Cuban missiles as a "bargaining chip"—a lever to employ in gaining Western concessions on issues.[60] Such a strategy would have been perfectly in keeping with the Khrushchev diplomatic style.

The actual unfolding of the Cuban Missile Crisis is an oft-told tale, and only a bare outline need be given here.[61] The Soviets began their scenario in September, when Ambassador Dobrynin disingenuously assured President Kennedy that Moscow would cause no trouble in either Berlin or Cuba prior to the November Congressional elections. Still, there was heated political debate in the United States about the Russian activity in Cuba, and on October 14, a U-2 overflight of the island brought evidence that missile installations were being constructed. On October 18, the president held a scheduled meeting with Foreign Minister Gromyko, who baldly lied about the purpose of Soviet shipments to Cuba. And on October 20, in a distant but related development, a new border war broke out between China and India; the Soviets, not wanting to risk disunity in the socialist camp at this critical moment, intially supported China in the dispute.

On October 22, 1962, President Kennedy made a televised address in which he informed the American people and the world of the evidence of Soviet missile construction in Cuba. He declared ominously that the United States would consider an attack from Cuba as the equivalent of an attack from the USSR, thus shifting the burden squarely into Khrushchev's court, and announced the imposition of a naval blockade (officially, a "quarantine") to halt further Soviet shipment of missiles to Cuba. With several Soviet vessels then on their way to Cuba and work on the missile installations proceeding apace, the stage was set for a confrontation unlike any the nuclear age had yet seen.

With the imposition of the quarantine, Kennedy had seized the "ominous initiative"; American conventional and strategic strength was superior to that of the Soviets and there seemed no lack of will on the part of the administration to use it. Khrushchev was aware of this and set about mightily striving to salvage what he could of the situation. There is little doubt that his major concern was "to save the peace," but he hoped to do so without substantial loss of prestige. Threatening a counterattack in Berlin, where the Soviets had local conventional superiority, would hardly ease the strategic threat, although the threat of such a move might be sufficient to hold the Americans back from a hasty preemptive attack on the missiles in Cuba.

It was in this context that, on October 26, Khrushchev sent Kennedy a lengthy and rambling letter, almost frantic in its tone and intensely personal in its appeal, that contained the outline of a solution. Much of the letter constituted an appeal to the president to resist "intoxication and petty passions" and take regard of the utter calamity that nuclear war would bring to both the United States and the Soviet Union. Another section was a tortured explanation of the purpose of the Soviet missiles and a denial that they could be termed "offensive." Khrushchev assured the president that the weapons shipments had been completed and that Soviet vessels currently bound for Cuba contained only peaceful cargoes. The purpose of Soviet assistance to Cuba, he argued, had been only a humanitarian desire to assist these people in making their revolution without outside impediment. If the threat to Cuba's peaceful reconstruction (such as had been posed at the Bay of Pigs) were removed, then the need for armaments in Cuba would disappear "since, if there is no threat, then armaments are a burden for every people."

At last Khrushchev had come to his proposal:

Let us therefore show statesmanlike wisdom. I propose: We, for our part, will declare that our ships, bound for Cuba, will not carry any kind of armaments. You would declare that the United States will not invade Cuba with its forces and will not support any sort of forces which might intend to carry out an invasion of Cuba. Then the necessity for the presence of our military specialists in Cuba would disappear.[62]

Earlier that same day, Alexander S. Fomin, a counselor in the Soviet embassy, had lunched with an American television newsman, John Scali, and had outlined to him essentially the same proposition. In this disavowable channel, however, the Soviet proposal could be more specific; Fomin specified that the missile sites would be dismantled and shipped back to the USSR under United Nations supervision, that Castro would pledge to accept no more offensive weapons in the future, and that the United States in turn would pledge not to invade Cuba.

The situation was complicated the next day when a second letter arrived from Khrushchev, quite different in tone and substance from the first. The second letter seemed to pick up on a suggestion that had been made by columnist Walter Lippmann, that Soviet missiles in Cuba be removed in return for the removal of American missiles in Turkey. American Ambassador to the USSR, Llewellyn Thompson, speculated that the dispatch of the second letter might signal a split among the Kremlin leadership: that it was composed in haste was suggested by the fact that it appeared in the Soviet newspaper *Izvestiia* alongside a column (evidently written earlier) that rejected the notion of such a swap as "cynical bargaining."

On October 28, the American administration chose to ignore the second letter altogether and accept the offer conveyed in Khrushchev's first letter (and by Mr. Fomin). The Soviets accepted the offer and war was averted. Later, Khrushchev was to imply that it was Kennedy who had been in need of assistance in a time of grave political challenge (from a possible military coup) and that the solution to the Cuban crisis had been a gracious act on his part— a "triumph of common sense" as well as a "personal triumph," that had "forced the U.S. to demobilize and to recognize Cuba." He did not explain in his account why he had so charitably accepted the word of a "class-blinded" capitalist, nor did he explain what had happened to his determination to "equalize the balance of power." Clearly, allowed by the American president to "save face" in his retreat, Khrushchev was not inclined to refuse the opportunity.

Although he could take credit publicly for having "saved the peace," Khrushchev was now in even more serious trouble with his colleagues in the

Kremlin. There was fresh emphasis placed in Moscow on the "collective leadership" and signs appeared that Khrushchev was being forced to retreat on several fronts. Marshal Moskalenko, head of the strategic rocket forces, who had been ousted from his post in April (probably because of his opposition to the Cuban missile gamble) was restored to his position in November. Khrushchev was forced to backtrack on de-Stalinization and his efforts at economic liberalization and reorganization were scrapped. In the spring of 1963, there was also a brief interlude of detente with the Chinese (who had greeted Khrushchev's Caribbean escapade with simultaneous cries of "adventurism" and "capitulationism").

Khrushchev might well have been removed from office in the spring of 1963 had it not been for the sudden illness of Frol Kozlov, his rival and heir presumptive. This stroke of good fortune allowed Khrushchev to make a temporary recovery. The proposal for a peace treaty on Germany had been shelved indefinitely earlier in the year when Khrushchev had traveled to the GDR to inform his allies that the building of the wall had served to fulfill most of the communist objectives in Berlin. The matter of nuclear proliferation lingered, however, and Khrushchev—responding to President Kennedy's arms control initiative in a speech at the American University—moved to bring about progress on that front in the summer of 1963. Hard on the heels of the collapse of talks between the Soviets and Chinese, a treaty banning nuclear tests (except those conducted underground) was initialed in Moscow, London, and Washington. Although the Chinese (and the French) refused to sign, the Federal Republic of Germany was among the eventual signatories to the treaty. A year later, there were hints that Khrushchev might be planning a rapprochement with West Germany, in the hope of coping with the German threat through direct negotiations and compromise. A visit to Bonn in July 1964 by Khrushchev's son-in-law Alexei Adzhubei was reportedly made in preparation for a trip by Khrushchev himself the coming autumn.

In the aftermath of the Cuban Missile Crisis, Khrushchev's efforts seem to have been focused on restoring an atmosphere of relaxation of tensions with the West and searching for negotiated solutions to some problems, particularly in the realm of arms control, while holding others on the "back burner." Both the signing of the limited test ban treaty and the conclusion, in June 1963, of a Soviet-American agreement to establish a direct communication link ("hot line") seemed to signal a developing East-West detente. Having sought to gain at least the illusion of strategic parity or superiority—first through deception and then through an equalization of the balance "on the cheap"— the Soviet leaders were now apparently reconciled to making the painful investments in military hardware that would be necessary for the achievement of genuine parity. They were also being forced to expend a far greater amount of their energy and concern in management of the affairs of the socialist bloc, as the split with China had moved to the point of open break, fragmenting the international communist movement in the process.

Although foreign policy issues in general did not rank high on the list of "errors" for which Khrushchev was ousted, his management of relationships in the socialist bloc and his gamble in Cuba are possible exceptions. Rather, the chief substantive failures of Khrushchev were domestic, including most notably his mismanagement of Soviet agriculture and his reorganizations of the Soviet party and government bureaucracies. But it was Khrushchev's style as much as the failure of policies which disturbed his more bureaucratic-minded colleagues; his frequent reorganizations and campaigns left an aura of unsettledness and inefficiency, his intervention in areas where his expertise was questionable had alienated key interests, and he was increasingly given to taking action without consulting his colleagues in advance (such as his conferral of the award, "Hero of the USSR," on Arab leaders Ben Bella and Nasser, and the dispatch of Adzhubei to Bonn).

On October 14, 1964, Khrushchev was summoned to Moscow from his Black Sea vacation home to hear the indictments against him and to face the demand that he tender his resignation from all his posts "at his own request" and "due to advancing age and deteriorating health." The conspirators had done their homework; the army and police had apparently cooperated in the plot, and the Central Committee had already been summoned to accept Khrushchev's resignation. It was all over quickly. Only a sparse and indirect explanation was made to the Soviet people, who read in a *Pravda* editorial on October 17:

subjectivism and complacency . . . harebrained scheming, hasty conclusions, rash decisions, and actions based on wishful thinking, boasting and empty words, bureaucratism, the refusal to take into account all the achievements of science and practical technology—all these defects are alien to the Party.[63]

Khrushchev spent his retirement as a virtual "unperson." His name appeared in the Soviet press only two times after his "resignation." On the first occasion, he was quoted in 1970 as having denied that he had "passed on material of a memoir nature" to Western publishing houses. (The statement denying his personal involvement was strictly true, though made under duress. The memoirs have been definitely established as his own words.)[64] The second brief, matter-of-fact press notice, in September 1971, recorded his death:

The C.P.S.U. Central Committee and the USSR Council of Ministers announce with regret that personal pensioner Nikita Sergeyevich Khrushchev, formerly First Secretary of the C.P.S.U. Central Committee and Chairman of the USSR Council of Ministers, died September 11, 1971, at the age of 78, after a grave and prolonged illness.[65]

He might have been struck by the irony that the obituaries in the Western press were both more voluminous and more laudatory than was the recognition allowed him by his lieutenants and successors in his own native land.

NOTES

1. *Khrushchev Remembers,* with an introduction, commentary, and notes by Edward Crankshaw, trans. and ed. by Strobe Talbott (Boston: Little, Brown and Company, 1970), p. 392. (Hereafter, *Khrushchev I.*)
2. For details of the Korean armistice negotiations, see C. Turner Joy, *How Communists Negotiate* (New York: MacMillan, 1955).
3. Excerpted in Myron Rush, ed., *The International Situation and Soviet Foreign Policy* (Columbus, Ohio: Charles E. Merrill, 1970), p. 160.
4. Ibid., p. 162.
5. *Khrushchev I,* pp. 393-394.
6. *Department of State Bulletin, 30,* no. 767 (March 8, 1954): 344.
7. *New Times,* no. 49 (December 4, 1954), Supplement, p. 72.
8. For further details, see David J. Dallin, *Soviet Foreign Policy After Stalin* (Philadelphia: Lippincott, 1961), pp. 148-150.
9. See ibid., pp. 150-155, and J. M. Mackintosh, *Strategy and Tactics of Soviet Foreign Policy* (New York: Oxford University Press, 1963), pp. 79-85.
10. *Khrushchev I,* pp. 482-483.
11. *Pravda,* March 13, 1954. For more details, see Mackintosh, *Strategy and Tactics,* pp. 88-104, and H. S. Dinerstein, *War and the Soviet Union,* rev. ed. (New York: Praeger, 1962), especially pp. 91-166.
12. *Izvestiia,* April 27, 1954.
13. *Pravda,* March 27, 1955.
14. Quoted in Mackintosh, *Strategy and Tactics,* p. 93.
15. For details of the Khrushchev-Molotov quarrel, see Dallin, *Soviet Foreign Policy After Stalin,* pp. 228-233.
16. *Khrushchev I,* p. 393.
17. Ibid., p. 395.
18. *Khrushchev I,* p. 398, and *Khrushchev Remembers: The Last Testament,* trans. and ed. Strobe Talbott, with a Foreword by Edward Crankshaw and an Introduction by Jerrold L. Schecter (Boston: Little, Brown and Company, 1974), pp. 362-363. (Hereafter, *Khrushchev II.*)
19. *Khrushchev I,* p. 400.
20. Cited in Dwight D. Eisenhower, *The White House Years: Mandate for Change 1953-1956* (Garden City: Doubleday, 1963), p. 526.
21. Quoted in Dallin, *Soviet Foreign Policy After Stalin,* p. 283.

22. Eisenhower, *The White House Years,* p. 529.
23. *Khrushchev I,* p. 358.
24. Dallin, *Soviet Foreign Policy After Stalin,* pp. 261-269.
25. Ibid., p. 238.
26. Excerpts from the speech are found in Rush, *The International Situation,* pp. 166-185.
27. Roy A. and Zhores A. Medvedev, *Khrushchev: The Years in Power* (New York: Columbia University Press, 1976), p. 20.
28. See Dallin, *Soviet Foreign Policy After Stalin,* pp. 326-327.
29. *Khrushchev I,* p. 432.
30. *Pravda,* November 6, 1956, quoted in Dallin, *Soviet Foreign Policy After Stalin,* p. 416.
31. *Khrushchev I,* p. 431.
32. Dallin draws the connection between the Suez crisis and the dismissal of Shepilov in *Soviet Foreign Policy After Stalin,* p. 420. Shepilov was replaced by Andrei Gromyko, a career diplomat.
33. For a complete list, see ibid., pp. 332-333.
34. W. E. Griffith, *The Sino-Soviet Rift* (Cambridge, Mass.: MIT Press, 1964), pp. 16-17.
35. Arnold L. Horelick and Myron Rush, *Strategic Power and Soviet Foreign Policy* (Chicago: University of Chicago Press, 1966), p. 43.
36. *Documents on International Affairs 1957* (London: Royal Institute of International Affairs, 1960), p. 39.
37. For a persuasive statement of the "missile deception" thesis, see Horelick and Rush, *Strategic Power.* The material in this section summarizes their argument.
38. Ibid., pp. 37-38.
39. *Khrushchev II,* p. 533.
40. See, for example, *New York Times,* January 12, 1959, p. 1, and Horelick and Rush, *Strategic Power,* pp. 63-64.
41. Stanley Hoffmann, *The State of War* (New York: Praeger, 1965), p. 237.
42. *Khrushchev I,* p. 453.
43. *Khrushchev II,* p. 411.
44. Ibid., p. 415, and Keesing's Research Report, *The Sino-Soviet Dispute,* (New York: Charles Scribner's Sons, 1969), p. 20.
45. The speech is excerpted in Rush, *The International Situation,* pp. 206-226.
46. Thomas W. Wolfe, *Soviet Power and Europe 1945-1970,* (Baltimore: Johns Hopkins University Press, 1970), p. 153.
47. *Khrushchev II,* pp. 443-446.
48. Michel Tatu, *Power in the Kremlin: From Khrushchev to Kosygin* (New York: Viking, 1967), pp. 41-68. Khrushchev's rivals Frol Kozlov and

Alexei Kosygin were the main beneficiaries; his client Leonid Brezhnev was the chief loser in this realignment.

49. *Khrushchev II,* p. 461.
50. *Khrushchev I,* pp. 488–491.
51. For Khrushchev's account of the Vienna meeting, see *Khrushchev II,* pp. 487–501.
52. Arthur Schlesinger, Jr., *A Thousand Days: John F. Kennedy in the White House* (Boston: Houghton Mifflin, 1965), pp. 358–374.
53. The following account of the 1961 Berlin crisis is heavily indebted to Robert M. Slusser, *The Berlin Crisis of 1961: Soviet-American Relations and the Struggle for Power in the Kremlin* (Baltimore: Johns Hopkins University Press, 1973).
54. *Khrushchev II,* pp. 507–508; *Khrushchev I,* pp. 455–456.
55. For detailed documentation of this assertion, see Slusser, *The Berlin Crisis* pp. 157–169.
56. Slusser, *The Berlin Crisis,* pp. 207–210.
57. Ibid., chap. 9.
58. *Khrushchev II,* pp. 459–460, 529.
59. *Khrushchev I,* pp. 493–494.
60. Ulam's explanation, *Expansion and Coexistence: Soviet Foreign Policy 1917–1973* (New York: Praeger, 1974), pp. 668–677, focuses on the proposal for nuclear-free zones in Germany and the Far East.
61. The best accounts are Elie Abel, *The Missile Crisis* (New York: Bantam, 1966), and Graham T. Allison, *Essence of Decision: Explaining the Cuban Missile Crisis* (Boston: Little, Brown Company, 1971).
62. See Abel, *The Missile Crisis,* pp. 158–162, for a summary of the Khrushchev letter. The quotation is from a copy in the possession of one of the authors, obtained from the U.S. State Department after its declassification in 1971.
63. *Pravda,* October 17, 1964, p. 1.
64. *Khrushchev II,* pp. xiv–xv.
65. *Pravda,* September 13, 1971, p. 1.

Chapter 5
The Soviet Union and the Third World

KHRUSHCHEV AND THE LEGACIES OF LENIN AND STALIN

From the very beginning of the Bolshevik movement in Russia, its leaders avowed an appreciation of the importance of the "East" to the world revolutionary cause. Although Lenin and his colleagues, in the years immediately following the October Revolution, concentrated their attention in foreign policy on problems relating to the industrially advanced countries of Europe, they remained sensitive to the role that the "toiling masses of the East" could play in assisting the proletariat to achieve its victory over the world imperialist system. Still, it remained for the heirs of Stalin to make—as probably their most important foreign policy achievement—the first substantial and continuing Soviet investments in the area now commonly known as the Third World. Used here to refer to the less developed noncommunist countries of Asia, Africa, and Latin America, this area now comprises two-thirds of the world's states and almost half its population.

During the first years of the century Lenin saw, in the context of his theory of imperialism, the value of a temporary tactical alliance between communist forces and the "national-liberation movement" in the East. In 1916, he wrote that the proletariat must give "determined support to the more revolutionary elements in the bourgeois-democratic movements" in their agitation for national liberation.[1] Such bourgeois-led movements were deemed worthy of support not only because they created the internal conditions necessary for capitalist (and then socialist) development, but also because they were directed against the imperialist powers. Their success thus weakened the system of imperialism itself. This Leninist position, worked out before 1917, has continued to occupy a central place in the analyses of Soviet policymakers in the contemporary era.

When presented to the Second Congress of the Communist International in 1920, Lenin's theses directed both the European proletariat and the com-

130

munist parties in the colonial and "semicolonial" countries to lend their support to revolutionary bourgeois leaders of the national movement. Lenin acknowledged the diversity of conditions in the East and urged his communist brethren to remain flexible in their approach to these issues. Lenin recognized that his own position was a departure from the orthodox Marxist analysis and maintained that the priority of combatting the imperialist assault against the new Soviet state temporarily played in abeyance the orthodox position regarding the internal class alignments in preindustrial societies.

Stalin's disastrous experience in applying the united front strategy during the Chinese revolution of the 1920s had a lasting effect on Soviet perceptions. Chiang Kai-shek manipulated Soviet and Comintern support of the Kuomintang to defeat the Chinese communists. Unaccustomed to being used to serve the purposes of others, Stalin apparently vowed never again to assist Asian nationalist leaders who were not under his direct control. After the Chinese defeat, the Sixth Congress of the Comintern in 1928 directed communists to concentrate their fire on the "national bourgeoisie"—exposing its tendency to sell out to imperialism, discrediting it in the eyes of its mass followers, and joining with these proletarian and peasant masses in a "united front from below" against imperialism and capitalism.

The defeat of the Axis powers in the second World War brought the beginning of the end of the great colonial empires, especially in Asia. After the Soviet entry into the war, communist groups had moved to the forefront of the anti-Axis struggle, and, in the late 1940s, they capitalized on this reputation and on the fact that the Soviet Union was not identified in the eyes of Third World nationalists as a colonial power. The prevailing mood in these areas was for independence from imperialist rule and the "winds of change" were definitely blowing. Yet, even in the face of this opportunity for expanding Soviet influence, Stalin was extremely cautious at first, not wishing to alienate his erstwhile wartime allies by actively aiding in the disintegration of their empires while seeking their acquiescence to his new-found sphere of influence in Eastern Europe. Only in 1947, with the cold war clearly under way, did the Soviets direct their attention to what Zhdanov proclaimed as the "crisis of the colonial system."[2] But this authoritative speech, by asserting a stark bipolar division of the world into "two camps," denied the possibility that the emerging forces of the Third World could remain neutral between them. The postwar Stalinist stance toward the national-liberation movement embodied the assertion that "he who is not unconditionally with us is therefore against us."

As the Chinese communists moved toward victory, the communist parties of Asia were directed to undertake militant antiimperialist struggle, including as their targets not only the colonial powers but also their "national-bourgeois lackeys." Not only were the noncommunist leaders of the newly independent countries not exempt from this attack, but their declarations of political independence were denounced as shams, their professions of nonalignment in the cold war struggle were proclaimed illusory, and their proclamations of noncommunist doctrines of development were labeled worthless. True independence, declared the Soviet Orientalist "scholars," could be achieved only under the hegemony of the proletariat and its vanguard party. Moscow's leading Africanist, Professor I. I. Potekhin, wrote in 1950 that:

A complete and final victory of a colonial revolution is possible only under the direction of the proletariat. . . . Only the working class leading the national front of all the antiimperialist forces is capable of carrying out a consistent struggle for independence.[3]

But in countries where the proletariat hardly existed and the communist parties' slogans were alien to the masses, such a dogmatic approach inexorably led to the isolation and defeat of communist forces or, where there were no parties (as in much of Africa), to the total isolation of the USSR from the national independence movement.

By 1951, with stalemate in Korea following upon the East-West deadlock in Europe, there did appear fragmentary signs of Soviet attention to the new regimes outside the "main arena." A few overtures were made by Moscow toward opening trade relations with the new nations, and there were hints of a dawning appreciation of the antiimperialist potential of the foreign policies of some of the new leaders. But it was only after the death of Stalin that a shift in Soviet policy could be discerned. Malenkov's August 1953 speech to the Supreme Soviet paid special tribute to India's contribution to the Korean settlement, and the new Soviet premier voiced the hope for the growth of "friendly cooperation" both with that country and with the Arab states.[4]

The initial thrust of the active Soviet reentry into the countries of the East came in seeming response to the policies both of Moscow's American rival and of the new Soviet ally in Beijing. Washington's efforts in 1954-55 to enlarge the ring of containment by enlisting allies on the Soviet Union's southern periphery (Pakistan, Iraq, Iran) alarmed the Soviets, and the hostile reaction to the American policy on the part of the emerging "neutralist" nations encouraged Moscow to counterattack. Moreover, Zhou Enlai's success in capitalizing on the antiimperialist mood at the Bandung Conference of Asian and African States held in Indonesia in April 1955, demonstrated anew the possipossibilities for a communist-nationalist alliance against the imperialist designs.

Thus by 1955 there was a reawakened appreciation in Moscow of the importance of the Third World as the vital "strategic reserve" of imperialism and as an arena in which the Soviets could wage the bipolar struggle with solid prospects of success (but at a lower level of risk than would be posed by a direct challenge in the "main arena" of confrontation). The year's significant events foreshadowed the Soviet priorities and techniques in this new arena: Moscow's entry into the Middle East by means of the arms deal with Nasser's Egypt; the visit of India's Prime Minister Nehru to Moscow and the return trip by Khrushchev and Bulganin to India, Burma, and Afghanistan; the dramatic announcement that the Soviets would finance and construct a giant steel mill at Bhilai in India. These early targets of Soviet activity were chosen for their strategic importance in the struggle with the West rather than for any particular features of their internal development, and, with great optimism but little sophisticated knowledge of the domestic affairs of the Third World states, the Soviets soon set about to revise the doctrinal bases of their new policy.

As we have seen, Lenin prepared the ideological foundations for the communist alliance with the forces of national liberation, but in its early years the besieged Soviet state lacked the resources for an operational commitment in the East. Stalin had more resources at his command, but his own experiences and attitudes blunted and distorted the Leninist perception of strategic opportunity in the imperialist reserve. It took the new Soviet leadership, at the helm of the world's second mightiest state and eager to demonstrate the continued revolutionary vitality of its ideology, to provide the fresh doctrinal approach to undergird the new operational initiatives in the Third World.

Like Lenin, Khrushchev sensed that as long as the brunt of the independence movement was aimed against the "imperialist" West, it would serve the interests of the communist East. There was a sufficient community of interest to provide the basis for a temporary alliance against the common enermy—a new "Zone of Peace," he called it. As for the future, it was Khrushchev's confident assertion that aid from the socialist bloc could allow the Third World countries to break away from the imperialist economic grip and launch their plans for industrialized and truly independent national economies. The inevitable result of this process would be the emergence of a class-conscious proletariat ready to respond to the political program of its communist vanguard and—once the "national bourgeoisie" had revealed the compromising side of its dual nature—to assume political power, even by peaceful means. Khrushchev asserted this perspective in his landmark speech to the Twentieth Congress of the CPSU in February 1956 and emphasized to his listeners that:

Whatever the form of transition to socialism, the decisive and indispensable factor is the political leadership of the working class headed by its vanguard. Without this there can be no transition to socialism.[5]

But (to paraphrase a remark that Soviet writers would later aim at Third World leaders) to proclaim the prospects for socialism is easier than to achieve it. Only a few years after their initial plunge into Asia and Africa, the Soviets were discovering that their initial optimism concerning the enlargement of the camp of socialism was misplaced. With only rare exceptions (such as Indonesia), the communist parties in these regions were still either nonexistent, weak, or persecuted by the new nationalist allies of the Soviet Union. Some Afro-Asian communist leaders were bold enough to voice their frustration at this state of affairs. But the primary problem was the reluctance of the nationalist and revolutionary elites in the new nations to adhere to Marxism-Leninism or "scientific socialism" or to proclaim their willingness to establish "people's democracies" in their countries. The fiercely nationalistic leaders of Asia and Africa had their own goals for political and economic progress, and although many of them were influenced by Marxist thought and "socialist" ideals, they were loathe to accept the Soviet approach and model. Naturally, those leaders who spurned formal communist affiliation were uncomfortable with a Soviet policy that proclaimed their inevitable removal from power.

At the root of this dilemma was a woeful ignorance on the part of Soviet politicians and their advisers of the actual social and economic conditions prevailing in the Third World. Khrushchev's initial proclamation of the "Zone of Peace" strategy had asserted as the sole criterion for Soviet support of the new regimes the degree of antiimperialist content in their foreign policies, but as the Soviets and the nationalist leaders themselves increasingly turned their attention to the problems of development, the artificiality of the orthodox Soviet approach became even more evident. It was not until the Twentieth Party Congress freed the Soviet analysis of the sterile formulas of Stalin and directed Soviet scholars to devise new concepts and categories that a more flexible doctrine could be evolved. In terms of sheer volume, the results of this resurgence of "scholarly" investigation were striking. A study of Soviet publications on Africa reveals that whereas 100 articles appeared in 40 different journals in 1950, in 1956, there were 400 articles in 80 journals, and by 1960 fully 1000 articles were published in 140 journals.[6]

As a first result of this reappraisal, in the statement issued by the Moscow Conference of Communist Parties in December 1960 a new concept of an intermediate stage of development toward socialism appeared, which took account of internal as well as foreign policy characteristics. This concoction, the "state of national democracy," represented an attempt in a single doctrinal formula to take account of a multiplicity of interests: the aspirations of nationalist leaders, the interests of local communist parties, and the requirements of Soviet foreign policy. According to the Moscow Statement, all patriotic forces in a developing country should unite in a single national-democratic front based on an alliance of the working class and peasantry, who would play the leading role in solving the problems of noncapitalist development. While the "national bourgeoisie" could participate in such an alliance, it was too unstable a force to be conceded a monopoly of leadership. The goal of this united front was the creation of a state of national democracy:

a state which consistently upholds its political and economic independence, fights against imperialism and its military blocs, against military bases on its territory; a state which fights against the new forms of colonialism and the penetration of imperialist capital; a state in which the people are ensured broad democratic rights and freedoms . . . the opportunity to work for the enactment of an agrarian reform and other domestic and social changes, and for participation in shaping government policy.[7]

The concept, thus, set forth a new intermediate objective, seemingly more attainable than establishment of "people's democracy," which constituted a sort of way station on the road to socialism and which guaranteed an active role both to the working class (that is, the communist party) and to the bourgeoisie. As the Soviets interpreted it, the national democratic state was an objective that made the entry of the new states into the noncapitalist path possible, although their actual transformation to socialism would require further preparation and revolutionary struggle.[8]

Although the Moscow Statement was a major attempt to compromise the diverging Soviet and Chinese assessments of communist objectives, the concept of national democracy was simply ignored by the Chinese, who evidently considered it an unworthy objective for proletarian struggle. Disillusioned with some of the nationalist leaders of South Asia and the Middle East, the Beijing comrades simply denied the acceptability of intermediate forms of state organization under the leadership of noncommunist elements. As the Sino-Soviet dispute developed, the Soviet attempts to bend communist doctrine to take account of the interests of cooperation with Third World nationalists were loudly denounced by the Chinese communists. The Soviets, they charged, were engaged in a betrayal of the national-liberation movement, sacrificing it on the altar of their own enrichment and thereby playing into the hands of the imperialists. In Chinese parlance, the Soviet leaders became the "New Tsars" who were restoring capitalism in their own country and seeking to impose their own "social-imperialist" hegemony on the Third World. Moscow's counterattack portrayed the Chinese as "adventurists," wedded to the dangerous and often fruitless path of armed struggle and attempting to create their own racially based grouping which would simply isolate the national-liberation movement from the world socialist center. The ideological dispute spilled over into a frantic competition between the USSR and China, resulting in their staking out rival spheres of influence in the Third World and causing splits in the communist parties of the area.

Not only did the concept of national democracy fail to heal the Sino-Soviet rift over communist strategy in the Third World, it also proved to be largely irrelevant to the dynamic situation there. One problem was that there was no model "state of national democracy," although Cuba briefly served that role until Castro's abrupt proclamation of socialism. In the most "progressive" Asian and African states, nationalist leaders proved thoroughly uninterested in sharing power through a united front between their own parties and the communists, and in fact, in most of these states, all rivals to the single ruling parties were proscribed. The fundamental problem was that the new concept was still wedded to a class-based analysis increasingly artificial in its applicability to the Third World—especially to Africa, where there was neither a "national bourgeoisie" nor a proletariat. Revolutionary nationalism in Africa was primarily a movement of the intelligentsia, but Marxist-Leninist analysis portrayed this group as a "free-floating stratum"—of no great consequence to the revolutionary struggle. Under such leadership, the antiimperialist states of Africa, often the most responsive to Soviet overtures, were condemned by the concept to a sort of limbo.

In the early 1960s, the call for the application of "creative Marxism" in further research by Soviet scholars led to a great deal of experimentation with the doctrine and a surprising willingness to invent new categories of social forces and more forms of organization by which new states could make the transition to noncapitalist development. The result of this reassessment was the concept of "revolutionary democracy" and a doctrine so flexible that it could justify almost any course of action by suggesting that any state, no matter how backward, could, under the proper leadership, be said to be moving toward socialism. In the absence of a proletariat and a communist party, three basic alternatives for noncapitalist development were said to exist: (1) nonproletarian leaders ("revolutionary democrats") could adopt "working-class viewpoints"; (2) a "progressive" single party could lead its country on the path to noncapitalist development; or (3) the proletariat of the advanced countries (i.e., the Soviet Union) could substitute its own leadership for that of the absent proletariat.[9]

The general spirit of this reassessment was neatly summed up by one writer, who said: "If a revolutionary democrat or a member of the national bourgeoisie is willing to take one step forward, it is the duty of the Marxists to help him take two."[10] Given the proper relationship to the Soviet Union, Moscow seemed to be saying, neither proletarian leadership nor the direction of a communist party was an inviolable prerequisite for the transformation to socialism. By citing the Cuban precedent, an article in the CPSU Central Committee's theoretical journal claimed that "the experience of history shows that national leaders of revolutionary inclination can implement a general democratic program and lead their countries to socialism."[11]

The development of the flexible concept of intermediate stages, proceeding under the direction of broad united fronts, provided Soviet leaders with the ideological justification for continuing their support of the development efforts of the new states. In December 1963, an important editorial in *Pravda* acknowledged that even certain national or regional varieties of "socialist" doctrine, previously condemned as petty-bourgeois or utopian, could play a "positive role."[12] And in the same month Khrushchev himself, stressing that "there is no universal recipe suitable for all countries," endorsed measures taken by "revolutionary-democratic statesmen . . . [who] declare their determination to build socialism."[13] The following spring, the Soviet leader gave concrete form to these notions, hailing the Algerian National Liberation Front (FLN) as a "fraternal" party and awarding its leader ("Comrade" Ben Bella) the "Hero of the Soviet Union" medal. The next month, he bestowed this same award on Egypt's President Nasser and Vice President Amer, again hailing them as "comrades" and declaring that their country "was embarking on the path of socialist construction."

This optimistic emphasis on way stations or shortcuts to socialism was flattering to the egos of Third World leaders and satisfying to Khrushchev's own desire to proclaim new victories in the building of socialism, but it maddened the Chinese "dogmatists," further frustrated the local communist cadres, and even irritated some of Khrushchev's own colleagues in the Kremlin. More significantly, it was soon to run aground in the Third World itself, shattering on the enormous and persistent obstacles that lay in the path of development.

THE KHRUSHCHEV APPROACH: TACTICS AND TECHNIQUES

The Soviet Union's approach to the Third World has truly been opportunistic, not only in its willingness to modify the Marxist-Leninist doctrine to suit a variety of circumstances, but also in its use of a wide range of instruments for establishing its presence and extending its influence. Often based in bilateral agreements of variable duration, Moscow's relations with the nations of the Third World are spread broadly in the political, economic, military, and cultural spheres. They reach beyond government-to-government dealings to include relationships with both communist and noncommunist parties; contacts and exchanges among trade union, student, scientific, artistic, and other groups (both directly through the Soviet counterpart organization and through various international communist-front organizations); the massive dissemination of both printed material and radio propaganda; the on-the-scene activities of tens of thousands of Soviet technicians and advisers, both civilian and military, and so forth.

Taken as a whole, the Soviet contacts with Third World countries fully exemplify the techniques of what Andrew Scott has termed "informal penetration"—"means by which the agents or instruments of one country gain access to the population (or parts of it) or processes of another country" and in which "the special nature of cold warfare must be sought."[14] As Scott analyzes it, this phenomenon has increased in frequency and importance for several reasons, among which are the greater role of public opinion in many nations, the development of ideological struggle, the technological revolution in communication and transportation, the increased destructiveness of full-scale warfare, and the emergence of a large number of new nations in the postwar era. Although also employed by the United States (as well as by China and a number of smaller countries, including Egypt and Cuba), the Soviet Union's use of the techniques of informal penetration has been, by virtue of its Leninist ideology and the totalitarian structure of its own state system, more coordinated and massive than any rival effort.

The first and more direct means for establishing contact with a Third World government and gaining access to its population is through the establishment of a diplomatic presence. Unusually large numbers of "diplomats" have been sent to these countries from the Soviet Union; for the two or three sent to Moscow by each African state, hundreds are sent in return. In Togo, for example, which had a population in 1960 of slightly over one million, there was one Soviet diplomat for every 18,000 inhabitants. The Soviets, faced with the absence of Communist parties in many such countries, have employed this large diplomatic corps, operating under diplomatic immunity, to gather information, make political contacts, and serve as a point of departure for training and organizing future communist cadres.[15] It should be noted that host governments do not always welcome this large flock of official visitors, and there have been a number of cases, including Ghana, Mexico, and the Congo (Zaire), where Soviet "diplomats" have been expelled for espionage or attempted subversion.

Propaganda was recognized by Lenin as a central instrument in the revolutionary arsenal and his heirs have remained true to his legacy by flooding the Third World with cheap and widely accessible books, pamphlets, magazines, and newspapers, and by broadcasting hundreds of hours weekly on the radio in a host of languages. Through the use of themes for which there is wide popular sympathy in the emerging nations, the purposes of the Soviet propaganda effort are to highlight the achievements of the Soviet state, to downgrade the accomplishments of the West (and the Chinese), and to encourage listeners to exert pressure for "progressive" internal reforms and government support of Soviet foreign policy objectives.

The establishment of cultural relations also helps evoke an image of Soviet achievement as well as flattering the national pride of the target country. Soviet ballet and dance troupes and exhibitions of literary and artistic achievement have been sent throughout the world; these will often feature representatives of the Soviet Asian or Turkic nationalities in prominent roles. Two-way exchanges of this type are usually fostered by "friendship societies," which themselves serve as networks for penetrating the country involved.

Target groups of special importance in the less developed countries are intellectuals, students, and military personnel; these have been the object of intensive training, education, and exchange programs. An estimated 26,500 students from Third World countries attended educational institutions in the USSR at the beginning of 1979; many of these were enrolled in Patrice Lumumba Friendship University in Moscow, which serves African, Asian, and Latin American students exclusively. Moreover, in the 23-year period ending in 1978, about 43,790 military personnel from the Third World were trained in the Soviet Union. Many more Third World nationals are trained by Soviet and East European economic and military technicians stationed throughout the world; they numbered almost 85,000 in 1978.[16] These programs not only provide training in educational skills but seek also to demonstrate Soviet technological strength and impart a certain "political" orientation.

The provision of economic aid is a technique that has been made possible for the Soviets not only by the post-Stalin change in perception and strategy but by the growth in Soviet economic resources and capabilities as well. Only a very limited amount of activity was conducted in this sphere prior to 1955, but the magnitude and nature of the Soviet aid program since then has been impressive. In absolute terms, the Soviet foreign aid program (just under $20 billion in the first two and one-half decades) is dwarfed by that of the United States, and measured by effort as a proportion of gross national product (0.05 percent in 1974) the Soviet effort has lagged far behind United Nations targets or the efforts of some smaller industrialized states.

The key feature of the Soviet aid program, which has enhanced its effectiveness, has been its concentrated and selective nature, especially as compared with the American program. The bulk of Soviet aid has gone to countries in the Middle East and South Asia, and in fact two countries—India and Egypt—have received over one-fifth of the total amount extended since 1955. (See Table 5.1 for a complete regional breakdown.) Another significant characteristic of Soviet aid is its timing; in contrast to the relatively small and steady annual disbursements often found in Western programs, the Soviets like to announce larger totals of credits to be drawn over an extended period. These announcements are often timed to coincide with the visit of a high-ranking politician to one or another capital, and (especially in the early days) Soviet aid has been offered for high-prestige projects immediately after they have been spurned by "imperialist" donors. Egypt's Aswan Dam and India's Bokaro steel mill were two Soviet-aided projects that had originally been refused by American aid officials. Another Indian project, the Bhilai steel mill, was funded and built by the Soviets in a much ballyhooed atmosphere of competition with the British and Germans, who were simultaneously constructing mills at other sites in India. The contrasts drawn by Soviet officials and media between their own aid and "so-called capitalist aid" center on the supposedly

Table 5.1. Soviet Economic Credits and Grants Extended to Noncommunist and Less Developed Countries, By Region, 1954-1978 and Years 1977 and 1978 (in Millions of U.S. Dollars).

Region	1954-1978	1977	1978
North Africa (excluding Egypt)	2918	–	2000
Sub-Saharan Africa	1071	31	11
East Asia	261	–	–
South Asia	4956	341	283
Middle East	6918	–	1399
Latin America	964	30	15
Total	17,088	402	3708

Source: National Foreign Assessment Center, Central Intelligence Agency, *Communist Aid Activities in Non-Communist Less Developed Countries 1978,* September 1979, pp. 7–10.

"disinterested" nature of their assistance and its concentration on large-scale industrial projects in the public sector (as opposed to the long-standing American preference for private enterprise).

Amidst references to unnamed persons who "grumbled" about his aid program, Khrushchev's memoirs record both the alleged economic disinterestedness of Soviet assistance and its starkly political purposes. In specific reference to Afghanistan, he argues that if the Soviets had not given aid, the Americans would have been glad to take their place and "bait a hook" for the Afghans. The amount of money expended by the Soviets in aid to Kabul was thus "a drop in the ocean," compared to the price Moscow would have had to pay to counter the threat that an American military base in Afghanistan would have posed: "We must be statesmen, not misers, in our approach to neighboring countries. We must be willing to make advance payments which promise in the future to bring us enormous returns in the form of peace and friendship."[17]

Contrary to an impression often conveyed by Soviet propaganda, Soviet economic aid has not been in the form of grants, which actually comprise less than 5 percent of the total, but primarily in the form of long-term credits bearing (unlike China's loans) varying amounts of interest (at first, 2.5 percent, but recently higher). Nor is Soviet aid extended to the less developed countries for the free purchase of needed commodities; it is strictly "tied" to Soviet goods, and then usually in the context of approved projects. It is this latter feature that accounts largely for the fact that less than one-half of the Soviet economic credits offered to the Third World have actually been utilized by the recipients; in many cases, their absorptive capacity is too low or their infrastructure too little developed to implement the project, or they lack the capital needed to finance the local costs of the project. But this low rate of "draw down" has not meant that Soviet aid clients have not overextended themselves;

indeed, a number of the most prominent Soviet aid recipients (including Egypt, Indonesia, and Mali) had by the early 1960s greatly surpassed their abilities to borrow or to absorb the aid they had accepted, and their economies were reeling under the heavy debt burdens.

The "tied" nature of Soviet aid links it very closely with Soviet trade. Soviet aid is counted in with Third World imports as repayments are with exports; it is not at all surprising that the USSR's major aid recipients are precisely the Third World countries with whom it does most of its trading. Likewise, Soviet trade with the Third World has greatly expanded with the evolving aid program; in 1955, the USSR traded with only 18 Third World countries, but this number had grown to 60 by the end of the 1960s. Prominent among the USSR's exports are industrial and agricultural machinery and industrial raw materials; it imports raw materials, certain foodstuffs, and a growing volume of goods from Soviet-aided plants. The Soviet currency is nonconvertible outside the bloc and Soviet trade with the Third World is almost entirely conducted on a barter basis. This has led to a number of disputes between Moscow and its trading partners concerning the valuation of trade goods and a few acute problems have arisen over the Soviet practice of acquiring a large quantity of a certain material in payment for its own aid or exports and then proceeding to resell it for a higher world market price (thus earning for itself and depriving its client of the hard currency value of the product).

Trade with the Soviet Union constitutes only about 5 percent of the total Third World volume; as a share of the Soviet total, this trade amounts to between 10 and 15 percent. As with aid, however, these figures can be misleading for the concentrated nature of Soviet trade means that there are a few states for whom it constitutes one-quarter to one-third of their total turnover. Egypt and Syria are prime examples of countries that developed a substantial trade dependency on the Soviet Union, and although the impact varies with circumstances, this has potentially great political significance.

We have yet to mention the product that has recently been the chief export of the Soviet Union to certain areas of the Third World: military weaponry. As Table 5.2 indicates, Soviet military aid has far surpassed Soviet economic assistance in dollar value; the volume more than doubled between 1973 and 1978, and in recent years it has constituted over half of the total value of Soviet exports to the Third World.[18] Not surprisingly, it too is heavily concentrated; about three-fourths of total Soviet military aid in the two decades since the first arms deal with Egypt went to the Middle East. As we have already seen, military aid relationships often include a component of training of Third World personnel in the USSR and/or the stationing of Soviet military technicians in the recipient country. For favored clients, military aid is not difficult to obtain; the credits are easy (as are the debts), the prices are low (at least, initially) and the deliveries are fairly rapid (if the Soviets wish them to be).

Table 5.2. Soviet Military Aid Agreements with Noncommunist Less Developed Countries, By Region and Selected Country, 1956–1978 (in Millions of U.S. Dollars)

Region	1956–1978	1977	1978
North Africa (excluding Egypt)	4965	1800	315
Sub-Saharan Africa	3900	1415	845
East Asia	890	–	–
South Asia	4290	655	505
Middle East	14,960	1235	100
Latin America	650	110	–
Total	29,655	5215	1765

Source: National Foreign Assessment Center, Central Intelligence Agency, *Communist Aid Activities in Non-Communist Less Developed Countries 1978,* September 1979, p. 3.

Clearly, both sides in the military aid relationship perceive certain benefits in it. There is a mutual interest in breaking the Western arms monopoly and in countering an American military alliance (which often entails for the Soviet client the arming of a regional rival). The supply of arms adds prestige for the recipient, especially if, as is often the case, it is headed by a military elite. And there is mutual benefit to the extent that military aid enhances the client's position in a regional conflict and enables it to pursue objectives that will satisfy both itself and its patron. We shall see that it is not rare for the supplier's and the recipient's interests to diverge in such situations, sometimes producing substantial grief for Moscow, given the proven difficulty of exercising leverage in such situations. Moreover, there is always the possibility that a Soviet-aided state will be defeated in a regional conflict, in which case costly demands can be made for resupply or, even more dangerous, for the Soviet Union to escalate its own commitments in the conflict. Thus the military aid relationships presents many tempting opportunities to the Soviet Union: to extend its influence with key states, to enhance the strength of its clients, to expand its own military presence and capabilities, and even to produce a favorable shift in the international balance of power. The projected benefits have certainly been alluring enough to draw the USSR heavily into the provision of such aid, but the costs have not been absent, and over time this has had a certain sobering effect on the Soviet leadership.

A final instrument employed by the USSR in its approach to the Third World has been the provision of political and diplomatic support for certain issues of importance to the developing world. Efforts to speed up the dismantling of colonial empires, to restrict the "imperialist" economic and political practices of the West, or to divert resources from armaments to the pursuit of peace and development have been among the causes to which the Soviets have lent support or have advanced their own initiatives. Moscow has also been willing to throw its support to one side in a regional conflict where it perceives a possible gain in popularity or possible embarrassment for the West. Such political support not only flatters the egos of Third World leaders, it also provides the Soviets with an opportunity to seek reciprocation on their own favored causes. The occasion of a high-level visit is almost always concluded by the issuance of a joint communique listing a whole series of issues on which "identity" and "similarity" of views was achieved between a Soviet leader and his Third World counterpart.

During the Khrushchev era in particular, the USSR considered the United Nations a favorable venue for such activity. This had not always been the case; originally the organization was seen by the Soviets strictly in terms of its security functions. Like the world as a whole, the United Nations was portrayed by the USSR in the Stalinist zero-sum imagery of tight bipolarity. As a seemingly permanent minority, Moscow and its few allies, protected by the Soviet veto, sought to prevent the organization from being used by the majority in an anti-Soviet way or from expanding its powers in a supranational direction.

In 1955, the long East-West deadlock on the admission of new members was broken, and in the next decade 46 new members were admitted to the United Nations, of whom 34 were African states. The composition of the United Nations was changing and so were the issues with which the new Third World majority sought to engage the organization. But the Afro-Asian "bloc" was cohesive only on issues of anticolonialism, disarmament, and the diversion of resources from North to South; it was divided on questions of Cold War conflict as well as by fratricidal quarrels within the Third World.

Mirroring their objectives and activity in the world outside, the Soviets' behavior in the United Nations shifted from a defensive to an offensive orientation. They began to see that the organization could be useful in exacerbating the split between the West and the Third World, and for the first time in the late 1950s, the USSR began to take initiatives in this forum. But the United Nations reflected the world itself in another way: the Third World states were disinclined to be manipulated or to allow cold war considerations to penetrate their sphere of interest. The summer 1960 crisis in the former Belgian Congo saw the new U.N. majority, encouraged and abetted by Secretary-General Hammarskjöld, seek to use the United Nations as a force for insulating a Third World conflict from the cold war competition.

Since this effort flew in the face of a dramatic attempt by the Soviets to extend their own presence and influence in Africa, it drew Moscow into renewed conflict with the international organization. The villain in the piece was Hammarskjöld, whom the Soviets bitterly denounced as an agent of the imperialists. But Khrushchev assured the General Assembly in his speech of September 1960 that the problem was not with just this particular Secretary-

General; no single person could stand above the ideological conflict and behave in a perfectly neutral fashion. "It is said that God alone was able to combine three persons in one. But then, no one has ever seen him, and so let him remain in the imaginations of the people who invented him. But we can see the Secretary-General."[19]

The Soviets insisted that the solution was the replacement of a single Secretary-General by a three-headed Secretariat (dubbed the "troika"). Each of the three would represent a definite group—East, West, and Third World—and would be able to guarantee (through the application of a rule of unanimity) that the actions of the Secretariat were not detrimental to the interests of "his" bloc. Khrushchev generously suggested that Hammarskjöld could remain as the representative of the Western bloc; the USSR, however, would no longer recognize him as the legitimate Secretary-General.

Although the troika proposal was calculated by the Soviets to appeal to the interests of the Afro-Asian bloc, it failed to gain much support. The Third World states correctly perceived Moscow's plan as an attempt to hamstring the United Nations. Once they had achieved a General Assembly majority, they were in no mood to limit the United Nations' powers by introducing the ideological conflict into the Secretariat—the very organ capable of expressing a "world" viewpoint. While the Soviets soon recognized that they could not yet achieve the ouster of Hammarskjöld, they continued their vitriolic attacks against him. The Secretary-General's death in a plane crash in the Congo in September 1961 presented Moscow with another opportunity to press its plan. The Soviets for a while threatened to block the choice of a single successor, but lack of Third World support eventually caused them to drop the troika proposal and accede in the selection of a representative of an Asian neutral, U Thant of Burma.

Khrushchev's record in the United Nations was similar to the balance sheet of his activities in the larger effort to penetrate the Third World: Soviet achievements under his leadership fell far short of his initial optimistic expectations, but he created the ideological and operational foundations for sustained involvement over the long haul. Although his ambition greatly exceeded Moscow's reach, Khrushchev plunged the USSR into *global* involvement; he extended the bipolar struggle into the "imperialist reserve" and left the United States unchallenged in no area of the world. Active ties were forged with the more radical members of the Third World, for whom Moscow represented an alternative source of economic and military capabilities. One result was that Western alliance systems were disrupted and the United States was forced onto the defensive; often the Soviet presence was expanded by means of the inflammation of regional conflicts.

But it did not all happen precisely as Khrushchev planned it. Although Marxist-Leninist ideology was bent to justify Soviet opportunism, thereby further alienating not only the Chinese but also many local communist cadres, the complexity of Third World politics was not easily encompassed by the new formulations of "creative Marxism." Lavish Soviet aid and the encouragement of radical socioeconomic change often left economic and political chaos in its wake. Khrushchev's most promising clients—Sukarno, Ben Bella, Nkrumah— were toppled only shortly after Khrushchev himself. Despite the failures, Khrushchev's lasting accomplishment was to expand the horizons of Soviet foreign policy beyond the narrow confines to which Stalin had confined it and to reenliven the appeal of Soviet doctrine beyond the rigid formulations of his predecessor. In so doing, Khrushchev won for the Soviets some valuable footholds in strategically prized and previously uncharted territories.

THE BREZHNEV ERA: A LOWERED PROFILE

In ousting Khrushchev, his lieutenants and heirs showed their irritation at his excessive optimism and flamboyant style; they resented his lavish aid (especially when he failed to consult them), his loose rhetoric (as in his accolades to the Egyptians and Algerians), and his impulsive behavior (such as the unseemly shoe-banging at the United Nations), but they shared the basic objectives of his strategy in the Third World and only gradually brought about a new approach through a shift in tactics and the adoption of a more cautious and pragmatic style.

The doctrinal assessment of Third World regimes did not change overnight. In August 1965, *Pravda* reaffirmed the Khrushchevian view that communists and the working class would continue to give support to all "progressive" social forces that were sincerely striving to build socialism, and that it would be "sectarian" to reject cooperation with adherents of non-Marxist socialism.[20] An article appearing in *Kommunist* at the beginning of 1966, written by the deputy chief of the Central Committee's International Department, reasserted the possibility of a gradual transition from the "general democratic" to the socialist stage of a revolution, beginning without a national proletarian dictatorship or even an organized Marxist-Leninist party. But the article stressed that as the struggle developed further, some form of "vanguard party" would have to be created.[21] Finally, the Central Committee's May Day and October Anniversary slogans continued to characterize several Third World regimes as "national democracies," said to be fighting for "socialist development" or building "people's democratic" states.[22]

Gradually, however, and more noticeably after the fall of leading "revolutionary democrats," a subtle shift in emphasis began to appear. A justification for nonintervention on behalf of such erstwhile clients and a signal of a decline in Soviet activism in the Third World was provided in a *Pravda* editorial of

October 1965. It stated that the forcible implementation of one country's will upon another not only was alien to Marxism-Leninism, but, worse yet, could lead to thermonuclear war. The peoples of the socialist countries should concentrate their main efforts on the building of socialism and communism in their own countries, for this was their chief contribution to and the decisive precondition for development of the liberation movement.[23]

The emphasis in Soviet pronouncements was soon on the lengthy time-table that would be required for the new states to achieve the heights of socialism. As Brezhnev himself put it in an address marking the 100th anniversary of Lenin's birth, the path toward socialist development in the Third World was not likely to be an immediate or direct one. In his opinion, "this road of development, as Lenin said, must include a whole series of 'gradual preliminary stages,' of 'special transitional measures.'"[24] This explicit recognition of the complex and extended nature of social change in the Third World, the result of a decade and a half of full-scale Soviet activity in Asia and Africa, is a far cry from the confident optimism concerning the prospects for rapid development toward socialism that had characterized the Khrushchev years.

One of the most respected of Soviet Orientalists, E. M. Zhukov, wrote about this change in mood among his colleagues quite candidly. The relative ease with which the first stage of the national-liberation movement—the achievement of political independence—had been achieved had created "illusions" about the possibility of a "similarly simple and one-act solution" for the second stage—the achievement of economic independence. But the further progress of the movement had proved "much more drawn out than some political leaders and scientists had expected." In some countries there had been "reckless" attempts by petty bourgeois leaders to skip stages of development or to ignore the absence of "objective conditions" for revolutionary advance. Zhukov frankly declared: "Proclaiming socialism is not the same thing as building it." Yet, even while condemning such impatience, Zhukov did not seem to be advising Soviet policymakers to withdraw support in these circumstances. Rather, he was saying, they needed to be more realistic concerning the likely slow pace of further advance toward socialism in the third world.[25]

The labors of the "creative Marxist-Leninists," however, did not cease. There was simply less emphasis placed on prescribing a desirable form of state power or insisting upon a particular composition for a ruling elite, and there was more attention to the mix and direction of policies adopted by "progressive" regime. Soviet analysts advised caution in nationalizing private trade, narrowing the united front, or cutting off all ties with the imperialist market. The task of regimes taking the noncapitalist path was said to be the creation of the prerequisites for socialist development; the achievement of the transition itself, Moscow implied, lay in the far distant future. It was as though the Soviets were saying that they could be more comfortable with existing friendly but noncommunist regimes than with putative successor states which, though ideologically more orthodox, might pose heavier burdens of "fraternal assistance" and might more readily fall prey to the temptations of Maoist dogmatism.

This preoccupation with domestic development policies and warning against rushing ahead too rapidly was a product of the immense economic difficulties faced by some of the Soviet clients (including Cuba, which was proving to be an enormous economic burden to Moscow). The Soviet concern was reflected in a new approach toward economic assistance, which placed greater stress on the economic feasibility of new projects. Soviet economists began to preach the virtues of sustained and balanced development, recognizing the positive immediate contributions of the private sector, of agricultural development, and even of Western assistance. In a fashion consistent with the neo-Liberman emphasis on improving the efficiency of the Soviet economy, Prime Minister Kosygin personally inspected aid projects in locations such as India and lectured his hosts on the need for improved performance in the state sector.

Soviet aid and trade agreements began to be cast in a longer-range framework, institutionalized through bilateral economic commissions and allowing for greater integration with the Soviet and East European plans for development. In a growing number of cases, imports from the less developed countries were utilized as alternatives to domestic investment in the exploitation of raw materials. Extravagant claims regarding the accomplishments of foreign aid were abandoned, to be replaced by an emphais on the limitations of what could be accomplished by Soviet resources. As Foreign Minister Gromyko put it:

It is natural, however, that the Soviet Union's potential for rendering economic assistance is not infinite. Of course, the Soviet state cannot fail to be concerned for the well being of its own people. The Soviet Union . . . allocates funds to render the developing countries economic and technical assistance on the basis of its own capabilities.[26]

Increasingly, the motivations for Soviet aid and trade were expressed in terms of *mutual* economic benefit, including the joint exploration and production of raw materials (for example, oil and natural gas), with repayment provided through shipments of the product itself. Prime Minister Kosygin described this to the Twenty-Fourth Party Congress in 1971:

Our trade and economic cooperation with many [Third World countries] are entering a stage at which one can begin to speak of stably founded, mutually advantageous economic relations. Our cooperation with them is based on the principles of equality and respect for mutual interests . . . and is acquiring the characteristics of a stable distribution of labor. . . . At the same time, by expanding trade with the developing countries, the Soviet Union will gain the opportunity of satisfying more fully the requirements of its own national economy.[27]

In the opinion of one respected Western observer of the Soviet scene, this new emphasis on creating firm and beneficial ties between the economies of the developing countries and the USSR amounts to an effort to fight imperialism by adopting imperialist techniques—a strategy which has has labeled "counter-imperialism."[28]

Soviet aid and trade relations remain concentrated in a few areas, but there is little doubt that these are chosen according to considerations of strategic benefit rather than by criteria of "progressiveness" alone. Even in cases where radical pro-Soviet regimes have been replaced by more moderate and less friendly governments, the Soviets have demonstrated a concern for protecting their considerable investments by maintaining "businesslike relations." In addition to economic factors such as debt repayment, the acquisition of new markets, or access to raw materials, in choosing their targets, the Soviets consider strategic factors such as the degree of Chinese or Western interest in a country, its importance to Soviet security, or its ability to provide support facilities—including airports, harbors, or sites for communication stations—for Soviet military activities.

These latter factors have assumed greater importance in recent years as the Soviet Union has deployed a substantial naval force in the oceans and seas surrounding the Third World and as it has sought to use this new capability not merely for military defense but for the political purpose of "protecting state interests in time of peace." Prior to the Second World War, the Soviet Union played the role of a "land power" and lacked a significant naval capability, as had Russia before it. But in the postwar period Moscow invested heavily in a large navy whose mission has been essentially defensive in nature. The post-Stalin development of Soviet surface and submarine vessels, armed with tactical cruise missiles, has been designed primarily to neutralize the perceived threat posed first by the U.S. aircraft carriers and, more recently, by the American strategic missile submarine force, which the USSR has sought to counter through a massive antisubmarine warfare deployment, while adding a formidable sea-based attack capability of its own.

In addition to these purposes of defense and strategic deterrence, in the last decade, the Soviets have also deployed their navy in a way that would support foreign policy objectives, most notably in the Third World. In both the Mediterranean Sea and the Indian Ocean, they have sought to establish a peacetime naval "presence," featuring frequent calls at the ports of the littoral countries, both to demonstrate their interest in these areas and to signal their resolve in times of crisis.

An interesting and significant illustration of this evolving purpose has been provided in the last decade by the Soviet naval presence in the Indian Ocean. First manifested with the appearance of two vessels in 1968, the Soviet deployment has slowly but steadily increased in both size and visibility. In recent years, the Soviets have maintained a permanent squadron of 15 to 20 vessels, with occasional "surges" in times of crisis to a squadron of more than 30. The original Soviet deployment was based on a combination of factors: both a military strategic concern over a potential submarine threat from the United States and the internal bureaucratic needs and organizational routines of the Soviet Navy.

Once established, however, the Soviets found the naval presence useful both in safeguarding their growing commerce and as an instrument in the heightening political competition with Washington and Beijing. Thus, for most of the period, the primary purpose of the Soviet naval activity has been the building and maintenance of political and economic influence in the littoral states. At times this activity has focused on particularly strategic countries as the Soviets have sought to solidify their relations and express a commitment without provoking an overt military reaction from their global rivals. Moreover, the Soviets have on occasion utilized this capability for dramatic demonstrations of their resolve to back up their own and their clients' interests in times of crisis (for example, the Bangladesh war of 1971, the Iraq-Kuwait conflict of 1973, and the period following the 1973 Middle East war).[29]

Direct confirmation that the Soviets are using their naval capabilities as a means of projecting their prestige and influence into this region can be found in the recent writings of the naval commander-in-chief, Admiral Sergei Gorshkov. In a series of articles advocating naval deployments for the purpose of "protection of state interest in times of peace," he wrote:

the friendly visits of Soviet navy men make it possible for the peoples of many countries to become convinced with their own eyes of the creativity of the ideas of Communism. . . . They see warships as embodying the achievements of Soviet science, technology, and industry.[30]

Soviet Admiral Grishanov has written in a similar vein that the cruises of Soviet ships to foreign ports "serve the noble purpose of improving mutual understanding between nations . . . enhancing the international prestige of the homeland, and strengthening the political influence of the Soviet Union."[31]

In utilizing its expanded naval capability for the purpose of "showing the flag" and supporting its foreign policy objectives, the Soviet leadership seems to be following the examples of the "imperialist" British and American navies and the teachings of their nineteenth-century mentor, Admiral Alfred Thayer Mahan. Their activities demonstrate that they have mastered the principle that subjective *perception* of strength and relative superiority weighs heavily in the competition for influence. Admiral Stansfield Turner, in an article published just prior to his appointment as Director of the U.S. Central Intelligence Agency, expressed the point well:

though the United States can wield the presence tool more effectively, the Soviets have been playing the game well. Realizing that they are dealing with perceptions, they are gaining maximum advantage from the fact that any change is news. . . . And as our Navy constricts and draws back from traditional deployment patterns, the Soviet Navy has been demonstrating increasingly imaginative and frequent global deployment of forces in response to developments in international politics—as in Angola, Mozambique, the Indian Ocean and West Africa. It seems a confirmation of the claim that we are a declining sea power and that they are a growing and restive one. The invalidity of that claim is academic if it is universally believed.[32]

Addressing the naval balance, Admiral Turner proceeded to demonstrate that, in terms of specific objectives and missions, the U.S. Navy remains adequate to the task. The Soviet Navy has achieved wide-ranging capabilities in strategic deterrence and naval presence, but it remains inferior in its mission of sea control—capable of denial only and not of assertion—and in its ability to project power ashore through amphibious and tactical air capabilities.[33] Nevertheless, the expansion of the Soviet Navy in the Brezhnev era has signaled Moscow's determination to achieve the status of a global superpower—not confined to the Eurasian land mass but capable of projecting its power far beyond its own borders. In pursuit of this objective, the Soviets have given renewed importance to the achievement of a strong position in strategic areas of the Third World.

HIGH STAKES IN THE MIDDLE EAST

The Soviet Union was virtually uninvolved in the affairs of the Middle East from the time of the collapse of Stalin's efforts to establish a communist enclave in neighboring Iran (see chapter 3) until the Soviet dictator's death in 1953. Moscow viewed the Arab Middle East in particular as solidly within the Western sphere of influence; it regarded existing regimes as reactionary and proimperialist (even after the coup in which Naguib and Nasser ousted King Farouk in 1952). The communist parties in the region were weak, and the Soviets had no available channels for penetrating the area even had they wished to do so. Even the 1953 overthrow of the leftist Iranian premier Mossadegh and ensuing persecution of the Iranian communist party (Tudeh) was greeted by Moscow with only routine protest and invective. After Stalin's death, Malenkov did refer in his August 1953 speech to a desire for furthering "friendly cooperation" with the Arab states, and the Soviet government the same year dropped its territorial claims against Turkey, but there was no visible sign of Soviet activity in the area for another two years.

Apart from the general motivations leading them toward a new Third World policy in 1955, the Soviets had a particular defensive security consideration that accelerated their move into the Middle East that year. This was the American-sponsored effort to erect anti-Soviet "collective security" agreements in the "Northern Tier" of states along the southern borders of the USSR. At the urging of Secretary of State Dulles, bilateral pacts were concluded between Turkey and Pakistan (April 1954), the United States and Pakistan (May 1954), and Turkey and Iraq (February 1955). With the adherence of Britain (April 1955) and Iran (October 1955) to the latter agreement, the entire arrangement came to be known as the Baghdad Pact.

Each stage of this process was greeted by loud protests from Moscow, which recognized it as clearly aimed against the USSR. A foreign ministry statement issued in April, 1955 declared that "the Soviet Union cannot remain indifferent to the situation arising in the region of the Near and Middle East, since the formation of these blocs and the establishment of foreign military bases on the territory of the countries of the Near and Middle East have a direct bearing on the security of the USSR."[34] The conclusion of the agreements and the active role of Iraq in their formulation also produced severe uneasiness in Egypt, where Colonel Nasser aspired to forge a united Arab bloc under his own leadership. Nasser perceived Iraq as his major rival in this effort and desired to discourage other Arab states from adhering to the Baghdad Pact; he needed weapons in order to enhance Egypt's regional credibility and prestige but was not likely to find willing salesmen in the West. He did locate them in Czechoslovakia (which acted, he admitted the following year, only as a surrogate for the USSR). The Czech-Egyptian arms sale agreement, which began as a commercial transaction, was concluded in September 1955 and produced considerable disquiet in both Iraq and the United States, who recognized it as permitting the Soviets to "leapfrog" the Northern Tier.

The Soviets were immensely pleased with the results of this bargain and followed it the next year with arms deals with Syria and Yemen. The latter state, which was engaged in a struggle to oust the British from the neighboring strategic port of Aden, also received an agreement from Moscow to assist in the modernization of its own port of Hodeida. Apparently the USSR's involvement was not initially in response to signs of "progressive" political development in the region (Yemen was a feudal monarchy), nor was it at first meant to align Moscow with the Arabs in their dispute with Israel (with whom the Soviets had resumed relations in 1953). But the Soviets were drawn into this conflict (though not to the Arab goal of liquidating the Israeli state) by their involvement in the Suez crisis in 1956 (see chapter 4), and they soon began to pay more attention to signs of internal political change in the region. Nasser's dispute with the West spurred his turn toward the left, and a change of government early in 1957 in Syria (which had the strongest communist party in the region) brought a leftist regime to power there.

The United States was also spurred to action by these signs, and in January 1957 a Congressional resolution (known as the Eisenhower Declaration) authorized the president to render economic and military aid to Middle Eastern countires that requested it and promised to give American military help "to secure and protect the territorial integrity and political independence of such nations, requesting such aid, against overt armed aggression from any nation controlled by International Communism."[35] The burgeoning leftist influence in Syria and the actions of Cairo and Damascus in promoting a challenge to the monarchy in Jordan, amidst rumors (fanned in the Soviet press) of Turkish troop concentrations on the border with Syria led on September 7 1957, to an American warning to Syria that it was approaching the state of procommunist domination specified in the Eisenhower Doctrine.

This threat from Washington was countered the following week by a note sent by Premier Bulganin to Turkish Premier Menderes, warning of the consequences of aggression against Syria and threatening Soviet retaliation. Menderes replied that he had no such plans, and the crisis abated until mid-October. At that point the Soviets heated it up for one final round, during which they announced their readiness to help "crush aggression" with their military forces. By the end of the month, the Soviets had turned down the heat again.[36] Moscow apparently felt that it had made its point, which was to demonstrate its great-power role as the patron of Syria, countering a putative American effort to apply the Eisenhower Doctrine.

The Syrian crisis of 1957 was followed early in the next year by the merger of Syria and Egypt into the United Arab Republic (UAR). Although this event posed a setback to promising Soviet prospects in Syria (whose communist party was dissolved and pro-Soviet politicians shoved into the background by Nasser), it by no means brought calm to the Middle Eastern scene. The outbreak of political crises in pro-Western Lebanon and Jordan, apparently fanned by pro-Nasser agitators, was followed in July by a bloody coup, led by the left-leaning General Kassem, which overturned Iraq's Hashemite monarchy (and, in the process, the Baghdad Pact). Fearing that their moderate protegés might also topple, the British and Americans immediately sent troops into Jordan and Lebanon, at the request of the governments there. Apparently caught by surprise by both the coup and its aftermath, Khrushchev sought to make the best of the situation by staging military maneuvers on the Soviet border with Turkey and Iran and issuing an appeal for a summit conference "to take measures to terminate the military conflict." But the Soviets' ability to capitalize on the situation was limited by the Arabs themselves. A session of the General Assembly in August, instead of condemning the Anglo-American intervention, passed an Arab-authored resolution calling for a settlement of the conflict by the states of the region alone.

The image of the Soviet Union as the powerful protector of the Arab states against imperialist intervention was tarnished by the ease with which the West was able to demonstrate its capability and resolve during the 1958 Middle Eastern crisis. Nevertheless, the Soviets had scored a net gain by the collapse of the Baghdad Pact and the overthrow of the pro-Western regime in Iraq by a group that had quickly professed its friendship for the USSR and legalized the communist party. Fascinated by the potential in this situation, the Soviets began to lavish their attention on Iraq. But Nasser, who had aspirations to draw Iraq into the UAR, was alarmed by the upsurge of communist activity there. In a well-publicized speech in December, he hurled angry denunciations at the communists, as opponents of Arab unity, and shortly thereafter began arresting communist cadres in Egypt. The Soviets, who were then in a mood of disillusionment with "bourgeois nationalist" leaders, answered in kind. Khrushchev, in a speech to the Twenty-first CPSU Congress, condemned Nasser's actions as "a reactionary business," and later he denounced the UAR president as "a passionate, hot-headed young man." But the Soviets had no viable alternative to the Arab nationalist leaders and thus chose not to burn their bridges entirely; Khrushchev assured the Congress delegates that ideological differences would not prevent the development of further friendly relations in the area.

The situation, however, was to get worse for the Soviets in the Middle East before it again turned upward. The Shah of Iran, who had developed good trade relations with the Soviets and had paid a friendly visit to Moscow in 1956, concluded a defense agreement with the United States in March 1959, in apparent reaction to the turn of events in neighboring Iraq. Moreover, the Iraqi government itself began to turn away from Moscow. General Kassem began to trim the sails of the Iraqi communists in mid-1959, and by 1960 he had begun to move his government toward a more neutral foreign policy stance amidst growing criticism in the Soviet press. Soviet-Iraqi relations were further complicated by the government's military action in 1961 against the Kurds, who had long been under Soviet patronage.

The Soviets were beginning to learn that the political situation in the Middle East was extremely volatile; friendly regimes might be toppled by unfriendly ones but those too would soon pass away. In September 1961 Syria withdrew from the UAR, and in the next five years there were eight coups in Damascus. The net result was a lessening of Soviet involvement in Syria, particularly during the periods when the anticommunist right wing of the Ba'ath Party was in command there. As Syria turned rightward, however, Nasser was again moving to the left. Oppressed by growing economic difficulties, he began to talk more of socialism, and by 1963 he was again viewed in Moscow as "progressive." But, as we have seen, the pace of doctrinal reassessment was moving as quickly in Moscow during this period as were the political tides in the Middle East. The original concept of "national democracy" had rapidly proved inapplicable in the region, where communist parties were generally not allowed to function freely. As the Soviet approach became more flexible and pragmatic, however, Moscow began to build its ties with the area's "progressive" ruling parties, such as the Arab Socialist Union (ASU) in Cairo and the National Liberation Front (FLN) in Algeria. Relations with the latter group had developed slowly, due in large part to the heavy support given by Moscow to the rival Algerian Communist Party during Algeria's independence struggle. During this period, the Soviets were also having to build their ties with the Algerians and other Arabs in active competition with the Chinese, who had begun to pursue an active campaign of diplomacy and economic assistance in the Middle East.

Yet another setback to the prospects of Arab communists occurred early in 1963, when the regime of General Kassem was overthrown by a rightist Ba'ath group, which then unleashed a bloody terror that virtually obliterated the Iraqi communists. This regime lasted only nine months and was succeeded by a government far friendlier to the Soviet Union, but the damage to local communist prospects endured nonetheless. An additional "hotbed of tension" during this period existed in Yemen, where Nasser and the Soviets (as well as the Chinese) were heavily involved as patrons and suppliers of weapons in a savage and costly civil war.

It was in the midst of such a tumultuous situation that Khrushchev appeared in the Middle East in May 1964 to bestow his exuberant blessing on the Egyptian regime "for embarking on a path of socialist construction." To celebrate the occasion, Nasser released the jailed Egyptian communists; the following year, they "voluntarily" dissolved their party and joined the Arab Socialist Union. Similar accolades were bestowed in the spring of 1964 on Algeria's President Ben Bella; shortly thereafter the Soviet Communist Party established ties with the FLN and allowed the Algerian communists to slip into obscurity.

As noted, Moscow's policy of establishing itself as the patron of radical but noncommunist Arab regimes did not change with Khrushchev's removal. The July 1965 coup in Algeria, which replaced Ben Bella with Boumediènne, produced no reorientation of Soviet policy toward that state, which along with Egypt and Syria (after the February 1966 coup) was held up as a model practitioner of noncapitalist development.

One significant change wrought by Khrushchev's successors in the direction of Soviet policy in the Middle East was the intensification of a campaign to strengthen Moscow's relations with the states of the "Northern Tier"—Turkey, Iran, and Pakistan. In each case, the Soviets were taking advantage of the reduction in East-West tensions and the growing American involvement in Vietnam to encourage Washington's clients in demonstrating a more neutral position. In the case of Turkey, the new Soviet leaders also capitalized on Ankara's alienation from Washington following the 1964 crisis in Cyprus by assuming a position of neutrality in the Cyprus dispute. Soviet-Turkish relations were warmed in this period by the conclusion of substantial aid and trade agreements and the exchange of high-level visits, including a trip by Kosygin to Ankara at the end of 1966.

In the case of Iran, the Soviets had welcomed the Shah's program of reforms and his pledge that no American missile bases would be allowed on Iranian territory. In June 1965 the Iranian monarch visited Moscow and concluded a $290 million credit agreement. The following year the Soviets signed an agreement with Iran which called for the delivery of natural gas to the USSR, and a five-year trading pact was negotiated in 1967. While the emphasis in this relationship was on the development of commercial ties, there was also a political payoff to the extent that Teheran's ties to (and dependence upon) Washington appeared to be weakened in the process.

While Moscow was in the process of solidifying its ties with its southern neighbors, a new crisis was developing in the Arab lands of the Middle East, which led to the Six-Day War of 1967. In January 1964 the first Arab summit conference had resulted in a heightening militancy toward Israel as the leaders agreed to press Palestinian claims more vigorously. Although the Soviets virtually ignored the Palestinians, they did escalate their sale of arms to the region. In his memoirs, Khrushchev claims that, during his visit of May 1964, he strongly urged Nasser not to try to take on the Israelis again, declaring: "The state of Israel exists and we must both accept that fact." Interestingly, the former Soviet leader placed less blame for the subsequent military disaster on the Arabs themselves than on the Soviet regime, which, he says, should have exerted its influence to restrain the Egyptians from demonstrating their belligerence.[37]

The Soviet leaders, caught up in the campaign to increase their influence among the Arab clients, apparently did not take the gathering war clouds seriously. Moscow was evidently unwilling to spend its political capital in an effort to restrain the Arabs on an issue of such salience to them. As Michel Tatu puts it, "The Arabs had the initiative and they drew their Moscow protectors in deeper and deeper after them."[38] As the crisis deepened, the Soviets continued to miscalculate, misunderstanding the volatility of the situation and overestimating both the military strength of their clients and the willingness of the Israelis to tolerate Arab provocations.

The origins of the 1967 war can be found in the February 1966 coup in Syria, which brought to power a militant but politically insecure regime that began to step up provocative activity against Israel and Jordan. The Damascus government seemed to thrive on the growing war scare and the Soviets, delighted at the return of a friendly regime in Syria, helped fan the tensions in the region. Israeli responses to Syrian and Palestinian attacks escalated steadily, and in April 1967 Israel delivered a particularly humiliating retaliatory blow at the Syrian capital itself. Syria called on the Egyptians and Soviets for support; Moscow complied with verbal assaults on Israel but Cairo's actions were more challenging. In a series of escalatory moves, Nasser moved his troops into the Sinai peninsula, demanded the removal of United Nations peace-keeping forces, and finally blockaded the Straits of Tiran, closing this vital waterway to Israeli shipping. Nasser was evidently relying on the Soviet Union to deter the United States from giving assistance to Israel, and Moscow cooperated with an ambiguous statement that declared that aggression would receive a "firm riposte" from the Soviet Union.

That the Soviets underestimated the danger of war is evident from the fact that Brezhnev, Kosygin, and Defense Minister Grechko departed the Soviet capital on May 31 for a leisurely four-day fleet inspection visit to Murmansk and Archangel. Moscow was thus caught completely off guard by the June 5 preemptive Israeli attack on Egyptian and Syrian forces. Reeling from the devastating Israeli blow, in a patent effort to force a commitment from Moscow, a desperate Nasser claimed that American planes had joined Israeli aircraft in the attack. The Soviets, however, wanted no part in this propaganda and the Kremlin leaders made use of the "hot line" to reassure Washington that they sought no military confrontation with the United States in the Middle East. In the hope of staving off a total Arab collapse, they worked frantically with the Americans to produce a ceasefire. At the same time the Soviets sought to demonstrate support of their clients (without incurring the risk of war). Moscow broke off relations with the Israeli government (thereby isolating itself from subsequent peace-making efforts) and undertook a massive effort to replace the captured and destroyed Arab armaments (which amounted to over three-fourths of their clients' total arsenals). In a tactic reminiscent of previous crises, the Soviets threatened direct intervention only after the main danger had passed and they had American agreement to a ceasefire; the threat was aimed at forcing Israel to accept the ceasefire prior to completing its military campaign against the Syrians.

In addition to their arsenals, the Arabs had lost substantial amounts of territory to the Israelis: the Sinai Peninsula and Gaza Strip were captured from Egypt, the West Bank from Jordan, and the Golan Heights from Syria. In the wake of this monumental defeat, the Soviet Union pursued active diplomatic and propaganda campaigns designed to regain for its clients their lost territories. The Soviet media denounced the Israeli "aggressors" in the strongest terms, accusing them of "Hitlerite tactics," and Kosygin himself led a delegation to the United Nations to demand Israeli withdrawal from the captured lands. While in the United States, the Soviet premier traveled to Glassboro State College in New Jersey to meet with President Johnson. Although the summit meeting made no progress toward settling the conflict in the Middle East, it did seem to demonstrate to the world the USSR's equal status with the United States in assuming responsibility for world affairs. (The symbolism of parity even extended to the selection of a site, which was deemed to be exactly halfway between Washington and the United Nations.)

Soviet President Podgorny and a series of high-ranking military officials visited the Middle East in June and July to arrange for the rearming of the Arab belligerents. The amount of weapons provided during the balance of 1967 and 1968 totalled $2.5 billion—nearly as much as had been supplied during the preceding 12 years. And though Nasser was later to claim that the resupply was provided by the Soviets without charge, Moscow did demand a greater voice for Soviet advisers in the equipping and training of the Arab armies as a price for its weaponry.

There is no doubt that Moscow regarded the June war as a serious defeat; a group of "hawks" in the Soviet leadership who apparently dared criticize the Politburo majority for its handling of the crisis was purged in its aftermath. The Kremlin leaders were also sharply criticized by the Algerians and Syrians for their insufficient assistance during the war and relations between Moscow and the two radical Arab regimes were badly strained in the immediate wake of the conflict.

The Soviets had by no means lost everything; in a way, with the Arabs more dependent on them and more bitterly alienated from the Americans than ever before, the Soviets were in a position to seek even more influence in the Middle East. Moscow's rearming of its clients was designed to strengthen their defenses and bring them to a state of parity with Israel; the objective was not, as the Soviets saw it, to prepare for another round of war but to strengthen the Arab hand for the political bargaining that lay ahead. And yet the Arabs saw it differently; their primary objective was not the maintenance of peace but the recovery of their territories, and if the Soviets wished to carry weight in the Arab capitals, they would have to assist in the realization of this objective, whatever means would have to be used. In the final analysis, the superpower was in danger of becoming a prisoner of its clients' objectives, rather than the other way round.

One other postwar development that affected the future balance of power in the Middle East was occurring in the area of the Persian Gulf—the growing international importance of Middle Eastern oil. During the June war the Arabs had already sought to use the "oil weapon" against the friends of Israel; Saudi Arabia, Kuwait, Libya, and Iraq had enforced a brief blockade but Western dependence was not yet at the point where a blockade could be effective. The petroleum supply-and-demand situation was changing rapidly, however, and the Middle East was rapidly becoming the vital center of international energy production. Apart from its interest in the oil weapon as an instrument to be used against the West, the Soviet Union was developing its own positive interest in Middle Eastern oil and natural gas. Although its own reserves were substantial, the costs of exploiting them were also large. For years, most of the Soviet oil and gas exports had gone to Eastern Europe, but as the world price began to rise, Moscow developed an interest in diverting its East European customers to the Middle East, so that it could export its own petroleum to the West in exchange for hard currency or advanced technology.

As the Arabian peninsula and Persian Gulf area became economically more attractive to the Soviets, it also became more politically tempting. Britain's announcement of its intention to abandon its military installations "east of Suez" by 1970 stirred talk of a "power vacuum" in the area and the Soviets were determined to have a hand in the division of the spoils. In late 1967, Moscow stepped up its aid to republican forces in Yemen, in the wake of the withdrawal of forces by the financially strapped Egyptians. The British pulled out of the strategic port of Aden in November and the Soviets promptly recognized the Marxist-oriented People's Republic of South Yemen. The Chinese were also very active in Aden, and for the next few years the two communist states sought to outbid each other in competition for the favor of the new regime.

Not surprisingly, the conflict on the Arab-Israeli front soon heated up again, and by the spring of 1970 the Egyptians were approaching desperation at the porous state of their defenses in the escalating War of Attrition that they had initiated against Israel. In response, the Soviets escalated their own commitment, installing surface-to-air missiles (SAM-3) sites, manned by Soviet "advisers," and providing Soviet pilots to fly Egypt's MiG-21 interceptors in combat missions against the Israeli Phantom jets. At this point, there were approximately 20,000 Soviet military personnel stationed in Egypt, and the size of the Mediterranean naval squadron had been increased as well. Clearly the Russians felt that they could not afford to have their clients humiliated but they also feared that further escalation of the conflict might soon involve them in a direct confrontation with the United States. To avoid this outcome, once the defensive installations were in place, Moscow acquiesced in the American drive for a ceasefire in the war of attrition; this was achieved in August 1970.

One risky element in this situation was particularly difficult to control: the Palestinian factor. Both the radical Arab regimes and the Chinese had stepped up their support for the Palestine Liberation Organization (PLO), and this necessarily stirred new Soviet interest in the Palestinians. But despite its professed growing sympathy for PLO objectives, Moscow objected strenuously to the terrorist tactics practiced by Palestinian guerrillas, including airplane hijacking. The guerrilla capture of three "jumbo" aircraft and their passengers in September 1970 had far-reaching consequences. The aircraft were parked in the Jordanian desert, in a flagrant demonstration of fedayeen power in that state. King Hussein reacted angrily and a virtual civil war erupted involving both the Syrians and the Americans and resulting in a severe defeat for the Palestinians and their patrons. Nevertheless, the Soviets continued to provide military aid to the PLO, while pressing on it the necessity for a political solution. After the October 1973 war, Moscow moved even closer to the Palestinians and began to support the creation of a Palestinian state in the West Bank and Gaza Strip for the first time.

Another risk that the Soviet strategy courted was that the Arabs would become utterly disillusioned with a continuing state of controlled tension: "no war, no peace." The political situation moved further out of Soviet control with Nasser's sudden death in September 1970. His successor, Anwar Sadat, was less than secure in his new position and desperately needed a victory in the conflict with Israel to stabilize his regime. The Soviets, with no contacts or influence in Israel, could not oblige him, and in February 1971 Sadat opened negotiations with the United States for an "interim solution" to the conflict. In May the situation took a rapid turn, with both the visit to Egypt of Secretary of State Rogers and a dramatic purge of his regime by Sadat, resulting in the dismissal of Moscow's closest friend in the leadership, Ali Sabri.

Alarmed over the internal trends and the growing American role, the Kremlin dispatched President Podgornyi and a high-level government, party, and military delegation to Cairo on May 25. After only two days of intensive negotiations, Podgorny and Sadat signed a 15-year Treaty of Friendship and Cooperation. Modeled after Soviet treaties with the Warsaw Pact allies, the treaty called for regular consultations and extended military cooperation. Apparently initiated at Moscow's behest, the treaty provided the Soviets with an institutionalization of their presence in Egypt at a time when they feared a growing U.S. involvement, while Sadat gained a formalization and enlargement of the Russian military commitment and an implied Soviet assurance of noninterference in Egypt's internal affairs.[39]

Sadat announced to his people in July that 1971 was the "year of decision" in the conflict with Israel. Yet simultaneously, and largely hidden from public view, his relations with his Russian patrons were worsening. Sadat greatly displeased the Soviets by his actions in helping reverse a coup supported by the communist party against the government of neighboring Sudan, which took place on July 19. This event, which virtually destroyed Moscow's position of influence with Sudanese President Nimeiry, demonstrated anew the aversion of Arab elites to communism in their region. Continuing Soviet-Egyptian difficulties were signaled by the communique issued after Sadat's visit to Moscow in October, which characterized the discussions as occurring in a "spirit of frankness." The Soviets were particularly irritated by Sadat's revelation that his new association with the Americans would be stepped up by President Nixon's visit to Cairo the following May.

In December, the Soviets had an opportunity to demonstrate their displeasure with Sadat (and their continuing aversion to another Middle East war), when a shipment of arms promised to Egypt was diverted to India (then engaged in a war with Pakistan). By the end of the month, Sadat was forced to announce to the Egyptians that the "year of decision" would have to be postponed. Sadat visited Moscow twice more in the first four months of 1972 in search of further commitments in the struggle against Israel, and twice more he found his hosts insufficiently responsive.

Finally, in a dramatic speech on July 18, Sadat announced that he was expelling the entire Soviet military mission from Egypt. Moscow's public reaction was one of relative equanimity; it announced simply that the mission had "completed its functions." Sadat's public explanation excoriated the Russians for the failure to deliver offensive weapons but in fact this charge was not entirely fair to Moscow and the underlying reasons for his expulsion of the Soviets apparently lay both with his desire to solidify his internal position by boosting the morale of his people and soothing the ruffled feathers of his military leaders, and with his hopes for further improving relations with the United States and the conservative Arab oil monarchies.[40]

After their setback in Egypt, the Soviets moved quickly to strengthen their ties with the regimes in Syria and Iraq. In April 1972 they had concluded a long-term treaty with Baghdad, and they proceeded later in the year to increase their military and economic assistance to the Iraqis, substantially. This assistance strengthened the Baghdad regime in its regional conflicts with Kuwait and Iran and in its confrontation with the Western oil companies.

Chapter 7 will describe the collapse of the Rogers Plan for an Arab-Israeli settlement and the events of the October 1973 war in the Middle East. While the Soviets eventually acquiesced to another war, its ironic result was to make even clearer to the Arabs that while Moscow could help them wage war, only the United States could help bring peace and a return of their lost territories. Kissinger's post-October diplomacy isolated the Soviet Union from this process. The Soviet-Egyptian relationship subsequently worsened considerably as Moscow cut off its military aid and refused to reschedule Egypt's huge debt. Sadat responded in 1976 by abrogating the 1971 treaty and denying the Soviets use of Egyptian facilities on the Mediterranean Sea.

One clear reason in this complex relationship is that the USSR clearly does not "call the shots" in the Arab world, and yet its presence is well established and hard to displace. Sadat's new relationship with the United States and the oil monarchs can provide him with diplomatic and financial support, and thereby reduce his dependence on the Soviet Union in these realms, but it is apparently unable to supply his military needs. The Soviet Union's large role and military presence continue in the Middle East, and although the balance of dependence has shifted, there continue to be real limits to the influence of *both* superpowers in this rapidly changing situation. Soviet efforts to forge ideological bonds with the Arabs have also foundered and it is evident that Moscow's continuing role in the area rests less on its professed doctrine than on its superpower status.

It is hazardous to attempt to predict the future of the Soviet Union's relationship with the countries of the Middle East. The politics of the region remain extremely volatile and seemingly resistant to Soviet influence, as the bloody 1976 civil war in Lebanon showed again. That conflict left Moscow closer to the Palestinians and estranged from the Syrians and also greatly inflamed the intra-Arab conflict, especially the bitter feud between Syria and Iraq. But the Israeli political scene was also in transition, with the triumph of the hardline Likud in the 1977 elections again underlining the obstacles on the road to a lasting political settlement of the Arab-Israeli conflict. As long as these conflicts persist, there will be new opportunities for the Soviets to exploit and continuing dangers to world peace.

BALANCING ACT IN SOUTH AND SOUTHEAST ASIA

South Asia has been second only to the Middle East as the site of the largest sustained Soviet attention to and investment in the Third World. As in the Middle East, the Soviets have on occasion been drawn into severe regional conflicts, as a result of which they have been left with a substantial regional role but not with the comfortable position of a patron dealing with obedient clients. Moreover, to a much greater extent than in the Middle East, Asia has been the site of bitter rivalry with the People's Republic of China. At times, such as during the December 1971 Indo-Pakistani war, the situation in South Asia has mirrored almost perfectly the consequences of the shift from global bipolarity to the new triangular competition between Moscow, Washington, and Beijing.

As in Egypt, the beginning of Soviet involvement in the Indian subcontinent was motivated not primarily by changes occurring within India (though the ruling Congress Party did declare its dedication to socialism in 1955), but rather by the extension to the area of Moscow's bipolar competition with Washington and its nascent rivalry with Beijing. In particular, Soviet activity in India followed upon the conclusion of the 1954 U.S.-Pakistani defense agreement and the agreement on Tibet concluded the same year between Zhou Enlai and Nehru, which proclaimed that Sino-Indian relations would be governed by the "five principles of peaceful coexistence."

Prime Minister Nehru had already demonstrated his actively neutralist foreign policy and his aversion to the sins of "imperialism," and this behavior had also attracted the attention of the Soviet leaders. In February 1955 they concluded a substantial aid agreement with the Indians and in June, Nehru was given an unprecedented lavish reception on the occasion of his visit to the USSR. This trip was followed at the end of the year by the journey of Bulganin and Khrushchev to India, Afghanistan, and Burma. While in India, Khrushchev offered his hosts reassurance that strengthened relations need not be hindered by differences in the two states' social systems: "We do not force anything upon anyone; we are not seeking to impose any political obligations."[41] The Soviet leaders also bestowed generous praise on India's struggle for independence and on her late leader, Mahatma Gandhi (who had earlier been denounced by Moscow as a benighted reactionary). India's present ambitions were flattered by the Soviet leaders' assertions that she had been denied by the imperialists her deserved ranking as a "great power." Finally, Khrushchev lent support to India on the issue embroiling her in conflict with Pakistan and most crucial to her national pride, declaring that the people themselves had already decided that Kashmir was part of India. On their return to Moscow, however, the Soviet leaders were careful to make a statement that left the door open for a warming of Soviet-Pakistani relations, should that state return to an "independent" policy. But for the moment it appeared to serve Soviet purposes to seek to build influence by intervening in a regional quarrel on behalf of the party engaged in struggle against "imperialism and its lackeys."

Over the next few years, there was a proliferation of exchanges between India and the USSR; almost 200 Indian delegations of various sorts traveled to the Soviet Union between 1954 and 1957. An ever-increasing volume of books, pamphlets, and magazines made their way from the Soviet Union to India; whereas 17,000 books were sent in 1955, the figure had climbed to 4 million copies by 1958.[42] Of equal if not greater importance in achieving for the Soviet Union a profound impact on Indian consciousness were the offers of economic assistance. The volume of economic contacts rose steadily and by the 1960s India had become the USSR's most important noncommunist trading partner. Through the combined effect of this activity, the Soviets sought to wrest India from the economic and cultural orbit of the "imperialist" world.

India's foreign policy was said to be one of "positive neutrality," featuring nonalignment with military blocs and an active struggle against colonialism and warmongering. In Moscow's eyes, since these causes were most actively supported by the USSR, the ideal "neutral" would be consistently pro-Soviet, without actually being a member of the socialist camp. And indeed, India sided with the Soviet Union in the United Nations in 1956 on the Hungarian issue, and she was rewarded the following year when Moscow cast a veto in the Security Council on behalf of India's interests in the Kashmir dispute.

Moscow's discovery that the "national-bourgeois" government in New Delhi, formerly held to be an agent of the imperialists, was indeed a progressive and peace-loving friend of the Soviet Union led to a rapid reversal in its assessment of the regime's policies. Positions once denounced as hopelessly procapitalist were now viewed paternalistically as the basis on which more progressive policies could be built. There were, however, difficulties in fitting Marxist-Leninist categories to this analysis; an attempt by one Soviet analyst to characterize India as taking a step toward socialism brought a bitter protest to Moscow from the Communist Party of India (CPI). That party was influenced to adjust its own political program, discarding its earlier critical stance toward the Congress government and declaring itself an adherent of the "peaceful path to socialism."

This relatively happy picture of warming relations was shattered in the later 1950s by the burgeoning Chinese challenge to both Moscow and New Delhi. According to a Soviet diplomat who defected to the West from the embassy in Rangoon in 1959, a "gentleman's agreement" in 1955–56 that had recognized Southeast Asia as a "Chinese sphere" and India, Afghanistan, and points west as a "Soviet sphere" was considered by the Soviets to have been breached in 1958 by Chinese "intervention" in India.[43] In the spring of 1959, China charged "Indian expansionists" with having incited and aided a shortlived rebellion in Tibet, and in the summer and fall there were outbreaks of fighting along disputed areas of the Sino-Indian border.

The timing of the Chinese attacks had wider significance, since Khrushchev was at this time about to embark on his visit to the United States, where he hoped for results that would show the Chinese that detente and peaceful competition could serve the communist cause better than military force. But if the Chinese sought to sabotage the detente by forcing Khrushchev into a militant stand in support of Chinese claims in India, Khrushchev's reaction was far from obliging. On September 10, a TASS statement was issued from Moscow expressing regret over the border conflict, asserting that the USSR enjoyed "friendly relations" with both parties, condemning those unnamed forces who would disrupt friendship among peoples, and urging prompt negotiations. The Chinese were indignant at the attitude of studied neutrality reflected in this statement, which they interpreted as siding with a "bourgeois" country against a socialist ally. Nehru found the TASS statement both "fair and unusual." Khrushchev was given a warm reception in India in January 1960, and on this occasion he proclaimed that Indo-Soviet relations "have never before rested on a more solid basis of friendship and understanding."

This Soviet stance emboldened Nehru to adopt a "forward policy" on the Sino-Indian border, thus contributing to the heightening of Sino-Indian tensions. And in August 1962 he announced that he had accepted an offer made by the Soviets in May to supply MiG-21 fighter planes (which had not been supplied to China). The mounting conflict erupted on October 20 in fighting along the northeastern frontier of India, which turned in mid-November into a general Chinese offensive thoroughly defeating India's army and causing Nehru to appeal to Britain and the United States for military aid. In this second round of the Sino-Indian border conflict, the Soviet Union seemed at first to side with China, but it must be remembered that the fighting had broken out almost simultaneously with the Cuban Missile Crisis, and in this delicate period Khrushchev dared not risk provoking disunity in the communist camp. With the resolution of the Cuban crisis, however, the Soviets returned to a position of neutrality on the Sino-Indian conflict, complaining that only the imperialists could benefit from it.

Now that it had demonstrated the ability of its army to drive as far as it wished into India, China accepted a ceasefire on November 21 and unilaterally withdrew to positions behind the August 1959 lines of control. The major Chinese objectives had been accomplished; they had demonstrated the "sham" nature of Nehru's nonalignment, they damaged his prestige and had upset his ambitions to develop India as a model to the Third World, and they had forced him to begin diverting a much larger share of India's resources to defense expenditures. In subsequent months the Chinese media denounced Nehru as an imperialist lackey following "anti-people" policies, and urged Indian progressives to launch an all-out struggle against the "reactionary" government.

In the wake of the crisis, the Soviets sent a note to the Chinese complaining that "years of hard striving for Indian friendship and Indian neutrality" had gone for nothing as a result of Beijing's actions. Because of their initial vacillations, the Soviets had certainly lost standing with Indian popular opinion, while the influence of the United States and Britain had risen. The conflict had polarized the Indian political scene (forcing Nehru to expel a key leftist from his government and to jail hundreds of Indian communists) and had precipitated a conflict within the CPI that resulted in an open split in April 1964. It dramatized for the world the growing breach between Moscow and Beijing and itself became the cause of a further intensification of that conflict.

With the growing Chinese challenge, the Soviets were forced to give doctrinal justification for their support of the regime of Nehru (who died in May 1964) and his successors. This was not an easy task. India's leaders could not qualify as "revolutionary democrats," nor could their policies be characterized as leading to the "noncapitalist path." In the presence of a genuine proletariat and a long-suffering communist party, direct support could not justifiably be given to the Congress Party as a revolutionary alternative. That the Soviets continued nevertheless to give aid and support to the "bourgeois" Congress regime in India was testimony to the continued preeminence of the foreign-policy criterion in determining Soviet policy. It was evidence as well both of the increased Soviet fear of Chinese hegemony in Asia and of Moscow's calculation that a less forthcoming policy might well have opened India to even greater Western influence.

As Soviet ideologists saw it, the vital task for India was to interrupt capitalist development and transfer the country onto the "rails of noncapitalist development." This was clearly impossible as long as the national bourgeoisie continued to monopolize political power. Thus, the Soviets urged progressive forces in India to work for the formation of a democratic coalition of the left wing of the Congress and the CPI, which would then establish a "state of national democracy."

A consequence of the 1962 border war had been the warming of relations between India's two major adversaries—China and Pakistan. While Moscow was determined to retain the friendship of India, it was loathe to abandon Pakistan to the exclusive blandishments of Beijing and Washington. Thus, as part of the larger campaign to woo the states of the "Northern Tier," the USSR began to improve its relations with Pakistan. In April 1965 President Ayub Khan visited Moscow, and the resulting communique seemed to move the USSR toward a position of neutrality on the Kashmir question.

The Pakistanis had been emboldened by the changing situation on the sub-continent to press their claims to Kashmir, and in August 1965 a war erupted over the issue. The conflict was ignored at first in the Soviet press but then Moscow issued an appeal for an end to the conflict, expressing its desire for Indo-Pakistani relations to be a stabilizing factor in Asia. When China demonstrated its support for Pakistan and made threatening demands on New Delhi regarding the Sino-Indian frontier, the Soviets issued a stern warning to China not to stir up trouble on the subcontinent.

On September 17, Premier Kosygin volunteered to provide the "good offices" of the Soviet Union in helping settle the conflict. This dramatic gesture, in stark contrast to earlier Soviet behavior in fanning Indo-Pakistani strife, showed how far Moscow had come in its desire to bring stability to South Asia. The Soviets expressed fear that the conflict would only play into the hands of "extremists" both in the belligerent states and abroad, and they also calculated (though not publicly) that it could eventuate in the destruction of the quite substantial investment Moscow had built up in the governments and economies of the two states. The offer posed the risk of failure, but the stakes were sufficiently high to warrant it. If a Soviet-sponsored mediation could produce the beginnings of a rapprochement between India and Pakistan, then it would have contributed enormously to Moscow's primary aim in South Asia: the containment of Chinese influence and expansionism.

Kosygin met with Prime Minister Shastri (Nehru's successor) and President Ayub in the city of Tashkent in Soviet Uzbekistan in January 1966, and though his mediation did not succeed in settling the political future of Kashmir, it did defuse the immediate conflict. Shastri's death at the conclusion of the conference helped to galvanize Indian support for the Tashkent Declaration, and his successor, Indira Gandhi, Nehru's daughter, pledged to continue to work for peaceful resolution of Indo-Pakistani differences. The Soviets were widely praised for their efforts at mediation and managed to derive great propaganda advantage from the image they projected as a peace-loving great power endeavoring, while others aggravated conflict, to bring security to a troubled subcontinent.

The great hopes engendered at Tashkent were not to come to fruition. Indian and Pakistani leaders were caught in a web of their own making: long years of fanning popular hatred and suspicion were not easily overcome, nor were the large amounts of prestige invested by each side in the emotional issue of Kashmir easily sacrificed by either state. The continuation of the conflict was evidenced in the spiraling arms race that entrapped the great-power patrons of the two combatants. The United States sought to extricate itself, suspending arms shipments after the 1965 war. But India called on the Soviets for more arms and in May 1968, Moscow responded with a shipment of 100 SU-7 fighter-bombers. In the face of a vigorous protest from Pakistan (and fearing that she might move closer to Beijing), the Soviets agreed in the summer of 1968, following Ayub's cancellation of the lease on the U.S. intelligence base in Peshawar, to sell weapons to Pakistan. The announcement of this deal produced protests and riots in New Delhi in its turn, demonstrating anew the unpopularity that can be reaped by a supplier to both sides in an arms race.

Improving Soviet-Pakistani diplomatic and trade relations were derailed in the spring of 1971 by the outbreak of a severe civil conflict in East Pakistan which soon developed to near genocide. On April 2, President Podgornyi requested that Pakistani President Yahya Khan (who had succeeded Ayub two years earlier) "take the most urgent measures to stop the bloodshed and repressions against the population" in East Pakistan. As the conflict continued, however, millions of refugees streamed across the border into India, further straining its already tight economy and stimulating demands for Indian military action to help create an independent Bangladesh. Alarmed at the prospect that the conflict might again embroil the subcontinent in an enervating war, in which Pakistan might be supported by China, the Soviets moved decisively in an attempt to extend their influence and deter a war.

It is in the context of the larger campaign for "collective security" against China that the Soviet-Indian treaty, signed on August 9, 1971, must be viewed. Negotiations had actually begun two years before, in the context of sharp Sino-Soviet conflict and splits in Mrs. Gandhi's Congress Party. The Indians were apparently motivated by the increasing strain of the Pakistani civil war to resume the discussions in the summer of 1971. The other decisive new element in the situation was Henry Kissinger's trip to Beijing in July 1972—a journey facilitated by Pakistan. Thus, with the cooperation of India's sworn enemy, the American president was making overtures for a new relationship with China, India's second major antagonist in Asia. This dramatic shift raised serious doubts in New Delhi about the American role Pakistani conflict.

The Soviets, no less concerned over the prospect of a ᴏᵢᵢ. prochement, saw the Indian dilemma as an opportunity both to gain influence in New Delhi and to deter another wasteful and destabilizing war on the sub-continent, from which they thought only China might gain. The formal linkage of Soviet and Indian interests by means of a treaty might succeed in deterring the Chinese from providing military backing for Pakistan, while placing additional pressure on Yahya to reach a political solution. The formal obligations the Soviets incurred from the treaty were minimal; its main purpose, from the Soviet point of view, was to formalize and extend Russian influence for the immediate purpose of stabilizing the situation in South Asia.[44]

Article 10 of the treaty stated ambiguously that, in the event of an attack or threat directed toward either party by a third state, they would "immediately start mutual consultations with a view to eliminating this threat." The first consultations under the treaty took place in September in Moscow. There, Kosygin reportedly lectured Mrs. Gandhi about the need for the Pakistani people to decide their own future: "It is not a question for India to decide. You agreed to this. Therefore, we appeal that this problem has to be solved by peaceful political means."[45] Although Soviet statements later in the fall grew steadily more critical of Pakistan, Moscow still urged a peaceful solution to the conflict. Nevertheless, the Soviets rushed substantial quantities of arms to India, thus ensuring that their client would be well armed should she find a military solution necessary. In the meantime, the Soviets were putting heavy pressure on the Pakistanis to make political concessions to Sheik Mujibur Rahman's party in the East. Washington was also heavily engaged in the effort to restrain the two parties from going to war.

Nevertheless, India moved her troops into East Pakistan at the end of November. The brief war ended in mid-December with the unconditional surrender of Pakistani troops in the East and a ceasefire on the western front. But while the fighting on the subcontinent was proceeding, as well as in its aftermath, a torrent of impassioned words poured forth from Moscow, Beijing, and Washington, and acrimonious, around-the-clock debates occurred at the United Nations. Soviet Ambassador Malik, arguing that Pakistan bore full responsibility for the conflict, used his vetoes in the Security Council to block ceasefire resolutions while the Indians completed their military operations in East Pakistan. The United States, pressing for a ceasefire, claimed that India had attacked without justification while the United States was in the process of promoting a political settlement. As for the Soviets, Washington charged that by failing to restrain India they had pursued unilateral military advantage in the subcontinent. The Chinese went further—though not to the point of actual military intervention—in their attacks on Moscow and New Delhi, charging that the Soviets had "stage-managed" the whole plot and warning India that "he who plays with fire will be consumed by fire."[46]

In the immediate aftermath of the war, the Soviets had every reason to be exultant. Though they had failed to effect the removal of the refugee burden from India by peaceful means, they had at least played an essential role in India's victory over Pakistan, while their American and Chinese rivals—in the first test of the new "anti-Soviet axis"—had both lined up on the side of the loser. As American influence in India had declined dramatically, so Soviet influence had never been greater.

The Soviets moved rapidly to build their ties with the new state of Bangladesh. Sheik Mujib visited Moscow in March 1972, concluding agreements on economic assistance that were soon to lead to a substantial Soviet presence in Bangladesh. Two weeks later Pakistan's new leader, President Bhutto, was received in the Soviet capital for a "frank and useful exchange" on the prospects for rebuilding Soviet-Pakistani relations. In subsequent meetings with officials of all three states of the subcontinent, the Soviets consistently exerted their influence in an effort to foster reconciliation. The Simla Agreement of July 1972, in which India and Pakistan pledged their mutual desire for normalization of relations, the New Delhi Agreement of August 1973, which achieved a three-way repatriation of prisoners and refugees from the 1971 war, and subsequent agreements restoring relations between India and Pakistan were all welcomed by the Soviets as positive developments helping to restore stability to South Asia.

In the changed circumstances of the postwar period, however, Pakistan and Bangladesh were overshadowed on the subcontinent by a strengthened and confident India. For the Soviets, the essential point was that whereas prior to 1971 the balance of forces had dictated the nearly impossible task of uniting India and Pakistan in a common grouping against Chinese influence, the situation after the December war seemed far more manageable. By Moscow's reckoning, India, grateful for Soviet assistance and dependent on further aid, would be in the new circumstances an even more valuable partner in the effort to outflank China. But Soviet calculations projecting a firm and lasting partnership with an increasingly left-leaning India have been upset by subsequent events, and most notably by India's evident fierce determination to be the client of no other state.

A survey of post-1971 Soviet-Indian relations reveals that Soviet influence has been subject to considerable limitations. India's leaders have strongly reaffirmed their continuing nonalignment, and not only have they failed to echo the warm references made in Moscow to the Indo-Soviet Treaty, but they have in fact made statements strongly critical of "superpower hegemony." India has taken steps to improve her long-damaged relationships with both Washington and Beijing. She has resisted Soviet requests for naval cooperation and has even refused (despite Brezhnev's personal plea during his visit to New Delhi in November 1973) to give explicit endorsement to the Soviet plan for "collective security in Asia." The Indians did sign a 15-year agreement designed to put their economic relationships with the Soviets on a stable long-term basis, but they have denied rumors that they plan to seek formal association with the Soviet trading bloc (COMECON). And there are signs that further growth in Soviet-Indian trade may be limited due both to noncomplementarity in the two economies and to Soviet unwillingness to provide certain raw materials needed by India. There are also limits to expansion of Soviet-Indian military cooperation; through the treaty, the Soviets have already extended their pledge of support, and by virtue of her victory in the December war, India now faces a much reduced threat. In a determined fashion, India has been seeking self-sufficiency in arms production and her progress in building a nuclear capability—viewed with a notable lack of enthusiasm in Moscow—suggests that she may be capable of achieving it.

On balance, the Soviet-Indian relationship and the degree of Moscow's influence in New Delhi probably reached a peak in 1971. In the period since then, India's dependence has lessened and the Soviets may now need India's support more than New Delhi needs Moscow's. If India were to become hostile or indifferent, Moscow would be left with no major asset in South Asia.

In fact, the events of the mid-1970s have represented a setback for Soviet interests in the subcontinent. The overthrow of the pro-Soviet government of Mujib in Bangladesh in the summer of 1975, and its replacement by a more pro-Western (and anti-Indian) regime was viewed with apprehension in Moscow. The 1975 political crisis in India, culminating in Mrs. Gandhi's proclamation of emergency rule in June, was at first welcomed by the Soviets for its seeming reversal of a mounting "reactionary" tide. But the period of the emergency freed Mrs. Gandhi of any parliamentary dependence on the CPI, and the harsh restrictions on political freedom limited the capabilities of communists as well as other parties. The lifting of the emergency and Mrs. Gandhi's defeat in the spring 1977 elections seemed as surprising to the Soviet Union as to the rest of the world; the net effect of these events was a further loss in influence for the USSR. Thus, although Moscow's stake, presence, and influence in South Asia are still sizeable, the future of the relationship between New Delhi and Moscow—like the Soviet-Egyptian alliance—has been called into serious question by the events of recent years.

The temporary removal of Mrs. Gandhi and the fall of Sheik Mujib were not nearly such spectacular losses as was the demise of another of Moscow's Asian friends—President Sukarno of Indonesia, who was once the repository of great Soviet hopes in Southeast Asia. The Soviet friendship with Sukarno was relatively late in developing. As in India, the Indonesian Communist Party (PKI) had been at odds with nationalist leaders in the late 1940s and had even attempted a coup d'état in 1948. When Indonesia attained independence in December 1949, its relations with the Soviet Union were anything but cordial, and ambassadors were not exchanged until 1954. But Sukarno's performance at the Bandung Conference in 1955 heralded the adoption of strongly nationalistic and "antiimperialist" foreign and domestic policies in Indonesia, and Moscow's relations with Indonesia soon began to warm. The first trade agreement was signed in August 1956, and Sukarno visited Moscow the following month. Soon Indonesia was receiving massive aid from the Soviet Union (amounting to over $1.5 billion in credits)—most of which had no positive effect on Indonesia's development.

There was great praise in the Soviet press for Sukarno's steadily more radical policies: his nationalization measures of 1958, the proclamation of "guided democracy" in 1959, and his eight-year plan for strengthening the state sector, announced in 1960. Especially as compared to India, Indonesia's domestic policies seemed worthy of enthusiastic support to the Soviets. In this atmosphere, the PKI (as one of the few legalized communist parties in the Soviet client states) fared extremely well, and it had over two million members by 1960.

As the most populous state in Southeast Asia, Indonesia had special regional significance that was intensified by Sukarno's burning desire to be a major world figure. Khrushchev was willing to help feed this ambition, and he was generous with Soviet assistance in bolstering Indonesia's military capabilities. The USSR also gave Sukarno diplomatic and propaganda backing in his noisy campaign to absorb Dutch-held West Irian. Khrushchev's memoirs record how Sukarno managed to extract a pledge of Soviet military assistance in the planned attack on West Irian, and then "leaked" this information to the United States in an effort to persuade Washington to pressure the Dutch to concede the territory. The late Soviet leader's reminiscences also describe his 1960 visit to Indonesia, where he was reportedly overwhelmed by Sukarno's "theatrical streak," his obsession with pompous displays and grand processions, and his well-known "weakness for women."[47]

Khrushchev wistfully observes in this account that if the PKI leadership had "acted wisely," showing more resistance to the seductions of Mao Zedong, Indonesia might have chosen the "correct course" and become one of the world's most powerful socialist countries. His reference is to the fact that in the early 1960s the PKI began to lean toward the Chinese side in the Sino-Soviet dispute, managing in the process to carry Sukarno with it. The Soviets watched helplessly as Sukarno began to adopt even more reckless policies, the most notable of which was his campaign to "crush Malaysia." Unlike the successful drive to acquire West Irian, this confrontation was not an anticolonial conflict, and Sukarno's heated rhetoric and military preparations (much of which was probably designed to satisfy internal political needs) caused the

Soviets to fear a possible East-West confrontation. A militant Indonesia, once regarded in Moscow as serving the "antiimperialist" purposes of the USSR, now appeared only to be playing into the hands of Beijing. With China's encouragement, Sukarno withdrew Indonesia from the United Nations and announced his intention to join with China in a New Emerging Forces Organization. Although Sukarno's objectives were thus radically divergent from those of Moscow, the Soviets were reluctant to extricate themselves from the relationship, thereby abandoning Indonesia to the exclusive courtship of Beijing.

This situation was drastically altered with the events of September 30, 1965. An attempted coup by the PKI and its leftist allies in the Indonesian military was foiled by more moderate officers, and the result was not only the removal of Sukarno to a figurehead position but also a massive slaughter of the PKI. The toll in this extended massacre reached into the hundreds of thousands, and although it was met in Moscow by harsh denunciations and a cutoff of aid, the Soviets' sense of loss was undoubtedly mitigated by the realization that the big loser in Indonesia was China. The events there, together with the setback to China's prestige resulting from the Indo-Pakistani war and the move toward neutrality in the Sino-Soviet dispute by her two allies among the Asian ruling communist parties (North Vietnam and North Korea), combined to make 1965 a year of disaster for Beijing's strategy in Asia.

The new Indonisian regime of General Suharto adopted a pro-Western foreign policy orientation along with its virulent domestic anticommunism. By virtue of its previous massive aid, however, the Soviet Union continued to be involved in Indonesia. Negotiations opened in 1966 on the subject of rescheduling Jakarta's enormous debt to Moscow, but no agreement was reached until 1970. Gradually Indonesia's large military machine almost ground to a halt due to Jakarta's inability to obtain spare parts for the Soviet-supplied equipment.

As the Chinese emerged from a hiatus in their diplomacy caused by the cultural revolution, and particularly with the opening of the Sino-American relationship, Moscow has shown renewed interest in establishing a presence in Indonesia, if only to act as a balancer in the new triangular competition in Asia. Diplomatic relations with Jakarta were reopened in 1972, and a new aid agreement was negotiated two years later, accompanied by an increase in Soviet-Indonesian trade. Despite this revival of activity, however, Indonesia has not recovered its former place as a high priority in Soviet policy in the Third World.

Indochina is another area in which Soviet policy in recent years has responded to the strategic needs of the triangular competition with the United States and China. Moscow's influence in North Vietnam (the DRV) had declined at the beginning of the 1960s as Hanoi increasingly sided with China and Khrushchev moved to disengage the USSR from the heightened conflict in the area. Not only did the Soviets agree to the neutralization of Laos in 1962, but they appeared to perceive no benefit for themselves in the revival of armed struggle in South Vietnam. As the United States stepped up its own military involvement there, and as it steadily focused on China as its primary antagonist in Asia, the Soviets seemed content to watch from the sidelines.

With the ouster of Khrushchev, however, the Soviet Union began to move toward more active engagement in Indochina. The beginning of the American bombing of North Vietnam in the midst of Prime Minister Kosygin's visit to that country in February 1965 evoked from Moscow a larger commitment of aid in Hanoi. The Soviets were apparently motivated both by their "fraternal obligation" to stave off the collapse of a communist regime and by their desire to entice Hanoi away from its pro-Beijing stance in the Sino-Soviet dispute. On the other hand, the Soviet leaders seemed to discourage a further escalation of the fighting in Vietnam, fearing that they might be drawn into direct confrontation with the United States. Soviet assistance was thus calculated to enable Hanoi to hold its own in the conflict, tying down American forces until Washington's will was broken and a satisfactory political settlement could be achieved.

The signing of the Vietnam peace agreements in 1973 was hailed by the Soviets as an important antiimperalist victory, which both gave "graphic evidence of the effectiveness of the internationalism of the Soviet Union" and opened up "new possibilities" for "extending detente."[48] In subsequent meetings with Le Duan and other North Vietnamese leaders, the Soviets steadily increased their influence in the DRV, primarily by means of the provision of large-scale assistance for economic reconstruction. By 1975, when communist forces had achieved complete victory in Indochina, the North Vietnamese had moved even closer to the Soviet position in the Sino-Soviet dispute, while expressing their support of Moscow's efforts "toward peace and social progress" that were "making the course of detente irreversible."[49]

But by the late 1970s, it was only in Vietnam, of all the countries or communist parties of Southeast Asia, in which the Soviet Union enjoyed greater influence than its great-power rivals. The reductions in the levels of Soviet assistance and involvement (except in the DRV) signaled that Southeast Asia was not regarded as a high priority area in Soviet calculations. In Laos, the Soviets established a presence competitive with China's in the new communist state, but in communist Cambodia Moscow had virtually no influence, due both to ideological antipathy and to the Pol Pot regime's resentment of the unseemly Soviet delay in breaking with the predecessor government. This situation had changed at the end of the decade, by virtue of the establishment of Vietnamese hegemony over Laos and Cambodia, but Moscow's influence there was indirect and depended almost entirely on the maintenance of its friendship with Hanoi. In Burma, Moscow's influence and activities have been limited by Rangoon's strong desire to maintain its neutrality. In Malaysia and the Philippines, the Soviets have only recently opened diplomatic relations (in 1968 with Malaysia and in 1975 with Manila), and although commercial relations have expanded rapidly with Kuala Lumpur, the Soviet role is primarily as a "balancer" to American and Chinese influence.

The centerpiece of Moscow's recent diplomacy in South and Southeast Asia has been the campaign, originated in 1969, for the establishment of a "system of collective security in Asia." The thrust of this effort has been the containment of China's influence in Asia; Beijing itself has characterized the Soviet plan as a "sinister" scheme picked up "from the garbage heap of the notorious warmonger Dulles."[50] Moscow has denied that its proposal was aimed against China, but it has been deliberately ambiguous about what the purpose or form of the proposed "collective security system" might be. On a very modest level, the proposal was an effective way of reminding the world that the Soviet Union considers itself an Asian as well as a European power, and that it intends to play an active role in Asian security matters. A second motive has been to serve notice that the Soviets are aware of the changing military balance in Asia, beginning with the British withdrawal from "east of Suez," and to alert smaller Asian states to the danger of allowing American or Japanese "imperialism" to take up the British role. Even if no Soviet-sponsored "collective security system" were to result, by promoting the erosion of existing security arrangements (such as the bilateral American pacts with Pakistan, Thailand, and the Philippines), the Soviets have achieved a net gain.

Despite their loud protestations against the notion that they are seeking to "fill a vacuum," the behavior of the Soviets in the Indian Ocean has indicated that they are sensitive to such an opportunity. The Soviets can already calculate an increased political impact from the present limited naval force which, with the reopening of the Suez Canal, can be linked with the more formidable force in the Mediterranean. In the context of this expanded presence, the Soviet proposal may be seen as an invitation to the states of the area to discuss with Moscow, either collectively or individually, cooperative security arrangements for the post-Vietnam era. Significantly, none of the noncommunist states of Asia has given an unambiguous endorsement to the Soviet proposal. Nevertheless, Moscow has continued to ennunciate it as a symbol both of its continuing concern over the threats represented by Beijing and Washington and its own dedication to "peace and stability" on the continent.[51]

INCURSIONS INTO AMERICA'S BACKYARD

Parallel with the relatively limited scope of Soviet activity in China's backyard—Southeast Asia—the Soviets have also maintained a rather low level of involvement in the primary sphere of influence of the United States—Latin America. Especially in its earlier activity in the Third World, Moscow apparently proceeded from the assumption that the United States would retain its domination in the lands to the south. Khrushchev's formulation of the "Zone of Peace" in 1956 omitted Latin America altogether, as did the primary Soviet-sponsored front organization in the Third World, the Afro-Asian People's Solidarity Organization. Moscow's "geographic fatalism" reflected both a calculation of American strength and of its own limited resources to support activities in that area. Events such as the U.S. intervention in Guatemala in 1954 in support of the removal of the leftist Arbenz government only served to confirm the Soviet perception.

Fidel Castro's Cuban revolution, which triumphed on New Year's Day 1959, was to bring about a change in Moscow's perceptions both of Soviet opportunities and capabilities in Latin America and of Washington's ability to insulate the hemisphere from communist influence. At the beginning of the 1960s, the USSR launched a more active policy to encourage anti-American sentiment and activity in Latin America, and in the process it began gradually to incorporate the area into the overall strategy for the Third World.

From a doctrinal standpoint, however, Latin America was still differentiated from Asia and Africa by the relatively greater extent of capitalist development as well as by the relative absence of struggles for political independence. Although this area is characterized by a great political and economic diversity, this fact was not always recognized by Soviet analysts. On the whole, the Soviets did not seek to apply to Latin America the special categories and tactics developed by "creative Marxist-Leninists" in the mid-1960s. The director of the Soviet Institute for Latin America declared in 1970 that:

Socio-economic backwardness in these countries, plus the domination by latifundism and the presence of strong precapitalist relations in the countryside, oppression by foreign monopolies—all this testifies to the fact that the road to socialism on the continent lies basically through a people's democratic revolution.[52]

According to this analysis, the objective and subjective conditions for such a transformation were said already to exist in five countries: Argentina, Brazil, Chile, Mexico, and Uruguay.

By this time, of course, Cuba had long since declared its own dedication to the path of socialist transformation and it stood as the USSR's sole ally in the hemisphere. But the development of Soviet-Cuban relations had by no means been smooth; almost a decade of mistrust and tension preceded the metamorphosis of Fidel Castro into an avowed member of the Soviet orbit. Castro had developed his own distinctive approach to Marxism-Leninism, which

rejected a strong institutionalized communist party, prescribed a rapid transformation of the economy, and projected a different strategy for revolution
in Latin America than the path preferred by the Soviets. This, together
with Castro's strong nationalistic wariness of "strings" in dealings with other
states and his suspicion of Moscow's "superpower" interests (a legacy of the
Cuban Missile Crisis) made for an uneasy relationship between Moscow and
Havana.

At the end of the 1950s, the Soviet Union had established diplomatic relations in Latin America only with Argentina, Brazil, Mexico, and Uruguay.
Moscow was thus without official representation in Havana in 1959, and even
the Cuban Communist Party had been relatively isolated from Castro's guerrilla forces in the Sierra Maestre. The first official Soviet contact with the new
regime came in the form of a visit by Anastas Mikoyan early in 1960; the occasion was marked by restraint on the part of the Soviets, who were not eager
to stir up American resentment in the months prior to the Paris summit conference. But in the wake of the decline in U.S.-Soviet relations following the
U-2 incident, the Soviets were willing to be more forthcoming in their approach
to Castro. In July 1960, accusing the United States of planning "criminal
steps" against Cuba, Khrushchev warned that Soviet artillerymen could support the island nation with their rocketfire, and he offered to break the U.S.
economic boycott against Castro by purchasing Cuban sugar. A few months
later, with Ché Guevara's trip to Moscow (and Beijing), Cuba began to build
its ideological ties with the communist countries.

Following the unsuccessful attempt to overthrow Castro at the Bay of Pigs,
Moscow offered to support Castro with all necessary assistance. There ensued
a rapid buildup of trade and aid ties between Cuba and the Soviet bloc. In
1959, Cuba had done 68 percent of its trade with the United States and only
2 percent with the Soviet bloc, but by 1962 this pattern had been sharply
reversed—trade with Washington was embargoed and almost 83 percent of
Cuba's trade was with the USSR and its East European allies.

This warming relationship suffered a sharp setback in the aftermath of the
missile crisis, when Castro openly attacked Khrushchev for his attempt to save
the peace by pledging to remove Soviet offensive weapons from Cuba. Castro
showed his pique by only belatedly supporting Moscow in its quarrel with
China and by disregarding Soviet advice on the development of the Cuban
economy. Despite the rapid deterioration of the economy Castro proved unwilling to toe the Soviet line, and in 1966-67 he disavowed the use of material
incentives in the economy, launched an attack on "bureaucratism" in economic
decision making, and declared that Cuba was embarking on the stage of building
communism. At the same time he stepped up his efforts to export Cuban-style
revolution elsewhere in Latin America. The Soviets showed relative patience
with this behavior; they did not attempt to cut off economic aid or trade,

but neither did they give Castro a blank check by formalizing the Soviet commitment to the defense of Cuba.

This phase of Castro's policies came to an end with the death of Ché Guevara in the Bolivian jungles in 1967. But the Cuban dictator was still not ready to act the part of a dutiful client of Moscow. He turned his endorsement of the Warsaw Pact invasion of Czechslovakia into a complaint at the lack of a firm defense commitment: "Will they send the divisions of the Warsaw Pact to Cuba if the Yankee imperialists attack our country, or even in the event of threat . . . if our country requests it?"[53] He continued to pursue policies disruptive of stable economic development, and in the process accumulated a trade deficit with the USSR amounting to $2.687 billion by 1973. In an effort to reverse the pattern of below-plan sugar harvests, in 1970 he launched a nationwide campaign for a 10 million-ton harvest and, while failing to achieve the target, managed to disrupt the economy even more.

Castro failed to rid himself of dependence on Moscow and therefore had no option but to seek to rebuild his ties to the Soviet Union. In April 1970 his brother Raul went to Moscow to negotiate a resumption of Soviet military aid, and Fidel himself made two visits to the USSR in 1972. By means of Cuba's admission to COMECON, Castro submitted the Cuban economy to the discipline of integration with the Soviet and East European economies. And though he still failed to achieve a bilateral defense pact, Castro did extract from Brezhnev a strong pledge of support: "Socialist Cuba is not alone, is a strong constituent part of the world system of socialism safeguarded by Soviet support."[54] An increase of Soviet naval visits to Cuba, however, provoked a diplomatic crisis with the United States in the fall of 1970, which resulted in a Soviet agreement not to seek to use the Cuban port of Cienfuegos as a base for missile-carrying submarines.

By the time of the September 1973 meeting of nonaligned nations at Algiers, Castro was the Third World's strongest defender of the Soviet Union, and he proved his loyalty with his fiery rebuttals to attacks made on Moscow at that meeting. His support was rewarded the following January with a visit to Havana from Soviet party leader Brezhnev. The Russian used the occasion to proclaim that the goals of superpower detente superseded but did not contradict the goals of revolution—in effect telling Castro that Soviet-U.S. detente did not threaten Cuba's independence. While denouncing as "inadmissable and criminal" any attempts to export counterrevolution, Brezhnev also declared: "Nor are the communists supporters of the 'export of revolution.' A revolution matures on the domestic soil of this or that country." How or when it breaks out, he indicated, and what forms and methods it employs, are matters for the people of the given country to decide. After delivering this lecture to Castro, Brezhnev added a message for the United States: "We know well, as others evidently know too, that Soviet weapons in the hands of Cubans are not weapons for attacking anybody, not a means of aggravating the international situation," but serve the "just cause" of "defending the revolutionary gains" of Cuba.[55]

With reassurrances such as this, the Soviets hope eventually to gain American recognition of the Castro regime, symbolizing Washington's acquiescence to the irreversibility of communism in Cuba and its tacit recognition of the legitimacy of the Soviet presence. Soviet statements suggest that they perceive that the United States is increasingly isolated in Latin America on this question, and that Washington will before long be driven to concede the point. Although the resumption of Cuban-American trade might ease the Soviet economic burden somewhat, it is not likely to alter the situation radically. Cuba currently ranks about sixth or seventh on the list of Soviet trading partners; she is almost totally dependent on the USSR for her petroleum imports and imports large quantities of industrial and agricultural machinery, fertilizer, and grain. Such dependence is not easy to erase, especially in light of the enormous debt (refinanced in 1972) that Cuba owes to Moscow.

Castro's well-known reluctance to step out of the spotlight may have prompted the Soviets to enlist his assistance in the growing communist drive in southern Africa. There is little doubt that Moscow is more willing to have Cuban soldiers actively assisting the revolutionary cause in Africa than under the nose of the United States in Latin America. The Soviet Union does not regard the Cuban model as applicable in the western hemisphere, where it prefers to sponsor broad united fronts in which communist parties collaborate with other leftist groups in an antiimperialist alliance using primarily peaceful and parliamentary tactics. On numerous occasions, the Soviets have shown their contempt for the "ultra-left" groups (such as the Tupamaros in Uruguay) who employ violent "gangster tactics" and thereby play into the hands of the "reactionaries."

The seeming embodiment of the Soviet-preferred model for Latin American revolution appeared in Chile, where in September 1970 the Socialist party candidate, Marxist physician Salvador Allende, was elected president as the head of a leftist coalition in a three-way race. Allende had pledged to create a nationalist, popular, democratic, and revolutionary government in Chile that would move the country toward socialism but without totalitarian methods. His victory was hailed by the Soviets as an event of historical significance for Latin America, demonstrating the effectiveness of united-front tactics in that setting. During Allende's tenure in office, Soviet analysts even concluded that the Chilean model had validity beyond the hemisphere, and might also be successfully applied in West European settings such as Portugal.

From the time of Allende's election, his Soviet supporters appeared to be nervous about his staying power, and they emphasized the continuing tasks of antiimperialist and anticapitalist struggle that lay ahead for Allende's regime.

In accordance with the prevailing Soviet mood regarding Third World radicals, a leading Soviet analyst warned in April 1971 against tendencies on the part of the "radical-democratic intelligentsia . . . to underestimate the difficulties in building socialism." The Chilean revolutionary forces were reminded of the importance of enlisting the support of the socialist states and of all progressive forces (that is, of building firm ties to the USSR) and of activating the working people and creating an advanced political organization (that is, of giving a major role to the Chilean Communist Party).[56]

Soviet-Chilean ties were indeed advanced the following month by the visit to Moscow of the Chilean foreign minister, and in June, in a meeting with representatives of Allende's Chilean Socialist Party, Brezhnev sought to strengthen that party's bonds with communists in both Chile and the USSR. Allende himself visited Moscow at the end of 1972. The Soviets extended assistance to the new Chilean regime, but their caution was reflected in the limited amount that they gave. In October an important article by CPSU Party Secretary Boris Ponomarev, generally optimistic in tone, pointed to six lessons that could be found in the evolving Chilean situation: Allende's experience, he said, demonstrated that: (1) the working class is the main force of the revolution; (2) the unity of the working class, and especially of communists and socialists, is a valuable condition of success; (3) a democratic government can assume power peacefully (though its electoral activity must be combined with mass activity); (4) a correct economic policy is important; (5) the moral support of the socialist countries is vital; and (6) the revolution must know "how to defend itself."[57]

Although pronouncements such as this one usually contained warnings that the process of revolution in Chile was not "irreversible," the Soviets none-theless appear to have been caught by surprise by Allende's overthrow in September 1973. But Moscow quickly insisted that the failure in Chile was not due to any flaw in the doctrinal prescription; rather, Allende had ignored its emphasis on retaining the support of the middle classes, and he had fallen prey to the excesses of radical leftists. From the perspective of the following summer, Ponomarev found a new lesson in the Chilean experience: "the tre-mendous importance of being prepared to change promptly the forms of struggle, peaceful and non-peaceful, and of the ability to repel the counter-revolutionary violence of the bourgeoisie with revolutionary violence."[58] Allende, the Soviets decided, had made a mistake in dealing with the key ques-tion of the conquest of power; he should have neutralized the danger of a coup in advance by infiltrating the army in order to "democratize" it. More-over, he had failed to heed Soviet advice on economic policy, and by proceeding too fast toward socialism, he had alienated key sections of the population.

The Soviet Union severed its relations with the Pinochet junta and pro-ceeded to flood its media with denunciations of the Chilean "fascists" and the horrors they committed against democracy. Appealing for the unity of revolutionary forces and seeking to isolate the junta internationally and domestically, the Soviets made the release of Chilean Communist leader Luis Corvalan the central slogan in their propaganda campaign. In an unusual move, Moscow and Santiago assented at the end of 1976 to an exchange (negotiated by Amnesty International) of Soviet dissident Vladimir Bukovskii for the imprisoned Corvalan.

After the Chilean coup, the USSR's interest in Latin America continued at a very low level. Moscow's warmest relations were with the leftist military regime in Peru. The Soviets had once viewed juntas with undifferentiated distaste, but they belatedly discovered in the 1970s that some military regimes might show "revolutionary-democratic" tendencies that accelerated a leftward course of development. Emphasizing in particular Peru's "antiimperialist" policies, Moscow developed close economic ties with the Peruvian government, which became the first South American regime to receive military assistance from the Soviet Union. In this case as in general, however, the USSR was cautious in extending its commitments, taking advantage of such opportunities as might arise in Latin America, but keeping a wary eye on the effects of its activities on its relations with the United States.

AFRICAN ADVENTURES

More than in any other region of the Third World, communist parties in Africa were virtually nonexistent in the Stalinist era, and yet there too the Soviets denounced noncommunist nationalists as puppets and prescribed an orthodox strategy stressing "proletarian" revolutionary activity. Only with the Khrushchev reassessment in the mid-1950s did the Soviets become sensitive to the anti-Western political and economic potential of the independence movements in Black Africa. Moscow's first embassies in the area were opened in 1958 in Ghana and Guinea. The latter was judged a more promising target for Soviet influence, for it had broken with French plans to join the former African colonies in a French Community, and it was consequently being subjected to substantial pressure. To Guinea's plea for aid Moscow replied with credits and trade, and within a few years the communist bloc was providing over 85 percent of the capital needs for Guinea's development plan.

In Guinea as in many other African states the nationalist elite soon formed one-party regimes, and the Soviets adjusted their strategy to accommodate the development of party-to-party ties between the CPSU and the more radical ruling parties of the continent. In a break with precedent, delegations from the single parties of Ghana, Guinea, and Mali were invited to attend the Twenty-second Congress of the CPSU in 1961. By 1964, some of the more optimistic

Soviet analysts were proclaiming that the "revolutionary-democratic" leaders of such states could proceed directly to the building of socialism, as though the absence of capitalist patterns of ownership in these countries were an advantage to their more rapid transformation.

The boldest attempt by Moscow to capitalize on the independence struggle in order to establish a revolutionary foothold in Africa came not in these West African states but in the Belgian Congo (now Zaire). Little prepared by the Belgian colonialists for political independence, the Congo's declaration of independence in July 1960 was hailed by the Soviets as a major victory over colonialism. The new prime minister, Patrice Lumumba, announced that he was a nationalist, not a communist, and he declared a policy of "positive neutrality." But the new state's independence day confidence was soon shattered by a mutiny of the Belgian-trained army, followed shortly by the announced secession of the strategic copper-producing province of Katanga. Though uninvited, Belgium dispatched paratroopers to the Congo to protect its citizens (and their economic holdings). The Soviet Union charged that the entire incident had been instigated by Belgium and its NATO allies and offered to take "decisive measures to stop the aggression," but Lumumba appealed instead to the United Nations for assistance. A Security Council resolution authorized the Secretary-General to create an emergency peace-keeping force for the Congo (ONUC), but when these troops failed immediately to expel the Belgians or end the Katangan secession, a desperate Lumumba denounced the United Nations's handling of the crisis and accepted Khrushchev's offer of assistance. But the limited amounts of Soviet aid that reached the Congo were not able to stabilize Lumumba's regime, and in September, amidst growing chaos, General Mobutu seized power, displacing the prime minister and ordering the Soviets out of the country.

Moscow's effort to capitalize on the instability in the Congo in order to gain unilateral political advantage against the West deeply alarmed the Afro-Asian majority at the United Nations. Together with Secretary-General Hammarskjöld, the General Assembly majority, seeking to use the international organization to insulate the Congo from cold war competition, called for all assistance to the country to be channeled through the U.N. forces. The USSR broke with Hammarskjöld over this issue, and in December it threw its support in the Congo to Vice-Premier Antoine Gizenga, who declared his regime in the provincial capital of Stanleyville the legitimate successor to the Lumumba government. Gizenga, who had graduated from a Marxist-Leninist training school in Guinea and traveled in the communist bloc, launched a civil war against the central military regime. The Soviets sensed the opportunity to establish their influence in a left-leaning enclave and sought to rush additional military assistance to Gizenga's forces, but their shipments were halted by the Sudanese government.

Without the capability for logistical support of the leftist regime, Moscow sought to broaden its diplomatic support among the Afro-Asian states. The Soviet campaign was greatly aided by Lumumba's murder in captivity; this event was used by Soviet propaganda to focus hostility on both the central government and Hammarskjöld, who was still withholding the ONUC forces from participation in the civil conflict.

Amidst growing Soviet-sponsored diplomatic support and increasing military success, Gizenga suddenly disbanded his Stanleyville regime in August 1961 and rejoined the newly constituted civilian government under Prime Minister Adoula. He soon became disillusioned and later unsuccessfully sought to re-establish his leftist enclave.

As the new central government gained strength, it succeeded at the beginning of 1963, with ONUC's help, in reintegrating Katanga. In the fall of that year the entire Soviet diplomatic staff, still engaged in efforts to cultivate left-leaning Congolese politicians, was expelled for espionage by the Adoula government.

Not only did the Congo crisis have significance for the African independence movement, the East-West struggle, and the United Nations, it also should have taught the Soviet Union some valuable lessons regarding its involvement in Africa. The badly bungled effort to channel Soviet military assistance to the radical faction in the Congo pointed up not only the limits on Soviet capabilities but also the unpredictability of radical-nationalist politicians. The frequent shifts in composition of the central government in the Congo pointed up the volatility of postindependence politics in Africa and the riskiness of making substantial political investments there. And finally, the hostile reaction on the part of many Afro-Asian states to the Soviet effort to intervene unilaterally in the internal affairs of one of their number should have demonstrated to the Soviets that Russians too can be regarded by Africans as unwelcome white-skinned perpetrators of great-power political schemes.

Subsequent years have brought many more demonstrations of the mortality of Soviet-aided politicians in Africa, from the ouster of Ghana's Nkrumah in 1966 and of Mali's Keita in 1968 to the assassination of President Ngoubai of the People's Republic of the Congo (Brazzaville) in 1977. Post-Khrushchev Soviet strategy in Africa places more emphasis in the choice of targets on a country's strategic importance than its ideological potential and thus the Soviets have not generally allowed the ouster of their leftist friends to interfere with the continuation of profitable political and economic relationships. As one example of the triumph of expedience and strategic benefit over ideological principle, Moscow gave military aid and diplomatic support to the central government in Nigeria in the late 1960s in its struggle against breakaway Biafra, even though Soviet analysts regarded the Biafran leaders as more "progressive." By siding with the likely (and eventual) winner in this conflict, the USSR managed to increase its influence in one of the largest and most strategically important African countries.

Excellent harbors and a strategic position at the junction of the Red Sea and the Indian Ocean give the "Horn" of Africa a special importance in Soviet calculations, particularly in the period since 1968 when the Soviet navy has sought facilities for its Indian Ocean squadron. Moscow's special relationship with Somalia, institutionalized through the 1974 treaty of friendship and cooperation, was thus founded not only on that country's "progressive" leanings, but, more importantly, on its willingness to allow the Soviets to expand and make use of the facilities at the port of Berbera, including an airfield, drydock, fuel tanks, communication station, and ammunition dump, as well as berthing facilities. Yet despite the heavy assistance Moscow provided the Somalis, its position there was fragile; in dealings with the United States and with Saudi Arabia, the Somalis showed signs in 1976 of seeking to balance their relationships to avoid overdependence on the USSR. For its part, Moscow's willingness to sponsor and support the Marxist-oriented regime in neighboring Ethiopia was a sign of the Soviet Union's desire to "hedge its bets." With the outbreak of war between Somalia and Ethiopia in the summer of 1977 in the disputed Ogaden territory it also represented a risk that the Soviet military investment in these two rival states might go up in smoke. And indeed, by the end of the year the Somali government had abrogated its friendship treaty with the USSR and ousted Soviet personnel from the country, terminating the Soviet presence at Berbera.

The Soviets have made seemingly great strides in southern Africa since 1974 by again enlisting the revolutionary impulse as a principal tactic in the effort to extend their influence into strategically important areas. In Angola, the Popular Movement for the Liberation of Angola (MPLA) had been receiving Soviet support since the early 1960s. Moscow stepped up its assistance in 1974 as the triumph of the Armed Forces Movement in Portugal presaged the end of Lisbon's colonial rule in Africa and intensified the struggle among the MPLA and two other nationalist factions for control of the country. Angola's vast natural resources and strategic location made it a particularly valued prize; fearing that it would fall under exclusive Soviet influence, the United States and China soon increased their own assistance to a rival faction.

In contrast to 1960, the Soviets now had the capabilities to render massive amounts of military assistance to their African friends; in 1975–76 an estimated $300 million in military aid (including 122-mm. rocket launchers, tanks, and MiG-21 fighters) reached the Soviet-backed forces. Most significant, however, was the introduction in May 1975 of Cuban military advisers, followed by large numbers of troops (eventually totaling between 15,000 and 20,000 men).[59] The Cuban presence, made possible only by the logistical and material support of the Soviet Union, not only tipped the scales in favor of the MPLA but also infuriated the Ford Administration, causing it to charge Moscow with violating the "rules of the game" of detente.

Its advantage in ability to supply arms was also enabling Moscow to win out over Beijing in the competition for influence with the liberation forces (FRELIMO) in Mozambique. By 1976, Soviet-aided and Marxist-oriented governments were in power in both of these former Portuguese colonies, which now were open to use as bases for further "liberation struggle" against the white-dominated regimes of Rhodesia (Zimbabwe), Southwest Africa (Namibia), and South Africa. By 1977 both states had signed long-term treaties of mutual cooperation with the USSR, and their ruling parties, affirming a Marxist-Leninist orientation, had concluded cooperative agreements with the CPSU.

Aware that the tide of Soviet influence was rising with the continuation of illegal minority rule in Zimbabwe and Namibia, and that an open racial war in southern Africa could destroy moderate forces on both sides, Secretary of State Kissinger joined American efforts to those of Britain in a concerted effort to achieve a negotiated settlement in the fall of 1976. The changed American position threatened the prior Soviet advantage, and Moscow's press and diplomats launched an angry attack on Kissinger's peace-making mission, labeling it as an "imperialist-racist plot." The seeming collapse of the Western effort to negotiate a settlement was followed by simultaneous and well-publicized tours of East and South Africa in the spring of 1977 by Soviet President Podgornyi and Cuban Premier Castro, concluded by a meeting between Castro and Brezhnev in Moscow.

Clearly the Soviets, in concert with their Cuban allies, were making a major effort in the second half of the 1970s to capitalize on the unstable situation in southern Africa in order to increase communist influence in this strategic area of the continent. Moscow seemed to have overcome the logistical limitations that had afflicted its strategy in the Congo years before. And yet the other limitations to Soviet (or, more generally, great-power) influence in Africa remained: the volatility of political regimes and affiliations and the fierce nationalism of Africa elites, which makes them wary of dependence on any outside power.

SOVIET POLICY AND THE CHALLENGES OF THE FUTURE

In two decades of active involvement, the Soviet Union has acquired a considerable stake in areas of the Third World. We should not make the mistake, however, of assuming that this large investment implies that the Third World is an objective of highest priority for the Soviet leaders. The Soviets also have vital interests elsewhere in the world. The compatibility of one of them—the detente relationship with the United States—with the promotion of a national-liberation struggle" in southern Africa has been actively challenged by the United States ever since the closing months of the Ford Administration. The Soviets, however, have denied that a conflict existed between their obligations under detente and their commitment to the "liberation struggle." As Secretary Brezhnev put it at the Twenty-fifth Party Congress in 1976:

Detente does not in the slightest way abolish, and cannot abolish or change the laws of the class struggle. We do not conceal the fact that we see detente as a way to create more *favorable* conditions for peaceful socialist and com-munist construction.[60]

Indeed, he might have added, support of Third World "liberation" movements remains a primary means for the Soviets to demonstrate—at a time when they are under heavy challenge—their continuing ideological *bona fides* and loyalty to revolutionary obligation. We need not, however, accept at face value Brezhnev's bald claim that this is the *only* Soviet motivation:

The Soviet Union is not looking for any benefits for itself, is not hunting for concessions, is not trying to gain political supremacy and is not seeking any military bases. We are acting as our revolutionary conscience and our com-munist convictions permit us.[61]

In fact, the Brezhnev-era approach seems much more attuned to precisely such factors as the satisfaction of Soviet military and economic interests, just as it has lowered the expectation that Third World regimes are viable can-didates for the rapid transformation in socialism. The Soviet timetable is longer and the style more cautious than it was in Khrushchev's time, and in addition to such general and long-standing objectives of increasing Moscow's own influence, there are now more concrete goals such as gaining access to key resources or support facilities for naval expeditions or trade routes. For these objectives and the supporting range of tactics the term "counterimperialism" indeed seems most appropriate. This complex of interests, much more than the revolutionary impulse of ideological affinity, seems to provide Moscow's major criteria for the concentration of its energies and resources in the Third World.

In fact, the assumptions underlying the "revolutionary conscience" and "communist convictions" of the Soviet leaders have been under constant challenge in the Third World, and the wells of "creative Marxism-Leninism" seem to have run dry in the effort to salvage them. Socioeconomic change occurs in the Third World in ways quite different from the Soviet expectations; political change has been notoriously resistant to the neat categorization of Marxist analysis.

Ironically, states that are judged most "progressive" by one set of measures may still prove very reluctant to follow the ideological prescriptions or policy advice of the Soviet Union. The record of Soviet relations with states such as Egypt, India, Indonesia, and Ghana is replete with instances of Moscow's inability to influence its supposed friends and clients. When the issue is of marginal importance to it, a state might be disposed to follow its patron's lead, but in cases where its vital interests diverge from those of its great-power friend, the Third World state will frequently pursue an independent course. Given its own stake in the region and its fear of being displaced by a great-power rival, the patron is usually unable or unwilling to dictate or compel in such circumstances. As a recent study of Soviet and Chinese influence in the Third World concluded: "Soviet and Chinese policies seem to have made adjustments to the needs of Third World countries more often than the latters' decisions have yielded to the preferences of the Communist courters."[62]

The powerful force of nationalism has thus been a major obstacle to Moscow's effort to enlist the resources and support of the countries of the Third World behind its own vital objectives. Moreover, the Third World's growing determination to exert full political and economic sovereignty has recently underscored the large degree of incompatibility between its own purposes and preferences and those of the industrialized "great powers." At the United Nations and in special settings such as the May 1976 Nairobi U.N. Conference on Trade and Development (UNCTAD IV) or the August 1976 Colombo Conference of Non-Aligned Nations, the USSR has been finding itself in the uncomfortable position of being lumped together with other developed countries (the "North") and forced by the Third World (the "South") into a defensive position regarding its policies and tactics.

In response to this challenge, Moscow has sought to emphasize its own economic strength and developmental experience as resources freely available to the less developed countries and to reinforce the notion that there is a natural community of interests between itself and the Third World. The problems of underdevelopment, including food scarcity, overpopulation, illiteracy, mass underemployment, are all portrayed as consequences of the "crisis of capitalism" and the neocolonialist policies of the Western imperialists. To the extent that the program for a "New International Economic Order" attacks the policies and practices of the West, the Soviets are willing to give it their full support. And yet its sponsors (the "Group of 77," which included 111 countries at the time of UNCTAD IV) have also included in their platform demands for changes in the policies and behavior of the USSR and its East European allies. The barter system of trade, the noncovertibility of communist-bloc currencies, and the refusal of the bloc to grant trade preferences to Third World products have been particular objects of Third World dissatisfaction. The efforts of Soviet representatives to deny that the USSR bears any specific "obligation" or shares any collective responsibility for the worsening economic plight of the Third World are increasingly resented by spokesmen for the less developed countries.

What these trends suggest is that as the "South" collectively mobilizes its strength and resources in order to pursue its platform of demands against the industrialized "North," the Soviet leaders may find it increasingly difficult to define their interests in a way that is compatible with those of Third World states. Despite their efforts to distance themselves from the "imperialist" West, the Soviets are increasingly associated with "the other superpower" in the eyes of the world's "have-nots." The major challenge for Soviet policy in the coming decade may lie in Moscow's ability to adjust its doctrine and strategy to take account of this growing North-South conflict. And whether and how the Soviets accomplish this may well determine whether that conflict evolves into constructive dialogue or destructive confrontation.

NOTES

1. V. I. Lenin, "The Socialist Revolution and the Right of Nations to Self-Determination," in *The National-Liberation Movement in the East* (Moscow, 1957), p. 109. For a further discussion of the Leninist legacy, see Robert H. Donaldson, *Soviet Policy toward India: Ideology and Strategy* (Cambridge, Mass.: Harvard University Press, 1974), chap. 1.
2. In his speech to the founding Congress of the Cominform, quoted in Myron Rush, ed., *The International Situation and Soviet Foreign Policy* (Columbus, Ohio: Charles E. Merrill, 1970), p. 127.
3. I. I. Potekhin, "Stalinskaia teoriia kolonial'noi revoliutsii i natsional'no-osvoboditel'noe dvizhenie v tropicheskoi i iuznoi Afrike," [The Stalinist Theory of Colonial Revolution and the National Liberation Movement in Tropical and South Africa] *Sovetskaia etnografiia* [Soviet Ethnography], no. 1 (1950): 24-40.
4. Quoted in Rush, *The International Situation*, pp. 159-160.
5. Quoted in ibid., p. 184.
6. Christopher Bird, "Scholarship and Propaganda," *Problems of Communism*, March-April 1962, p. 37.
7. The Moscow Statement is reprinted in G. F. Hudson, et al., *The Sino-Soviet Dispute* (New York: Praeger, 1961), pp. 177-205.
8. B. N. Ponomarev, "O gosudarstve natsional'noi demokratii," [Concerning the National-Democratic State] *Kommunist*, no. 8 (1961) 33-48.
9. For a more detailed discussion, see Donaldson, *Soviet Policy toward India*, pp. 173-179.
10. A. Sobolev, "National Democracy—The Way to Social Progress," *World Marxist Review 6*, no. 2 (1963):41-42.

11. G. B. Starushenko, "Cherez obshchedemokraticheskie preobrazovaniia k sotsialisticheskim" [Through General-democratic Transformation to Socialist Transformation] *Kommunist,* no. 13 (1962): 108.
12. "For the Unity and Solidarity of the International Communist Movement," *Pravda,* December 6, 1963, pp. 2–5.
13. "N. S. Khrushchev's Replies to Questions Put by the Ghanaian Times, Alger Republicain, Le Peuple, and Botataung," *New Times* (supplement), no. 52 (1963): 42, 45.
14. Andrew M. Scott, *The Revolution in Statecraft: Informal Penetration* (New York: Random House, 1965), especially chapter 1.
15. Nicolas Lang, "'Diplomates' communistes en Afrique," *Est et Ouest,* November 16–30, 1961, p. 6.
16. These figures are from National Foreign Assessment Center, Central Intelligence Agency, *Communist Aid Activities in Non-Communist Less Developed Countries 1978: A Research Paper,* ER79-10412U, September 1979 (Washington: Central Intelligence Agency, 1979), and from Senior Specialists Division, Congressional Research Service, Library of Congress, *The Soviet Union and the Third World: A Watershed in Great Power Policy?,* Report to the Committee on International Relations, House of Representatives, 95th Congress, 1st Session, May 8, 1977 (Washington: Government Printing Office, 1977). (Hereafter, *The Soviet Union and the Third World*)
17. *Khrushchev Remembers: The Last Testament,* trans. and ed., Strobe Talbott, with a Foreword by Edward Crankshaw and an Introduction by Jerrold L. Schecter (Boston: Little, Brown and Company, 1974), p. 300 (Hereafter, *Khrushchev II*)
18. *The Soviet Union and the Third World,* pp. 66–69.
19. *New York Times,* September 25, 1960, p. 37.
20. *Pravda,* August 15, 1965, pp. 3–4.
21. R. A. Ul'ianovskii, "Nekotorye voprosy nekapitalisticheskogo razvitiia osvobodivshikhsia stran," [Some Problems of the Non-capitalist Development of the Liberated Countries] *Kommunist,* no. 1 (1966): 112.
22. Citations for these slogans may be found in Donaldson, *Soviet Policy toward India,* p. 301, fn. 69.
23. "The Supreme International Duty of a Socialist Country," *Pravda,* October 27, 1965, pp. 3–4, in *Current Digest of the Soviet Press 17,* 43 (1965): 6–9. Of course the implementation by force of one country's will upon another is not considered alien to Marxism-Leninism when the defense of the Soviet periphery is felt to be in danger, as the Czechoslovaks can attest.
24. L. I. Brezhnev, "The Cause of Lenin Lives on and Triumphs," *New Times,* (1970), p. 19.

25. E. M. Zhukov, "Contemporary Pace of Development of National-Liberation Revolution," in "Immediate Problems of the National-Liberation Movement," *International Affairs* (Moscow) no. 5 (1967): 52–54.
26. *Pravda,* October 5, 1976, p. 4.
27. *Pravda,* April 7, 1971, p. 6.
28. Richard Lowenthal, "Soviet Counterimperialism," *Problems of Communism 25,* no. 6 (November–December 1976): 52–63.
29. For a more detailed explication of this view of Soviet activity in the Indian Ocean, see Geoffrey Jukes, *The Indian Ocean in Soviet Naval Policy,* Adelphi Papers, no. 87, May 1972 (London: IISS), 30 pp.; Oles Smolanski, "Soviet Policy in the Persian Gulf," in Michael MccGwire, Ken Booth, and John McDonnell, eds., *Soviet Naval Policy: Objectives and Restraints* (New York: Praeger, 1975), pp. 278–286; and James McConnell, "The Soviet Navy in the Indian Ocean," in Michael MccGwire, ed., *Soviet Naval Developments: Capability and Context* (New York: Praeger, 1973), pp. 389–406.
30. Sergei Gorshkov, "Navies in War and Peace," *Morskoi sbornik,* no. 12, 1973, quoted in MccGwire, Booth and McDonnell, *Soviet Naval Policy,* p. 334.
31. Cited in McConnell, *The Soviet Navy,* p. 395.
32. Admiral Stansfield Turner, "The Naval Balance: Not Just a Numbers Game," *Foreign Affairs 55,* no. 2 (January, 1977): 346.
33. Ibid., especially pp. 342–344.
34. Quoted in A. Z. Rubinstein, *Red Star on the Nile* (Princeton, N.J.: Princeton University Press, 1977), p. 4.
35. Royal Institute of International Affairs, *Documents on International Affairs 1957* (London: RIIA, 1960), p. 238.
36. For further details, see Malcolm Mackintosh, *Strategy and Tactics of Soviet Foreign Policy* (New York: Oxford University Press, 1962), pp. 225–232.
37. *Khrushchev II,* pp. 344–345.
38. Michel Tatu, *Power in the Kremlin: From Khrushchev to Kosygin* (New York: Viking, 1967), p. 534.
39. See Rubinstein, *Red Star on the Nile,* pp. 144–153.
40. Ibid., pp. 192–202.
41. "Statements by N. A. Bulganin and N. S. Khrushchev in India, Burma and Afghanistan," *New Times,* Supplement, no. 52 (1955): 22.
42. Donaldson, *Soviet Policy toward India,* p. 118.
43. Alexander Kaznacheev, *Inside a Soviet Embassy: Experiences of a Russian Diplomat in Burma* (Philadelphia: Lippincott, 1962), p. 142.
44. This section draws on Donaldson, *Soviet Policy toward India,* pp. 225–227.
45. *Hindustan Times,* September 30, 1971.
46. This sections draws on Donaldson, *Soviet Policy toward India,* pp. 231–234.

47. *Khrushchev II*, pp. 314, 326–327.
48. *Pravda*, January 31, 1973.
49. *Pravda*, October 31, 1975.
50. "'System of Collective Security in Asia' Soviet Revisionism's Tattered Flag for Anti-China Military Alliance," *Peking Review 12*, no. 27 (1969): 22–23, 32–33.
51. For more on this subject, see Arnold L. Horelick, *The Soviet Union's 'Asian Collective Security' Proposal: A Club in Search of Members*, RAND Corporation Paper P-5195, March 1974, and Alexander O. Ghebhardt, "The Soviet System of Collective Security in Asia," *Asian Survey 13* (1973): 1075–1091.
52. *Pravda*, June 27, 1970.
53. Quoted in Leon Goure and Morris Rothenberg, *Soviet Penetration of Latin America* (Miami: University of Miami, 1975), p. 30.
54. *Pravda*, June 28, 1972.
55. *Pravda*, January 31, 1974.
56. R. A. Ul'ianovskii, in *Izvestiia*, April 25, 1971.
57. Boris Ponomarev, "Topical Problems in the Theory of the Revolutionary Process," *Kommunist*, no. 15 (October 1971), quoted in Goure and Rothenberg, *Soviet Penetration*, pp. 100–101.
58. Boris Ponomarev, "The World Situation and the Revolutionary Process," *World Marxist Review*, no. 6 (June 1974): 10.
59. *The Soviet Union and the Third World*, p. 107.
60. In *Documents and Resolutions: XXVth Congress of the CPSU* (Moscow: Novosti, 1976), p. 39.
61. In ibid., p. 16.
62. Alvin Z. Rubinstein, ed., *Soviet and Chinese Influence in the Third World* (New York: Praeger, 1975), p. 223.

Chapter 6
The Socialist System Becomes Polycentric

The Soviet Union operates within three networks of relationships all of which are interrelated: as a great power in the international system, as the leading member of the socialist state system, and as one of the two dominant parties of the world communist movement. The socialist state system, which can be considered a subsystem of the international system, became organized in the aftermath of World War II with the creation of the peoples democracies in Eastern Europe. Before that time the only socialist states were the Soviet Union and Mongolia (which became a peoples republic on November 26, 1924). The world communist movement, antedating the Russian Revolution, comprises all the communist parties throughout the world whether in or out of power. Only those parties in power—numbering 16 today—make up the world socialist system. These distinctions are important because the rules governing Soviet behavior in each arena—the international system, the socialist state system, and the world communist movement—are different, or at least partially different.

From the moment the Red Army started moving across Eastern Europe in 1944, laying the foundations for communist rule in the liberated countries, the Soviet leadership was confronted with the problem of defining the relationship between the Soviet Union and other socialist states. There was never the slightest doubt that Stalin intended to subordinate the peoples democracies to Soviet rule, but there were different ways by which this might be accomplished. One solution, of course, was simply to incorporate the Eastern European states as union-republics in an enlarged USSR. Stalin did in fact consider that possibility, ultimately rejecting it presumably as premature.[1] Equally effective control at perhaps less cost could have been achieved by installing leaders who would be completely subject to Stalin's directives in the different countries. These elites would be, in effect, puppets. Another approach toward the same end might be to permit a degree of internal autonomy but to maintain pressure by the traditional means available to great powers

190

to insure that the socialist states pursued pro-Soviet policies. Soviet control in such a relationship would put the countries of Eastern Europe in a position somewhere between that of a satellite or simply within the Soviet sphere of influence. As will be shown below, Stalin's techniques of control changed at different periods of time.

Stalin's techniques were not so readily available to his successors. A combination of circumstances forced both Khrushchev and Brezhnev to pursue more flexible policies toward the countries of Eastern Europe. Indeed, Stalin's successors were continuously faced with the problem of reexamining the rightful and proper relationship between socialist states, large and small. Clearly they were not ready to concede genuine independence to their neighbors, but they were prepared to abandon the near total control of Stalin for a high degree of influence instead. The socialist countries could pursue domestic economic policies different from those in the Soviet Union and, up to a point, they could even take an independent line in foreign policy, but only up to a point.

PROLETARIAN AND SOCIALIST INTERNATIONALISM

The question of defining the relationship between the Soviet Union and other socialist states is a doctrinal as well as a practical problem. Theory alone has never guided Soviet policy; quite the contrary, the doctrine has consistently been molded to meet the needs of policy. But because Soviet leaders claim Marxist-Leninist theory as the basis of their political system and all its policies, they are obliged to formulate some doctrinal construct for everything they do. They need the ideology to legitimize both their domestic and foreign policies.

As we have already observed, Marxism contains no theory of interstate relations. Lenin's theory of imperialism describes relations between capitalist nations under certain conditions but is irrelevant to the issue of interstate relations between socialist countries. The only theoretical concept that could be adapted to explain the relationship between socialist states was "proletarian internationalism." As conceived by Marx (and by Lenin before the revolution), proletarian internationalism referred to the unity of the working class. It assumed that the proletariat everywhere had a common interest in the overthrow of the bourgeoisie, that it had no loyalty to any particular nation or country. "Proletarian internationalism," said Lenin, "demands firstly that the interests of the proletarian struggle in one country be subordinated to the interests of the struggle on a world-wide basis, and secondly that a nation which has achieved victory over the bourgeoisie be able and willing to make the greatest national sacrifice for the sake of the overthrowing of international capital."[2] Implicit in this formulation was the idea of revolutionary war with which

Lenin did flirt for a brief period. After the Bolshevik revolution, proletarian internationalism increasingly came to mean devotion by the toilers of the world to the Soviet Union. Joseph Stalin with characteristic bluntness expressed that idea: "He is an internationalist who unreservedly, unhesitatingly and unconditionally is prepared to defend the U.S.S.R., because the U.S.S.R. is the base of the world revolutionary movement."[3] In addition to the defense of the socialist fatherland, proletarian internationalism in the interwar period came to be identified with Soviet nationality policies. Soviet theorists described the relationship between the various minorities and nationalities comprising the union republics as governed by the principle of proletarian internationalism, meaning the displacement of national antagonism with mutual assistance and cooperation.

There still was no need for a theory of relations between socialist states as long as the Soviet Union constituted the sole bastion of the dictatorship of the proletariat (since the 1920s, Mongolia was virtually a satellite of Soviet Russia). Nevertheless, in anticipation of that time when the revolution would spread, Soviet theorists expanded proletariat internationalism to cover relations between socialist states. While still close to the seat of Soviet power, Nikolai Bukharin wrote an article in which he referred to "the system of proletarian states." He asserted that "there is no clash of real interests between proletarian states whatsoever; on the contrary, their real interest is in maximum cooperation."[4] That essentially was the heart of the concept when the post-World War II period saw the realization of Bukharin's dream of a "system of proletarian states."

Proletarian internationalism may have served Stalin adequately but his successors eventually found the concept inadequate. Khrushchev and Brezhnev both confronted very different problems regarding intersocialist relations. Their foreign policies were largely efforts to adapt to the changing realities of the 1950s and 1960s. Part of that adaptation involved a modification of theory in order to meet the new realities. But the substance of the realities facing Khrushchev and those facing Brezhnev were quite different. Khrushchev was confronted with a need to recognize a greater independence and autonomy within the socialist camp. So was Brezhnev. The Czechoslovak crisis of the later 1960s, however, posed for the Russians the question of how much independence to concede to Eastern Europe and Brezhnev was forced to justify placing limits on the autonomy of a socialist state.

The ideological answer to these diverse needs was "socialist internationalism." This concept was developed under Khrushchev's administration to explain what was called a new type of international relations resulting from the creation of a community of socialist states. In the words of a Soviet specialist on international law, "Socialist internationalism is proletarian internationalism extended into the sphere of relations among sovereign socialist states."[5] Like its predecessor, socialist internationalism assumes an identity of vital interests between socialist states, an identiy not shared with capitalist states. The socialist states share common goals, a common ideology, a common enemy. There are two fundamental aspects to socialist internationalism. One recognizes the equality, independence, and territorial sovereignty of each socialist state. The other affirms the need for unity and the obligation of mutual assistance of all socialist states.[6]

In practice there is a potential incompatibility between the principles of sovereignty and unity embodied in socialist internationalism. The unity of the communist camp might not always permit each member to exercise its sovereignty as it desired. There is no doubt that Stalin's successors genuinely wanted to find a more flexible means of cooperation between the states of the communist camp, but they were never prepared to go so far as to permit any one of them to leave the camp. Thus in their 1957 Declaration the representatives of the Socialist states observed:

The Socialist countries base their relations on principles of complete equality, respect for territorial integrity, state independence and sovereignty, and non-interference in one another's affairs. These are vital principles. However, they do not exhaust the essence of relations between them. Fraternal mutual aid is part and parcel of these relations. This aid is a striking expression of Socialist internationalism.[7]

After the Czechoslovak crisis in 1968 Soviet theorists increasingly stressed the importance of "fraternal assistance." In the words of the concluding Document of the 1969 meeting of world communist parties: "Each Communist Party is responsible for its activity to its own working class and people and *at the same time,* to the international working class."[8] Not surprisingly, the ideological justification given by Leonid Brezhnev for the Soviet invasion of Czechoslovakia has come to be popularly known as the doctrine of "limited sovereignty." This doctrine as well as the events that precipitated it are examined below.

THE STALINIST INTERNATIONAL SYSTEM

There were two important forces that could prevent total Soviet domination of the countries of Eastern Europe: (1) the Western powers, notably Great Britain and the United States; and (2) nationalistic sentiment within the region itself. For almost two years these forces did indeed manage to secure some degree of autonomy for some of Soviet Russia's neighbors. Actually, only limited credit can be given to the Western powers for the relative freedom that prevailed initially east of the Iron Curtain. Roosevelt and

Churchill had extracted promises from Stalin at Yalta to support democratic and representative governments in Eastern Europe, and although allied diplomacy did exert pressure to admit noncommunists to governing coalitions, the fact remains that there was really little that the British or Americans were able or willing to do to stop the Russians from exercising their power in the area. Perhaps more significant was Soviet fear about what the West might do, if the Soviets acted too swiftly. Stalin was uncertain what limits the Americans might set to Communist control. As one close observer notes:

Stalin's behavior and his communications to the Yugoslav and Polish comrades suggest that the Soviet leaders feared that rash actions might precipitate a Western reaction or even induce the West to sign a separate agreement with some "bourgeois" anti-Nazi German elements, thereby depriving the USSR of its rightful share of the spoils of victory. In order to prevent concerted efforts to contain the Soviet Union, the task of the Communists outside the USSR were to make themselves an inseparable part of any postwar political structure and to participate in the reconstruction of the occupied states. A form of popular front was the very minimum which the USSR expected in East Europe.[9]

A more potent limitation on Soviet power was the force of Eastern European nationalism. Anti-Russian and anticommunist sentiment was sufficiently strong in the region to cause Stalin to move with some circumspection. Although prewar bourgeois political parties were greatly weakened by the war, the majority of workers identified with moderate socialist parties while the peasant parties remained strongly hostile to communism. With the possible exception of Bulgaria, the peoples of Eastern Europe opposed the idea of incorporation into the Soviet Union, the fate not too many years previously of Latvia, Lithuania, and Estonia. Even the local communist parties affirmed the importance of national independence. They denounced talk of a future union with the USSR as a bourgeois slander.

Stalin accordingly pursued a comparatively moderate course in bringing the area under control during the period from 1945 through 1947. No attempt was made to socialize the economies of Eastern Europe or to collectivize agriculture on a large scale. The constitutional structures of the Peoples Democracies varied considerably; and some remained a coalition of communist and noncommunist elements. More important, the national communist leaders during this period maintained an air of independence and on many issues acted independently of Moscow. A considerable diversity of policy was permitted among the nations of the region.

The theory of the Peoples Democracies provided an ideological justification for the nations of Eastern Europe to pursue social and economic policies that differed from those of the Soviet Union. In Marxist terminology a "Peoples

Democracy" had cast off bourgeois rule, thus permitting the beginning of popular reform, but had not yet established the "dictatorship of the prole- tariat" as had the Soviet Union. Thus it was not necessary for these countries to follow the USSR slavishly as a model—not yet. Zbigniew Brzezinski char- acterized communist policy during this period as one of "caution," "elasticity," and "camouflage."

In 1947, however, Soviet policy changed. Stalin apparently became surer of the international situation and the conditions within Eastern Europe. It became increasingly clear that the Western powers would not interfere how- ever far Stalin might go. Furthermore, the Soviet Union shortly became the dominant military power on the continent. Western power declined precipi- tiously as demobilization proceeded at a rapid pace in the United States while the Soviet Union was taking energetic steps to recover from the ravages of the war. Within the Soviet sphere of influence, Stalin was pleasantly surprised to observe that the noncommunist forces were considerably weaker than he had anticipated.

The official signal for the change in Soviet policy was the establishment of the Communist Information Bureau (Cominform) in September 1947 in the Polish resort town of Szklarska Poreba (near Warsaw). Ironically, the only opposition to the creation of the Cominform came from Wladyslaw Gomulka, representing the host party. (In retrospect, Gomulka's dissent appears to be one of the first instances of national communist opposition to Russian domi- nation of the socialist camp.) Another irony of the Cominform's origins was the strong support given to it by Josip Broz-Tito, head of Yugoslavia's Com- munist Party. The principal function of the new communist international organization was ostensibly to promote the construction of communism by an exchange of information among Europe's leading parties. It was not sup- posed to be a policymaking body like its predecessor, the Comintern. Besides the Soviet Union, membership in the organization included the parties of Yugoslavia, Poland, Hungary, Rumania, Bulgaria, and Czechoslovakia, as well as the powerful Western parties of Italy and France. (Albania was not included because it was scheduled to be incorporated into Yugoslavia.) To promote an exchange of information among Cominform members, a biweekly news- paper (later a weekly) was established with the cumbersome name, *For a Lasting Peace, For a People's Democracy*. It is believed that Stalin personally selected the name so that every time it was repeated by a Western source renewed cur- rency would be given to the current slogan of Soviet policy. It was at the Cominform's founding meeting that Andrei Zhdanov made the vitriolic speech, noted above, that heralded a new Soviet hard line toward the West.

The real significance of the Cominform had less to do with relations be- tween the Soviet Union and the West than it had to do with those between the Soviet Union and its Eastern European neighbors. Its functions were to curb the nationalistic and independent tendencies that had been growing within the communist elites of Europe and to accelerate the speedy takeover of power by Communists in Czechoslovakia and Hungary.[10] Though its accomplishments were meager at best, it marked the beginning of a uniform system of satellite states. Between 1947 and 1953 (the year of Stalin's death), the socialist states underwent a profound economic and political revolution that in effect converted them to genuine satellites of the Soviet Union. One might say that Stalin tried to do to them what he did to his own country in the 1930s.

Politically, this period witnessed the complete elimination of all domestic opposition and civil liberties in each country. Left wing and socialist parties were forced to merge with the Communists and all other political parties were outlawed. One by one, using the USSR constitution as a model, the Peoples Democracies adopted new consitutions. Bulgaria proclaimed a new constitution on November 4, 1947; Rumania did so on April 13, 1948; Czechoslovakia followed suit on May 9, 1948; Hungary adopted its consitution on August 20, 1949; and Poland revised its on July 22, 1952. The latter two constitutions actually praised the Soviet Union in their texts. Yugoslavia's constitution was modeled on the Soviet Union from the outset (1946). Only East Germany followed a different constitutional path because it was technically still an occupied country and in theory to be governed as a unit. So, East Germany became in October 1949 a "Democratic Republic" while the five other satellites (and Yugoslavia and Albania) were Peoples Democracies. On July 23, 1952, the East German constitution was remodeled on the Soviet type though the name did not change. Behind the facade of these constitutional changes lay the reality of one-party dictatorships. As had been the case in the Soviet prototype, the state institutions of government declined to the point of impotence. Popular assemblies that represented the people in theory now played only a nominal role. Effective power was located in the various party committees which in turn were subordinated to central authorities of the party.

There remained the question of who would rule these parties. Stalin had determined to replace those party cadres who came to power in the aftermath of the war because many of them showed unmistakable signs of nationalistic identification with their own peoples. He replaced them with henchmen who understood that their first loyalty was to Moscow—not to Warsaw or Budapest or Bucharest or Prague or Sofia. The means to bring about the change in leadership was the same that Stalin had utilized some dozen years earlier in his own country: the purge.

Between 1949 and 1952 the leadership and thousands of party members in each country were liquidated. The purges were tied in with Stalin's fight against Titoism which is described below. None of those liquidated was in any sense defiant of Soviet authority, but in Stalin's eyes they had a potential for defiance. The purges were particularly violent in Hungary, Bulgaria, and

Czechoslovakia. The chief victim in Hungary was Laszlo Rajk, politburo member and minister of the interior. Tried in September 1949 for being, among other things, a CIA agent, Rajk was promised clemency for confessing, which he did. But to no avail; he was executed by garroting. In Bulgaria, Traicho Kostov, deputy prime minister and member of the politburo, was tried in March 1949 also on charges of treason. Kostov unexpectedly repudiated his confession in court, but that did not save him from the hangman. The most extensive purges took place in Czechoslovakia during the period 1950-52. Among the leading defendants were Foreign Minister Vladimir Clementis and Deputy Prime Minister and former Party Secretary-General, Rudolf Slansky. A particular feature of the Czech trials were the openly anti-Semitic appeals of the prosecution. There were comparable trials in Rumania, Poland, and East Germany but they were less extensive and less bloody. Wladyslaw Gomulka of Poland, for example, was eliminated from power but permitted to live. The common thread of all these purges was the elimination of individuals who were presumed to have the potential of opposing such dedicated Stalinist rulers as Rakosi in Hungary, Chervenkov in Bulgaria, Gottwald in Czechoslovakia, Gheorghiu-Dej in Rumania, and Bierut in Poland.

Finally, these changes in the political structure and personnel were accompanied by domestic policies leading to a throughgoing "socialist construction." The Soviet Union was to be the model for each country: collectivization of agriculture and industrialization were intensified. One by one, the six countries adopted five-year plans for economic development including the use of a state budget to guide the overall direction of a socialist economy. As in the USSR, the turnover tax became the main source of state revenue.

Historically, political domination has implied economic exploitation and "socialist internationalism" notwithstanding, this relationship was no different. The principal technique of exploitation was the joint stock company, an arrangement that permitted Soviet management to control selected satellite industries directly. Each of the joint stock companies was established on a bilateral basis: sixteen in Rumania, six in Hungary, seven in Bulgaria. The Czechoslovakian uranium industry, which had particular importance for the Soviet military, was made the subject of secret agreements between the two countries. All in all, it is estimated that in the period 1945-56, the Soviet Union extracted approximately $20 billion from the economies of Eastern Europe.[11]

The Council on Mutual Economic Cooperation (COMECON) was formed during this period (January 1949) largely as a response to the Marshall Plan. It too was an instrument under Stalin for economic exploitation although its main activity was originally limited to coordinating trade among the satellites. The founding members were the Soviet Union, Poland, Hungary, Bulgaria, Rumania, and Czechoslovakia. They were joined subsequently by Albania (which broke away in 1961), East Germany, Mongolia, and Cuba. In 1950 the ruble became the standard currency for international transactions within COMECOM, making the USSR the arbiter of all rates of exchange.

In sum then, Stalin created a socialist system that was truly monolithic. Eastern Europe became part of a Soviet bloc whose center was Moscow. While he lived, Stalin controlled this empire through a variety of informal techniques. Chief among these was his personal selection or approval of every satellite leader. Those who held power did so not because they had indigenous support but solely by virtue of Stalin's approval. The Kremlin's control extended throughout party and government apparatus including each country's secret police and military. The Soviet ambassadors to the satellites exercised the powers of proconsuls with direct access to anyone of importance in the country to which they were accredited. Speaking for Stalin they could advise, warn, and command.

What impelled Stalin toward such total control? Apologists argue the necessity of security. The Soviet Union had paid an enormous price to defend itself from a Western onslaught and was determined never again to be so exposed. The security argument, however, really begs the question. No one questioned the right of the USSR to prevent any part of Eastern Europe from being used as a staging ground for an attack, nor did any one doubt that the region politically fell within the Soviet "sphere of influence." Certainly both Churchill and Roosevelt conceded that the governments of Eastern Europe would have to be pro-Soviet. Security alone could neither justify nor explain the totality of Stalinist domination.

Ideologists contend that Soviet behavior had its roots in the Marxist-Leninist compulsion to expand the revolutionary cause of communism. This explanation too is unconvincing. As discussed in chapter 2, Soviet behavior is only partially influenced by ideology. From the standpoint of ideology, the basic fact is that the political and economic systems created in eastern Europe are no more adequately described by Marxist theory than they are by laissez-faire theory. They simply defy categorization in any ideological terms. They are called "socialist" only because Stalin and his agents called them that.

A better clue toward an understanding of the origins of the Soviet bloc is the totalitarian edifice that had been constructed in the USSR itself. The socialist state system was essentially an extension of domestic Stalinism. The Soviet autocrat knew no other kind of political relationship except that of domination-subordination, so it was natural that he should expand Soviet control as far as he was able. Within the domain of that control Stalin duplicated the features of what his successors would call "the cult of the personality." Thus, the official Czech newspaper *Rude Pravo* could assert, as the purges culminated in Czechoslovakia:

Love of the Soviet Union does not tolerate the slightest reservation. The road into the morass of treason indeed begins on the inclined plane of reservations and doubts regarding the correctness of the policy of the Soviet Union.[12]

More than any one event, the schism between Yugoslavia and the Soviet Union exposed the totalitarian mainspring of socialist internationalism under Stalin.

TITOISM: THE ORIGINS OF NATIONAL COMMUNISM

In 1948 a schism developed between the head of the Yugoslav Communist Party, Josip Broz-Tito, and Stalin that was to have profound repercussions for the socialist system. As discussed below, the historical trend of relations between socialist states has been toward polycentrism, that is, the growth of autonomous independent centers of decision making. Paradoxically, while the Soviet bloc was becoming monolithic, the seeds of disintegration of that monolith were being sown in Yugoslavia.

There is a real irony in the fact that Tito should be the one to challenge Stalin's autocracy within the socialist camp for of all the communist leaders to acquire power after the war none was more like Stalin himself than Tito. Indeed Tito considered himself second only to Stalin as a leader of world communism. Until the break with the USSR, Tito had pushed Yugoslavia further than any other of the Peoples Democracies (except perhaps Bulgaria) in socialist construction. In the late 1940s, Yugoslavia had one of the highest rates of collectivization of agriculture in Eastern Europe. No one was more vitriolic in condemning the West, none more aggressive in the pursuit of foreign policy. Tito had no hesitation in demanding the use of force to recover all of Trieste for Yugoslavia and was chagrined that Stalin might hesitate to wage war with the West for this lofty expansion of communism.[13] More than most communists, Tito demanded that the Peoples Democracies accept the Soviet Union as a model and he welcomed the establishment of the Cominform as a means of assuring unity within the communist bloc.

Another parallel with Stalin was Tito's imperialistic ambitions. After the war, Albania became a Yugoslav satellite whose ultimate fate would probably have been absorption into its larger neighbor had not the split with the USSR occurred. Stalin in a rather crude manner informed the Yugoslavs in 1947 "We agree to Yugoslavia swallowing Albania! . . . the sooner the better."[14] But Tito had even more grandiose designs. He planned to create a South Slav confederation that would unite Albania and Bulgaria with Yugoslavia. Although power would have been shared with Georgi Dimitrov, the Bulgarian leader, Tito would undoubtedly have dominated this Balkan Federation. This plan seemed to have had Stalin's support until January 1948 when the Soviet press unexpectedly attacked the idea.[15] That was one of the first outward signs of the crisis in Yugoslav-Soviet relations.

The cause of the crisis was Stalin's determination to replace the leaders of Yugoslavia's party and state apparatus with men who would be subject to Stalin's—not Tito's—direction. The first of Stalin's demands was simply that two Yugoslav diplomatic officers be dismissed as traitors. Tito resisted. As the crisis unfolded, it became apparent that Stalin wanted much more: a complete change of leadership in Yugoslavia, replacing Tito with an arch rival, Andrija Hebrang. Tito turned the trick on Stalin by arresting Hebrang. In March and April 1948, Tito won the support of the Yugoslav Communist Party to challenge the right of the Soviet party to interfere in Yugoslavia's internal affairs. The world first learned of the split on June 28, when the Cominform openly condemned Tito for nationalist deviations at its Budapest conference. The news came as a shock.

"I will shake my little finger—and there will be no more Tito. He will fall," Stalin is reported by Khrushchev to have said.[16] But Tito didn't fall. Why not? Tito survived because, alone among the satellite leaders, he was complete master of his party and state, most particularly of the army and secret police. His support rested upon the loyalty felt not only by the party hierarchy but the nation at large for his role in combatting the Nazis. Moreover, unlike many other states of the region, Yugoslavia had no Soviet troops on its territory; the Yugoslav army had a monopoly of force in the land. Stalin may have made a tactical error in not resorting to force to overthrow Tito. An invasion might have worked in 1948, but it become too risky by 1950. Titoism, then, was the assertion of a communist party to be master in its own house. It certainly did not imply anticommunism or even anti-Russianism. The central point was as Adam Ulam noted: "Who was to have political power in Yugoslavia?"[17]

Although Titoism did not constitute a doctrine at the time of the break, by 1950 Yugoslav theorists began developing an ideological basis for Yugoslav policies. They condemned Stalin's brand of communism as "revisionism." They objected specifically to Stalin's "theory of two camps" which they said gave rise to the dogma of a "leading" socialist country. As a substitute for the idea that one country should serve as a model for all, Titoists asserted the principle of "different roads to communism." Titoism also condemned the highly centralized state and party bureaucracy in the USSR which it described as "state capitalism." Yugoslav theorists argued that the transition from the lower phase of communism (socialism) toward the higher (pure) communism should be accompanied by the transformation of state ownership of property to "socialist ownership." By that they meant the decentralization of the economy and economic self-management.[18]

There is little doubt that Stalin's provocation of Tito was a monumental blunder. The consequences were both long and short term. One was an intensification of the purges in the satellites to eliminate any leaders suspected of having Titoist sympathies or nationalistic inclinations. As we have indicated above, these purges followed from the dynamics of Stalin's totalitarian rule. They would have taken place even without the Yugoslav rebellion, although they might not have been so intense. Another direct consequence of the Titoist schism was the collapse of the communist insurgency in Greece. Because the leaders of the Greek rebels were close to Tito, Stalin had them purged immediately. Yugoslavia ceased aiding the Greek partisans altogether in 1949. It seems safe to presume, however, that the most important consequence of Tito's defection was the long-term effect upon the socialist state system. Yugoslavia was the first socialist state to challenge Soviet hegemony and to get away with it. In so doing, it laid the moral and psychological basis for the development of polycentrism in the socialist state system.

KHRUSHCHEV AND THE CRISIS OF DE-STALINIZATION

Joseph Stalin's death in March 1953 was bound to have a profound effect on the socialist international system. Just as he had been the lynchpin of totalitarianism in the Soviet Union, Stalin was the bond that welded together the countries of the Soviet bloc. No small part of that bond was the personal fear engendered by the man himself. There would be an inevitable weakening of Moscow's grip unless and until a comparable personality acquired power in the Kremlin. As it turned out, his successors were no Stalins.

It would, however, be entirely misleading to attribute all the changes in the communist camp to the absence of Stalin. International politics underwent significant changes in the 1950s, changes that would have inevitably affected Soviet-Eastern European relations no matter who was at the helm. Foremost among them was the stalemate that had developed in the cold war. A temporary equilibrium was formed in Europe and Asia, bringing with it a general easing of international tensions. Concurrent with this stabilization of international politics was a change in administrations in the leading powers of both camps.

Stalin was succeeded by a collective leadership, initially led by Georgi Malenkov, but after 1955 by Nikita Khrushchev. Both men, though committed to maintaining the Stalinist political system at home and abroad, were nonetheless aware of the necessity to adjust to the realities of the world situation. Both favored substantial changes in Soviet foreign policy, particularly in the tactics used by Stalin. On the other hand, not all the soviet policymakers were in agreement with Malenkov or Khrushchev. Stalin had many heirs in the Kremlin. Precisely because the leadership was collective, it had to pursue a cautious, uncertain, and at times contradictory foreign policy. Looked at broadly, Soviet policy in the mid-1950s displayed an incredible picture of contradictions. On the one hand, there were important measures of accomodation such as the Korean armistice (1953), the Geneva conference on Indochina (1954), and the Austrian State Treaty (1955). In sharp contrast stood such actions as the suppression of the Berlin uprising (1953), the formation of the Warsaw Pact (1955), and the suppression of the Hungarian revolution (1956). There was a fundamental consistency behind the apparent contradictions of Soviet policy during this period. The underlying logic of Soviet foreign policy lay in its attempt to retain the basic features of the Stalinist system while at the same time making those adjustments necessitated by a changing world environment.

Stalin's successors introduced three policies that proved powerful stimuli to the development of polycentrism or national communism: (1) the "New Course" program of economic liberalization; (2) Tito's rehabilitation; and (3) the de-Stalinization campaign. Each of these policies was designed to cope with a different set of problems. None had as its goal the undermining of the cohesion of the Soviet bloc, yet that is what they inadvertently produced.

One of the legacies of Stalinist rule in Eastern Europe was a deteriorating economy that created widespread popular unrest. In June 1953 there were serious popular disturbances in Czechoslovakia and East Germany. The workers strike at the former Skoda works in Pilsen was easily contained by Czech authorities but, in Berlin, a general strike led to widespead disturbances that eventually required the Red Army forces to quell. It was to alleviate the harshness of the Stalinist economic policies that Malenkov introduced his New Course on August 8, 1953. His objectives for the satellites were the same as for the Soviet Union itself: to ease the crushing burden of taxation and to improve the standard of living through an increase in consumer goods production.

East Germany was the first to initiate a new economic course. The radical socialization begun in 1952 was halted. Delivery quotas and taxes were reduced. Subsequently, the Soviet Union agreed to return German enterprises managed by the USSR to East German control. Reparations payments to the Soviet Union were also soon terminated. A noticeable improvement in the standard of living took place as a result. The next state to adopt the New Course and the one most badly in need of it was Hungary. Here the forced industrialization on a less developed economy had worked a brutal hardship on the Hungarian workers and peasants. Popular resentment was intense. The Stalinist party boss most responsible, Matyas Rakosi, was summoned to Moscow in June where he was sharply castigated for economic excesses that were driving the country to ruin. He was forced to step down as premier in favor of the liberal reformer, Imre Nagy. In spite of his strong committment to reform—he introduced price reductions and wage increases and sanctioned the withdrawal from collective farms—Nagy was unable to overcome the economic ills of his country or to relieve the underlying popular hostility toward the regime. Next to introduce economic reforms were Rumania, Bulgaria, and Czechoslovakia. In the fall of 1953, Poland became the last to do so.

It is a measure of the change in relations between socialist countries that the New Course in each of these countries was applied differently depending upon the peculiar circumstances of each country. Some programs were at least partially successful. Those in Poland and Hungary were notably unsuccessful. The subversive consequence of economic liberalization was that it stimulated a desire among many for political liberalization. If, some reasoned, there could be economic liberalization, why should there not be political liberalization as well? Conversely, where economic liberalization failed, it focused the attention of the population on the political sphere as people realized that economic change could only occur if the political leaders were changed as well. The economic liberalization also exposed the fallibility of Communist Party leaders who, as it turned out, could make serious policy errors and be held responsible (at least by Moscow) for them.

Another contribution to the erosion of the Stalinist system in eastern Europe was the rehabilitation of Tito in the communist community. Almost as soon as Stalin was buried, the Kremlin initiated inquiries toward bringing about a rapprochement with Yugoslavia. Economic steps preceded political ones. In September 1954 the two countries signed a barter agreement. On May 6, 1955, Moscow made the startling announcement that a high-level Soviet delegation led by Nikita Khrushchev would visit Belgrade in June. In a rare public statement of contrition Khrushchev noted: "We sincerely regret what happened and resolutely reject the things that occurred."[19] This act has been described as a 20th-century Canossa. However much the Soviet leaders wanted to restore normal relations with Yugoslavia, they were not prepared to admit that all of the ideological error charged to Tito had been erroneous. Tito therefore responded to the Soviet embrace with some caution. The declaration agreed upon by both sides stressed the resolution of interstate as opposed to interparty relations. Soviet Russia agreed in the Belgrade Declaration of June 2 on the principle of "mutual respect and non-interference in one another's internal affairs for whatever reason, whether of an economic, political or ideological nature, inasmuch as questions of internal organization, difference of social systems, and difference in the concrete forms of socialist development are exclusively the concern of the peoples of the respective countries."[20] Eventually both sides agreed to extend the principle of noninterference to party affairs as well. One year after the Belgrade Declaration, another declaration was agreed upon between the two parties in which they affirmed that "the path of socialist development differs in various countries" and "that any tendency of imposing one's opinions on the ways and forms of socialist development is alien to both."[21] Tito's victory was complete. Khrushchev formalized Soviet policy with an endorsement of the idea of "Many roads to socialism" in his address before the Twentieth Party Congress in February 1956 and the dissolution of the Cominform on April 17, 1956.

Ironically, even in repudiating Stalin's behavior, his successors to some extent emulated it. Pressure was exerted on each of the satellites to reverse their own previous anti-Tito orientations. Under Soviet encouragement, Bulgaria, Hungary, and Albania were among the first to enter into negotiations with Yugoslavia. In April 1956 the Czech party formally apologized to Tito for "unfounded accusations" made during the 1952 political trials. Many of those who had been executed as "Titoists" during the earlier purges underwent that unique reversal of historical judgment periodically engaged in by communist parties: they were rehabilitated (posthumously). Most notable among the resurrected reputations were Rajk of Hungary and Kostov of Bulgaria. The political significance of Tito's comeback was not lost on many politically sophisticated Eastern Europeans. Tito had engaged in outright political opposition to the Kremlin and had not only survived, but was vindicated. The implications of this could only further weaken the Soviet hold on its allies.

One important countervailing development that took place during this period was the formation of the Warsaw Treaty Organization on May 14, 1955. The Warsaw Pact was in part a response to Western plans to rearm the Federal Republic of Germany and make it a full member of NATO. The original pact members included all of European communist countries except Yugoslavia (Albania ceased to participate in 1962 and formally withdrew in 1968). There has always been serious question about the military effectiveness of the Warsaw Pact but its political significance is considerable. From its inception the pact has constituted the single most vital commitment binding the Eastern European states to the Soviet Union. It establishes the legal framework for the presence of Soviet troops on the members' territory and precludes each country from participating in any other military alliance.

The Warsaw Treaty Organization had hardly begun to build the web that might further bind the Soviet bloc, however, when the whole structure was shattered by popular upheaval. In the fall of 1956 popular upheavals occurred in Poland and Hungary threatening to rupture Soviet control not only over these two countries but possibly all of Eastern Europe as well. The question of national communism was at stake.

A direct cause of the unrest in Eastern Europe was the campaign of de-Stalinization introduced by Nikita Khrushchev at the Twentieth Party Congress. On February 25, 1956, Khrushchev delivered a lengthy speech to a closed session of the Party's Congress in which he bitterly condemned the abuses of Stalin's long rule.[22] His purposes were undoubtedly multiple. He was unquestionably reaching out to establish his own undisputed leadership of the Party. But Khrushchev must also have been convinced that communist rule could meet its ends in a more rational and humane manner than it had under his predecessor.

The secret speech itself did not go into the issue of Soviet-Eastern bloc relations but the vigorous attack on rigid Stalinist attitudes was meant to apply to communists outside as well as inside the USSR.[23] Khrushchev intended change not only within Soviet society but with respect to relations with communist states as well. He was not proposing to abandon Soviet primacy but rather to base that supremacy on a more acceptable and hence durable basis. In his formal public address to the Congress, Khrushchev had acknowledged that there were different roads to socialism and that the Peoples Democracies as well as the Soviet model were viable forms of organizing society. Clearly he recognized the national differences in style, behavior, and policy. But still the problem remained: How much freedom, how much autonomy for the satellites?

Throughout the spring and summer of 1956, Khrushchev imposed his de-Stalinization program on the countries of eastern Europe, resulting in the purge of numerous old-line Stalinists. Among those who were forced out of power or demoted were Vulko Chervenkov in Bulgaria, Jacob Berman in Poland, and Matyas Rakosi in Hungary. In their place were elevated party leaders identified with a more popular, national line such as Wladyslaw Gomulka and, during the Hungarian revolt, Imre Nagy. In Poland an amnesty bill was published in April promising the release of 30,000 prisoners and a sentence reduction for 40,000 additional prisoners. The satellite parties were thoroughly revamped under Moscow's new directives. De-Stalinization had its greatest impact on the party elites at first. In June, however, the publication of the "secret" speech in the West enlarged the number of people affected. Stalin's dethronement struck a popular chord among the masses and led to consequences Khrushchev surely did not intend.

Of the two revolutions in Eastern Europe, one, the Polish uprising that began with the Poznan riots on June 28 and ended with the election of Gomulka as Communist Party chief on October 21st, proved a victory for national communism. The Hungarian revolution witnessed the defeat not only of national communism but national self-determination as well. The Soviet leadership refrained from the use of force in the former case; in the latter they used it. What accounted for the differences in these two revolutions?

Both upheavals involved genuinely popular uprisings. In late June a workers strike in the city of Poznan was suddenly joined in the streets by thousands of citizens, converting a worker's protest into a mass demonstration against the regime. Before order was finally restored, 53 people were killed, over 300 injured and 323 were arrested. Instead of responding with repression, the government accepted the validity of at least some of the workers' complaints and introduced a series of financial concessions to them in early July. Later that month, the Polish Workers Party (Poland's Communist Party) openly acknowledged "the existence of serious disturbances between the party and various sections of the working class."[24] By siding with the workers, the Polish Party was able to ride the crest of popular dissatisfaction and even assume a role of leadership. What is more, by rejecting the Soviet line that "foreign agents," not workers' grievances, had caused the riots, the communist party became a spokesman for Polish nationalism. Never before had there been such a divergence in position between the party leaders of both countries. Between July and September the Polish leadership took a series of measures completely independently of Moscow. On August 4, Wladyslaw Gomulka was readmitted to the Party. Measures were taken to raise the standard of living and reduce consumer prices for industrial workers. The trials in September of the Poznan rioters resulted in the release of most of those arrested with only minor sentences for a few who were convicted. These events produced a wave of popular enthusiasm for the regime and stimulated a desire for even greater reforms. They also brought the personality of Gomulka to the fore as the popular choice for political leadership.

The crisis reached a climax on October 19, as the Central Committee met to select a new leadership. Suddenly, with no advanced notification, Khrushchev and a high-level team of Soviet Party leaders descended in Warsaw to confer with Polish party leaders now led by Gomulka. The discussions were reported to have been heated. The Polish delegation refused to back down on the composition of the party leadership although they apparently gave the Russians assurances about Soviet-Polish relations. It is reported that the Poles threatened to order the Polish army to resist if the Russians attempted to move Russian troops into Warsaw. In the end the Russians backed down. On October 20, Khrushchev returned to Moscow and on the next day Gomulka was formally elected First Secretary of the Party. J. M. Mackintosh speculates that Khrushchev reasoned that a Soviet military move under the circumstances might have subjugated the Poles, but it would have killed communism forever in Poland.[25] In sum, the critical factors that worked for Poland were: (1) the Communist Party was in firm control of events and its rule was never in danger; (2) the party leadership was united, had popular backing, and the support of the army; (3) the party's reforms were limited to domestic affairs; and (4) in spite of widespread popular anti-Russian feeling Poland remained committed to its alliance with the Soviet Union. Poland's retention of the Oder-Neisse frontier with Germany required the continued support of its Eastern neighbor.

Hungary posed a different kind of problem. Like Poland, the stimulus for change came from among the masses, but in Hungary, hostility to communism and rule by the Communist Party were more intense and permeated almost every segment of the population. Forced industrialization coupled with incredible economic mismanagement—particularly in agriculture and coal mining—had produced great hardship on Hungary's proletariat, thus alienating what should have been the basis of class support for the regime. Furthermore, unlike Poland, which could at least look to the Soviet Union for support against a revanchist Germany, Hungary saw Russia as hostile to its national interests. Hungarians also remembered the transfer of northern Transylvania to Rumania that Russia imposed upon them after the war.

Like Poland, the Hungarian people had in Imre Nagy a national leader to whom they could turn. He had been removed as premier in the spring of 1955 and remained out of office until he was recalled as premier on October 24, 1956. Nagy had come to the conclusion that Hungary's interests were not always compatible with Soviet purposes and where the two conflicted the former should prevail. He was impressed with the principles of independence, sovereignty, equality, noninterference in internal affairs, and self-determination that emerged from the Bandung Conference in 1955, and argued that they should be applied to the Soviet camp, not just the Third World. Ultimately, as Soviet troops invaded his country, Nagy came to the position that Hungary should adopt a neutral stance between the two superpower blocs.[26]

Events in October in Poland had an electrifying effect on popular sentiment in Hungary. Gomulka's accession to power was widely interpreted in Hungary to signify Soviet willingness to remove all vestiges of Stalinism in Eastern Europe. Irresolution on the part of the government only encouraged students and intellectuals to intensify their demands for reform. On October 23, 1956, a demonstration led by students and workers swelled by the general populace of Budapest into a mass demonstration of hostility to the government. Popular hatred of the regime was symbolized by the smashing of the giant statue of Stalin in Budapest. Soviet armed forces tried futilely for four days to restore order in the Hungarian capital. Meanwhile the revolution began to sweep across the country. Nagy was able to negotiate a ceasefire and a withdrawal of Soviet troops as of October 28. During the last week of October the fury of the popular uprising, particularly against the hated political police, the AVO, completely destroyed government authority. Throughout the country there arose unofficial elected workers' councils that demanded a new, democratic regime and the end of the communist one-party dictatorship. Nagy moved increasingly toward support of the growing radical demands of his countrymen. On October 30 a multiparty system was restored. The ultimate treason from the Soviet point of view came on November 1 when—as Soviet troops in large numbers were entering Hungary—Nagy announced Hungary's withdrawal from the Warsaw Pact and proclaimed the country's complete neutrality in the cold war. Nagy's protests were met with deceptive responses by the Soviet Union concerning the purpose of the troop movements. Early in the morning of November 4, Soviet forces launched a general offensive on Hungarian forces in Budapest and throughout the country.

Bitter fighting ensued for days but the ultimate fate of the revolution was never in doubt. Imre Nagy was arrested, to be executed later. A new government under Janos Kadar was forcibly installed and remains in power today.

The vital issue in Hungary was not the relationship between one socialist country and another. This was not a question of proletarian internationalism. The Hungarian uprising was a spontaneous, popular, anticommunist revolt whose objective was the overthrow of the one-party dictatorship. At issue was the question: Could a "peoples democracy" revert back to a bourgeois democracy? Could a member of the Soviet bloc leave the bloc? The question was fundamentally one of national self-determination. Khrushchev had demonstrated in his behavior toward Poland and Yugoslavia that the Soviet Union was prepared to accept some divergence from the Soviet model. His response to the events in Hungary, however, made it clear that there were limits to such divergence. Soviet interests and influence had to be preserved whatever the cost.

In November of 1957, a meeting of the leaders of the eastern European parties and the ruling Asian parties was convened in Moscow. They unanimously declared that the Soviet Union was the leader of the socialist camp. Mao Zedong at this time endorsed the idea of Soviet leadership. In a few years his position would change. The late 1950s constitute a watershed in the relationship between the Soviet Union and the other socialist states. While the contours of its relationship with the European allies were being shaped into a fairly stable mold, the relationship with the parties of Asia were undergoing major changes.

THE SINO-SOVIET SCHISM

No one development has so profoundly altered the structure of the international communist movement as the Sino-Soviet schism. It is no exaggeration to say that since the second World War nothing except the nuclear weapon has affected the general orientation of Soviet foreign policy as much as the split with China. The implications for the socialist international system and for the larger international system have been enormous. Yugoslavia demonstrated that a communist country could retain its national sovereignty. Poland showed the possitiblities of independent domestic policies within the framework of Soviet external control. China was to explode entirely the myth of proletarian internationalism by revealing that communist countries can become bitter antagonists.

There are problems in dating the beginning of the schism as well as in identifying the causes. At the risk of putting the cart before the horse, we might first consider the causes. Most analysts agree that they were multiple, some general, some specific, some short, and others long term. It is important to keep in mind that the schism took place within a changing structure of international relations that not only made the split possible, but to some extent dictated it. International politics had moved away from the bipolarity of the postwar era by the late 1950s. The ideological and propagandistic antagonism emanating from both camps was beginning to subside. Pressures were generated within the two alliances that undermined their cohesiveness. The leaders of both blocs became increasingly aware of the benefits of cooperation. Their relationship gradually changed from one of total enmity toward a more complex one of limited hostility and occasional cooperation. An important factor producing this change in the international structure was the development of nuclear stockpiles, the means to deliver nuclear weapons, and the strategy of deterrence. War was becoming extraordinarily lethal, with the consequence that the superpowers were unable to convert their military power into political power, or in other words, to control events or nations around them as they had in the past.

If bipolarity was passing, what was taking its place? Even today political scientists are unable to agree on the structure that has succeeded bipolarity.[27] The consensus is that international politics in the 1960s and 1970s became more multipolar. The schism between the two communist giants was, thus, a part of a larger change that resulted in an increase in the number of great powers (polar actors) in international politics. It seems quite probable that as China became a great power, it was destined to become a rival to Soviet Russia irrespective of the internal political makeup of either nation.

To suggest that the change in the international socialist system was a consequence of changes in the global system (of which the former was a part) is not to deny the importance of a number of specific differences between the two parties. They include such factors as a conflict in ideology, the personality clash of Khrushchev and Mao Zedong, antagonistic nationalisms, the conflict of different levels of economic development, the rivalry for leadership of the socialist camp, the interaction of provocative and inept diplomacy, and last, but certainly not least, traditional national conflicts of interest. All of these were relevant to some degree. No one factor can be considered decisive.

Some of the causes of the schism are more important than others, which presupposes, of course, that some were of lesser importance. The personalities of the two chief antagonists certainly entered into the picture. Mao, who encouraged his own "personality cult", possessed a towering ego that must have more than once rubbed the populist Khrushchev the wrong way. But the peripheral role of personality is evident by the fact that Khrushchev's overthrow in 1964 and Mao's death in 1976 made no fundamental change in the Sino-Soviet relationship. Ideological differences, too, sparked much of the polemics between both sides. That both parties took their respective positions seriously is beyond doubt. But one must be careful to distinguish theory as the cause of conflict and ideological posturing as a consequence of other differences. Mao, for example, became a bitter opponent of what he called Yugoslav revisionism though he had earlier applauded many of Tito's ideas. Nationalism, likewise, cannot explain the bitterness that enveloped the antagonists, even though profound cultural differences between the Russians and the Chinese are undeniable. Many witnesses have testified to the xenophobia of both sides, particularly of the widespread Russian fear of the "yellow peril." But, again, the fact remains that despite these cultural differences, the Soviets were able to establish close ties with Mao before the split and with Chiang Kai-shek before him. We are faced, thus, with a complex phenomenon that has ideological, economic, national, personal, idiosyncratic, and political dimensions.

One can trace the roots of the Sino-Soviet conflict in the history of both countries as far back as the conquest of Russia by the Mongol Tartars during the 13th and 14th centuries. Some see this two century domination of Russia by the ancestors of today's Chinese as the source of a deep-seated fear by the Russians of their oriental neighbor. More recent history witnessed a complete reversal of fortunes for both societies. In the 19th century, Russia annexed large areas of land formerly under Chinese suzerainty. As a result of Chinese weakness the Russian Tsar imposed on the Manchu Emperor the so-called "unequal treaties", ceding to Russia vast territories north of the Amur and east of the Ussuri rivers.[28] After the Russian revolution the Soviet Government declared all secret and unequal treaties null and void and renounced all seizure of Chinese territory by the Tsars, but nothing ever came of this declaration; no land was ever actually returned.

Joseph Stalin consistently sacrificed the interests of the Chinese communists and the People's Republic of China to those of the Soviet Union. In the 1920s he supported the Kuomintang (led by Chiang Kai-shek) in hopes that a unified China—even under a nationalist regime—might be a barrier to Japanese expansion. He made Mongolia a Soviet satellite. After the war Soviet forces commandeered every piece of industrial equipment in Manchuria before they turned the territory over to communist forces. Stalin drove a very hard bargain with Mao in February 1950 when the Sino-Soviet Treaty of Alliance was negotiated. At that time Stalin agreed to lend China 300 million dollars at 1 percent interest. Shortly before, he had loaned Poland 450 million dollars with no interest. There is considerable evidence that the Korean War created serious friction between both powers.[29] Certaintly the Chinese resented the obligation to repay the Soviet aid received for the conduct of what was supposed to be a common struggle in Korea. In the face of all this it is amazing that the formal Chinese line regarding Stalin remains favorable.

The events that led directly to the Sino-Soviet rupture occurred in the post-Stalin period. They took place in three phases, each constituting an intensification of the crisis. The first phase occurred roughly in the period 1956 to 1960. Soviet-Chinese differences during this period were expressed confidentially within the framework of the world socialist system. Sometime between 1960 and 1964—the second phase—the dispute became a schism. By 1964, the socialist system had split into two separate systems. Although never formally expelled from the communist camp, China came to see itself and was perceived by others as operating independently of the Soviet-led camp. Sino-Soviet relations since 1964 have further deteriorated to the point of conflict. The issue since the 1960s is largely the conflict between two great powers, a struggle that transcends their doctrinal differences within the communist world. Today China and Russia see themselves as, and are in fact, rivals in a global political struggle.

Chinese dissatisfaction with the Soviets developed early in Khrushchev's administration. In his policies of detente, they perceived a threat to the unity of the communist movement, to the advancement of the worldwide proletarian revolution and, not insignificantly, to their own national interests. Khrushchev's condemnation of Stalin—undertaken without prior consultation with the Chinese—was seen as intemperate and damaging to the communist cause. After all, Mao was developing his own personality cult and could not have relished seeing a fellow prophet toppled so brutally. Notwithstanding these reservations, the Chinese loyally supported Khrushchev during the Eastern European crisis in the fall of 1956. One of the consequences of that support was the setting of a precedent for Chinese involvement in Communist affairs in Europe, a development the Soviets would later regret.

In November 1957 the Soviets organized a conference of bloc states in Moscow to meet in connection with celebrations of the 40th anniversary of the Revolution. Khrushchev wanted to obtain undisputed recognition of Soviet leadership over the communist camp. Toward this end he made an agreement on October 15th to provide China with assistance in weapons development. Although he did not give the Chinese an atomic bomb, as they would have liked, Khrushchev did commit his government to give some aid in nuclear development. Apparently the Chinese were satisfied because Mao Zedong personally gave the Soviet Union the endorsement, which Khrushchev so badly wanted, as "head" of the socialist camp.

Events in 1958 badly strained Sino-Soviet relations. Mao had never liked Khrushchev's economic reforms and obviously suspected that peaceful co-existence meant in effect a relaxation of the struggle against imperialism. Political crises in the Middle and Far East in the summer of 1958 seemed to confirm his suspicions. In July, American marines were sent to Lebanon and British parachute troops to Jordan to support these governments against suspected subversion. On July 19, Khrushchev proposed a heads of government conference consisting of the USSR, the United States, Britain, France, and *India* to deal with the Middle-Eastern crisis. In addition to the injury of including India rather than China in such a conference, Khruchshev committed the insult of accepting an Eisenhower counterproposal that a conference take place within the framework of the United Nations Security Council. This would have brought in Nationalist China (then holding a permanent seat on the Security Council) into the picture. Khrushchev visited Beijing later that same month. It can be assumed that the Chinese made their objections known because on his return the Soviet premier withdrew his support for a summit meeting within the framework of the Security Council.

More serious was the crisis that developed in the fall as a result of Chinese bombardment of the Nationalist-held island of Quemoy. American Secretary of State Dulles declared that U.S. forces would protect Quemoy if necessary and followed his warning with a deployment of air and naval forces in the Pacific. Khrushchev, on the other hand, though he gave verbal support to his ally, maintained a very cautious stance. The Chinese were disturbed by the lack of Soviet aggressiveness on their behalf. They had been persuaded by the launching of the first Soviet ICBM and the orbiting of its Sputnik around the moon in the summer and fall of 1957 that the global balance of power had shifted in favor of communism. They were convinced that a more aggressive stance by the Soviet Union would force American-led imperalism to retreat. Zbigniew Brzezinski paraphrases the differences in perspective that were developing during this time as follows:

The Soviets to the Chinese: "You overestimate the ability of the imperialists to initiate a war, hence war is not inevitable; you underestimate the destructiveness of war and our deterrent capabilities; you underestimate the danger of a total war developing out of local conflicts; you underestimate the world wide appeal of socialism as a powerful force and the global significance of the economic power of the world socialist system." The Chinese to the Soviets: "You overestimate the destructiveness of war; you overestimate the willingness of the imperialists to make peaceful concessions; you underestimate the militant revolutionary opportunities and the dangers of coexistence to the revolutionary zeal of the international Communist movements; you underestimate the ability of the socialist camp to win local wars or to force the imperialists to desist when they start one. Finally, you underestimate the possibility of the imperialists plunging the world into war, either out of despair or duplicity, and hence, there is a continuing danger of war."[30]

If the Chinese found the Russians too conservative, the Soviets were appalled by Chinese brashness. In May 1958 Chinese politics took a sharp turn toward the left with the initiation of the Great Leap Forward. In a sharp break with the Soviet model of development, the Chinese claimed a formula for moving quickly into the stage of full communism. They proposed to substitute mass enthusiasm and total mobilization of the population for their lack of material-technical resources. In the fall a program of peoples communes was organized on a nation-wide basis. By virtue of these communes China sought to become the first state in history to reach communism. The Soviets considered the communes economic folly. But worse, the Chinese were using the Great Leap Forward as a basis to claim ideological preeminence in the world socialist camp. Obviously, these claims constituted a serious threat to the legitimacy of Soviet preeminence in the socialist camp inasmuch as the Soviet claim to leadership rested in large part on its role as ideological leader.[31]

Sometime during 1959—probably after the Soviet Twenty-first Party Congress in February—the irreconcilability of their national objectives became evident to Mao and Khrushchev. China sought control over Formosa and the offshore islands, domination of Tibet, and favorable adjustments on the Sino-Indian border. In addition the Chinese wanted a greater voice within the socialist camp and recognition as a great power. Khrushchev's foreign policy objectives at the time focused primarily upon relations with the West. First and foremost he sought recognition by the United States as coequal in status as a world power. He wanted to resolve the basic conflicts of the cold war and thereby reduce the possiblity of a military clash with the United States. Toward this end he initiated a vigorous campaign of summit diplomacy such as his visit to the United States in the fall of 1959. That trip was followed by a visit to Beijing in October where the Soviet premier proposed to the Chinese that they abandon their claim to Formosa and accept a "Two Chinas" formula. Certainly Khrushchev's application of peaceful coexistence must have appeared to Mao as a Soviet effort to reach an accommodation with the West at the expense of China. Not all of Khrushchev's goals, however, were tension-reducing. He sought to pressure the West into making concessions in Europe, particularly over Berlin. He courted the neutralist Third World to undermine Western influence. Even his efforts to thwart the West in Asia and Africa did not necessarily meet with Chinese approval. One of Khrushchev's main targets was India, which in this period was more hostile to China than to the West. When several incidents took place along the Sino-Indian border in the fall of 1959 Khrushchev sacrificed his obligations to socialist solidarity to declare Soviet neutrality. The Chinese were outraged.

While there was some overlapping of national interest between the giants of the communist world, it was becoming clear to each that many of their interests clashed. China felt betrayed by Khrushchev's willingness, even occasional eagerness, to court the imperialist United States and the neutralist countries. Proletarian internationalism, the Chinese believed, should have produced a different set of priorities for a socialist state. The Russians, on the other hand, were annoyed and at times frightened by the aggressiveness of Chinese demands which appeared to be an impediment to the execution of what some have called Khrushchev's "grand design."[32] An unmistakable sign of its distrust of the Chinese was the Soviet government's unilateral abrogation in June 1959 of the 1957 military aid agreement in which it had promised to give China technical data for the manufacture of the atomic bomb. Obviously, China was becoming a potential rival who could not be trusted. The termination of military aid did not automatically bring with it an end to economic assistance. In the summer of 1960, however, economic assistance was abruptly curtailed with severe economic repercussions for China. Between 2–3,000 Soviet specialists suddenly left China, removing or destroying the blueprints of their projects. China would later claim that Moscow's action "inflicted enormous losses upon China's socialist construction." By now the dispute was moving toward a schism. The socialist camp was disintegrating even if the forms of unity were retained on the surface.

There is a strong possibility that Khrushchev may have tried to influence the Chinese by involving himself in Chinese intraparty politics. In mid-1959 Chinese Defense Minister Peng Teh-huia openly challenged both Mao's domestic and foreign policies. His critique was part of an internal crisis comparable to the Soviet "anti-Party" crisis of 1957. Peng is believed to have been in personal contact with Khrushchev. It is quite likely that the Chinese thought so. His opposition, however, was crushed by Mao at the eighth plenum of the Central Committee at Lushan in July and August. [33]

During the early 1960s the split deepened as both sides attempted to mobilize support within the communist camp. The odds strongly favored the Russians. Sino-Soviet differences were fought out in private until 1960. It fell to the Chinese to hang socialism's dirty linen on the line for all to see. On the occasion of the 90th anniversary of Lenin's birth in April 1960, the Chinese published a lengthy critique of the Russians under the title "Long Live Leninism." The thesis of this publication was that they, not the Russians, were the true standard bearers of Lenin's revolutionary tradition. From polemic by pen the debate escalated to verbal diatribe. The first head-on confrontation took place at a meeting of the Rumanian Party Congress in June 1960. A verbal slugfest between Khrushchev and P'eng Chen publicly forced the communist delegates to take a stand on one side or another, much to the distaste of several of them. All that they could agree on was to hold a major conference of all parties in Moscow in November. The meeting of 81 communist parties in Moscow was an historic event for the socialist camp. The Soviet leadership found itself for the first time condemned in its own backyard before an international audience. In an unprecedented way it had to politic among lesser members of the camp to rally support for its position. No longer could Moscow automatically assume complete compliance by the entire camp with the prevailing Soviet line. Only a dozen parties supported the Chinese position but that was enough to introduce a new pattern in the process of intracommunist politics. On the surface, this meeting continued to maintain the facade of unity but it was the last such conclave to do so. As Zbigniew Brzezinski observes, the 1960 Moscow meeting was a watershed in the evolution of the communist camp.[34]

Sino-Soviet relations deteriorated further during the 1960s. The split was characterized by polemical exchanges in a variety of forms and forums: international conferences, the press, radio broadcasts, party letters, and diplomatic dispatches. At first much of the public debate focused on Albania and Yugoslavia as proxies for the main contestants. Albania, as China's strongest (in fact, its only) ally in Europe, received the brunt of Soviet criticism. Khrushchev utilized the Twenty-second Congress of the Soviet Party to lash out against the Albanian Party leadership as well as Joseph Stalin. The Soviets broke diplomatic relations with Albania shortly afterwards. Soon, however, the thrusts against each other were made directly. China openly criticized Khrushchev's capitulation to President Kennedy during the Cuban missile crisis. They were even angrier over Khrushchev's tacit support of India during the Sino-Indian war that occurred almost simultaneously. These two crises confirmed Chinese suspicions about Soviet weakness in the face of imperialism and its fidelity to the cause of revolution. Additional confirmation came with the signing of the test ban treaty in August 1963. This treaty was the first important arms control measure between the superpowers in the postwar era. While the treaty itself did not cause the deterioration in relations between China and the Soviet Union that followed its signing, it did symbolize the changing complexity of international relations. That complexity was forcing the leaders of world communism and capitalism to come to terms with each other even against the interests of their own partners: France opposed the treaty as much as China. After the collapse of talks in Moscow to bridge Sino-Soviet differences, the Chinese in July 1963 published a scathing attack on Soviet policy.

During this phase of the schism several new features appeared. First, the ideological clash expanded to include accusations of internal as well as external deviation. Hitherto the doctrinal debate had focused on how best to cope with imperialism; now the two sides included criticism of each others internal regimes. The Soviet Union was found to be moving toward the restoration of capitalism in Russia, and Mao was accused of building a military dictatorship. Secondly, the quarrel was extended to include governmental as well as party elements. More and more Sino-Soviet differences covered the whole spectrum of their relationships. Finally, an important development of this period was the raising of territorial claims by China and the escalation of clashes along their common border in Asia. Here was a major factor in the transformation of the schism into a conflict.

Although not publicized at the time, border incidents occurred as early as July 1960. The Chinese first publicly suggested a revision of the frontiers in March 1963 when they responded to chiding by Khrushchev for permitting the colonies of Macao and Hong Kong to remain in "imperialist" hands. The *Peoples Daily* cited nine treaties that had been forced upon the Chinese by the Tsars and inquired: "In raising questions of this kind do you intend to raise all the questions of unequal treaties and invite a general settlement?" Khrushchev displayed some willingness to negotiate minor border differences but as regarded any substantial concessions of territory, the Soviet government was quite clear:

there would be none. In a statement issued in September the Soviet government warned, "[T]he artificial creation of any territorial problems in our
times, especially between Socialist countries, would be tantamount to embarking on a very dangerous path."[35] Boundary negotiations did take place
in Beijing from February through May 1964 but were suspended following
the Soviet refusal to consider the Chinese claim to some 580,000 square miles
of Soviet territory in the Far East.

Border difficulties were not limited to Chinese claims along the Soviet Far
Eastern frontier. Periodically, tension arose along the Central Asian frontier
which divided the Chinese province of Sinkiang from the Soviet republics
of Tadjikistan, Kirghizia, and Kazakhstan. During the early 1960s, China accused Soviet personnel of conducting "largescale subversive activities" in the
Ili region of Sinkiang and inciting and coercing tens of thousands of Chinese
to flee to the Soviet Union. Moscow charged in response that the Chinese
persecuted Kazakhs, Uighurs, and other nationalities causing some 50,000
Kazakhs and other tribesmen to seek refuge in the USSR. On and off through
the decade both sides accused the other of provoking incidents.

It is difficult to pinpoint the time when the two countries reached the conclusion that the other constituted the single greatest threat to itself, but that
point was almost certainly reached by the mid-1960s. Very early in his administration, Khrushchev advised his colleagues that "Conflict with China is
inevitable."[36] Shortly before his overthrow in October of 1964 he began preparations for a showdown with the Chinese Party at a planned world conference
of communist parties. Had Khrushchev remained in power it is likely the
Chinese would have been formally expelled from the world communist movement in 1965. The Chinese would probably have shifted their primary hostility
from the United States to the Soviet Union earlier had it not been for the
Vietnam war. But that conflict, at most, only delayed the ordering of enmities
by the Chinese. Around 1966 the Soviet Union came to be identified as China's
number one threat.[37] In March 1966 the Soviet Communist Party convened
its Twenty-third Party Congress, the first Congress boycotted by the Chinese.
In their letter rejecting the invitation, the Chinese asserted that "Russia . . .
used to be the centre of the international working-class movement." Now, however, "The leadership of the C.P.S.U. has become the centre of modern revisionism."[38]

Relations with China reached a nadir during the Great Proletarian Cultural
Revolution, officially inaugurated in August 1966. China's domestic and foreign
policies were in a state of turmoil for the next three years. Those in command
of Chinese politics went to extraordinary—at times bizarre—lengths to show
their hostility and contempt for the Russians, and the Soviets were not loath
to reply in kind. Demonstrations were organized outside embassies; students
and journalists were expelled. Eventually, diplomatic representation was

virtually severed. The "Svirsk" incident in the summer of 1967 illustrates the intensity of Chinese xenophobia. The second officer of a Soviet merchant ship, the *Svirsk,* in Dairen was accused of refusing to wear a badge bearing a portrait of Mao Zedong, throwing it into the sea instead. When the captain went ashore for clearance papers to leave the port he was arrested. While he was paraded through the streets in a lorry, his ship was invaded by Red Guards who destroyed equipment and painted anti-Soviet slogans all over it. Only after Aleksei Kosygin himself sent a telegram to Zhou Enlai did the Chinese agree to "deport" the Soviet captain and his ship. This was only one of many incidents that flared up between both countries.

As the Cultural Revolution began to wind down, a clash erupted between Soviet and Chinese forces which seriously raised the specter of war between the two countries for the first time. On March 2, 1969, a sizeable contingent of Chinese soldiers attacked some Soviet frontier guards on Damansky Island, a small uninhabited island in the Ussuri River which demarcates part of the Far Eastern Sino-Soviet boundary. The island—known to the Chinese as Chenpao—was one of several contested pieces of territory. Soviet casualties included the death of several score border guards. Strongly worded protest notes were sent by both sides followed by very emotional mass protest demonstrations in the capitals of both countries. As a lesson and a warning to the Chinese, on March 15, the Russians launched a sharp attack with heavy artillery units including missiles and tanks. They penetrated deep into Chinese territory for a short period of time. No official figures of casualties were given by either side, but they were believed to be heavy.

Although both sides were guilty of provocation in the Ussuri River crisis, it was clear that neither wanted to push the issue to extremes. For some days after the March 15 fighting the press of both countries published virulent and bellicose attacks on the other country's leaders, but the protest demonstrations were not renewed. The seriousness of the confrontation must have given pause to the leaders of both camps. A Soviet proposal to resume the boundary negotiations that had been broken off in 1964 was accepted. Later that year Aleksei Kosygin stopped off in Beijing following a trip to Hanoi to attend the funderal of Ho Chi Minh. At first it was unclear whether or not Beijing would welcome him. Shortly after Kosygin's visit both sides agreed to a resumption of diplomatic relations. Though nothing between them had been resolved, neither side wanted more overt clashes.

One might have expected the Vietnam war to have drawn the two communist powers together, but, if anything, it had the opposite effect. The competition for influence in Hanoi became so intense that it only widened their differences. During the early years of American involvement the Soviet Union made several efforts to encourage a negotiated settlement. At that time the Chinese were pushing the North Vietnamese to oppose any suggestions of a compromise. China's perception of American involvement in Vietnam and Asia, however, changed as her relationship with the Soviet Union worsened. Initially the American presence in Indochina could only be viewed as a direct threat to the Peoples Republic of China. Over time the menace of American "imperialism" began to appear less deadly in comparison to the Soviet threat. Coinciding with the Great Proletarian Cultural Revolution the Soviet Union began a massive buildup of military forces along the Chinese border and gave indications for several years that these forces might be used in a preemptive attack. By 1969 Mao could see that American power in the Pacific might constitute an important counterweight to the Soviet Union in the Asian balance of power. At this time Brezhnev, too, was thinking in terms of an Asian balance of power, and his conclusions were the obverse of Mao's. The answer to the Soviet problem of security was containment of the Peoples Republic. Thus, at a convocation of communist parties throughout the world in June 1969, Leonid Brezhnev introduced the idea of an Asian collective security pact. One might think of his proposal as a Soviet version of SEATO. Ironically the Soviet leader found himself in the same position vis à vis China as Secretary of State Dulles had in the 1950s, and his response was remarkably similar. But Brezhnev found few takers among the countries of Asia.

By the end of the 1960s the Sino-Soviet conflict had become one of the central factors in international politics. From the perspective of balance-of-power politics the logic of the situation called for both sides to turn to the United States for assistance against the other. And that is precisely what each did, and they did it at almost the same time. Perhaps the Chinese were slightly ahead. As early as October 1968, while the Cultural Revolution was in full gear, the Twelfth Plenum of the Chinese Communist Party agreed to seek an improvement in relations with the United States.[39] Because of the change in administrations in the United States as well as the Vietnam war, the Chinese had to move slowly. It was not until 1971 that substantial movement toward a rapprochement could take place. In January, U.S.-Chinese ambassadorial talks were resumed in Warsaw. In April an American ping pong team was invited to play in the Peoples Republic. Unknown to the public at the time, Henry Kissinger would make two trips to Beijing that year to prepare the ground for President Nixon's visit to China in 1972.

The same logic that propelled the Chinese toward a rapprochement with the United States guided the USSR toward "detente." It is not known precisely when Brezhnev and the Politburo decided to embark on a concerted effort to improve relations with the United States, but the Soviet intention to do so was made known at the Twenty-fourth Soviet Party Congress in March 1971. Thus, international politics as a consequence of the Sino-Soviet conflict had become triangular. The triangular relationship of the three great powers would dominate international politics into the 1970s and beyond.

CZECHOSLOVAKIA AND THE LIMITS OF POLYCENTRISM

The Soviet Union's conflict with China had a liberalizing effect upon Soviet relations with Eastern Europe. Moscow found itself having to court Eastern European support and votes at meetings of world communist parties. For Nikita Khrushchev, periodic conferences of communist parties were substituted for the Comintern or Cominform as the mechanism for hammering out the general line of the movement. After de-Stalinization Moscow's word was no longer automatically law. The Kremlin had to woo and cajole for those votes it got. Thus, at the 1960 meeting of world communist parties, Khrushchev's theses were largely adopted but only after an energetic political campaign.

Soviet hegemony in Eastern Europe continued but after the events in Hungary and Poland in 1956 it rested upon more subtle and complex means than before. The basis of Soviet control rested only in part upon the army (via the Warsaw Pact) and upon economic linkages (via COMECON) to the USSR. The most essential ingredient was Moscow's capacity to select those individuals holding high-ranking positions in the party and state bureaucracy or, at the least, to ensure that those who were selected were loyal to Moscow. Where possible the Soviets encouraged a sensitivity to the Kremlin by inducing rising Eastern European bureaucrats to attend Soviet party and technical schools for advanced training. "It is likely," notes Christopher Jones of this period, "that the Soviet diplomatic and intelligence services attentively flatter, bribe, and cajole these and other officials in the East European parties into placing themselves under obligations to Moscow."[40]

There were three circumstances that could undermine Soviet hegemony over the states in the socialist state system. One would be the coming to power of party elites who would be completely or substantially independent of Moscow from the beginning of communist rule. These elites would have to rely on domestic sources for their power. A second situation would be for a party leader originally installed by Moscow to move gradually away from Soviet influence. To accomplish this, a leader with nationalistic tendencies would have to acquire control gradually over the lower, then the middle and finally the upper echelons of the party apparatus. Eventually a renegade leader would need a secure domestic base of popular support. Thirdly, a party could become autonomous as a result of an intraparty struggle between a faction loyal to Moscow and a reform faction with indigenous support in which the latter won out.[41] In the decade after the Hungarian and Polish uprisings, the growth of polycentrism took place under each of these three different sets of circumstances. The socialist states achieving the greatest degree of independence from the Soviet Union were Yugoslavia, Albania, Rumania, and for a while, Czechoslovakia.

Yugoslavia and Albania illustrate communist regimes whose leaders took control independently of Soviet action. We have already seen how Tito removed Yugoslavia from the Soviet bloc and how subsequently without re-entering the bloc he became reintegrated into the communist movement. Tito remained committed to socialism throughout his long life although his relations with the Soviet Union alternated between hot and cold. Notwithstanding Tito's refusal to join either COMECON or the Warsaw Pact, Khrushchev publicly recognized Yugoslavia as a "socialist state" and as a member of the "socialist commonwealth." Tito was one of those rare party leaders able to have his cake and eat it too: in the delicate balance between east and west, he managed to maintain relations with the Soviet Union on his own, not Khrushchev's or Brezhnev's, terms.

Fear and hatred of Yugoslavia has been so central to Albania's foreign policy outlook that its relations with the Soviet Union were bound to deteriorate as Soviet relations with Yugoslavia improved. Albanians knew only too well that only Stalin's break with Tito spared them absorption into the Yugoslav republic. Thus, when the Sino-Soviet dispute developed into a schism and China made Yugoslavia one of its prime targets, it was only natural that Enver Hoxha should grasp the hand of a potential ally. In return for China's economic aid and political support, Hoxha became one of Khrushchev's bitterest critics in the communist camp. He could give vent to his natural fanaticism, secure in the knowledge that Albania's geographical isolation from the Red Army protected his regime. Khrushchev could do little more than reply with verbal abuse which he did, most notably at the Twenty-second Congress of the Communist Party in October 1961. Shortly thereafter diplomatic relations between the two countries were ruptured. To this day Albania operates as an independent communist state outside of the Soviet bloc. By the late 1970s even Albanian relations with China deteriorated as Sino-American relations improved.

Rumania's movement toward polycentrism illustrates the second pattern, that of a leadership originally solidly in the Soviet camp that gradually moved away. Gheorghe Gheorghiu-Dej, who became first secretary of the Rumanian Communist Party after the war, was one of a small group of Rumanian communists who did not, like so many other Eastern European communists, spend the war in exile in Moscow. There is a strong anti-Russian tradition in that country which looks upon itself as possessing a Western culture. The Soviet annexation of Bessarabia during the war intensified Rumanian anti-Russian nationalism. Gheorghiu-Dej, although a dedicated neo-Stalinist, succeeded in harnessing the support of domestic nationalism. He encouraged the replacement of Russian by Latin cultural influences, steered a neutral course in the Sino-Soviet dispute, and most importantly, he maintained Rumania's economic independence in the face of Soviet pressures to integrate the economies of Eastern Europe.

In June 1962, at a meeting in Moscow, Khrushchev obtained a commitment of the Eastern European First Secretaries, to a proposal for joint planning of the economies of the COMECON countries. Khrushchev's plan was to develop further the industrial base of the Soviet Union, Czechoslovakia, and East Germany while encouraging Rumania, Bulgaria, Poland, and Hungary to become primary raw material producers. Gheorghiu-Dej, accurately seeing this as an impediment to Rumania's becoming a fully industrialized country, quietly voiced his objections. Early in 1963 at a meeting of the Executive Council of COMECON, Rumanian resistance to integration was expressed more vigorously. At the same time Rumania was increasing its trade with both the West and the People's Republic of China. On April 22, 1964, in a virtual "declaration of independence," Gheorghiu-Dej completely rejected the Soviet moves to integrate the economies of the region. Because all COMECON decisions must be unanimous the idea had to be abandoned. At his death in 1965, Gheorghiu-Dej was succeeded by Nicolae Ceauescu, who continued his predecessor's skillful balancing act between good relations with Moscow and autonomy. Until the advent of the "Czech Spring" in 1968, Rumania was the most independent of any member of the Soviet bloc, and unlike Czechoslovakia, it has succeeded in retaining its autonomy.[42] Much of that success is because of the rigid control maintained by the Rumanian Communist Party and the maintenance by the party leadership of very orthodox domestic policies.

The Czech crisis in 1968 confronted the Kremlin with an unprecedented challenge to its leadership. Leonid Brezhnev and his colleagues in the Politburo were willing to concede a substantial independence in foreign policy—early in April 1967, Rumania had radically breached Soviet bloc discipline by establishing diplomatic relations with West Germany—as long as membership in the Warsaw Pact remained unimpaired. Developments in Czechoslovakia, however, introduced two particularly disturbing elements for the Soviets: first, they saw control of the Czech communist party fall into the hands of a reform faction completely independent of Moscow; and second, they feared that party control over the political system would erode as a result of a number of democratic changes being made in the country.

In 1968, Czechoslovakia was ripe for reform. For 15 years the country had been badly governed under the authoritarian rule of Antonin Novotny, who for a long period combined the offices of president of the country and first secretary of the Party. The most serious problem was the economy. As a result of extreme centralization, economic growth had declined significantly with production in some years actually falling. Goods were scarce, prices high, and initiative stifled. Another source of dissatisfaction was the general political repression under Novotny's rule. Czech intellectuals in particular resented the lack of artistic, cultural, and literary freedom. Unlike the rest of Eastern

Europe, Czechoslovakia did have, even if only briefly, a heritage of democratic government and freedom. The liberal tradition of Thomas Masaryk, the founder of the Czech state, had by no means been obliterated by two decades of communist rule. Finally, there was the problem of widespread Slovak unhappiness over their subordinate position within the Czechoslovak state. They wanted more autonomy. Conditions in the country were so bad by late 1967 that the Soviets were probably not unhappy to see Novotny go. When Leonid Brezhnev visited Prague in December he must have been aware of widespread hostility to Novotny, and there is no evidence that he moved in any way to prop him up.

The first step in the revolution was taken when, on January 5, Novotny was pressured to resign as First Secretary.[43] He was succeeded by Alexander Dubcek, the First Secretary of the Slovak Communist Party. There is no evidence that Dubcek assumed office with a preplanned program for liberalizing Czech society. Indeed, as a Moscow-trained communist he possessed all the credentials for a thoroughly reliable client. And in some ways he was. During the early months of 1968 Dubcek displayed uncertainty over how to respond to pressure from outside the Party for liberalization. His caution, even diffidence, hardly seemed characteristic of a revolutionary leader. His leadership of the reform faction of the party resulted, it would appear, less from his own initiative than from circumstances that simply thrust him toward the forefront. Throughout this period, Dubcek stressed his commitment to two cardinal conditions that he knew were vital to Moscow: (1) maintenance of communist party domination of Czech politics, and (2) membership in the Warsaw Pact. On April 24, the Czeckoslovak Government declared before the National Assembly:

The Czechoslovak Socialist Republic is a socialist country. The permanent foundation of Czechoslovak foreign policy is friendship and close cooperation with the Soviet Union and the other socialist countries. Our alliance with the Soviet Union belongs to those permanent, firm values whose purity has been fully confirmed by the critical examination of all values in our current revival process. This is so because our friendship with the Soviet Union arises organically from a number of experiences paid for so dearly by our nations, because we were brought to it by the very logic of historical development, the vital interests and needs of our homeland, because it is supported by the will, needs, and feelings of our people.[44]

Communist theoreticians, however, emphasize what they call the "objective" factors determining policy. What increasingly disturbed the Russians was the possibility that objective circumstances in Czechoslovakia might remove that country entirely from the Socialist camp. Two factors pointed in that direction: the seizure of the party organization by a faction hostile to Moscow's control and the establishment of new political freedoms that might lead to the displacement of Communist Party control of the government.

When Dubcek became First Secretary the party was divided between progressive and conservative factions, neither of which controlled the central party organs. It was through the Novotny group—the conservatives—that Moscow had been able to control the Czech party. In the struggle for power, which lasted through the spring and summer, the progressives, led by Dubcek, relied increasingly on the rank-and-file party membership and the public at large. This was a dangerous tactic because there was always the possibility that public opinion would demand more than Moscow would permit the progressives to deliver. Indeed, between January and August, Dubcek and his group had to toe a very thin line at times. In a show of strength on March 22, the reformers succeeded in forcing Novotny to resign as President. The Kremlin was less disturbed by this than by the growing tendency of the reform wing to assume control over cadre decisions, a step that could ultimately make that wing independent of Moscow.

To consolidate their early victories, the reformers knew they would have to win absolute control over the central organs of the party, the presidium, and the central committee. A Plenum of the central committee in April brought them some success when several conservatives were purged from the presidium. Of 11 members the progressives had a solid 5, the conservatives 3, with the rest essentially centrists. To consummate their victory, the progressives wanted to call a special party congress that would elect a new central committee that would in turn control the presidium. At a plenum of the central committee in May they successfully outmaneuvered the conservatives and got a majority to vote for the convocation of the Party's 14th congress on September 9th. From that point on a vigorous campaign ensued for the support of the 1.7 million members of the Czech Communist Party. Just prior to the election of delegates to the party congress in late June the press published an appeal entitled "2,000 words to the workers, farmers, scientists, artists and everyone" which urged popular support for the progressive wing of the party. The election gave the progressives an overwhelming victory.

Brezhnev found the prospects of a reform-controlled party congress extremely disturbing. In mid-July he mobilized five of the Eastern European countries—the same five who were to invade Czechoslovakia in August—for a meeting in Warsaw. Out of this meeting came a joint "Warsaw Letter" which called upon the "healthy" forces of the Czech party to purge the progressives and postpone the impending Congress. It was a futile effort. Meanwhile Brezhnev tried another approach: he pressured Dubcek and his colleagues to meet with Soviet leaders in Moscow. Dubcek would not agree to a meeting on Soviet territory, but an arrangement was worked out for a meeting of the Czech and Soviet party leaders at Cierna on the Czechoslovak side of the border on July 29th. It proved inconclusive. Another meeting was convened at Bratislava which brought together five of the Eastern European party leaders with the Czechs. Although nothing was resolved at this meeting they were all able to agree to a common declaration. Apparently the Czechs made the erroneous assumption that they had satisfied the Russians. The Bratislava Statement resolved:

The conference participants expressed the firm desire to do everything in their power to intensify all-round cooperation among their countries, based on the principles of equality, respect for sovereignty and national independence, territorial integrity and fraternal mutual aid and solidarity.[45]

At the same time that the Moscovite faction was losing control of the party the reformers were so liberalizing Czechoslovak society that an erosion of communist party control over the entire political system became possible. This was the prospect given by the Soviet Union as justification for its military intervention. It claimed that the Czechoslovak party had abandoned its "leading role" and had lost control of political developments throughout the country. During the early months of 1968 the process of democratization moved slowly. At the end of February government censorship was abandoned in practice. Legally, the powers of the government censor remained; they simply ceased to be used. This proved an important step in the democratizing process because the press became the principal instrument for the changes that were to follow.

A major step was taken on April 16 when the central committee of the party adopted what for a communist society can only be described as a radical program. This "Action Program" covered a broad spectrum of policies that in their totality sought to institutionalize a division of power within the political system. For the first time since the communist take-over in 1948, the communist party acknowledged an important role for other political parties. Although it reaffirmed the leading role of the communist party, the program also provided that "The whole *National Front,* the political parties which form it and the social organizations will take part in the creation of state policy."[46]

In the following months the movement toward democratization accelerated, now spurred on by widespread popular demands for greater freedom. On June 20, the government legally abolished all advanced censorship. Compared to "bourgeois" rights, this was hardly freedom of the press; publishers were still held accountable for what they printed, but, again, in the socialist state system this was unprecedented. In the summer the government adopted the policy of granting passports to citizens as a matter of right. The culmination of this trend came on August 10 when *Rude Pravo* published the "Draft Statutes of the Czechoslovak Communist Party" for consideration by the impending party congress. These statutes would have permitted secret voting in party activities, protected the right of minorities to adhere to dissenting views, and limited the term of office for party leaders. Although the draft affirmed the principle of "democratic centralism," the changes introduced would have in fact ended democratic centralism as developed by Lenin and practiced by every other party in power. They would have legitimized the sin of sins in party activity: factionalism.[47] At this point there seems to have been little doubt that the breach with the Soviet party had become irreparable.

One other factor contributed to the Soviet decision to destroy Dubcek's rule forcibly and that was Czechoslovakia's policy toward West Germany. At the Karlovy Vary conference of the previous year the Soviet Union had made it absolutely clear that no Warsaw Pact power was to emulate Rumania's establishment of diplomatic relations with West Germany. East Germany's party boss, Walter Ulbricht, was desperately fighting to avoid political isolation as West Germany engaged in a vigorous campaign to build political bridges to Eastern Europe. Alexander Dubcek fully realized the importance to the Soviet Union of this issue but he was under considerable pressure to open up relations with West Germany. For one thing, the East German regime of Walter Ulbricht was intensely unpopular with the Czechoslovak populace, not because West Germany was so particularly admired, but Ulbricht so greatly represented the kind of authoritarianism from which the Czechs were trying to escape. But perhaps of greater significance was the need for hard currency to build up the economy. Dubcek's government did at one point consider seeking a loan from West Germany. There was an increasing exchange of high-level visitors between Prague and Bonn, much to the consternation of Moscow and Pankow. Among the Warsaw Pact countries, none more vigorously urged a military solution to end the "Prague Spring" then East Germany.

There is considerable uncertainty as to when the Soviet Union made its decision to invade. The smoothness of the military operation that began on August 20–21, coupled with the clumsiness of the political preparations, suggest an indecisiveness on the part of the policymakers in the Kremlin.[48] The August invasion had been preceded in June by Warsaw Pact maneuvers in Czechoslovakia. Although these maneuvers had been prearranged with the Czechoslovak government, the presence of Soviet troops on Czechoslovakian territory beyond the scheduled date of departure constituted a form of coercion. At the meeting in Cierna, the Soviet leaders promised to withdraw their forces, a fact that may have led Dubcek to believe that the crisis in Czech-Soviet relations was ebbing. Some believe that the Soviet participation in the Cierna and Bratislava meetings was essentially a ruse to deceive the Dubcek regime.[49]

Czechoslovakia offered no military resistance to the Soviet invasion. Instead the government and people met Soviet troops and tanks with passive resistance. "We call on all the people," declared the Czech National Assembly on August

21 (in a unanimous vote), "not to take any violent action against the occupation armies and not [to] let themselves be provoked by various forces which want to gather proof for the justification of the intervention and use the situation for self-appointed actions."[50] To their embarrassment, the Soviets could find no individual or group willing to form an alternative government. The Soviet operation generated close to a nationwide animosity to the Russians and destroyed any political legitimacy the conservatives (the pro-Moscovites) might have hoped to acquire. Dubcek and a delegation of Czech leaders were brought to Moscow where, on August 26, they were coerced into signing a "Moscow Protocol" which invalidated the 14th party congress and committed the Czechs to purge the party of its progressives, reestablish censorship of the press, ban the Social Democratic Party, and order the removal of the issue from the agenda of the United Nations Security Council.[51] To promise a purge of the progressives was one thing; to bring to the fore a cadre of pro-Moscow leaders— who would have been Quislings in the eyes of the Czech people—was another thing. When the central committee met on August 30 to elect a new presidium the progressives again won a majority. In the face of powerful resistance both among the masses and within the communist party the Soviet Union moved slowly, though inexorably. On October 16, the government in Prague signed a treaty that legitimized the presence of Soviet forces in Czechoslovakia, but even with Soviet pressure the conservatives required eight months of maneuvering before they could take control of the party. Not until April 1969 did the relatively moderate pro-Moscow Slovak Gustav Husak replace Alexander Dubcek as First Secretary. He remains in power to this day.

The Soviet justification and rationalization for its invasion of Czechoslovakia is known in the West as the Brezhnev Doctrine, though Soviet authorities deny the existence of any such doctrine. It was published in *Pravda* on September 26, 1968 as an article entitled "Sovereignty and the International Obligations of Socialist Countries."[52] The article accused the Czechoslovak progressives of underdermining the principles of Marxism-Leninism. "Under the guise of 'democratization' these elements were shattering the socialist state step by step." The heart of the doctrine is the following argument:

There is no doubt that the peoples of the socialist countries and the Communist Parties have and must have freedom to determine their country's path of development. However, any decision of theirs must damage neither socialism in their own country nor the fundamental interests of the other socialist countries nor the worldwide workers movement, which is waging a struggle for socialism. This means that every Communist Party is responsible not only to its own people but also to all the socialist countries and to the entire Communist movement. Whoever forgets this is placing sole emphasis on the autonomy and independence of Communist Parties lapses into onesidedness, shirking his internationalist obligations.

Sovereignty, *Pravda* asserted, cannot be considered in an "abstract" or "non-class" or "legalistic" manner. Those who condemned the Soviet invasion as illegal "forget that in a class society there is and can be no such thing as non-class law." Proletarian internationalism thus sets a limit to polycentrism within the Soviet bloc. No socialist state may leave the Warsaw Pact (though Dubcek emphatically rejected the idea of doing so, the Kremlin accused him of aspiring toward "neutrality"). The Communist Party must maintain a monopoly of power. (Its leading role in Czechoslovakia was never questioned by the reformers though they were prepared to permit lesser roles for other parties.) And finally, no party can fall under a leadership completely independent of Moscow. This was Alexander Dubcek's cardinal sin.

The Czech crisis left the socialist international system in a state of disarray. Only East Germany and Poland actively supported military intervention. Bulgaria complied loyally, Hungary somewhat reluctantly. Rumania, though a Warsaw Pact member, refused to participate in the "fraternal invasion." For Albania, Yugoslavia, and Rumania the implications of the Brezhnev Doctrine were ominous and each publicly condemned it. They were joined in their criticisms by the nonruling communist parties in Western Europe. Cuba supported it but with qualifications. Among the Asian parties, China condemned the action; North Korea, North Vietnam, and Mongolia supported it.

During 1968 a nascent special relationship between Rumania, Yugoslavia, and Czechoslovakia had begun to take shape as Belgrade and Bucharest responded sympathetically to Prague's independent behavior. A common desire to be independent of Moscow united this potential alliance of revisionist powers. Their domestic policies had little in common. Neither Yugoslavia nor Rumania showed any tendencies toward emulating Czechoslovakia's experiment in democracy. After the invasion, both Rumania and Yugoslavia took steps to strengthen their own defenses, even going so far as to propose to undertake joint defense arrangements against the potential threat from the East. Bucharest vigorously opposed Soviet postinvasion proposals to restructure the Warsaw Pact command system along supranational lines that would have enhanced Moscow's control over the organization. With the Czechoslovak experience fresh in mind, the Rumanians also successfully resisted Soviet pressure to stage military maneuvers on Rumanian territory.

Moscow needed more than ever to restore its authority over the socialist camp, and, if possible, to establish a general line for the movement. The only mechanism for achieving this was an international conference of the world's communist parties. The Soviet Union had attempted to promote such a conference since 1966, but the resistance of numerous parties to Moscow's position on China frustrated its efforts. Leonid Brezhnev argued for an international conference at the jubilee 50th anniversary celebrations of the Revolution. All that he could obtain was agreement on a preparatory consultative conference that was held in Budapest in February 1968. Though it required considerable maneuvering Moscow did obtain at Budapest the international conference it had long sought. The conference met on June 5, 1969, in Moscow.

What had been intended as a "unity" conference turned out to be a demonstration of communist polycentrism. The world communist movement had split into several groupings in the decade since the last international conference. In competition with the Soviet brand of orthodoxy were Maoism, Castroism, and the Eastern European reformers. Five of the fourteen ruling parties (China, North Korea, North Vietnam, Albania, and Yugoslavia) boycotted the conference. Thirteen Asian nonruling parties chose not to attend. As if reflecting the schism between the two communist giants, the movement itself had become split into European and Asian centers. Brezhnev's sharp attack on China violated a preconference pledge and angered several delegations, including those of Rumania and Italy.

The main document summarizing the work of the conference was a compromise. While it endorsed the main features of Soviet foreign policy it did not censure China by name and it pointedly observed that there was "no leading center of the international communist movement."[53] Of the 75 parties in attendance, 61 signed the main document without reservations, 14 had reservations or were opposed. The most obvious message of the conference was that polycentrism had become a permanent feature of the socialist system as well as the communist movement.

EUROCOMMUNISM

The Eurocommunism of the 1970s was an extension of the polycentric trend in international communism of the 1960s. The basic meaning of Eurocommunism is the right of each communist party to pursue its political destiny without interference from Moscow.[54] In principle, the idea is not limited to European or nonruling communist parties, but in practice the term has become virtually synonymous with the struggle of three West European communist parties—the French, the Italian, and the Spanish—to maintain a political stance independent of, and in some instances in opposition to, the Communist Party of the Soviet Union. What distinguished these three parties in the 1970s was the prospect of acquiring political power at home through democratic parliamentary elections.[55] In order to establish their legitimacy as genuine national parties (as opposed to Soviet surrogates), these three parties, in different degrees, were under pressure to disassociate themselves from the Soviet Union and its policies.

Leonid Brezhnev had not abandoned hope that Moscow might yet be able to reestablish the primacy of Soviet authority over the communist movement and possibly even engineer a condemnation of China by the European communist parties. In October 1974, Moscow proposed a summit meeting of European communist party leaders. There was strong resistance from the

"Eurocommunists" in the West and from Yugoslavia and Rumania in the East. A preparatory meeting in November 1975 broke up in a deadlock, dashing the Soviet leader's hope for a grand meeting before the Twenty-fifth Party Congress. Soviet persistance, however, led to the convocation in late June 1976 of an all-European meeting in East Berlin. Leaders from 29 communist parties attended—only Iceland and Albania did not attend. Even Yugoslavia's Marshal Tito attended—his first international communist meeting since his excommunication in 1948.

The East Berlin conference turned out to be a landmark in the evolution of polycentrism. Convoked to affirm Moscow's leadership of the international communist movement, it ended by denying it. The final document of the conference deliberately avoided any reference to "proletarian internationalism," Brezhnev's codeword for Russian hegemony. Instead, it affirmed that Europe's communist parties

will develop their internationalist, comradely and voluntary cooperation and solidarity on the basis of the great ideas of Marx, Engels, and Lenin, strictly adhering to the principles of equality and sovereign independence of each party, noninterference in internal affairs and respect for their free choice of different roads in the struggle for social change of a progressive nature and for socialism.[56]

As watered down as the final document was, it evoked little enthusiasm from anyone. It was neither signed nor voted upon at the end of the conference; it was simply approved in silence. Afterwards, Italian, French, and Yugoslav leaders all openly regretted attending the meeting and insisted they would not attend another like it in the future. Tito was quoted as saying that the 1976 conference "must have no past and no future"—that is, it was not to be considered the beginning of any new international communist structure nor the revival of any old one.[57]

Eurocommunism continues to be a thorn in the Soviet struggle for "proletarian internationalism." Moscow is bound by ties of history and ideology to the communist parties of Western Europe. In the words of one authority, "They represent what is left of the vision of capitalism's demise and the proletarian revolution consummated. Since the Soviet leaders base much of their own system's legitimacy on this vision, they care profoundly how these parties serve it."[58] Moscow wants and needs Western Europe's communist parties as allies in the world communist movement. Some, however, refuse to behave as allies. At one end of the Eurocommunist spectrum is the French Party, one of Europe's largest and generally loyal to the USSR. At the other end has been the Spanish Communist Party under the leadership of Santiago Carillo. In his book *Eurocommunism and the State,* Carillo not only defends Spain's right to an independent road to socialism, but he attacks the legitimacy of the Soviet state as un-Marxist and condemns Soviet domination of the Eastern European states. From Moscow's perspective, Carillo went too far.[59]

The Soviet Union, while implicitly recognizing that the movement has lost the unity it once had, has never completely abandoned the effort to forge a unified line against "capitalist imperialism." During the spring of 1980, in the aftermath of the Afghanistan crisis (discussed below in chapter 8) Moscow again sought to mobilize the European parties around a "peace program" reminiscent of the "peace appeals" of a generation earlier. The French and Polish parties invited Europe's communists to a conference in Paris in April. It was the first meeting of its kind to be held outside of a communist country. Twenty-two parties participated, but the meeting was boycotted by the Rumanian, Yugoslav, Italian, Spanish, British, and Swedish parties. Their attitude was expressed by a leader of the Italian Party, who noted, "We as Communists refuse to accept that anyone is a guide for other parties."[60]

The Eurocommunist rejection of a guiding center in the world communist movement poses a constant challenge to the Kremlin. More is at stake than the mere loss of influence over Western Europe's communist parties. By providing an alternative model of socialism, Eurocommunists threaten to undermine the bureaucratic regimes of Eastern Europe and, as Charles Gati notes, "Eurocommunism is a primary source of ideological justification and political leverage in their [East European] search for more independence from Moscow."[61] Perhaps, however, the most serious challenge is to the bureaucratic dictatorial apparatus in the Soviet Union itself, for Eurocommunism threatens Moscow's efforts to legitimize its own power and revolutionary internationalism. The legitimation of Soviet power is one of the main functions of world communist conferences, and it can be presumed that Moscow will continue to strive for recognition as communism's global leader through such conferences.[62]

NOTES

1. Teresa Rakowska-Harmstone. "'Socialist Internationalism' and Eastern Europe—A New Stage," *Survey 22,* no. 1 (Winter 1976): 43.
2. Quoted in Jan F. Triska, "The Socialist World System in Search of a Theory," in *The New Communisms,* ed., Dan N. Jacobs (New York: Harper and Row, 1969), p. 19.
3. Quoted in Robert C. Tucker, *The Soviet Political Mind* (New York: Praeger, 1963), p. 173.
4. N. Bukharin, "Imperialism and Communism," in *The Soviet Union 1922-1962, A Foreign Affairs Reader,* ed., Phillip E. Mosely (New York: Praeger, 1963), p. 151.

5. E. Usenko, "International Legal Principles of Relations Between Socialist Countries," *International Affairs,* Moscow (August 1973), p. 50.

6. Triska, "The Socialist World System," contains a good analysis of Socialist Internationalism. Cf. pp. 25–44. For the Soviet description of the concept, see Shalva Sanakoyev, *The World Communist System.* (Moscow: Progress Publishers, 1972); also V. V. Zagladin, ed., *The World Communist Movement, Outline of Strategy and Tactics* (Moscow: Progress Publishers, 1973).

7. I. Dudinsky, "A Community of Equal and Sovereign Nations," *International Affairs* (November 1964), p. 6.

8. Quoted in Zagladin, *The World Communist Movement,* p. 464. Emphasis added.

9. Zbigniew Brzezinski, *The Soviet Bloc, Unity and Conflict,* rev. ed. (Cambridge, Mass.: Harvard University Press, 1971), p. 50. Much of the description of the pattern of Stalinist control is taken from this book.

10. Adam Ulam. *Titoism and the Cominform* (Cambridge, Mass.: Harvard University Press, 1952), p. 48. Much of the analysis of Titoism is taken from this book.

11. Brzezinski, *The Soviet Bloc,* p. 127.

12. Ibid., p. 67. This interpretation of the Stalinist interstate system is developed on pp. 134-138.

13. Hostility to the West, particularly the United States, has consistently been a dominant theme of Yugoslav foreign policy under Tito. See Lawrence Silberman, "Yugoslavia's 'Old' Communism," *Foreign Policy* no. 26 (Spring 1977): pp. 3-27.

14. Milovan Djilas. *Conversations With Stalin* (New York: Harcourt, Brace and World, 1962), p. 143.

15. See Ulam, *Titoism,* pp. 87-95, and Andrew Gyorgy, *Soviet Governments of Danubian Europe* (New York: Rinehart and Co., 1949), pp. 256-262.

16. *The Anti-Stalin Campaign and International Communism, A Selection of Documents,* edited by the Russian Institute of Columbia University (New York: Columbia University Press, 1956), p. 62. This statement was made by Khrushchev in his secret speech before the Twentieth Party Congress.

17. Ulam, *Titoism,* p. 107.

18. *Yugoslav Communism, A Critical Study.* Committee Print, 87th Congress, 1st session. Prepared for the Subcommittee to investigate the Administration of the Internal Security Act and Other Internal Security Laws of the Committee on the Judiciary, United States Senate. October 18, 1961 (Washington: U.S. Government Printing Office, 1961), pp. 171-176.

19. Roger Pethybridge, ed., *The Development of the Communist Bloc* (Boston: D.C. Heath & Co., 1965), p. 134.

20. Paul Zinner, ed., *National Communism and Popular Revolt in Eastern Europe, A Selection of Documents on Events in Poland and Hungary, February-November 1956* (New York: Columbia University Press, 1956), p. 6.
21. Ibid., p. 13.
22. The text is contained in ibid., pp. 1–89.
23. Brzezinski, *The Soviet Bloc*, p. 182.
24. J. M. Mackintosh, *Strategy and Tactics of Soviet Foreign Policy* (London: Oxford University Press, 1962), p. 156. Chapter 13 contains a good summary of the Polish uprising.
25. Ibid., p. 164. Christopher Jones argues that the Soviet Union will not use force to remove the leadership of a rebellious party if that leadership is prepared to defend itself with military force. See "Soviet Hegemony in Eastern Europe: The Dynamics of Political Autonomy and Military Intervention," *World Politics 29*, no. 2 (January 1977): 216-241. Zbigniew Brzezinski does not believe that the Soviets were inhibited by the Polish threat to fight, but rather by the lack of a clearcut reason why they should. He feels that the Soviets were uncertain as to the real meaning of the events in Poland; see Brzezinski, *The Soviet Bloc*, p. 261.
26. Brzezinski, *The Soviet Bloc*, pp. 219-222.
27. For a discussion of this point, see Joseph L. Nogee, "Polarity: An Ambiguous Concept," *Orbis 18,* no. 4 (Winter 1975): 1194-1205.
28. The treaties of Aigun (1858) and Peking (1860) gave to Russia 380,000 square miles of territory in Siberia. Today that territory includes the important port of Vladivostok.
29. Robert R. Simmons, *The Strained Alliance, Peking, P'yongyang, Moscow and the Politics of the Korean Civil War* (New York: The Free Press, 1975), marshalls considerable evidence to support this conclusion, though many of his other judgments in the book are speculative and polemical.
30. Brzezinski, *The Soviet Bloc*, pp. 374-375.
31. The Soviet concern was not just theoretical. The Bulgarians displayed what Moscow considered an unhealthy interest in the Chinese communes.
32. See Brzezinski, *The Soviet Bloc*, pp. 374-378, and Adam Ulam, *Expansion and Coexistence, Soviet Foreign Policy 1917-1973*, 2nd ed. (New York: Praeger, 1974) chapter 11.
33. In the spring of 1959 Peng spent seven weeks traveling in the Soviet Union and Eastern Europe, and he was in Albania at the same time Khrushchev had an unusually lengthy stay there. David Floyd, *Mao Against Khrushchev* (New York: Praeger, 1963), p. 66. William Griffith believes that the Lushan Plenum was "probably the point of no return in Sino-Soviet relations." *The Sino-Soviet Rift* (Cambridge, Mass.: The MIT Press, 1964), p. 18.
34. Brzezinski, *The Soviet Bloc*, pp. 411-412.

35. Keesing's Research Report, *The Sino-Soviet Dispute* (New York: Charles Scribner's Sons, 1969), p. 111.
36. *Khrushchev Remembers,* trans. and ed., Strobe Talbott (Boston: Little Brown and Co., 1970), p. 466. This admonition was made in 1954. At that time it could not have been a premonition of military conflict.
37. Harrison E. Salisbury, *War Between Russia and China* (New York: Bantam Books, 1970), p. 105.
38. Keesing Research Report, p. 88.
39. Richard C. Thornton, "Soviet Strategy and the Vietnam War," *Asian Affairs,* No. 4 (March–April, 1974), p. 221.
40. Christopher Jones, "Soviet Hegemony in Eastern Europe," pp. 221–222.
41. See ibid., pp. 227–228.
42. See William E. Griffith, *The Sino-Soviet Rift* (Cambridge, Mass.: The MIT Press, 1964), pp. 137–142; William E. Griffith, ed., *Communism in Europe, Continuity, Change and the Sino-Soviet Dispute,* v. 2 (Cambridge, Mass.: The MIT Press, 1966), pp. 12–13.
43. Detailed accounts of the Czech revolution in 1968 can be found in Philip Windsor and Adam Roberts, *Czechoslovakia 1968, Reform, Repression and Resistance* (New York: Columbia University Press, 1969) and Christopher D. Jones, "Autonomy and Intervention: The CPSU and the Struggle for the Czechoslovak Communist Party, 1968," *Orbis 19* no. 2 (Summer 1975). The account here draws heavily on these two sources. A very useful collection of documents on the crisis is Robin Alison Remington, *Winter in Prague, Documents on Czechoslovak Communism in Crisis* (Cambridge, Mass.: The MIT Press, 1969).
44. Remington, *Winter in Prague,* Document 20, p. 155.
45. Ibid., Document 41, p. 258.
46. Ibid., Document 16, p. 103.
47. See ibid., Document 43, pp. 265–287.
48. This is the argument made by Philip Windsor in *Czechoslovakia 1968* pp. 62–79.
49. Christopher Jones believes the Politburo authorized military intervention on August 6 at the same time it approved the text of the Bratislava Declaration. Jones, "Autonomy and Intervention," p. 617.
50. Remington, *Winter in Prague,* Document 59, p. 383.
51. Ibid. See Document 58, pp. 379–382.
52. The text is in ibid., Document 65, pp. 412–416.
53. See *World Communism, 1967–1969: Soviet Efforts to Re-Establish Control,* A Study prepared for the Subcommittee to Investigate the Administration of the Internal Security Act and Other Internal Security Laws of the Committee on the Judiciary, United States Senate, 91 Congress, 2 sess. (Washington: U.S. Government Printing Office, 1970), p. 269.

54. Rudolf L. Tokes, ed., *Eurocommunism and Detente* (New York: New York University Press, 1978), p. 2.

55. The adoption of a democratic constitution in Spain in 1977 permitted the Communist Party for the first time since 1936 to compete for seats in the Spanish Parliament. In Italy and France the communist parties had for years been active competitors in the electoral process, but for the first time since the later 1940s both parties entertained prospects of coming to power. An alliance of communists and socialists in France won 53 percent of the vote in regional elections in March 1976. The Italian Communist Party was in the strongest position of the three. Elections to the National Assembly in 1976 brought them to within a fraction of displacing the Christian Democrats as Italy's leading political party. In all three countries, however, the early hopes of communist electoral success proved premature. In the June 1979 elections in Italy the CPI suffered a decline. The PCF in 1977 abandoned its alliance with the Socialist Party and suffered a reverse in the March 1978 elections in France. In the first general elections in Spain in 40 years in June 1977 the CPE won only a respectable 9.4 percent of the vote. See Edward Mortimer, Jonathan Story, and Paolo Filo Della Torre, "Whatever Happened to 'Eurocommunism'?" *International Affairs* (October 1979), pp. 575-582.

56. *The New York Times,* July 1, 1976.

57. *The New York Times,* June 30, 1976.

58. Robert Legvold, "The Soviet Union and West European Communism," in Tokes, p. 317.

59. Ibid., pp. 376-377.

60. *The New York Times,* May 5, 1980.

61. Charles Gati, "The Europeanization of Communism," *Foreign Affairs 55,* no. 3 (April 1977): 546.

62. Wolfgang Leonhard, *Eurocommunism, Challenge for East and West* (New York: Holt, Rinehart and Winston, 1979), pp. 316-317.

Chapter 7
The Struggle for Detente

As the Soviet Union moved into its second half-century, the leaders in the Kremlin were confronted with a political landscape of unprecedented contours. Those who had seized power in October 1964 continued briefly along the paths charted by Nikita Khrushchev but it was not long before they were compelled to respond to the pressures of a changed political environment. By the end of the 1960s, Brezhnev's world was as different from Khrushchev's as Khrushchev's had been from Stalin's. The changes affected both the internal structure of Soviet society and the external character of international relations.

Probably the most fundamental development concerned the general structure of the international system. We have already noted the decline of bipolarity and its replacement by multipolarity which became evident during the 1960s.[1] Largely as a result of the strategy of nuclear deterrence the two superpowers found themselves stalemated in the use of power against the other. Neither could use—or even threaten to use—military force directly against the other for fear that military conflict might escalate into a nuclear holocaust. The political consequence of this stalemate was a decline in the cohesion of both sides' alliances, contributing, as we have seen, to the Sino-Soviet schism. New actors such as Europe, Japan, China, and some of the nations of the Third World rose to play more prominent roles in world politics. This is the essential meaning of the term multipolarity.

By the beginning of the 1970s, the general configuration of the international system came more sharply into focus. Global politics were assuming a triangular pattern, with the United States, the Soviet Union, and China as the main centers of world power.[2] Chinese power, of course, was immensely inferior to that of the Soviet Union and the United States but the potential was clearly there. China had a population in excess of 800 million and all the resources necessary to become a self-sufficient industrial power. Her iron reserves were the fifth largest in the world, her coal reserves the second. Even with limited petroleum reserves, China ranked third in the world's production and consumption of energy in 1969. Her armed forces in 1971 were numerically second only to those of the Soviet Union, though they lacked the advanced weaponry of the super-powers. At the time that the USSR and the United States were perfecting their nuclear second strike capabilities, China was just beginning to accumulate a nuclear stockpile. It was estimated that in 1971 China had produced sufficient fissionable material for approximately 120 atomic and nuclear warheads.[3] In possession of an abundance of uranium, China too would inevitably acquire a credible deterrent.

China's potential power did not in itself create a tripolar relationship. Power had to be combined with political conflict which, as we have seen, is the direc-tion Sino-Soviet relations took in the 1960s. Moscow and Peking became ad-versaries as Moscow and Washington, and Peking and Washington had been for some time. All three powers in fact became limited adversaries. Their antag-onisms, however, were not of equal intensity, as Michael Tatu has observed in describing this triangular relationship:

There is no such thing in practice as a struggle on two fronts, conducted with equal means and equal intensity against two adversaries who are also hostile to each other. In the nature of things at some point or other each power must choose a principal opponent.[4]

Whereas a decade earlier the two communist powers clearly considered Wash-ington their principal opponent, by the 1970s each considered the other "enemy number one." At first this distinction was only hinted at; later it was made explicit.

Whatever China's rank as an enemy of the Soviet Union, there was no doubt that the greatest threat to Soviet security still came from the United States. In military terms the global struggle for power remained, as it probably would throughout the century, a contest between the Soviet Union and the United States. The year 1970, however, brought a fundamental change in the military relationship between the two superpowers. For the first time in history the Soviet Union achieved a military position of approximate parity with the United States.

From the beginning of the arms race during the cold war, the Soviets had suffered a seemingly permanent inferiority to the Americans. Khrushchev had attempted to bluff in the late 1950s by claiming a greater capability than he in fact had, but the real weakness of Soviet power was exposed at the time of the Cuban missile crisis. Determined never again to be so vulnerable, Khrushchev embarked on a program of military expansion which his successors continued. By the end of the 1960s Brezhnev had achieved a rough balance. In 1970 the Soviet Union for the first time pulled alongside the United States in the number of intercontinental ballistic missiles (ICBMs). A year later they surpassed the United States in ICBMs by 1300 to 1054.[5] The United States remained ahead in many categories of arms, but that did not obscure the fact that in overall military capability the United States could no longer be considered preeminent. The political implications of this development were significant. For one thing, it meant that in arms control negotiations the Soviet Union could now negotiate from a position of equality. It did not have to fear that a disarmament or arms control plan would freeze it in a position of permanent inferiority. Thus, ironically, this increase in arms opened the way for a genuine effort in arms reduction, or, if not that, a stabilization of the arms race.

A third fundamental factor guiding Soviet foreign policy in the 1970s was the state of the Soviet economy. As they prepared the ninth five-year plan for the period 1971-75, Soviet economic planners found the economy in a crisis condition. Brezhnev and Kosygin had made economic growth one of the top priorities of their administration. In 1965 the Soviet leadership introduced a series of economic reforms whose purpose was to modernize the economy, stimulate growth, and improve the quality and quantity of goods available to the Soviet consumer. These reforms involved a decentralization of economic administration and the limited introduction of techniques of "market socialism." By the end of the eighth five-year plan (1970), it was clear that the reforms were a failure. A few figures will show the pattern of decline. Between 1950 and 1958 the gross national product (GNP) of the country grew by 6.4 percent; from 1958 to 1967 the rate of GNP growth dropped to 5.3 percent, and in the period 1967-73, it plummeted to 3.7 percent.[6] At heart the problem was one of productivity: How to increase it? One answer might be to restructure the economic system radically. Another could be to import technology from the industrialized West, particularly the United States.

The alternatives facing the Kremlin were stark. To do nothing would be to court trouble. Popular dissatisfaction with the quantity and quality of consumer goods was widespread. Repeated government promises of increases in consumer goods had stimulated popular expectations that could not be indefinitely deferred. Khrushchev was overthrown in large part because of his failure to improve the economy, a fact his successors knew only too well. The members of the Politburo could not automatically assume that their control over the levers of power in the Soviet political system rendered them immune from forces beneath them. They may have observed with some apprehension the consequences of popular hostility to the government in Poland in 1970. There, economic mismanagement had created widespread shortages of food and consumer goods which led to rioting in the cities of Gydnia, Gdansk, and Sczcecin, leading in turn to the replacement of Wladyslaw Gomulka by Edward Gierek. If there was a lesson in the Polish events, it was that even in a one-party dictatorship, popular pressure could force a change in leadership. On the other hand, the Kremlin could choose to reform the economy radically, perhaps by abolishing the collective farm system and truly decentralizing industrial administration. To do that, however, would disrupt the power and benefits of established interests in Soviet society, a prospect the Kremlin could hardly have welcomed. Thus, increasing productivity through importing technology by means of trade may well have seemed the safest road to take. Not surprisingly, the 1971-75 five-year plan provided for a growth in foreign trade of 35 percent. The actual growth in foreign trade turned out to be an increase of 186 percent.[7]

These changes in the political framework confronting Moscow—the emerging global tripolarity, military parity with the United States, and the stagnation of the Soviet economy—necessitated a rethinking of Soviet foreign policy as the decade of the 1960s gave way to the 1970s. The direction they all pointed toward was detente. There was nothing new in the idea of a relaxation of tensions; Stalin himself had on occasion advocated and practiced cooperation with the West. Nikita Khrushchev had developed the concept of peaceful coexistence and made it a permanent part of the Soviet general line. What was new about detente? In principle, nothing. In communist theory Brezhnev's detente adds nothing to the concept of peaceful coexistence. But in practice it was to encompass a much closer degree of cooperation with those countries that had previously been looked upon as adversaries. It envisioned cooperation in areas of arms control, trade, crisis settlement, science, technology, and more. Brezhnev wanted not just the avoidance of conflict, he needed the active collaboration of the West.

But what of the expansionist and hegemonic tendencies of the Soviet Union, its global rivalry with the United States, its perceptions of the industrialized capitalist nations as "imperialistic" adversaries? What of the pressures of the military-industrial complex—the army and the "steel-eaters"—in Soviet society? Soviet policymaking under Brezhnev was not monolithic, if indeed, it ever had been. The fact is that Brezhnev had to struggle for detente. Sometimes he won and sometimes he didn't. Sometimes he put aside detente policies for other priorities. Throughout the 1970s and into the decade of the 1980s, Soviet policy was characterized by ambiguities and contradictions. In the end, detente did not survive his administration.

Brezhnev won support for his "peace program" at the Twenty-fourth Party Congress which met from March 30 to April 9, 1971. One indication of the importance of foreign policy was the unusually large number of foreign delegations participating in the Congress. Out of 101 delegations from 90 countries, there were 22 "national-democratic" and left-wing socialist (i.e., not communist parties) parties represented. The Report of the Central Committee delivered by Brezhnev revealed a dual approach: peaceful coexistence combined with resistance to imperalism. Thus he reported:

Our policy has always combined firm rebuffs to aggression with the constructive line of settling pressing international problems and maintaining normal, and, wherever the situation allows, good relations with states belonging to the other social system. As in the past, we have consistently stood up for the Leninist principle of peaceful coexistence of states, regardless of their social system. This principle has now become a real force of international development.[8]

DETENTE IN EUROPE

If detente was to replace the cold war, the major powers were going to have to come to grips with the problem of Germany, which in the beginning had been the core issue of the cold war. For a quarter of a century the German problem spawned a number of divisive questions: Under what conditions were East and West Germany to be united? How could the German Democratic Republic be politically isolated? Should either Germany be armed? Should the Federal Republic have access to nuclear weapons? How permanent was the Oder-Neisse boundary with Poland? What was to be the status of Berlin? What was Soviet responsibility for allied access to West Berlin? How were refugees from East Berlin to be stopped? These and related questions made up the agenda of many Big Four foreign ministers and heads-of-government meetings. Related to the problem (or problems) of Germany were the broader territorial changes in Eastern Europe—the Soviet Union's acquisition of parts of Germany, Finland, Czechoslovakia, Poland, and Rumania—that were made during and after the second World War. There was also, of course, Soviet concern about Western acceptance of the permanence of the socialist revolutions engineered in the countries of Eastern Europe. Leonid Brezhnev defined one of the basic tasks of the Soviet Communist Party at the Twenty-fourth Party Congress as the need to secure:

The final recognition of the territorial changes that took place in Europe as a result of the Second World War. To bring about a radical turn towards detente and peace on this continent. To ensure the convocation and success of an all-European conference.[9]

The overriding Soviet objective was to secure Western acceptance of the division of Germany and the territorial and political changes in Eastern Europe. Ideally, Moscow would have liked to see all of Berlin incorporated into the German Democratic Republic; a lesser goal would have been to neutralize West Berlin by making it an international city. The central question for Brezhnev was how many concessions would have to be made to achieve any or all of these objectives. The basic Soviet position on Berlin suffered from a fundamental inconsistency. Their argument for acceptance of the status quo was premised on the necessity to accept the realities of European conditions since the war. One of those realities, however, was the integration of West Berlin into the political, cultural, and economic life of the Federal Republic.

Several important steps toward resolving the problem of Germany were taken in 1969. In October the Social Democrats (in alliance with the Free Democrats) won control of the Bundestag for the first time. Willy Brandt, the new Federal Chancellor, abandoned the long-held Christian Democratic goal of German unification, substituting for it the aim of reconciliation. In his inaugural speech on October 28, Brandt announced his formula of two German states within one German nation. Before the end of the year the Federal Republic had signed the Non-Proliferation Treaty and negotiations were opened in Moscow for a German-Soviet treaty. As a parallel of these developments the British, French, and Americans pressed the Soviet government for talks on Berlin.

West Germany and the Soviet Union each had powerful reasons to seek an agreement normalizing Germany's relations in Europe. Chancellor Brandt was convinced of the unreality of the goal of German reunification. The Hallstein Doctrine of treating any country's recognition of the German Democratic Republic as a hostile act had not led to the isolation of East Germany; indeed, there loomed the possibility that the Federal Republic might itself become isolated. Strong opposition, even among its allies, to Germany's having a finger on the atomic trigger, had killed the plan for a multilateral nuclear force in the mid-1960s, leaving Bonn more isolated than ever. Her primary ally, the United States, was mired in Vietnam, riven by internal divisions, and showing signs of a potential neoisolationism. For Brandt the policy of *Ostpolitik* was a gamble and a hope. His aspiration was to break down the barriers between the two German populations, and if the regimes could not be fused, at least to reconcile their peoples.[10] As he was operating from a position of weakness, Brandt inevitably had to give more than the Soviets, but as he advised his countrymen over television, he was conceding nothing that had not already been lost years ago.

A landmark treaty between the Federal Republic and the Soviet Union was signed in Moscow on August 12, 1970. It constituted the closest thing to a peace treaty terminating the second World War that exists. Article I specifically identified "detente" as the object of Soviet-German policies. The treaty provided for a mutual renunciation of force and described the frontiers "of all States in Europe" as inviolable, including the Oder-Neisse line between Poland and the German Democratic Republic.[11] Thus West Germany confirmed the division of that nation into two states and the loss of prewar German lands in the east to Poland. Brezhnev had at long last attained the Soviet goals in Germany that had eluded his predecessors for so many years.

A companion agreement to the Treaty of Moscow, as it was called, was the Treaty of Warsaw signed on December 7, 1970, between the Federal Republic and Poland. Its substance confirmed the commitments made by Germany regarding the Oder-Neisse boundary. While the Treaty of Moscow tilted markedly in Moscow's favor, the Germans set as a *quid pro quo* for ratification of the treaty the conclusion of a satisfactory four-power agreement on Berlin. Subsequently the NATO ministers resolved that an acceptable Berlin agreement would be a prerequisite for a conference on security and cooperation in Europe, another of the Kremlin's long-sought goals.

Negotiations between Britain, France, the United States, and the Soviet Union over Berlin began on March 26, 1970. They were to be long and difficult.

The issue of Berlin was complicated by the hard line taken by Walter Ulbricht, head of East Germany's SED (communist) party. Ulbricht attempted unsuccessfully to compel the Federal Republic to recognize the German Democratic Republic as a sovereign state as a precondition for an agreement on Berlin. During the 1970–71 negotiations, several issues divided the two sides. The most basic concerned the legal relationship between West Berlin and the Federal Republic. The Western powers wanted the city to be recognized as one of the states of West Germany. Bonn's constitution—known as the Basic Law—made provision for this. Both logic and the facts of Berlin's postwar development supported this position. The Western powers felt that if they were prepared to acknowledge East Berlin as the capital of the German Democratic Republic, the Soviet Union should be compelled to recognize West Berlin as part of the Federal German Republic. Moscow's position, however, was that West Berlin should be an independent political entity. What the Soviet argument lacked in logic was more than compensated for by the fact of communist control over the access to the city.

That too was a source of controversy. The Western powers maintained that transit between West Berlin and the Federal Republic should be guaranteed by Soviet, not East German, authority and should be unhindered. The Soviet Union insisted that responsibility for traffic through East Germany rested with the German Democratic Republic whose sovereignty it wanted recognized by the West. Two other differences stemmed from the controversy over Berlin's legal status. West Germany insisted upon the maintenance of a "federal presence" in West Berlin which the Soviets considered provocative. The Western allies held that diplomatic representation of West Berlin abroad was the responsibility of the Federal Republic. The Soviet Union contended that West Berlin was an independent political entity and objected to that authority. Finally, the Western allies wanted the people of West Berlin to have the same rights to visit East Berlin and East Germany as the citizens of the Federal Republic possessed.

Negotiations remained at an impasse for well over a year. Not until after the Twenty-fourth Party Congress in the spring of 1971 did the Soviets take the steps necessary to break the deadlock. It is quite likely that they had engineered the replacement on May 3 of hard-liner Walter Ulbricht as first secretary of the East German Communist Party by the more moderate Erich Honecker in order to obtain the agreement that was signed on September 3. It called for East and West Germany to conclude the necessary accords on the movement of traffic; they did so in December. The Final Quadripartite Protocol was signed on June 3, 1972. On the basic question of West Berlin's legal status and its ties with the Federal Republic the agreement was ambiguous. The major Soviet gains were the concession that West Berlin was "not to be a constituent part of the Federal Republic of Germany" and the Western agreement to limitation of the Federal presence in that city. The concessions to the Western powers included the Soviet promise of "unimpeded" transit between West Germany and acknowledgment of

Moscow's responsibility in that area. The Soviets agreed that the special financial, cultural, and economic ties between West Berlin and the Federal Republic could be maintained and developed. They also conceded that West German authority could represent West Berlin in all international agreements that did not concern matters of security and status. And finally, West Berliners were to be given the same access to East Berlin and East Germany as the citizens of West Germany had.[12] So, for the first time since 1945 the issue of Berlin as a source of East-West tension seemed to end. It was a victory for Willy Brandt's *Ostpolitik* and Leonid Brezhnev's detente. Its ambiguities, however, still left ajar an opening for further controversy, should the political structure of detente be undermined as it subsequently was.

All that remained to complete the integration of Germany into European and world politics was for the two Germanies to come to terms with each other. In August 1972, talks were opened in Berlin between the Federal Republic and the Democratic Republic on a basic treaty that was signed on December 21. This treaty also represented a political compromise that did not attempt a definitive *de jure* settlement of Germany's status. Its main provisions were threefold: (1) an exchange of permanent missions (not to be considered as embassies), (2) preservation of the German Democratic Republic's exemption (under the European Economic Community's regulations on inter-German trade) from the EEC common tariff on goods exported to the Federal Republic, and (3) approval of the application of both states to the United Nations (which was effected in September 1973).

Defusing the German problem was a major triumph of Soviet diplomacy, but that was only half the mark in the Soviet quest for Western acceptance of the permanence of the postwar changes in Europe. There remained the question of the territorial and political changes that had been made within and between the countries of Eastern Europe. What Brezhnev wanted was formal Western acquiescence in the Soviet sphere, a *de facto* legitimization of Europe's new balance of power. The device used to achieve this was a conference on security and cooperation in Europe. An all-European conference would supplement the German treaties and Berlin Agreement in an important way. Those treaties had brought about recognition of the status quo on a bilateral basis. A multilateral acceptance of the inviolability of Europe's borders would enhance that recognition even more. Furthermore, participation in such a conference by East Germany would virtually complete the process of its legitimation.

Originally the Soviet campaign for an all-European conference was linked closely to the problem of Germany. The idea goes back to a Soviet proposal for an All-European Treaty on Collective Security, introduced by V. M. Molotov at the Berlin conference of foreign ministers in 1954.[13] It was revived more than a decade later in the aftermath of the unsuccessful American attempt to create a multilateral nuclear force for NATO. At that time an important motivation behind the idea was the desire to undermine American political influence and possibly reduce the American military presence in Europe. Between 1966 and 1969 the proposal was endorsed repeatedly by various conferences of communist parties. On occasion the proposal was linked to a plan for the mutual disbandment of NATO and the Warsaw Pact.

With a suspicion that the purpose behind these proposals was to exacerbate divisions among the members of NATO and to ratify the existing division of Europe, the Western powers responded negatively. It was not until the meeting in Brussels in December 1969 that the NATO ministers made their first positive response to the Communist call for a conference on European security.[14] They made their assent to the meeting conditional upon progress on the Germany and Berlin negotiations. The completion of those agreements removed a major Western objection to the idea. President Nixon, without much enthusiasm, made a formal commitment at the 1972 Moscow Summit to participate in a European Security Conference. This commitment, however, was clearly linked to Soviet agreement to a parallel set of negotiations on a reduction of troops and arms in Europe. A suggestion by the Finnish Government led to the selection of Helsinki as the site of the European Security Conference. The first phase of what was to be an intensive effort by representatives of 35 states (every European state except Albania joined by the United States and Canada) began on July 3, 1973.

An agreement was forged after long preparation. The Final Act of the Conference on Security and Cooperation in Europe, commonly known as the Helsinki Declaration, was signed on August 1, 1975, at a summit-level gathering of the 35 participants. Not since the Congress of Vienna a century and a half earlier had Europe witnessed such a diplomatic conclave. The Helsinki Conference was the nearest thing that there would be to a peace conference officially ending World War II, but its accomplishments were not entirely what everyone had originally expected or wanted. With no strong interest in the convocation of the conference from the outset, the Western powers had intended to link its support for a conference to Soviet agreement to a conference on a mutual and balanced reduction of arms in Europe, which for them offered more prospects for substantive gain. During the course of the parallel negotiations, the conference on arms reduction stalled, leaving the West with only the Helsinki Declaration.

That Declaration turned out to be less than the total victory Brezhnev had anticipated. True, the Declaration produced for him the long-sought affirmation of the legitimacy of Europe's status quo. In the words of the Final Act: "The participating states regard as inviolable all one another's frontiers as well as the frontiers of all states in Europe, and therefore they will refrain now and in the future from assaulting these frontiers."[15] But in addition a section was included—the "Basket Three"—that affirmed a number of human rights to which all Europeans were entitled. Initiated by the Western European governments, the idea of human rights found support even among some Eastern European delegations. Eventually the Soviets, against their better judgment, capitulated. The signatories of the Final Act pledged: to respect human rights and fundamental freedoms including freedom of thought, conscience, or religion; to facilitate freer movement and contacts for persons individually or collectively; to permit travel for family visits; to permit family reunification; to facilitate the free and wider dissemination of information of all kinds; to improve dissemination of newspapers and publications from other states; and to grant accredited journalists multiple visas. Obviously these commitments were more than the Soviets had originally bargained for. Their implementation in the USSR could clearly lead to profound changes in the Soviet political system. That Brezhnev had no intention to permit Basket Three to modify Soviet practices was made clear by his statement at the conference that, "No one should try to dictate to other people, on the basis of foreign policy considerations of one kind or another, the manner in which they ought to manage their internal affairs."[16] Basket Three was the price Brezhnev had to pay for what was uppermost in his mind: the affirmation in the Final Act that the participating states agree to "broaden, deepen and make continuing and lasting the process of detente."

DETENTE WITH THE UNITED STATES

The final acceptance of Europe's boundaries and regimes settled the central issue of the cold war, but that met only a part of Soviet Russia's concerns. By the 1970s, Europe had ceased to be the center of East-West conflict. The achievement of the Kremlin's larger objectives now required a detente with the United States. Three objectives in particular necessitated a fairly close working relationship with the United States. First, there was the imperative of avoiding a superpower nuclear confrontation. Second, the USSR wanted to obtain American technology in order to build its economy, and that required a stable trade relationship between the two countries. Third, the Kremlin needed to prevent collusion between the United States and China to maintain its position in the global balance of power. Thus, the key to Brezhnev's detente lay in developing a working relationship with the citadel of world capitalism (or as Marxists see the United States, the center of world imperialism.)

Ideologically and politically, detente with the United States provided a profound dilemma for the Soviets. Their doctrine required them to view capitalist America as an adversary. How can an adversary be a friend? At no time has any Soviet spokesman ever disavowed the underlying conflict that must characterize the relationship between communist Russia and capitalist America. A typical expression of this relationship is described by S. Sanakoyev in a widely distributed text published well after detente had become the hallmark of Soviet foreign policy:

Peaceful coexistence is a principle of relations between states which does not extend to relations between the exploited and the exploiters, the oppressed peoples and the colonialists. . . . Marxists-Leninists see in peaceful coexistence a special form of the class struggle between socialism and capitalism in the world, a principle whose implementation ensures the most favorable conditions for the world revolutionary process.[17]

Still, Soviet spokesmen insisted, cooperative relations could be established that would enhance the prospects for world peace and even contribute to the betterment of each other's society. The object of detente then was not to eliminate the struggle between the superpowers—that was inherent in their social systems— but to set the ground rules governing that struggle.

It was not surprising that many Americans were suspicious of Soviet intentions. Were they serious or not? Was not detente basically a trojan horse to undermine Western resistance to the spread of either communism or Soviet power? Throughout Brezhnev's administration, these doubts were to plague Soviet-American relations, nor were all the doubts on the American side. The United States administration that came into power on January 20, 1969, was headed by one of the original cold warriors. If one judged by Richard Nixon's past, one could have easily assumed a continuation of the hard-line policies of the earlier years of the cold war. Soviet analysts were uncertain at first how to take the new president's assertion in his inaugural address that "After a period of confrontation, we are entering an era of negotiations." As a test of United States intention, the Kremlin immediately answered that the Soviet Union was ready to "start a serious exchange of views" on limiting the nuclear arsenals of the two superpowers. "When the representatives of the Nixon Administration are ready to sit down," announced K. V. Novikov, Chief of the Department of International Organizations, "we are ready."[18]

The fact was that at about the same time that the Soviet Union was ready for detente, so was the United States. Objective conditions compelled the elites of both camps to put aside ideological preconceptions in order to come to terms with each other. But the process was slow and at times painful.

The overriding foreign policy objective of the Nixon Administration's first year in office was to extricate the United States from Vietnam under conditions that would not constitute an American defeat. Henry Kissinger, Nixon's Assistant for National Security Affairs and, after 1973, Secretary of State, was convinced that the Soviet Union held the key to peace in Vietnam. He was prepared to make concessions to the Kremlin in trade, credits, technology, a European Security Conference, arms reduction and more, provided the Kremlin would cooperate in areas of vital interest to the United States. As the Nixon Administration viewed it, the Soviets could not expect American cooperation on some issues without conceding it on others. This was the essence of Kissinger's theory of "linkage."[19]

Vietnam was the crucial test of the linkage theory. Washington wanted Moscow to use its influence to get Hanoi to accept a negotiated end to the war; in return the United States was prepared to offer the Soviet Union concessions on issues vital to it. Nixon and Kissinger repeatedly signaled to the Politburo that until the war in Vietnam was liquidated there was no possibility for detente to flourish. How much support did the Soviet Union give to United States efforts to negotiate a settlement? On July 24, 1973, five months after the Paris Agreements had been signaled, Leonid Brezhnev made the cryptic observation over American television that "The improvement of Soviet-American relations has undoubtedly played a part in helping to end the long Vietnam war."[20] The words "undoubtedly" and "a part" here were deliberately vague, but they did imply definite Soviet assistance. The public record of the negotiations reveals very little of what, if anything, the Kremlin actually did to assist United States efforts to negotiate an end to the fighting. Nevertheless, without being specific, Nixon and Kissinger have both publically credited the Soviets with playing a constructive role. "It is well known" said Nixon, "that the Soviet Union was helpful in terms of getting the Paris peace talks started (in 1969). . . . I believe the Soviet Union would like to use what influence it could appropriately to help bring the war to a conclusion."[21]

During 1972, the critical year of the negotiations, the Soviet Union did agree to serve as an intermediary between Hanoi and Washington. Henry Kissinger made several trips to Moscow to enlist Soviet support to put pressure on North Vietnam to settle for a compromise. One of these was a highly secret mission in April following a major communist offensive against South Vietnam. At this meeting, Kissinger informed Brezhnev of a substantial change in the United States position. For the first time the United States agreed to accept a ceasefire in South Vietnam without a prior withdrawal of North Vietnamese forces in the south. Kissinger unsuccessfully urged the Soviet leader to reduce arms deliveries to North Vietnam. Brezhnev argued that the Soviets had no choice but to support a fraternal ally. He suggested or implied some unhappiness with North Vietnam's strategy, particularly the timing of its offensive and its stubborn and rigid negotiating stance, but he insisted that Hanoi's policies were not subject to Soviet control. The most that he would commit himself to do would be to transmit the new American position to Hanoi. As it turned out, the North Vietnamese rejected the new American position and continued their offensive. The United States responded on May 8 by mining the harbor at Haiphong and instituting heavy bombing raids over Hanoi.

Nixon's escalation of the war was a calculated risk, coming as it did only two weeks before the first scheduled summit meeting in Moscow. It confronted the Soviets with a dilemma: if they called off the summit, they would lose a critical opportunity to advance the cause of detente; if they went ahead with the meeting with Nixon, they would appear to accept the intensified punishment of a socialist ally. An emergency session of the Politburo met to deal with the crisis. Reportedly led by Pyotr Shelest, the hard-liners argued for a cancellation of the meeting with Nixon. Brezhnev opposed the hard-liners' position, and he won out. Shelest was demoted by the Party just before the Moscow summit and expelled from the Politburo in 1973.[22]

Vietnam continued to be a major topic of debate at the Moscow summit. Nixon urged great power responsibility and restraint. Brezhnev, Kosygin, and Podgorny denounced the bombing and mining of North Vietnam in strong terms and insisted that the United States withdraw all its forces and negotiate on the basis of North Vietnam's peace program. Kissinger observed that the United States was determined to leave Indochina but the exit had to be a respectable one. While the Soviets were unwilling to concede any substantive points to the Americans, they made it clear that they did not consider the war in Vietnam as an obstacle to detente. They, unlike the Americans, could live with the existing situation in Vietnam. By implication, they were rejecting the Kissinger idea of linkage. Though the Moscow summit failed to reconcile their divergent positions, the two parties were not in total disagreement. In the words of Marvin and Bernard Kalb, two correspondents who have chronicled the Nixon foreign policy: "by a process of subtle bargaining, in which more was implied than stated, there emerged between Nixon and Brezhnev an understanding that it was in the interest of both superpowers to end the war in Vitnam quickly."[23]

As they had done previously, the Soviets offered to act as intermediaries in the complex shuttle of proposals and counterproposals between Washington and Hanoi. In the afternoon of May 25, according to Tad Szulc, Kissinger stunned the Russians with the announcement that the United States was prepared to support a tripartite electoral commission in South Victnam. It would not be the coalition government demanded by Hanoi but it would include elements from the Saigon government, the Vietcong, and the neutralists. Brezhnev agreed on May 30, the concluding day of the summit meeting, that Soviet President N. Podgorny would leave as soon as possible to convey the new American position to Hanoi. Kissinger told his associates the Russians "are going to help us."[24] As added insurance, Kissinger flew to Beijing to enlist what support he could for Chinese pressure on Hanoi. Chou Enlai, like the Russians, made no promises.

We do not know what Podgorny (or the Chinese) said to the North Vietnamese, but when the negotiations reconvened in Paris in July, Kissinger observed a distinct change in the tone of Le Duc Tho, his co-negotiator. There was a noticeable decline in Vietnamese polemics. In August, United States intelligence reported a slowdown in the delivery of Russian and Chinese supplies to North Vietnam. In October, Hanoi agreed for the first time to a ceasefire without demanding President's Thieu's removal as a prior condition. This concession paved the way for the truce that was signed on January 27, 1973. Had the

Soviets played a helpful role behind the scenes? Tad Szulc, in his careful reconstruction of the Vietnam negotiations, believes so. President Nixon apparently
also credited Soviet pressure at least partly for the changes in Hanoi's negotiating posture. [25]

DETENTE INSTITUTIONALIZED IN SUMMITRY

At the core of Russia's dilemma of whether or not to aid the United States in
getting out of Vietnam was China. Ever sensitive to Chinese accusations of
betrayal of the revolutionary cause, the Soviets could not appear to be collab-
orating with imperialism. Soviet Foreign Minister Andrei Gromyko was worried
about the speculation at the Moscow summit that the United States was linking
concession on trade with a peace in Vietnam. And yet, precisely because of
China, the Kremlin felt obliged to forge closer ties with the United States. As
the Sino-Soviet schism increasingly became a permanent feature of the international political environment, the Soviet Union showed more signs of concern
over the possibilities of collaboration between its two greatest adversaries.
Indeed the Soviets were probably the first to anticipate the possibilities of
a Nixon-Mao axis. On October 26, 1970, at a reception for Nicolae Ceausescu,
President Nixon referred to China as the "People's Republic of China."
No American chief executive had every publicly used China's proper name.
Most newsmen missed the significance of the expression but Soviet Ambassador Anatoly Dobrynin did not. He telephoned Henry Kissinger and asked
for an explanation.[26] Obviously the United States was reexamining its relations with China and just as clearly, the Soviet Union, sensing the coming
change, was disturbed. When Richard Nixon announced his forthcoming visit to
the People's Republic on July 15, like many others, the Russians were shocked.
Angry charges of Chinese-American collusion erupted out of Moscow.

Brezhnev's response was an invitation to Nixon to meet with him in Moscow.
In adopting this approach, Brezhnev was following the lines of his predecessor,
Khrushchev, who in his day was a grand advocate of summit meetings. The post-
Stalin Soviet leadership had shown a consistent awareness of the importance of
personal contact of heads of governments as a vital feature of international
diplomacy. Indeed, Brezhnev's use of summit diplomacy did not begin with the
United States. The first Western country to develop a detente with the USSR
was France, under the leadership of Charles DeGaulle. "France," said Foreign
Minister Gromyko, "was the first among Western powers to have embarked on
the road of cooperation and concord with the USSR on major foreign policy
issues. The momentum of this process is being kept up to a large degree due to
the positive results of regular exchange of visits by top leaders."[27] The Soviet
hope was to institutionalize detente in a regular series of meetings between the

leaders of the two superpowers. One can find a loose historical parallel with this design in the conference system of the nineteenth-century Concert of Europe.

From 1972 to 1980, there were five Soviet-American summits, more than in the entire half-century of Soviet-American relations, if the wartime conferences are excluded. Out of these sessions came more than two dozen agreements, some of relatively little significance but a few, such as the Anti-Ballistic Missile (ABM) and SALT I and II agreements, were very important. These agreements were an attempt to define the changing relationship between the two countries and to establish more or less the ground rules that were to govern their competition. During the heyday of detente in the early 1970s, it appeared that there was more of a consensus on the rules of the game than there in fact was. The cracks in detente were later to be exposed in the Third World.

In the months leading up to the first Moscow summit, agreements were reached on a variety of issues of varying degrees of importance. On August 23, 1971, the four occupying powers were able to announce an agreement on the Berlin issue after 33 rounds of talks. On September 30, two arms control agreements were signed in Washington. One was essentially a technical measure to update the "Hot Line" agreement by supplementing the communications link established in 1963 with a system of earth satellite communications. The other agreement was designed to reduce the risk of an accidental nuclear war between the superpowers. In it, the United States and the USSR pledged to take measures against accidental or unauthorized use of nuclear weapons, to notify the other side immediately should an unexplained nuclear incident occur, and to give advanced notification of planned missile launches in the direction of the other party. On January 5, 1972, the United States and the Soviet Union agreed to open consular missions in San Francisco and Leningrad. Then, just prior to the summit, both countries and Great Britain signed on April 10, a treaty outlawing biological warfare. Although not a real source of discord among the major powers—no one had used or was contemplating engaging in germ warfare—this measure is significant as the only genuine example of disarmament in the postwar years.

All of these measures, however, were just a prelude to the orgy of agreements signed by Nixon and Brezhnev in Moscow during the week of May 22–30 at the summit. Without any doubt the longest and most difficult of the Moscow talks concerned Vietnam and the Strategic Arms Limitation Talks (SALT). The former we have already noted. Out of the SALT deliberations came two very important agreements, both signed on May 26: an ABM Treaty limiting the number of ABM missiles each side could possess and a moratorium on the construction of new offensive strategic ballistic missiles (the SALT I agreement). These two measures will be examined below in a discussion of the arms control facet of detente.

While the senior level personnel at the summit argued over Vietnam and

SALT, the junior staff were hammering out the details of lesser agreements. Not a single day passed that did not see at least one signing. First there was a Medical Science and Public Health Cooperation Agreement that pledged cooperation on heart, cancer, and environmental ailments. This was followed by an Environmental Protection Agreement. On the next day, Kosygin and Nixon signed a Joint Scientific and Technological Endeavors Pact that provided for a joint space rendezvous and docking mission in 1975. On Thursday, May 25, the naval chiefs signed a Naval Agreement on the Prevention of Incidents on and over the High Seas. It was designed to reduce harassment and to avoid collisions on the high seas between the world's two largest navies. Finally, in the economic sphere, the two sides created a Joint U.S.-USSR Commercial Commission to arrange for credit, most-favored-nation treatment and other cooperative programs.

The number and variety of these agreements was unprecedented in Soviet diplomacy. They provided for collaboration in a wide variety of pursuits, linking the bureaucracies of both countries in endeavors never before shared. In staking his political future on the success of detente, Brezhnev was clearly going out on a limb. He could not be certain of the genuineness of Richard Nixon's commitment to cooperation nor of its feasibility even if endorsed by the American leadership. American politics were somewhat unpredictable, though no one would then have imagined the trauma awaiting the Nixon Administration a few years later. In both countries, the legacy of a quarter-century of cold war had hardened domestic opinion, creating large pockets of opposition to the new trends. But for Brezhnev, with China at his rear, there simply was no alternative.

One area of work not completed at the summit was Soviet-American trade, a subject of major concern to the Soviet Union. The Nixon Administration in its desperate need for Soviet help on the Vietnam issue was prepared to bargain generously with the Soviet Union on trade. Two issues stood in the way of opening up normal trade relations. One was the Lend Lease debt owed to the United States since the end of World War II. A settlement of that debt had to be made before the USSR could receive American credit. The other issue was the need to extend "most-favored-nation" (MFN) status to Soviet exports to the United States. MFN meant that the Soviet Union would pay a tariff on goods exported to the United States at a level no higher than the same goods coming from other MFN countries. Presumably the Soviets needed MFN status to sell to the American market in order to pay for the technology and grain that they wanted.

A new era in Soviet-American trade was thought to be underway with completion of the Trade Agreement on October 18, 1972. According to its terms, the Lend Lease debt was to be settled with the payment of $722 million (a Soviet concession). In return, President Nixon would ask for congressional authorization of MFN status for the Soviet Union. Several provisions were included in the act to facilitate trade. The Russians, for example, could establish a trade representative in Washington, while the United States would maintain a commercial office in Moscow.[28]

As it turned out, this was one agreement that did not survive the downturn in Soviet-American relations following Richard Nixon's resignation from office. The Congress of the United States (by means of the Jackson-Vanik amendment) refused to concede MFN to the Soviets unless they agreed to relax restrictions on the emigration of Jews and other minorities from the Soviet Union. It came as something of a shock to the Soviets to encounter so much American resistance to the possibilities of expanding trade between the two countries. Perhaps as a lingering prejudice of their Marxist orthodoxy, they just assumed that all capitalists would immediately jump wherever the profits might be. The Soviets angrily charged the United States with interfering in its internal affairs and with violating the terms of the 1972 pact, and in January 1975 the Kremlin repudiated the Trade Agreement.[29] Thus, trade became one of the first victims of the human rights differences between the two countries.

While the general structure of trade has not developed according to Soviet expectations, the Soviet Union was the beneficiary of an extraordinary grain transaction made in the fall of 1972. As a consequence of an extremely poor harvest in 1972, the Soviet Union needed to import large quantities of grain from the West. Soviet negotiators were able to obtain an agreement to purchase at least 750 million dollars worth of American grain over a three-year period to be financed by easy credit terms. The price paid by the Soviets eventually proved considerably below the world market price for grain during this period. In effect, the United States ended up subsidizing the purchase of wheat that Moscow was desperate to obtain at almost any price.

The Moscow summit proved a diplomatic success for the Soviet Union as well as a personal triumph for the General-Secretary of the Communist Party. It was agreed at Moscow that the two leaders would meet again in Washington in 1973. Brezhnev also made arrangements for a summit meeting in Bonn during 1973, the first time that the head of the CPSU had ever visited the Federal Republic of Germany. Shortly before these meetings were scheduled to take place—the Bonn visit from May 18 to 22 and the Washington meeting from June 18 to 25—Brezhnev took advantage of his enhanced prestige to strengthen his hold over the leadership of the CPSU. On April 27, 1973, the Party Central Committee was convened for the purposes of endorsing Brezhnev's detente and reshuffling the composition of its Politburo. Dropped from membership were G. I. Voronov and Pyotr Shelest. Added were Foreign Minister Andrei Gromyko, Defense Minister Marshall Andrei Grechko, and Chairman of the Committee on State Security (the KGB) Yuri Andropov. These changes were the first important modifications in the composition of the Politburo since the overthrow of Khrushchev, and their overall effect was to strengthen Brezhnev's

hand. (The presence of these three ministers in the Politburo was a clear indication of the increased importance of foreign policy in Soviet politics generally.) These personnel changes were accompanied by a Central Committee
resolution affirming the principle of peaceful coexistence as "a general norm"
of relations between states with different social systems. The favorable changes
that have taken place in international politics should, according to the resolution "acquire an irreversible character."[30]

Before Brezhnev embarked on his first visit to the United States, he sought
to strengthen his position as much as possible by intensifying his detente policies
in Europe. Thus, he met with French President George Pompidou near Minsk
in January. Later that month, Austria and the Soviet Union negotiated a ten-
year agreement on scientific, technical, and industrial cooperation. The Bonn
summit meeting in May was largely concerned with measures for economic
cooperation. A ten-year pact was signed, pledging economic, industrial, and
technological cooperation between the two countries. There were some in-
completely resolved differences over the authority of the Federal Republic to
represent West Berlin on consular matters, but Brezhnev and Prime Minister
Willy Brandt pledged support for the Four Power Agreement of September 3,
1971. Their differences were resolved by compromise in later negotiations
between their foreign ministers.

Perhaps the most significant development in Europe were the agreements
to begin negotiations regarding a mutual reduction of forces and armament in
Central Europe (reached in June) and the convocation (in July) of Europe's
foreign ministers to prepare for the long-heralded Conference on Security and
Cooperation. Initially these two sets of negotiations were linked, although
as we have seen above, they ultimately took different paths.

It should be noted that while Brezhnev was strengthening his hand in anticipation of the Washington summit, so was Richard Nixon. During February,
Henry Kissinger made another one of his extraordinary missions to Beijing,
again consulting with Mao Zedong. Out of this meeting came a Sino-American
agreement to set up liaison offices in Washington and Peking, establishing in
effect regular diplomatic relations between the two countries.

Brezhnev's visit to Washington in June 1973 turned out to be the high point
in his series of summit meetings with American leaders. The momentum that
began with Summit I continued through Summit II even though the agreements
reached in 1973 were not as substantial as those signed a year earlier. Now that
a peace agreement had been reached over Vietnam, a major source of contention between both countries appeared to be eliminated. Indeed, rarely
in the entire postwar period had there been such a lack of controversial issues
pitting the two countries against each other as there was in the first half of
1973. At that time the promise of expanding trade between the United States
and the Soviet Union seemed to be achieving fulfillment. The total trade turn-

over between them was almost four times greater in 1972–74 than it had been in 1969–71. in their joint communique signed on June 25, they pledged "to turn the development of friendship and cooperation between their peoples into a permanent factor for worldwide peace."[31] The introduction of the idea that United States-Soviet relations could become permanently friendly and cooperative carried the concept of detente further than ever before.

There were 11 agreements signed during Summit II of which the three most important concerned nuclear matters.[32] An agreement on basic principles for limiting strategic weapons set 1974 as the intended date for a comprehensive SALT II program. Both sides acknowledged that "efforts to obtain unilateral advantage, directly or indirectly, would be inconsistent with the strengthening of peaceful relations between the United States of America and the Union of Soviet Socialist Republics."[33] Another agreement, signed on the same day, established a U.S.-USSR Joint Committee on Cooperation in the Peaceful Uses of Atomic Energy.

From the Soviet point of view, the most important of the measures negotiated at Summit II was the "Agreement on the Prevention of Nuclear War." The Politburo and Council of Ministers resolved that, if implemented, this agreement "will have a truly historic significance for all mankind." At a news conference, Henry Kissinger also remarked that the agreement "could mark a landmark on the road toward the structure of peace."[34] The most important commitment in the agreement was Article IV which reads:

If at any time relations between the Parties or between either Party and other countries appear to involve the risk of a nuclear conflict, or if relations between countries not parties to this Agreement appear to involve the risk of nuclear war between the United States of America and the Union of Soviet Socialist Republics or between either Party and other countries, the United States and the Soviet Union, acting in accordance with the provisions of this Agreement, shall immediately enter into urgent consultations with each other and make every effort to avert this risk.[35]

There is little doubt that this article had potentially extraordinary implications for Soviet-American relations, depending of course on how it would be interpreted. The constant danger of the cold war had always been that the superpowers could be forced into a confrontation because of the actions of their allies or clients, over which neither country had full control. Korea and Vietnam to a lesser degree, and Israel and Egypt to a major degree, were cases in point. All posed the danger of direct superpower involvement should a client state be confronted with catastrophic defeat (as was North Korea in November 1950 and Egypt in June 1967 and October 1973). What was significant about this agreement was that it committed both countries to cooperate with each other if necessary, against the interests of an ally. Within less than four months this agreement would be put to its first test in the Yom Kippur War, and it would not pass that test.

Summit II was notable because of the extraordinary rapport between the two leaders. For their own personal political reasons, Brezhnev and Nixon wanted to stress the importance of the personal relations between them. In its review of the meeting afterwards, the CPSU Politburo noted "the great personal contribution of Comrade Brezhnev." The Republican administration was coming under increasing domestic pressure because of Watergate revelations and found itself relying upon foreign policy successes to compensate for domestic failure. Richard Nixon was spared the embarassing distraction of the Senate Watergate hearings only because the Senate Committee recessed so as not to interfere with the administration's international diplomacy.

The mood of the third summit in 1974 differed considerably from the atmosphere surrounding the preceding ones. By the time of the meeting (June 27 to July 3), Richard Nixon's position at home had declined precipitously. Ever a realist, Leonid Brezhnev understood the domestic weakness of his partner and the folly of linking his own fate too closely with the American. But there was more to the subdued character of Summit III than simply the politically precarious position of one of its leaders. Soviet-American relations in the period 1973-74 had been drifting downwards. The Yom Kippur War in the Middle East had threatened to bring about the kind of confrontation that detente had been specifically designed to prevent. It revealed at the very least the potential hollowness of some of the agreements of the previous meetings, notably the Declaration on Basic Principles (see below) and the Agreement on the Prevention of Nuclear War.

Detente seemed to be floundering. The root of the difficulty was not so much the existence of specific points of disagreement as the failure of the many agreements of earlier summits to consummate a relationship of friendship or even genuine trust. Americans were disturbed by the growing number of powerful Soviet strategic missiles. They were upset by Soviet suppression of its dissidents and particularly by its harassment of Jews who sought to leave the country. For their part, the Soviets were irked by the failure of Congress to grant them equal tariff treatment or to make large credits available. They were perplexed by the uncertainty that Watergate had made of American politics.

One issue dominated the negotiations: the completion of an agreement on limiting strategic weapons. Intensive discussions were held on setting a numerical limit on the number of strategic launchers, including a figure for the number of missiles that could be equipped with multiple independently targeted reentry vehicles (MIRVs). No breakthrough was achieved, so the negotiators had to defer signing a SALT II pact.

The limited number of agreements signed at Summit III reflected the sober and subdued tone of the negotiations. Relatively minor pacts were signed to promote cooperation in housing, research on non-nuclear energy, and on artificial hearts, but two significant arms control measures were revealed on the final day of the conference. Both were modifications of previous treaties. The ABM treaty of 1972 (see below) was modified to limit the number of ABM sites to one instead of the original two. The 1963 Nuclear Test Ban treaty was modified to prohibit underground nuclear tests larger than 150 kilotons (as of March 1976). Since the original treaty had already outlawed nuclear tests in the atmosphere, under water and in outer space, the only environment not permitted to the signatories was underground tests of 150 kilotons or less.[36]

Notwithstanding its limited accomplishments, Summit III strengthened Brezhnev's detente objectives. Three summit meetings in three years had established a diplomatic pattern of some regularity. Whether this routine would lead to a permanent diplomatic institution or not, it had the clear advantage for Moscow of encouraging close relations with the United States in a way that Beijing could not duplicate. In the strategic triangle between the three countries, China was being finessed. On a different level, the Kremlin benefited by the newly opened contacts with American businessmen, scientists, technicians, and academics while being able to maintain its traditional isolation of the Soviet masses from outside contact. In short, up to this point it appeared that the Kremlin could achieve the fruits of detente without having to make any substantial domestic reforms.

It is not surprising that Moscow looked with apprehension and even some suspicion at those elements in American politics attempting to bring about the impeachment of President Nixon. Some Soviet spokesmen saw in the Watergate scandal a conspiracy to discredit the foreign policy course of the Nixon Administration. And when Nixon did resign his office on August 9, 1974, some Soviet commentators claimed that he had been unfairly "hounded" from office.[37] Moscow, nevertheless, quickly reaffirmed its commitment to detente and to the unswerving fulfillment of the agreements that gave it substance. Brezhnev was particularly anxious to establish personal contact with President Ford. Arrangements were made for a fourth Soviet-American summit to take place less than four months after Nixon's successor took office.

Gerald Ford and Leonid Brezhnev met for a get-acquainted session in the Siberian port city of Vladivostok on November 23-24. The single most important issue under discussion was the unresolved problem of Summit III— namely the number of strategic launchers to be permitted each side in a SALT II agreement. Though their differences could not be reconciled in the short time available to them, both sides were able to agree on guidelines that would set maximum figures for a future SALT agreement. In principle, a limit of 2,400 launchers for each side was set, of which a maximum of 1,320 could be fitted with "MIRV'ed" warheads.

Vladivostok was to be Brezhnev's last summit meeting with the leadership of the Republican administration. Plans had been made for another American visit by Brezhnev in 1975 as part of an understanding with Nixon that their contacts would be placed on a regular footing. The year 1975, however, witnessed a cooling off in Soviet-American relations. In January, the Kremlin cancelled the 1972 Trade Agreement rejecting the Congressionally imposed conditions regarding Jewish emigration as unwarranted interference. In April the South Vietnam government collapsed and North Vietnamese troops occupied Saigon. The failure of North Vietnam to abide by the terms of the Paris Agreements, resulting in the collapse of American Indochina policy, produced a reaction in the United States to the idea of cooperating with a communist regime. Soviet-American detente was inevitably bound to suffer. As American politics heated up for the 1976 presidential year, Gerald Ford publicly announced that the word "detente" was no longer a part of his political vocabulary.

Some of the disillusionment with detente on both sides resulted from short-term or temporary disappointments, campaign rhetoric, or ideological posturing. But there were serious differences too. Unquestionably the major barrier to a further rapprochement in Soviet-American relations in the mid-1970s was the inability of both sides to agree on measures to end the arms race. To date, the question of arms control was both the greatest success and the greatest failure of detente.

AVOIDANCE OF NUCLEAR WAR:
CONTROL OF THE ARMS RACE

At the core of detente was the issue of arms control. We have already noted that by the early 1970s the Soviet Union had achieved an approximate strategic parity with the United States; this military balance made it easier for the USSR to consider a slowdown in the arms race because an agreement would no longer freeze it in a position of permanent military inferiority. The Kremlin now found itself moving toward a common perspective with the United States on the subject of arms control.

It might be useful here to distinguish between disarmament and arms control. They are related yet distinct. Disarmament refers to the partial or complete elimination of armies and the weapons of war. Every effort in the postwar period to negotiate a disarmament agreement has failed because the nations of the world—small, great, and superpowers alike—rely upon arms for their security.[38] As long as international politics are characterized by a struggle for power, nations will be reluctant to abandon their arms.

Nuclear weapons, however, have introduced a radical complication in the freedom of nations to go to war. For the nuclear powers, war against each other is no longer a rational option. The two superpowers have the weapons to destroy each other completely. Over time both countries have come to rely on a strategy of deterrence as the main guarantee against an attack by the other. The principle of deterrence is basically simple: each state is inhibited from attacking the other because of the fear of overwhelming destruction in a retaliatory attack. In essence, the populations (in the cities) of the two countries are hostage to the other country. Security thus rests upon a precarious balance of power.[39]

From the beginning of the nuclear age, the strategy of deterrence was never uncomplicated. There were always conditions or potential conditions that threatened the stability of the deterrent relationship. For example, a major threat to the stability of a retaliatory deterrent force was its vulnerability to a surprise attack. If one side could destroy the strategic force of another in a surprise attack, it might be tempted to initiate one. Aircraft as a means of delivering nuclear weapons are vulnerable because they can be destroyed on the ground or by an antiaircraft defense. Because they cannot easily be destroyed or stopped, missiles are less vulnerable and thus more stable as a deterrent. Other conditions, besides the vulnerability of the deterrent force, that can create instability in the balance of power are nuclear accidents, the possession of the bomb by irrational or fanatic leaders, miscalculation of an opponent's intentions, scientific breakthroughs that might destroy a retaliatory force, a defensive measure that could protect a population from a retaliatory strike (an ABM or civil defense, for example), to name a few. It is precisely to combat these threats to the stability of deterrence that arms control came into being. We would therefore define arms control as any measure that stabilizes the military environment so as to make a nuclear attack less likely. Arms control may or may not involve an actual reduction of arms (i.e., disarmament); in most instances it has not.

The early arms control treaties of the 1960s had little to do with nuclear deterrence as such. They were important primarily as confidence-building stepping stones to more substantial agreements. The first arms limitation agreement was the Antarctic Treaty of 1959 which demilitarized the Antarctic Continent. It was followed by the "Hot Line" agreement in June 1963 which established the first direct communication link between Washington and Moscow. In August 1963 the Soviet Union, together with Great Britain and the United States, took the first significant step toward curtailing the nuclear arms race by signing the treaty banning nuclear weapons tests in the atmosphere, outer space, and under water. That treaty failed to prohibit underground nuclear tests because of Soviet-American differences over whether onsite inspection was necessary to detect and verify underground explosions. Over a decade later, that treaty was modified to prohibit underground nuclear tests larger than 150 kilotons. Subsequent arms control treaties sought to limit the introduction of nuclear weapons into regions (such as Latin America in a treaty signed in February 1967) or into environments (such as outer space, 1967, and the ocean floor, 1971) which had hitherto been free of them. These agreements taken as a whole constituted an important web restricting the expansion or use of nuclear weapons but they did not come to grips with the major threats to international security and deterrent stability which were: (1) the spread of nuclear weapons to non-nuclear powers, and (2) the growing superpower arsenals of strategic weapons. These dangers are what some have called the problems of the horizontal and vertical proliferation of nuclear weapons.

Nuclear proliferation had been a particular concern of the United States from the time when it possessed a monopoly on the atomic bomb. The Soviet Union was the first country to break that monopoly in 1949, followed by the United Kingdom in 1952 and France in 1960. Early American efforts to engage the Soviet Union in a treaty to stop the spread of nuclear weapons were countered by the Soviet demand that it be coupled with a prohibition on stationing nuclear weapons in foreign countries. Because the United States would not relinquish its tactical nuclear component in NATO, the negotiations foundered. Soviet concern about nuclear proliferation in the 1960s focused on two countries: China and West Germany. Clearly one of the purposes of Khrushchev's termination of atomic aid to China in 1959 was to keep it from acquiring nuclear weapons. Soviet anxiety must have been intensified by the successful detonation of a nuclear device by China in the fall of 1964, but by then it was too late. Germany, however, might still be kept from acquiring the bomb. During the mid-1960s, the Soviet Union raised the nonproliferation issue in criticizing an American plan to create a multilateral nuclear force (MLF) under NATO control. The MLF, the Soviets contended, would put a German finger on the nuclear trigger and thereby preclude any possibility of a nonproliferation agreement. Only after the Western powers abandoned the MLF and the British alternative to it, the Atlantic Nuclear Force (ANC), did the Soviets begin serious negotiations toward a nonproliferation treaty. Private conversations between the American and Soviet co-chairmen of the Eighteen Nation Disarmament Committee in Geneva were begun in the fall of 1966.

The obstacles to a nonproliferation agreement were staggering and they came from every conceivable direction. The Soviets wanted every signatory to accept International Atomic Energy Agency (IAEA) safeguards, while the members of the European Atomic Energy Community (EURATOM) wanted only EURATOM control. America's NATO allies were concerned that a nonproliferation agreement would prohibit NATO consultation and planning on nuclear defense and ban deployment of U.S. owned and controlled nuclear weapons on the territory of non-nuclear NATO members. Many non-nuclear states voiced concern that abnegating a nuclear capability would put them at a commercial and technological disadvantage in developing nuclear energy for peaceful uses. Some non-nuclear states wanted guarantees that renunciation of nuclear weapons would not make them vulnerable to nuclear intimidation. Finally, there was a chorus of objections that a nonproliferation treaty would freeze the status quo with the nuclear powers still armed to the teeth.

These objections were gradually overcome. On July 1, 1968, the Non-Proliferation Treaty was signed by the Soviet Union, the United States, and the United Kingdom and 59 non-nuclear powers. Under its terms the nuclear powers agreed "not to transfer to any recipient whatsoever nuclear weapons" or to assist a non-nuclear state in the manufacture of nuclear devices. The obligations of the non-nuclear powers were the obverse: not to receive or construct nuclear devices. In addition, non-nuclear states had to accept international safeguards in order to prevent diversion of fissonable fuel for peaceful uses to nuclear weapons. For their part, the nuclear powers committed themselves "to pursue negotiations in good faith on effective measures relating to cessation of the nuclear arms race at an early date and to nuclear disarmament."[40]

One subject not covered by the treaty was the security concerns of the non-nuclear powers. The three nuclear powers sought to meet this concern with a resolution introduced before the United Nations Security Council on June 17 in which they promised "to act immediately through the Security Council" if a non-nuclear state were threatened by aggression with nuclear weapons.[41] What exactly they would do in such a contingency no one could say. No one took that guarantee very seriously. Indeed, however significant it is as a symbol of Soviet-Western collaboration, there was grave doubt that the Non-Proliferation Treaty could effectively stop the spread of the dreaded bombs. Adherence to the treaty has been less than overwhelming. By the time of the Review Conference in 1975 (specified in the Treaty), over 100 countries had signed and 87 had ratified the treaty, but the flaw was in the number of threshold nuclear powers—such as Argentina, Brazil, Israel, Egypt, Spain, South Africa, and Pakistan—that had not adhered to the treaty. India's detonation of a nuclear device in 1974 exposed the basic inadequacy of the bilaterally imposed safeguards. Atomic materials which had been provided to India for peaceful uses were diverted to produce the atomic detonation; India was not a signatory to the Non-Proliferation Treaty.

As serious as was the spread of nuclear weapons, the greater immediate danger confronting the superpowers was the growing strategic arsenals each possessed, for the hard reality was that the Soviet Union and the United States were vulnerable only to an attack by the other. By the beginning of the 1970s, there were three weapons developments that threatened to undermine the stability of the strategic balance. They were: first, computerized guidance systems capable of increasing missile accuracy; second, anti-ballistic missile

(ABM) defense systems; and third, multiple independently targeted reentry vehicles (MIRVs).

The danger with precise guidance systems was that when combined with intercontinental ballistic missiles (ICBMs) equipped with high yield warheads—in the megatonnage range—they could destroy land-based retaliatory ICBMs. The United States was particularly concerned about the powerful SS-9 missile of which the Soviets had an estimated 280 in 1970. When armed with a warhead of 3-5 megatons, the Soviet weapon threatened the Minuteman missile that was the heart of the American deterrent.

In its own way, the anti-ballistic missile had the potential to be just as destabilizing. Though ostensibly a defensive instrument, the ABM offered the prospect of sheltering a country's population from a retaliatory strike so that it might be free to engage in a first strike attack. A stable deterrent relationship presumes and requires that the populations of both sides be hostages against an attack by the other side. As early as 1966, the Soviet Union had begun to deploy an anti-ballistic missile defense around Moscow. In view of China's successful test of a ballistic missile that year, it is possible that the Kremlin was anticipating a future attack from the People's Republic of China as much as it might have anticipated one from the United States. The United States would inevitably respond with its own anti-ballistic missile defense. On September 18, 1967, the United States announced that it would begin deployment of a "thin" ABM system to defend certain American cities. Ironically, the reason given was the threat of a Chinese ICBM attack. Later the American ABM program was changed to protect ICBM missile sites rather than cities. At one point, a program of 12 ABM complexes was planned. It appeared that the superpowers were again headed toward a major escalation of the arms race.

From the Soviet perspective, the MIRV was particularly menacing. MIRV's made it possible for an individual missile to deliver a dozen or more nuclear warheads to separate targets. This technology had been originally developed to overcome the Soviet ABM defenses—in effect to overwhelm the defending missiles—which by the end of the 1960s numbered 67 around Moscow. Furthermore, the MIRV was a weapon the Soviet Union did not then possess.

In sum, both sides were involved in a deadly competition for strategic arms. Numerically, the Soviet Union was beginning to pull ahead of the United States in the number of ICBMs, deploying approximately 200 per annum. Since 1967, the number of United States strategic missiles had remained fixed at 1054 ICBMs and 656 submarine launched ballistic missiles (SLBMs). The Soviet Union also had an edge in the payload capacity ("throw weight") of its larger missiles. On the other hand, the United States, with its MIRV technology, far exceeded the Soviet capacity to deliver numbers of warheads and it maintained a substantial lead in long-range bombers. Both countries had ample reason to negotiate a limit to their competition.

Moscow was initially slow to respond to a United States proposal to engage in strategic arms limitations talks (SALT). It was not until June 1968, 18 months after the initial proposal by President Johnson that the Soviet Foreign Minister announced his government's agreement to the talks. They would have probably begun in 1968 had not the invasion of Czechoslovakia disrupted Soviet-American diplomacy. On January 20, 1969, the day of Richard Nixon's inauguration as president, Andrei Gromyko again announced his government's willingness to discuss strategic arms limitations. The talks finally began in November 1969 in Helsinki. For two and a half years the discussion of what was to become known as SALT I alternated between Helsinki and Vienna. Progress was slow and tortuous. Efforts to reach a comprehensive agreement limiting strategic weapons failed, so the negotiators settled for two lesser accords: a treaty limiting the building of ABM systems and an Interim Agreement setting a five-year moratorium on certain strategic delivery vehicles. The two agreements were signed in Moscow at the summit meeting between Richard Nixon and Leonid Brezhnev on May 26, 1972.[42]

The ABM Treaty limited both parties to two ABM sites of no more than 100 missile launchers each. One system could protect the country's capital and the other a part of its ICBM retaliatory force. At the third summit meeting in July 3, 1974, Nixon and Brezhnev signed a protocol to the ABM Treaty limiting ABM deployment to one site only, again at either the national capital or around an ICBM field. The Soviet Union has chosen to maintain but not to complete its ABM launchers around Moscow. The United States began construction of several ABM launchers at Grand Forks, North Dakota but subsequently abandoned the entire program. While the Treaty and its protocol have contributed to reducing tensions and perhaps allaying suspicions, the fact that neither party has gone as far in its ABM deployment as is permitted by treaty suggests that the ABM idea died because the benefits were not worth the cost.

The Interim Agreement was essentially a complex holding action intended to give both sides more time to negotiate a permanent limitation of strategic arms in SALT II. It froze the number of intercontinental missile launchers possessed by each side for a five-year period. At the time of signing, the United States had 1054 land-based ICBMs and 656 SLBMs in 41 submarines. Corresponding figures for the Soviet Union were 1618 ICBMs and 740 SLBMs. Neither party could start construction of additional land-based ICBM launchers, but some replacement for older missiles was permitted, including the substitution of SLBMs for retired ICBMs. Thus, the United States was permitted to reach a ceiling of 710 SLBMs on 44 submarines by replacing 54 older ICBMs. The Soviet Union was permitted to increase its SLBM launchers to 950 on 62 submarines. The potentially thorny issue of control was avoided by the specification that "each Party shall use national technical means of verification."

That meant, in essence, satellite observation, eliminating any need for inspectors on Soviet territory, the idea of which was anathema to the Kremlin. Both sides were forbidden to interfere with the other's aerial surveillance.[43]

SALT I was intended as the first of several agreements to bring the arms race in strategic weapons under control. Whatever their political differences, both countries shared a realization that a nuclear confrontation meant the loss of everything each sought to protect. This recognition was made explicit in a Declaration on Basic Principles signed by Nixon and Brezhnev on May 29 at the summit. It contained the following points:

in the nuclear age there is no alternative to conducting . . . relations on the basis of peaceful coexistence. . . . The USA and the USSR . . . will do their utmost to avoid military confrontations and to prevent the outbreak of nuclear war. They will always exercise restraint in their mutual relations. . . . Both sides recognize that efforts to obtain unilateral advantage at the expense of the other, directly or indirectly, are inconsistent with these objectives. The USA and the USSR have a special responsibility . . . to do everything in their power so that conflicts or situations will not arise which would serve to increase international tensions.[44]

SALT II, however, proved even more difficult to negotiate than SALT I had been. Part of the difficulty lay in the vagaries of American domestic politics, part in diplomatic ineptitude and part in the struggle of each party to maneuver for strategic advantage. By the time Richard Nixon participated in his third summit in Moscow, he was virtually submerged by the Watergate crisis. All that he and Brezhnev could do was agree that a SALT II treaty should extend through 1985. For the American president time had run out. In August, 1974 Richard Nixon was forced to resign.

President Gerald Ford moved quickly to confer with Leonid Brezhnev to work out guidelines for a SALT II agreement. They met in November in the Siberian city of Vladivostok and agreed to a limit of 2,400 strategic vehicles (ICBMs, SLBMs, and heavy bombers) of which 1,320 could be equipped with MIRV warheads. The 2,400 figure was above the level reached by either side and far higher than Secretary of State Kissinger had sought earlier, but it was the minimum acceptable at the time to the Soviet Union. Negotiations moved slowly after Vladivostok, eventually becoming enveloped in the presidential campaign of 1976 and the change from a Republican to a Democratic administration.

The superpowers assumed that they would be able to agree on a further limitation of strategic weapons within a five-year period after ratifying SALT I. That set October 1979 as the deadline for SALT II. Negotiations proved more difficult and complex than imagined with the result that October 1979 came and went without a successor agreement. What stymied SALT II, however, was not the technical complexities of the issue but the growing political discord between the architects of the SALT process. If detente faltered, SALT II would be one of the casualties.

NOTES

1. For a description of the change in the international structure during the 1960s, see John Spanier, *Games Nations Play* (New York: Praeger, 1975), Chap. 4.
2. See *International Negotiation, The Great Power Triangle, Selected Comment,* Subcommittee on National Security and International Operations of the Committee on Government Operations, United States Senate, 92 Congress, 1st Session. (Washington: U.S. Government Printing Office, 1971).
3. *The Military Balance, 1971-1972* (London: The Institute for Strategic Studies, 1971), p. 40. See also *Strategic Survey, 1971* (London: Institute for Strategic Studies, 1972), pp. 54-58.
4. Michael Tatu, "The Great Power Triangle: Washington-Moscow-Peking," in *International Negotiation*, p. 10.
5. See the ICBM/SLBM table in *The Military Balance, 1970-1971*, p. 106. In SLBMs, the Soviet Union remained far below the United States, 280 to 656.
6. See the Testimony of Herbert S. Levine before the Senate Foreign Relations Committee in *Detente*. Hearings before the Senate Foreign Relations Committee, U.S. Senate, 93 Congress, 2nd session, August 15, 20, 21, September 10, 12, 18, 19, 24, 25, October 1, 8, 1974 (Washington: U.S. Government Printing Office, 1975), pp. 19-30.
7. Daniel Yergin, "Politics and Soviet American Trade: The Three Questions." *Foreign Affairs 55*, no. 3 (April 1977): 522.
8. *24th Congress of the Communist Party of the Soviet Union, 1971, Documents* (Moscow, 1971), p. 29.
9. Ibid., p. 37.
10. See Josef Korbel, *Detente in Europe, Real or Imaginary?* (Princeton, N.J.: Princeton University Press, 1972), pp. 187-207.
11. The text of the treaty is in *The Treaty of August 12, 1970 between the Federal Republic of Germany and the Union of Soviet Socialist Republics* (Wiesbaden, Germany, 1970), pp. 7-9.
12. The text of the Quadripartite Agreement is in Dennis L. Bark, *Agreement on Berlin, A Study of the 1970-72 Quadripartite Negotiations* (Washington: American Enterprise Institute, 1974), pp. 117-119. This work also contains

a thorough analysis of the negotiations leading up to the agreement. See also Korbel, *Detente in Europe,* pp. 212-228.

13. For a review of the background to the Conference on Security and Cooperation in Europe, see Robert H. Donaldson, "Global Power Relationships in the Seventies: The View from the Kremlin," in *The Dynamics of Soviet Politics,* ed. Paul Cocks, Robert V. Daniels, and Nancy Whittier Heer (Cambridge, Mass.: Harvard University Press, 1976), pp. 329-333.

14. Robin Edmonds, *Soviet Foreign Policy 1962-1973* (London: Oxford University Press, 1975), p. 81.

15. *New York Times,* July 30, 1975. This issue contains an abbreviated version of the Helsinki Declaration.

16. Ibid., August 1, 1975.

17. Shalva Sanakeyev, *The World Socialist System* (Moscow, 1972), pp. 289-290.

18. Marvin Kalb and Bernard Kalb, *Kissinger* (New York: Dell, 1975), p. 120.

19. Henry Kissinger, *White House Years* (Boston: Little, Brown, 1979), pp. 129-130.

20. Leonid Brezhnev, *Peace, Detente, and Soviet-American Relations, A Collection of Public Statements* (New York: Harcourt, Brace Jovanovich, 1979), p. 25.

21. Kalb and Kalb, *Kissinger,* p. 149. Kissinger claims that in 1972 the United States did induce some cooperation from the Soviet Union, *White House Years,* p. 308.

22. See *New York Times,* May 22, 1972.

23. See their analysis in *Kissinger,* Chapters 7, 11, 12, 13, 14, and 15, and Tad Szulc's "Behind the Vietnam Cease-Fire Agreement," in *Foreign Policy,* no. 15 (Summer 1974), pp. 21-69 and Kissinger, *White House Years,* chapters 23, 25-27, 31-33.

24. Szulc, "Behind the Vietnam Cease-Fire," pp. 43-44.

25. Ibid., p. 23. Kalb and Kalb, *Kissinger,* p. 194.

26. Kalb and Kalb, *Kissinger,* p. 267.

27. Andrei Gromyko, "Peace Programme in Action," *International Affairs,* (Moscow), no. 12 (December 1975), p. 11.

28. Marshall I. Goldman. *Detente and Dollars, Doing Business with the Soviets* (New York: Basic Books, 1975), pp. 67-70, 156-158.

29. Daniel Yergin, "Politics and Soviet American Trade," p. 532, argues that it was not the Jackson-Vanik Amendment to the Trade Reform Act of 1974 that caused the Soviets to repudiate the Trade Agreement, but rather the Stevenson Amendment which limited American credit to the Soviet Union to a meager $300 million over a four-year period.

30. *Pravda,* April 28, 1973, quoted in Edmonds, *Soviet Foreign Policy,* p. 127.

31. *The Washington Summit: General Secretary Brezhnev's Visit to the United States, June 18-25, 1973.* (Washington: The Department of States, August 1973), p. 49. (Emphasis added.)

32. The non-nuclear agreements covered cooperation in the fields of agriculture, studies of the world's oceans, transportation, exchanges in science, technology, education and culture, a convention on taxation, and three protocols, one on the establishment of commercial representation in each other's capital, the establishment of a U.S.-USSR Chamber of Commerce, and one on the expansion of air services. Texts of the agreements can be found in *The Washington Summit* (*Department of State Bulletin*, July 23, 1974). The Soviet texts are available in *Documents of the USSR-USA Summit Talks,* June 1973. (Moscow: Novesti Press Agency Publishing House, 1973).

33. *The Washington Summit*, p. 17.

34. *Documents of the USSR-USA, Summit Talks,* p. 59; *The Washington Summit,* p. 32.

35. *The Washington Summit,* p. 30.

36. For texts of these agreements, see *Arms Control and Disarmament Agreements, Texts and History of Negotiations.* (Washington: U.S. Arms Control and Disarmament Agency, 1975), pp. 151-152, 155-156. Nuclear explosions for peaceful purposes were exempt from the provisions of this agreement.

37. Donaldson, "Global Power Relationships," p. 315.

38. The only disarmament measure agreed upon to date is the Convention on the Prohibition of the Development, Production and Stockpiling of Bacteriological and Toxic Weapons and their Destruction signed on April 10, 1972. This agreement resulted in the destruction of existing supplies of biological agents. Needless to say, none of the major powers has ever relied very much on "germ warfare." For a general discussion of why disarmament has been unsuccessful, see John Spanier and Joseph L. Nogee, *The Politics of Disarmament, A Study of Soviet-American Gamesmanship* (New York: Praeger, 1962).

39. Soviet reliance on this strategy is only implicit. Soviet strategists have never explicitly adopted the doctrine of "mutually assured destruction." See V. D. Sokolovsky, *Soviet Military Strategy,* ed. Harriet Fast Scott (New York: Crane, Russak and Co., 1976). For two authoritative but different interpretations of Soviet doctrine, see Richard Pipes, "Why the Soviet Union Thinks It Could Fight and Win a Nuclear War," *Commentary* (July 1977), pp. 21-34, and Raymond L. Garthoff, "Mutual Deterrence and Strategic Arms Limitations in Soviet Policy," *International Security* (Summer 1978), pp. 112-147.

40. The text of the treaty is contained in *Arms Control and Disarmament, Agreements, Texts and History of the Negotiations.* (Washington: United States Arms Control and Disarmament Agency, 1975), pp. 85-89.

41. William Epstein, *The Last Chance: Nuclear Proliferation and Arms Control* (New York: The Free Press, 1976), pp. 139-142.

42. For the diplomacy of SALT I, see John Newhouse, *Cold Dawn, The Story of SALT* (New York: Holt, Rinehart and Winston, 1973); also Thomas W. Wolfe, *The SALT Experience* (Cambridge, Mass.: Ballinger, 1979), chapters 1-3.

43. The texts of the ABM Treaty and the 1974 Protocol are in Roger P. Labrie, ed., *SALT Hand Book, Key Documents and Issues, 1972-1979* (Washington: American Enterprise Institute, 1979), pp. 15-19 and 246-248. The texts of the Interim Agreement on Strategic Offensive Arms and the protocol are on pp. 20-23.

44. "Basic Principles of U.S.-Soviet Relations, 29 May 1972," in ibid., pp. 50-52.

Chapter 8
Detente in Decline

From its inception the policy of detente involved contradictions. Brezhnev and his colleagues wanted cooperation from the West at the same time that they were undermining Western influence throughout the globe. Soviet spokesmen made it clear that they did not interpret detente as obligating the Soviet Union to accept a "freezing" of the status quo. "Peaceful coexistence" implied a combination of cooperative and competitive relations, the end result of which would be the inevitable triumph of the forces of socialism. Under conditions of the "relaxation of tensions," this struggle would be marked in the "main arena" of East-West relations by a diminution of crisis and military confrontation. While this was a shift of great importance from conditions of "cold war," it did not imply a quieting of forces of revolutionary change. On the contrary, in Brezhnev's words, it would "create more favorable conditions for the accomplishment of many other important tasks—national liberation, social progress, overcoming of the scandalous inequality between various countries."[1] In the Soviet view, whereas the cold war had provided a nutrient medium for imperialist blocs directed against the interests of the Third World, the relaxation of tensions was bringing about the weakening of such blocs and was creating more favorable conditions for pursuit of the national liberation and revolutionary struggles.[2] Thus it was in the Third World that detente was to face its most serious tests.

CONTRADICTIONS IN THE THIRD WORLD

The region of greatest conflict between the Soviet Union and the United States during the decade of the 1970s was the Middle East, that perennial "hotbed of tension." We have seen above in chapter 5 that Moscow was willing to press its clients to accept a ceasefire in the war of attrition in 1970 only after it had substantially increased its own direct military involvement in Egypt. And Soviet complicity with Cairo in the violation of the ceasefire agreements by the forward movement of surface-to-air missile emplacements only increased Washington's suspicions that Moscow was seeking "unilateral advantage" in the Middle East. For its part, the Soviet Union must have had similar doubts about American intentions, given Henry Kissinger's pronouncement in June of an intention to "expel" the Soviet military presence from the Middle East.

The conflict came to a head in September, 1970, with the crisis in Jordan, precipitated by King Hussein's reactions to the Palestinian hijackings. Moscow's assurances to Washington that Syrian forces would not seek to intervene in the ensuing civil war were belied by Damascus' actions. As Syrian tanks crossed the Jordanian border on September 18 and 19, Washington placed its military forces on selective alert and issued a stern warning to Moscow to restrain its client. At the urging of the United States, Israel prepared for a counterintervention against Syria, and the crisis threatened to erupt in a superpower confrontation. Fortunately for world peace, the Soviet Union chose to back away from the brink of war; a combination of Washington's and Moscow's pressure and Hussein's battlefield success forced Syrian troops to withdraw from Jordan and the crisis subsided.[3]

Almost simultaneous with the Syrian threat to Jordan, a political crisis was brewing in the Caribbean. A U-2 overflight to Cuba in September had uncovered signs that Moscow was engaged in the construction of a base for its nuclear submarines at the port of Cienfuegos. Washington warned the Soviets that it regarded such activity as a "hostile act," violating the 1962 Kennedy-Khrushchev understanding about offensive Soviet weapons in Cuba and threatening to bring on a new missile crisis. Soviet Ambassador Dobrynin assured Kissinger that no such offensive installations were planned, and the Soviets soon halted the construction activities.

Thus, on two occasions in the fall of 1970 the Soviet Union had acted to escalate its commitments to the Third World ally, in search of a more advantageous balance with the United States. In both cases stern American warnings and threats of counteractions had persuaded the Russians to back down. Larger Soviet interests, including the progress toward detente in Europe and the prospect for a more beneficial relationship with the United States, had prevailed. By the following autumn, these hopes seemed to be bearing out; breakthroughs had been achieved on Berlin and SALT, and the Soviet interest in detente had been spurred by the announcement of Nixon's impending visit to Peking.

Once again, however, a Soviet commitment to a Third World ally threatened to derail the progress in Soviet-American relations. As we have seen above, the 1971 Bangladesh war found the United States and the USSR on opposite sides of a Third World conflict. Although Washington had apparently failed to appreciate the extent to which Moscow had tried to restrain the Indians from a military solution to the crisis in East Pakistan (a misperception heightened by Nixon's evident dislike of Mrs. Gandhi and his gratitude to Yahya Khan), the massive shipments of Soviet arms to India angered the Americans.

When Washington perceived (again, probably mistakenly) that India was seeking to dismember West Pakistan, it again warned Moscow that Soviet-American relations (and even the Moscow summit) could be jeopardized by a continuation of the war.

An even greater threat to detente was posed by events in Indochina. We have already reviewed the crisis posed by the communist offensive in the spring of 1972, the desperate efforts by the Nixon administration to get the Russians to put pressue on the North Vietnamese, and the limited but apparently helpful role played by Moscow in facilitating negotiations in Paris. As they had in Geneva 18 years before, the Soviets (and also, it would seem, the Chinese) sacrificed the prospect of an immediate communist military victory in Indochina for the larger interests of East-West detente. In response to the pressure of its patrons, Hanoi compromised its stance, and by January 1973, the United States had achieved its peace settlement in Vietnam.

In the wake of the Paris agreements, Soviet spokesmen waxed enthusiastic about the improved prospects for the solution of other international problems, particularly including the Middle East. Such talk, together with the growing pace of Soviet-American cooperation, evidently aroused Arab fears that the two superpowers would impose a partial settlement to the conflict. Through the spring and summer of 1973, the political atmosphere between the Soviets and the Arabs—especially the Egyptians—was characterized by tension and mutual suspicion, despite the heavy shipments of sophisticated weapons that continued to flow between Moscow and the Arab states. But as late as August, the Soviets evidently had not overcome their doubts about Arab military capabilities:

The attempts of right-wing nationalistic quarters which parade pseudo-patriotic extremist slogans to impose their own conceptions on leading Arab countries and steer them into adventurist courses are meeting with no success. . . . The Arabs know the costs of bloodshed as well as anyone else.[4]

But the Arabs were determined to force the issue of the liberation of their occupied territories from Israeli control. That Moscow had advanced warning of imminent hostilities is evident from the fact that Soviet dependents began departing from Syria three days before fighting began on October 6. With no desire to destroy their influence and apparently calculating that a limited Arab victory could damage American standing in the area without destroying detente, the Soviets did not act to prevent the war. Taken by surprise, the Americans were angered at the Soviets but appealed for their cooperation in obtaining a ceasefire and containment of the fighting. Nixon sent a letter to Brezhnev to this effect, citing the Soviet-American agreements to prevent such conflicts which endangered world peace.

Although Brezhnev's reply to the American president was conciliatory, the surprising initial military successes seemed to elicit warm public support from Moscow for the Arab cause. A message sent by Brezhnev to Algerian President Boumediènne (unpublished in the USSR but leaked by the recipient) urged the Arabs to unite in giving all possible support to Egypt and Syria. American Secretary of State Kissinger, informing Ambassador Dobrynin that he was refraining from pro-Israeli actions in the hope of Soviet cooperation warned publicly that "detente cannot survive irresponsibility in any area, including the Middle East."[5] The warning seemed, however, to have no effect; on October 10, the USSR began its massive airlift of supplies to the Arabs, which by the end of the month had amounted to almost one thousand planeloads. Only on the eve of the Israeli counterattacks did the Soviets begin to urge a political settlement of the conflict. The ambassadors of Syria, Egypt, Iraq, Algeria, and Jordan in Moscow were summoned to meet with Gromyko and were reportedly nonplussed to hear him express Soviet determination to pursue every effort to obtain a just peace that would guarantee the security of all states in the Middle East. The same day, *Izvestiia* cited serious consequences for the entire international situation and termed the need for a settlement "urgent."

The Americans themselves had by this time begun a massive airlift of supplies to Israel. With the Arab military situation worsening, Kosygin traveled secretly to Cairo on October 16 for three days of talks devoted to working out the provisions of a ceasefire agreement that would be guaranteed by the United States and USSR. On Brezhnev's request, Kissinger flew to Moscow on October 20, where the two superpowers engaged in final negotiations on the terms of the agreement, with the Soviets conceding the point linking the ceasefire with direct negotiations between the Arabs and Israel. But Moscow's pleasure at playing a coequal role with the United States in containing the conflict was shattered by the breakdown of the U.N. ceasefire resolution of October 22, followed by the rapid Israeli military gains on the west bank of the Suez Canal.

The complete military collapse of the Egyptian army was averted only by a near confrontation between the United States and the Soviet Union. Sadat's October 24 call (reportedly solicited by the Soviets) for a joint U.S.-Soviet expeditionary force to enforce the ceasefire was accompanied by a note from Brezhnev to Nixon endorsing such an action. Alarmingly, American intelligence reported signs that, after pulling back most of its air force transports from the Middle East to their home bases, Moscow had placed seven divisions of airborne troops on standby alert. A second Brezhnev note to Nixon, described by the Americans as "harsh," "blunt," "leaving nothing to the imagination," threatened unilateral Soviet action: "I will say it straight, that if you find it impossible to act together with us in this matter, we should be faced with the necessity urgently to consider the questioning of taking appropriate steps unilaterally. Israel cannot be allowed to get away with these violations."[6] Soon thereafter the U.S.

military forces were put on worldwide alert status. In the tense hours that followed, Soviet and American diplomats worked out a new Security Council resolution that established a United Nations peacekeeping force for the Middle East, but excluded (contrary to Moscow's original desire) troop contributions from the major powers.

The Middle East crisis aroused widespread doubts in the West about the depth of the Soviet-U.S. detente and new suspicions in the Third World and Beijing about a Soviet-U.S. "condominium." It also posed both risks and opportunities for the Soviet Union. With respect to its relationship with the United States, the USSR seized the opportunity to denounce the "saber-rattling" of the U.S. alert and to take pleasure from the failure of support and alarm that greeted U.S. actions in the NATO capitals.[7]

The Soviets were particularly interested in reaping the maximum possible gains from their military and political support to the Arab side during the conflict. High-level diplomatic contacts between Moscow and the Arab capitals continued in the aftermath of the ceasefire. In the military sphere, Moscow proceeded to complete the rebuilding of Arab military strength through its massive shipments of arms. These Soviet actions, however, failed to quiet the Arab critics who charged Moscow with selling out the Arab states in quest of its own priorities. On balance, the Soviets had staked out a leading role in the Middle East, including their co-chairmanship of the Geneva Peace Conference that opened on December 21, 1973. But there were severe limitations on this role stemming from both their continuing lack of relations with Israel and the more intensive activity of Secretary Kissinger in communicating American proposals to both sides of the conflict. In fact, Kissinger's brilliant "shuttle diplomacy"—which achieved agreements on Egyptian-Israeli and Syrian-Israeli disengagement in January and May, 1974—dramatically brought home to the Arabs (and to Moscow) the realization that, whereas Moscow could supply the arms for war, only the United States apparently could achieve the peaceful return of Arab territories.

Even the Arab oil boycott, which Moscow's earlier propaganda had encouraged, proved a mixed blessing for the Soviet Union. On the positive side for Moscow were the gaping split in Western unity, the likelihood of increasing nationalization of Western oil interests in the area, and the higher prices that the Soviets were able to get for their own oil exports. On the other hand, it had not been the Soviet Union and its "progressive" Arab allies who brought about the boycott, but rather the anticommunist Saudi Arabians, whose role and stature in Arab politics were thereby enhanced. Thus, Moscow faced the possibility that the oil sheiks, rather than Soviet arms, might receive primary credit for any ultimate Arab successes. Moreover, cutbacks in the delivery of Mideast oil to Eastern Europe had forced the Soviets to divert some of their own exports from Western to Eastern Europe. This threatened both to lower their political standing in the West and to affect their reputation as reliable trading partners, in addition to the danger that their own economic prospects might be lessened by the disruption of Western economies.

But again risks for the Soviet Union were balanced with opportunties. The economic and political disruption brought about in Europe by the oil embargo provoked a discussion in Moscow about the relationship between detente and the opportunities for communist gains that were opened up by this "crisis of capitalism." *Pravda* noted in June 1974 that the relaxation of East-West tensions together with "the intensification of the political and economic instability of capitalism" opened up to the "workers and democratic movements of the capitalist countries unprecedented opportunities." In such a context, a revised version of the "popular front" strategy was appropriate, as attention should be directed to "establishing relations with socialists and social-democrats, setting up alliances with broad masses of religious believers, working with the young people, drawing the intelligentsia to the side of the workers' movement, and so forth."[8] In October, Party Secretary Boris Ponomarev echoed this theme, again citing conditions of detente and the crisis of capitalism as reasons to conclude that "At this time, we believe, the communist parties have greater opportunities and resources than ever before for influencing the course of events in Europe."[9]

The Soviet Union's greatest attention in this context was directed toward Portugal, where a right-wing dictatorship had been overthrown in April 1974 by the armed forces, an important section of which soon came under influence of the communists. By the end of the year, relations between the USSR and the left-wing government of General Goncalves had become sufficiently close that reports began to be heard of the possibilities that this NATO country might offer port facilities to the Soviet navy.

The United States observed these developments with great concern. Secretary Kissinger again raised the flag of "linkage," warning Moscow that the United States regarded Soviet nonintervention in Portugal as a requirement for the further advance of detente. Although Moscow had asserted that it "has not interfered and does not intend to interfere" in Portugal's internal affairs, the temptations for the USSR mounted in the summer of 1975 as the course of the struggle there turned against the communist party and its allies. The Soviet press denounced "interference" by NATO, European social-democrats, and the "forces of reaction." On August 19, drawing a parallel with the events of 1973 in Chile, *Pravda* declared that "no friend of democracy could remain indifferent" to the events in Portugal. It added, however, that the Soviet people, while displaying mass solidarity with their Portuguese comrades, would continue to hold to the principle of noninterference and to insist that the problems in Portugal should be solved by the people themselves.

The removal of General Goncalves in September 1975 was viewed in Moscow as the end of the "carnation revolution" and the beginning of a new period of acute class struggle. In the final analysis, the practical advice rendered to the Portuguese comrades by the Soviet press advocated caution: "Only revolutionaries who do not believe in themselves are incapable of understanding that talks and compromises are necessary in the sharp bends of the revolutionary path." Thus, it was necessary, for the present, to secure "a breathing space to repulse the onslaught of reaction and to consolidate the positions won."[10]

As it turned out, the fall of 1975 marked the end of Portugal's "lurch to the left."[11] In mid-November, Communist-led labor unions mounted a general strike in Lisbon followed shortly by an uprising of leftist military units. Armed forces loyal to the government crushed the uprising and from then on the prospects of a communist revolution in Portugal steadily receded. A new constitution officially came into being on April 25, 1976. In June, the elections for the country's first president under the new constitution were a disaster for the communists. General Antonio dos Santos Ramalho Eanes, backed by the Socialists, Popular Democrats, and Social Democrats, won an overwhelming victory. The communist-supported candidate gained only 7.6 percent of the vote.

ANGOLA TO AFGHANISTAN: DETENTE IN DECLINE

In the crisis in Portugal then, occurring as it did in the "main arena" of Soviet-American competition where Soviet capabilities were constrained and the danger of war greatest, Moscow ultimately demonstrated caution in the face of American warning. In contrast, the Soviet Union demonstrated much less restraint in Africa where, as a result of the April 1974 revolution, Portugal's colonies moved quickly toward independence. Events in Angola were to put a serious strain on detente.

When Angola became independent on November 11, 1975, the country was wracked by a civil war in which the main contenders were the Movement for the Popular Liberation of Angola (MPLA), the Front for the National Liberation of Angola (FNLA), and the Union for the Total Independence of Angola (UNITA). As we have noted above, Moscow had been involved in support of the MPLA for over a decade. Soviet military aid to Augustino Neto, the Marxist head of MPLA, increased substantially during 1975–76. According to Western sources, this assistance included T–34 and T–54 battle tanks, PT–76 amphibious light tanks and armored personnel carriers, MIG–15 and MIG–21 fighter bombers, 40-tubed 122 mm. rocket launchers, and large quantities of light weapons and ammunition.[12]

Equally if not more disturbing to the United States was the large-scale intervention of Cuban combat troops (numbering some 17,000 by the end of the war in March 1976) in support of the MPLA. Moscow's material aid, combined with Havana's soldiers, proved decisive in the outcome of Angola's civil war. Never before had Communist military forces intervened so massively and decisively in Africa. The aggressiveness of Moscow's actions in Angola was a notable deviation from the caution that had traditionally marked Soviet involvement in the Third World. To many in the West, Soviet military involvement in a region so far from the Soviet periphery seemed to reveal a new phase in Soviet policy in the Third World. In response to American charges that its actions contravened the goals of detente, Soviet authorities replied:

No one seeks to deny that the Soviet Union and other socialist countries render moral and material assistance to the Angolan people and its vanguard, the MPLA. This assistance contributed to the successes of the Angolan patriots in their armed struggle against colonial rule, and now helps them defend the sovereignty, independence, and territorial integrity of their country. As for the contention voiced from time to time even by responsible Western government leaders that this policy does not accord with the spirit of detente, it only testifies to a false understanding of the meaning of detente, which never implied and cannot imply giving a free hand to aggressors.[13]

The differences between the Soviet and American viewpoints on detente were thus clear, and though they had actually been present from the beginnings of the new relationship, the implications of the clash of interpretations were never so stark as during the crisis in Angola. In seeking the explanation for this situation, we may find more than a grain of truth in the reported comment of one unnamed Soviet analyst: "You Americans tried to sell detente like detergent and claimed it would do everything a detergent could do."[14]

The victory of Soviet arms in Angola came just as the Communist Party of the Soviet Union concluded its Twenty-fifth Congress in March 1976. Leonid Brezhnev used the Congress to reaffirm his leadership of the Party and to proclaim the success of Soviet foreign policy. His report on behalf of the Central Committee was dotted with a variety of successes—victory in Vietnam, treaties of friendship and cooperation with Iraq and India, normalization of relations with Germany—but in summing it up, the best he could report was that "the international position of the Soviet Union has never been more stable."[15]

One region, however, where the position of the Soviet Union was anything but stable was the Middle East. Indeed, the Twenty-fifth Congress had barely adjourned when Moscow suffered a major defeat inflicted by Egypt. Anwar Sadat determined that cooperation with the United States offered greater rewards than collusion with the Soviet Union, and on March 15, 1976, he unilaterally terminated the Treaty of Friendship and Cooperation between the USSR and Egypt. This action was the natural culmination of the trend that started with the expulsion in 1972 of Soviet troops and advisors in Egypt.

Sadat had increasingly aligned himself with anti-Soviet forces in the Middle East, even going so far as to approach the Israelis directly in order to freeze the Soviets out of the region. That, presumably, was one of the reasons for Sadat's dramatic visit to Jerusalem in November 1977. Just prior to Sadat's announcement of his visit to Jerusalem, the United States and the Soviet Union issued a joint statement calling for the resumption of the Geneva Conference. As co-chairman of the Geneva Conference, the Soviet Union would have had a significant role in any Middle Eastern settlement.[16] Sadat's action scuttled the Soviet-American initiative. The Jerusalem visit—the first of any Arab leader to Israel—set a train of events in motion that culminated in the Camp David accords of September 1978 and the Egyptian-Israeli peace treaty signed on March 26, 1979.[17] Sadat's willingness to sign a separate peace treaty with Israel heralded the virtual bankruptcy of Moscow's Egyptian policy.

Soviet difficulties in the Arab world were not limited to Egypt. Moscow discovered to its consternation that the substantial political and military support given to the Arab cause did not necessarily win the hearts and minds of the beneficiaries or even their gratitude. Similarly in Africa, the Soviet commitment to the black African cause of ending white rule in the southern part of the continent did not bring with it acceptance of Soviet influence. The MPLA victory in Angola added to Soviet prestige in Africa, particularly among the more militant regimes and movements, but it also intensified resistance to Soviet encroachments among those governments—such as Zaire, Sudan, and Egypt—already suspicious of Soviet motives. Sudan, for example, a long-time recipient of Soviet aid, suddenly reversed its position when President Nimeiry in May 1977 expelled all Soviet technicians and military advisers. Thereafter Sudan became one of the most active opponents of Soviet involvement in African affairs.

Part of the Soviet dilemma in the Middle East and Africa resulted from the volatility of politics in these areas. The Soviet Union often found itself supporting both sides in a bitter conflict. Thus it was in the Lebanese Civil War in 1976 after the Syrian intervention. Both the Syrians and the Palestine Liberation Organization (PLO) were fighting with Soviet-supplied arms. In the summer of 1977, Egypt and Libya fought a short war in which each was equipped with Soviet weapons. The largest conflict between African antagonists, in which each was equipped with Soviet arms, was the war between Ethiopia and Somalia in 1977–78.

Ethiopia had pursued a pro-Western foreign policy until a coup brought a Marxist military officer to power in 1977. In May, Lt. Col. Mengistu Haile Mariam was invited to Moscow where he was accorded red carpet treatment by the Kremlin. A military aid agreement of approximately half a billion dollars for modern weapons for Ethiopia was signed in May.[18] Initially, the Kremlin assumed that it could have good relations with both Ethiopia and Somalia;

in the spring of 1977, Moscow even proposed that Ethiopia and Somalia join South Yemen and independent Djibouti in a federation of Marxist states. Somalia rejected the plan. Moscow apparently did not anticipate that the territorial dispute between Ethiopia and Somalia would lead to the bitter fighting that erupted in the summer of 1977. Moscow's aid to Ethiopia caused Somalia to abrogate its 1974 Friendship Treaty with Moscow in November and subsequently to expel all Soviet advisers and deny Moscow the use of naval facilities at the port of Berbera.

On balance, Soviet involvement in the Horn of Africa brought more benefits than losses. Ethiopia, with the second largest population in Black Africa, is considerably more important in African affairs than Somalia. Even the loss of the port of Berbera could be partially compensated for by the Ethiopian ports of Assaba and Massawa. By March of 1978, Ethiopian forces, armed and advised by the Russians and joined by Cuban combat forces (numbering approximately 16,000), expelled Somali troops in the Ogaden. After Somalia's defeat, Ethiopia directed its efforts toward crushing the rebellion in the province of Eritrea.

The success of Soviet arms and Cuban troops in Ethiopia added to the prestige of Moscow and Havana in many areas of the Third World. By its support of the Ethiopian "Marxist" regime, Moscow had demonstrated its willingness to honor its "proletarian internationalist duty" but there was a price to pay, and the cost was in detente. Ethiopia, like Angola earlier, raised questions in the West about how far the Soviet Union was willing to involve itself militarily in regions of the Third World outside its traditional spheres of interest. There was renewed concern about the use of Cuban military forces as Soviet proxies. Even before the Middle Eastern crises in 1979, charges were widespread in the United States that detente was little more than a facade for Soviet expansion.

Soviet activity in the Third World was designed to undermine not only Western but Chinese influence as well. The death of China's two great leaders—Zhou Enlai and Mao Zedong—in 1976 led to a struggle for power which a "moderate" group under the leadership of Hua Guofeng and Deng Xiaoping won out over a radical element, the so-called "gang of four." The existence of a new leadership opened the possibilities of bridging the differences between the two communist giants. Immediately after Mao's death, Moscow sent its chief Sinologist, Deputy Foreign Minister Leonid F. Ilyichev, to resume border negotiations. His mission was fruitless. Beijing's new leadership continued to excoriate the Russians in much the same shrill tones as had its old leadership.

The failure of Soviet efforts to achieve a reconciliation with Post-Mao China was heralded in an authoritative article in *Pravda* published on May 14, 1977. The article warned the world that China constituted a real threat to peace. "China," it said, "is the only country in the world whose official circles advocate publicly and without any camouflage a new world slaughter." Western circles in particular were warned not to "delude themselves with the hope that they would be able to ward off Peking's expansionism from themselves and channel it to a different direction."[19] Here again was expressed the latent Soviet fear of being maneuvered into a military confrontation with China.

The Kremlin could hardly have anticipated the developments in Southeast Asia that within less than two years were to bring conflict with China perilously close to realization. Indeed, few could have imagined how quickly after the American withdrawal from Vietnam the victorious parties would be at each others' throats. Vietnam, now unified, moved deeper into the Soviet orbit while Cambodia became an ally of China. Soviet-Vietnamese relations were solidified in November 1978 with the signing of a 25-year Treaty of Friendship and Cooperation pledging the signatories "in case one of the parties becomes the object of attack or of threats of attack, to begin mutual consultations immediately for the purpose of removing that threat and taking appropriate effective measures to insure the peace and security of their countries."[20]

That comitment took on special meaning during 1978 and 1979 as relations deteriorated between Vietnam and Cambodia and China. In December 1978, Vietnamese armed forces invaded Cambodia in support of a Cambodian communist rebellion against the communist government of Pol Pot. Early in January 1979 a pro-Vietnamese government was firmly established in Phnom Penh. China reacted on February 17 by invading Vietnam with the avowed purpose of "punishing" Vietnam for its aggression against Cambodia. Moscow was furious. "Peking's aggression against socialist Vietnam," said TASS, "is a direct result of the policy of blackmail and pressure which the Chinese authorities have pursued in the course of a number of years vis-à-vis Southeast Asia in general and Vietnam in particular."[21] To the Russians it did not seem entirely coincidental that the Chinese invasion followed very shortly after the normalization of U.S.-Chinese relations and an official visit to the United States by China's Vice-Premier, Deng Xiaoping. Moscow, however, carefully avoided retaliating with military action against China. Clearly Soviet interests were better served by a reduction rather than an exacerbation of tension between the two countries. China too recognized the dangers of carrying its punitive action too far; in the spring, it terminated the crisis by withdrawing its forces from North Vietnam. The fighting in Indochina during 1978 and 1979 did not fundamentally alter Sino-Soviet relations but it did guarantee that a Sino-Soviet reconciliation would not come during Brezhnev's tenure in power.

As the decade of the 1970s came to a close, the arena of Soviet-American conflict shifted once again to the Middle East, this time to countries along the southern border of the Soviet Union. Crises stemming from internal instability in Iran and Afghanistan led to bitter political clashes between the two superpowers. During the latter half of 1978, Iran experienced a revolutionary upheaval that forced the Shah to leave the country in January 1979. During the early phase of the Iranian revolution, Moscow pursued a cautious policy.

As long as there was some possibility that the Shah might survive, the Soviet Union carefully avoided attacking him. The Kremlin clearly recognized, however, that the collapse of the Shah would be a major setback for the West. Consequently, the only clear objective of Soviet policy was to keep the United States from doing anything that might interfere with the revolutionary course of events taking place in Teheran. Leonid Brezhnev on November 18, 1978, warned the West: "It must be made clear that any interference, let alone military intervention in the affairs of Iran—a state which has a common frontier with the Soviet Union—would be regarded by the USSR as a matter affecting its security interests."[22]

This position had the advantage of inducing caution in Washington and making it possible for the Soviet Union to claim later that it had deterred Western intervention. As noted below, the Soviet role in preventing outside interference with revolutionary change in Iran was exactly the opposite of its role in Afghanistan where it used military force in order to oppose internal revolutionary change. Underneath this inconsistency of principle, of course, was the more fundamental principle of *Realpolitik:* the Soviet Union would support or undermine the status quo depending on how the status quo served Soviet interests. As the Shah's government collapsed, the Soviet Union abandoned its hesitancy and moved quickly toward approval of the revolution, being among the first to recognize the Ayatollah Khomeini's Islamic Republic on February 12, 1979.

While relations between Teheran and Moscow remained relatively stable during 1979, relations between Teheran and Washington seriously deteriorated. A crisis of major proportions in U.S.-Iranian relations developed in November when, as a reaction to the admission of the Shah to the United States for medical treatment, a group of youthful armed fanatics ("students") seized the U.S. Embassy and, apparently with the approval of Khomeini, made prisoners of some 50 American citizens. Their release became a central objective of United States diplomacy.

When the hostage crisis occurred, Moscow had clearly concluded that its strategic and economic interests would be better served by keeping on good terms with the Iranians than by supporting Washington on the issue of the sanctity of international law. For a month, the Soviet press avoided commentary on the issue although Soviet broadcasts in Persian indicated sympathy with the Iranians. "[T]he anger of the Iranian nation and its youth, who ask that a stop be put to U.S. imperialist interference in the country's affairs," reported radio Moscow two days after the seizure, "is totally understandable and logical."[23] Moscow's first formal statement came in a *Pravda* article on December 5. It acknowledged that the hostages were being held in violation of international law but found the U.S. response equally if not more reprehensible. The United States was accused of trying to "blackmail" Iran and of committing "a gross violation of international legal norms" by conducting naval maneuvers in the Arabian Sea. Secretary of State Cyrus Vance denounced *Pravda's* observations as "deplorable."[24] That Moscow had some doubts about Iranian behavior is evident by the fact that on December 4 the Soviet representative at the United Nations joined a unanimous Security Council in calling upon Iran to "release immediately" the American hostages. Also, on December 31, the Soviet representative abstained on a Security Council resolution that threatened Iran with economic sanctions unless it freed the hostages.

That same month the crisis in Iran was complicated by a crisis in Afghanistan. The Soviet invasion of a Moslem neighbor posed a dilemma for Iran as it did for many Third World countries that were generally sympathetic to the Soviet Union. Iran's Islamic religious leaders found themselves sharply at odds with both superpowers and thus in a bad position to balance one against the other should that become necessary. Moscow found itself in the contradictory position of supporting one Islamic revolution while opposing another in a neighboring country. One method of neutralizing opposition in Iran to Soviet actions in Afghanistan was to come down more firmly against the United States on the hostage issue. This is precisely the direction in which Soviet policy moved in the winter and spring of 1980. On January 13, the Soviet Union vetoed a U.S.-proposed resolution in the United Nations Security Council which called for economic sanctions against Iran. In the spring, when the United States attempted, unsuccessfully, a helicopter rescue of the hostages, TASS immediately condemned President Carter by name, accused him of bringing the United States to the "brink of insanity" and charged that "The hostages are only a pretext for pursuing an aggressive, hegemonistic American policy aimed at making Iran submit to its imperialistic diktat and bolstering the American presence in the Near and Middle East."[25] Clearly Moscow took advantage of the opportunity to shift attention away from its own military activities in Afghanistan.

Many of the details of the Soviet invasion of Afghanistan in December 1979 remain clouded in secrecy, although the general picture is clear. On December 27, following a sudden airlift of Soviet troops into Kabul, the government of Afghanistan's president, Hafizullah Amin, was overthrown in a coup. Amin was subsequently executed. On the following day, Radio Afghanistan reported that Babrak Karmal had been selected as Amin's successor. The theory that the coup was plotted in the Kremlin received credence from the fact that the radio broadcast of Karmal's election came from Soviet, not Afghan, territory and that Karmal himself did not arrive in Kabul until December 30.[26] By January 1980 the number of Soviet troops in Afghanistan exceeded 85,000.

Ironically, the regime overthrown by the Kremlin was a Marxist government. In April 1978 the government of President Mohammed Daud was overthrown in an unusually bloody coup.[27] Daud was replaced by Noor Mohammed Taraki, a leader of the Peoples Democratic Party of Afghanistan and a dedicated Marxist.

On December 5, 1978, Taraki signed a Treaty of Friendship with the Soviet Union. His government introduced a program of radical educational, social, and economic reforms that quickly stimulated widespread opposition, particularly among conservative Moslem tribesmen. On September 16, 1979, Taraki was himself the victim of a coup that brought his one time ally, Hafizullah Amin, to power. One TASS report claimed that Taraki was strangled by three of Amin's aids. Amin was even more oppressive than his predecessor, and the insurrection, which began under Taraki, spread. By the time of Amin's overthrow the Islamic insurrection had spread to virtually every province in the country, leaving the Communists in control of only the capital and at most four other urban centers. Moscow replaced Amin with Karmal in order to preserve a pro-Soviet socialist government in Afghanistan. The collapse of the Peoples Democratic Party of Afghanistan would have led to a third (with Iran and Pakistan) anticommunist Islamic republic on the periphery of Soviet Central Asia, a prospect that undoubtedly concerned Moscow.[28]

The use of large-scale military forces in Afghanistan came as a shock to much of the world, particularly to the United States. President Carter confessed that "This action of the Soviets had made a more dramatic change in my own opinion of what the Soviets' ultimate goals are than anything they've done in the previous time I've been in office."[29] The invasion was the first time that Moscow had sent combat forces into a country that was not a part of the Soviet bloc. Even by Soviet standards it was a cynical operation. When United States Ambassador Thomas Watson expressed concern early in December to Andrei Gromyko about reports of Soviet troop movements on the Afghanistan border, the Soviet Foreign Minister stated "The reports are wrong. We don't know what you're talking about."[30]

Moscow justified its action with the charge that the United States, Pakistan, and China were covertly supporting Islamic insurrection in Afghanistan. TASS even accused Amin of being "in the service of the CIA." *Pravda* reported on December 31, "our country made no secret of the fact that it would not allow Afghanistan to be transformed into a staging ground for the preparation of imperialist aggression against the Soviet Union."[31] Soviet behavior toward Afghanistan had all the earmarks of another application of the Brezhnev Doctrine.[32]

The reaction of individual governments to the Afghanistan invasion was largely predictable although it appears that the Soviet Union was surprised by the intensity of the response from some countries, particularly the United States. Within the Soviet bloc, there was general support except for Rumania whose criticism was implicit in its lack of active approval. China, of course, condemned the action. The communist parties of the Western democracies were divided, the Italian party being notably critical. The government of Indira Ghandi sided with Moscow, if quietly, and a few days after the Soviet invasion even voiced some cautious criticism of the USSR. Some of the sharpest public criticism of the Soviet Union was made in the United Nations. A resolution introduced in the Security Council condemning the Soviet Union for its invasion was thwarted only by a Soviet veto. On January 14, the General Assembly deplored the invasion by a vote of 104 to 18 (with 18 abstentions) and called for the immediate withdrawal of troops. Later that month, a conference of 36 Islamic states also condemned the invasion.

Negative reaction was strong within most of the Western countries. Early in January, President Carter announced a series of punitive measures designed to induce reconsideration in Moscow: the curtailment of grain sales, the suspension of high technology exports, the curtailment of fishing privileges in American waters, deferral of cultural and economic exchanges, an offer of military and economic aid to Pakistan, and a boycott of the 1980 Moscow Olympics. In his State of the Union address on January 23, Carter warned the Soviets that the oil supply routes of the Persian Gulf were sufficiently vital to American interests that the United States was prepared to go to war to protect them. As for detente, Carter warned, "The Soviet Union must realize that its decision to use military force in Afghanistan will be costly to every political and economic relationship it values."[33]

Was detente one of those political relationships the USSR valued? Officially, Moscow continued to identify detente as one of its foreign policy goals, but the leaders in the Kremlin appeared to have calculated that their actions in the Middle East would cost them little more than had already been lost before Afghanistan. Detente, in other words, had been in trouble for some time. From Moscow's perspective the emphasis Jimmy Carter placed in 1979 upon increasing military spending was particularly disturbing. They considered his approval of the MX missile a violation of the spirit of SALT.

There were two other developments in the military field that influenced Moscow's judgment. One was an American proposal to upgrade NATO's nuclear defenses by installing 572 modern medium-range nuclear missiles in Europe by 1983 (108 Pershing II and 464 land-based cruise missiles). In October, Leonid Brezhnev had made an effort to head off the plan by announcing a withdrawl of 20,000 Soviet soldiers and 1,000 tanks from East Germany and offering to reduce the number of medium-range nuclear missiles in the Western areas of the Soviet Union if NATO would forgo modernization of its missiles. The foreign and defense ministers of NATO refused the Soviet bait and approved the United States plan on December 12. The new missiles were in part compensation for the powerful Soviet SS-20 missiles. Significantly, the new NATO missiles would give Europe its first nuclear weapons capable of reaching Soviet territory. The other troublesome development was the declining fortunes of SALT, an issue whose progress we need briefly to review.

SALT IN ABEYANCE

SALT was from the beginning the centerpiece of detente. Although detente was already in an advanced state of deterioration when the Carter Administration took office in 1977, both the American president and the Soviet leader were determined to push for a SALT II agreement. Brezhnev saw SALT as an important element of detente that continued to be the general line of Soviet policy toward the United States. Carter supported SALT as a vital step toward curbing the arms race between the two superpowers. But there were problems, some of a strategic-technical nature, others of a more political character.

After SALT I, there were several important changes in military technology in both camps. The Interim Agreement in 1972 had balanced the Soviet superiority in ICBM numbers with an American superiority in deliverable warheads. At the time of SALT I, the largest of the Soviet ICBMs was the SS-9. It carried a warhead in the 25 megaton range, five times as powerful as Titan and more than 12 times the power of Minuteman. When the behemoth, nearly three times as long as Minuteman, was displayed in a parade in Red Square, it "took away the breath of the assembled Western military attachés."[34] In the summer of 1973, the Soviet Union began flight testing a new generation of ICBMs, all with payloads larger than American ICBMs and some of which were MIRV'd—that is, contained several warheads. The successor to the SS-9 was the SS-18, a giant capable of carrying ten independently targetable warheads. Somewhat smaller but in some ways more lethal because more accurate was the SS-19, which carried six warheads (six times as many as the Titan and twice as many as Minuteman). What disturbed the United States was the possibility that the Soviet heavy missiles, when MIRV'd, might be able to destroy the United States Minuteman in a surprise attack. The Soviet heavy missiles seemed to be designed as a counterforce weapon rather than as a retaliatory instrument. This raised the possibility that the Soviet Union might have in mind the use of its strategic arsenal for purposes other than deterrence.

Another disturbing addition to the Soviet arsenal was a new supersonic bomber of advanced variable wing design known as the Backfire. Produced before SALT I, the Backfire entered service in 1974 after years of testing and modification.[35] The Kremlin insisted that this bomber was a theater and not a strategic weapon because it could not hit targets in the United States and return to a Soviet base. By definition, a strategic weapon is one that can deliver a nuclear warhead to the territory of the enemy. By refueling in flight, however, the range of the Backfire could be extended to cover targets in the United States. One of the controversial issues of the SALT II negotiations was whether or not to include the Backfire among the strategic launchers permitted to the Soviet Union.

A development of major concern for the Soviets was the American built cruise missile. The cruise missile is a subsonic guided drone that flies close to the earth's surface, avoiding radar detection. It is guided by a radar system that can "read" the terrain over which it passes, compare the reading with a program of the terrain over which it should be passing, and automatically correct itself should it go off course. The cruise missile can be fired from land installations, submarines, or bombers. Its speed, distance, and payload are variable. The Soviets wanted limits placed on the range of the cruise missile and they wanted those mounted on bombers to be considered the equivalent of MIRV'd strategic weapons. They especially wanted limits placed on the distance permitted for ground-launched cruise missiles because of the possibility that cruise missiles located in West Germany could hit targets in the Soviet Union. This was of importance because Moscow had agreed that NATO forward-based systems in Europe would not be included among the SALT II limits.

Early in his administration, President Carter made a serious miscalculation by proposing a reduction in strategic weapons far below the 2,400 figure agreed upon at Vladivostok. In March 1977 the United States offered Moscow a choice of (1) a drastic reduction in strategic weapons to between 1,800 to 2,000 launchers of which 1,100 to 1,200 could be MIRV'd, or (2) agreement on the higher Vladivostok figures while deferring any action on the Backfire bomber or the cruise missile. Brezhnev was outraged at what appeared as an American effort to scuttle the Vladivostock accords. The lower numbers would have meant a much sharper cutback in its ICBM inventory for Moscow than for Washington. Brezhnev had to overcome considerable internal resistance to get agreement on the limit of 2,400. George Kornienko, Gromyko's deputy, later told U.S. negotiator Paul Warnke: "You shouldn't have disregarded the fact that Brezhnev had to spill political blood to get the Vladivostok accords."[36]

The failure of Carter's initial effort was a harbinger of the difficult negotiations to come. The five-year moratorium of SALT I expired in October without a successor agreement. It took almost a year after SALT I expired before a breakthrough was reduced that ultimately made the complex formulas of SALT II possible. The United States found that it could not force the Soviets to reduce their inventory of heavy missiles so it concentrated instead on setting limits to the number of MIRV'd warheads for those missiles. For their part, the Soviets could not stop the development of the cruise missile but they were able to obtain limitations on range, numbers, and timing of deployment. Agreement on the SALT II Treaty was announced in the spring of 1979. The formal signing took place in Vienna on June 18, 1979, at the often postponed and long-awaited summit meeting between Leonid Brezhnev and Jimmy Carter. This, the last summit meeting between Brezhnev and an American president, was lower keyed than previous summits, and though other issues were discussed, no agreements were signed in Vienna other than the SALT II Treaty.

The Treaty set two ceilings for strategic launchers (which included heavy bombers): until 1981 each side was allowed 2,400; after 1981 and until January 1, 1985, the maximum number of launchers permitted was 2,250. Under these overall ceilings were several sublimits. The maximum number of launchers which could be MIRV'd (i.e., fitted with more than one nuclear warhead) was 1,320. This figure included heavy bombers fitted with cruise missiles. Each side was free to determine its own combination of missiles with multiple warheads and heavy bombers with cruise missiles with two limitations: the total number of MIRV'd ICBMs and SLBMs together could not exceed 1,200 and the total number of MIRV'd ICBMs alone could not be larger than 820.

There were other restrictions in this complex agreement. The number of multiple warheads on missiles were limited to 10 for ICBMs and 14 on SLBMs. Heavy bombers were restricted to a total of 28 cruise missiles. Existing missile systems could be modernized but only within prescribed limits. Each side would be permitted to develop only one new type of launcher. A Protocol to the treaty prohibited (until December, 1981) the flight testing of ICBMs for mobile launchers and the deployment of ground and sea-launched cruise missiles with a range of more than 360 miles. Finally, as in SALT I, verification of compliance was specified "by national technical means" with the proviso that neither side was to interfere with the other's methods.[37]

The major benefits applied equally to both sides; the treaty would contribute to the stability of the deterrent relationship and reduce the risk of war; it would make each side's second strike forces more secure, and, of course, the limits on numbers could lower defense budgets. Some features of SALT II were beneficial to the Soviet Union. Moscow retained 308 of its heavy SS-18 missiles while the United States was prohibited from building a comparable ICBM. On the issue of the Backfire bomber, the Soviet position that it not be counted as a strategic bomber won out; but as a concession Leonid Brezhnev in a separate statement agreed not to give the Backfire an intercontinental capability and not to produce more than 30 a year. In general, SALT II froze a status quo that gave the USSR more powerful missiles with a greater throw-weight than any possessed by the United States.

Counterbalancing these advantages were several specific benefits to the United States. One American advantage that SALT II protected was a superiority in the total number of warheads the United States could deploy. Furthermore, the Treaty in no way affected U.S. theater bombers based in Europe that could deliver nuclear strikes against Soviet cities. Finally, as a result of the Treaty, the Soviet Union was compelled to abandon a larger number of new missile programs and to dismantle more strategic vehicles than the United States in order to meet the 2,250 ceiling. On balance, neither side achieved a decided advantage over the other.

Moscow probably felt that with the signing of the SALT II Treaty the most serious obstacles to an agreement limiting strategic weapons had been overcome.

The Soviets almost certainly assumed that in the last analysis the United States Senate would be compelled to back up the action of President Carter. Statements made by Politburo members to visiting U.S. congressmen indicated a fundamental lack of understanding of the American system of checks and balances.[38] The rulers in the Kremlin were certainly not subject to comparable restraints. Ratification of SALT II by the Supreme Soviet or its Presidium would have been a formality only. The institutions of government in the USSR are subordinated in the decision-making process to the ruling authorities of the Communist Party, of which the Politburo is the highest.

But as 1979 wore on, the prospects for strategic weapons limitations steadily declined. SALT II fell victim both to strong and persistent opposition in the United States and to the Soviet invasion of Afghanistan in late December. In the U.S. Senate, the opposition of Republican minority leader Howard Baker and Democratic arms control authority, Henry Jackson, appeared to guarantee that if the Treaty were approved at all, it would very likely be approved with reservations or amendments objectionable to Moscow. In the midst of the debate, the Carter administration's revelation of the presence of a Soviet combat brigade in Cuba hardened opposition to the Treaty and led some Senators to demand the withdrawal of Soviet combat forces in Cuba as a necessary condition for their support of SALT II. Moscow refused to accede to these demands. By all accounts, the issue in the Senate was still close in December when the Soviet Union began its airlift of troops into Kabul. President Carter, although arguing that ratification of SALT II remained in the long-term interest of the United States, bowed to the reality of Senate opposition and in early January, 1980 withdrew the Treaty from Senate consideration. Thus had collapsed, perhaps only temporarily, the centerpiece of detente. The implications of the failure of SALT II were enormous. Moscow and Washington now had to reassess their options with regard to the development of strategic weapons, and, more importantly, to reexamine the bases of the conflict that continued to pit each against the other.

HUMAN RIGHTS

Not all of the differences between Moscow and Washington involved conflicts of interest. Between the Brezhnev and Carter administrations, there was also a clash of values, and the central issue dividing them was that of human rights. It should be noted that American advocacy of human rights did not begin with Jimmy Carter, but from the moment of his inaugural proclamation, "Because we are free we can never be indifferent to the fate of freedom elsewhere," the issue became a measure of Soviet-American relations.[39] The launching of the human rights campaign in the United States produced an expression of concern in the

Soviet press about the future of Soviet-American cooperation.[40] Georgii A. Arbatov, a leading Soviet specialist on the United States, observed in the summer of 1977 that "the political atmosphere in relations between the two countries has changed for the worse. . . . This is a direct result of the anti-Soviet propaganda campaigns that are being carried out one after another in the United States and also of the attempts at interference in the internal affairs of the U.S.S.R. and other socialist countries under the pretext of 'defense of human rights' "[41]

There are several reasons why the Kremlin reacted so negatively to the human rights issue. The Soviet leadership undoubtedly saw the American stance as a propaganda ploy in the continual battle for men's minds throughout the world. Already on the defensive over its repression of dissidents in Soviet society, the Soviets certainly did not wish to be called on the carpet every time they undertook to stifle dissent at home. They were particularly concerned that the preparatory conference in the summer of 1977 and the October meeting in Belgrade to review compliance with the Final Act of the Helsinki Declaration should not become forums for anti-Soviet critiques on human rights questions. Nor did they relish the possible negative image that might be projected at the very time they were celebrating the glories of the 60th anniversary of the Bolshevik Revolution in November 1977.

More serious than propaganda alone, however, was the subversive character of the issue for the Soviet political system. Though the rhetoric of the campaign for human rights never defined precisely what those rights are or the conditions for their application, it is widely assumed that they included what might be classified as political rights, such as freedom of speech, assembly, fair trials, and the like. These are rights whose presence is clearly identified with democratic political systems and whose absence is most notable in authoritarian systems. Whether we classify the Soviet Union as a totalitarian society or simply an authoritarian or autocratic one,[42] there is little doubt that these political rights are absent in Soviet society. Indeed the political and philosophic foundations of the Soviet regime—that is, Leninism—oppose the implementation of these rights, often derided as "bourgeois rights" in Soviet writings, as fundamentally inimical to a communist society. Thus, open criticism of political leaders or their actions can be and have been punished under Soviet criminal law as "slander" against the Soviet system.

The point is that the issue of human rights cannot be divorced from the nature of a society's political system. To condemn a political system for denying these rights is to brand it nondemocratic. Yet if the Kremlin were to permit its citizens to exercise the rights urged upon them by the United States, the entire character of the Soviet regime would be fundamentally altered. The Soviet leaders probably understand this better than the Americans. It is precisely these democratic rights that have been so insistently demanded by such Soviet dissidents as Andrei Amalrik, Vladimir Bukovsky, Valerii Chalidze, Yurii

Galanskov, Alexander Ginsburg, Roy and Zhores Medvedev, Yurii Orlov, Andrei
Sakharov, Anatoly Shcharansky, and Andrei Tverdokhlebov, to name just a
few.[43] Thus Brezhnev and his colleagues in the Politburo rightly viewed American encouragement of the dissidents as subversive, or as Arbatov and others put
it, "interference in the internal affairs of the U.S.S.R."

There is a more profound significance to the issue of human rights than the
political consequences of their espousal. When pressed, Soviet spokesmen deny
that these rights are lacking in Soviet society, just as they insist that their
government is a democratic one. We are confronted with what would appear to
be a semantic problem: How are concepts, adjectives, terms, to be defined? In
Soviet eyes, for example, military occupation becomes "fraternal assistance,"
invasion may be "liberation," dictatorship can be "democracy." Obviously there
are different realities for the same event or circumstance: the communist reality
and the noncommunist reality. We are reminded of the argument made in defense of the Soviet invasion of Czechoslovakia in 1968:

Those who speak of the "illegality" of the allied socialist countries' actions in
Czechoslovakia forget that in a class society there is and can be no such thing as
nonclass law. Laws and the norms of law are subordinated to the laws of the
class struggle and the laws of social development. The class approach to the
matter cannot be discarded in the name of legalistic considerations.[44]

Truth, in effect, is determined by the purpose it serves.

Article 50 of the new Soviet constitution, approved in the fall of 1977,
guarantees to Soviet citizens the rights of speech, press, meeting, and assembly. These rights are identical to those guaranteed under the previous constitution (in Article 125); yet when 20–30 people demonstrated peacefully in
Pushkin Square in February 1967 protesting the imprisonment of four writers,
they were attacked by the police and five were arrested.[45] In 1968 an even
smaller, equally peaceful demonstration in protest of the Soviet invasion of
Czechoslovakia was broken up by the police with dire consequences for most
of the participants. Were these violations of human rights or rights protected by
the Soviet constitution? The problem in answering this question is that there
is no common measure by which Soviet and Western observers can evaluate the
actions of the Soviet state. In the realm of social behavior there are no standards
common to the Soviet and non-Soviet world by which the truth—objective
reality—can be determined. This difficulty may well be the most intractable of
all the dilemmas confronting Soviet relations with the West.

THE FUTURE OF SOVIET FOREIGN POLICY

As this study concludes, Soviet foreign policy is in a state of transition. The
detente of the early 1970s ceased to exist by the early 1980s. Will the Soviet

Union move into a long period of confrontation with the West reminiscent of the cold war or can the cooperative ties of a decade ago be restored? Clearly, in the complex world of international politics no one can assuredly predict the future. One can at best assess some of the factors likely to control future events, and speculate on likely trends.

We have already observed that Soviet foreign policy since World War II has alternated between periods of conflict and accommodation with other great powers. From its wartime collaboration with the Western democracies, the Soviet Union moved into a bitter confrontation with the West. The dates may be somewhat arbitrary but the cold war lasted for roughly a quarter of a century and was followed by a decade of detente. Within the broad general periods of Soviet policy we have observed numerous fluctuations between phases of limited cooperation (the Spirit of Geneva, the Test Ban Treaty, for example) and sharp confrontation (as in the Vietnam and Yom Kippur wars).

We have also noted some of the general factors that contributed to the continuity and change in Soviet foreign policy. We considered in chapter 2 the influence of the international system with its anarchical framework and communist ideology with its stress on the antagonistic character of political relations as enduring influences toward conflict between the Soviet Union and the West. In chapter 1, we surveyed the factors that led to important changes in Soviet foreign policy, viz., multipolarity in the international system, polycentrism in the world communist movement, nuclear weapons, nuclear parity with the United States, the change in the Soviet political system, and changes of the Soviet ruling elite.

Of these six factors, only one—the composition of the Soviet leadership—is certain to change in the 1980s. Leonid Brezhnev, President and Party General-Secretary, is in poor health. In December 1979 he celebrated his 73rd birthday. Although a political succession is imminent, we cannot say when it will take place or who the successor will be. One of the major weaknesses of the Soviet political system is the lack of a constitutional means for transferring power from one leader to the next. Previous successions have resulted from the death of the incumbent (Lenin and Stalin) or a political coup (Khrushchev); Leonid Brezhnev may well be the first Soviet leader to abandon power willingly and voluntarily go into retirement. His elevation to the presidency (replacing Nikolaii Podgorny) in June 1977 represented the culmination of a career rather than the acquisition of new power.

The forthcoming political succession will involve more than just the selection of a new leader. Executive authority in the Soviet system today is collective. The ruling oligarchy today consists of about 27 men who comprise the membership of the Politburo and the Secretariat. They are an elderly group. As of early 1980, ten of these top leaders are septuagenarians. One is in his 80s, another seven are older than 65, and only four are in their 50s. Thus, one can reasonably assume that almost half of the ruling oligarchy will be replaced during the 1980s.[46]

The succession is likely to take place in two stages. Brezhnev's immediate successor will probably be one of his own generation, possibly someone like A. P. Kirilenko (who, though in relatively good health, is actually a few months older than Brezhnev). Given the inevitability of the vicissitudes of age, a younger team will eventually assume power. If these new leaders do move Soviet policy in a new direction, it is not likely to be until the second stage of the political succession. Those of Brezhnev's generation share a common experience and perception in their guidance of Soviet policy since World War II. They are not likely to change in any important way. From them we can expect only a continuation of those policies that have reinvigorated the conflict between the Soviet Union and the West. But those who were born after 1930, whose political careers are not linked to Stalin, could conceivably bring new approaches and attitudes to Soviet foreign policy.

Another internal development with probable foreign policy consequences will be the adoption of the 11th Five-Year-Plan for 1981–1985, which is likely a major item of business for the 26th Party Congress. Almost certainly, the 11th Five-Year-Plan will make important changes in the productive process. After a long period of steady progress, the Soviet economy in the 1970s experienced a succession of serious problems. The economy suffered from declining output growth, inflation, slow technological progress and accumulated differences in housing and other public needs. Agriculture, with its inefficiency and high cost, continues to be a major weakness. Bad crop years periodically necessitate the purchase of food abroad, forcing the government to expend valuable hard currency. Because Soviet manufactured goods cannot compete in the hard currency markets, Moscow is compelled to rely upon the exports of raw materials such as oil. But recent estimates are that Soviet oil production will peak in the early 1980s, forcing the Soviet Union to become a net oil importer.

There are two basic directions in which economic change could go under the new economic plan: a shift toward a liberal policy or a re-Stalinization of economic administration.[47] A liberal scenario would involve permitting economic managers at the local level to have much more freedom than they now have. It would encourage innovation without drastically penalizing mistakes. Resources would be allocated according to market factors and less by administrative fiat. Labor and materials would be shifted to reflect the changing opportunity costs of production. One of the consequences of a liberalization of the economy would be a greater investment in light industry and consumer goods. An alternative scenario would be a reversion to more centralized controls from Moscow, a tightening of labor discipline, and a renewed emphasis upon quantitative quotas as a measure of enterprise success. As in the past, priority would be given to capital goods production, heavy industry, and military weapons.

There are foreign policy implications of both these approaches. A more liberal domestic orientation would encourage increased Soviet involvement in the world economy. If this led to an improvement in the quality of Soviet manufactured goods, the Soviet Union would become more competitive in a world market. At the same time, by making concessions to popular demand for greater quality in consumer items and a higher standard of living, the Soviet Union would be compelled to import more. Economic interdependence would presumably give the Kremlin a greater stake in peace and international stability. With less resources available for military construction, the Soviet Union would be more inclined to move toward more substantial cuts in armaments through disarmament and arms control negotiations. The foreign policy consequences of a shift toward a re-Stalinization of the economy would be just the opposite. It would portend economic autarky, international tension, and a heightening of the arms race.

While we cannot predict the outcome of the succession struggle or the direction of the 11th Five-Year-Plan, we can be fairly certain that the combined input of these two sets of internal changes will have some impact on foreign policy. It is quite probable that the coincidence of major changes in the economic and political sphere will have a synergistic effect on foreign policy, so that the end result will be greater than would have been the case had each development occurred at a different time.

Externally, the major variables affecting Soviet foreign policy portend a continuation of the tension between the Soviet Union and its adversaries, both East and West. Moscow will pursue its venture in Afghanistan until it has pacified the Moslem insurgents and stabilized a pro-Soviet government in Kabul. Whether, how soon, and to what extent the Soviet Union will use its position in Afghanistan to extend its influence into other areas of the Middle East will depend upon the cost of the Afghan operation and the response of the United States and its allies. It is plausible to assume that Moscow's decision to invade Afghanistan took into calculation the preoccupation of the United States with the Iranian crisis and the general reluctance of the United States since Vietnam to use military forces abroad.

There will be no lack of upheavals in the countries of the Third World in the coming decade. Moscow has made clear its determination to have a voice in the resolution of major conflicts anywhere in the world with a decisive voice in those regions close to Soviet borders. Soviet power today is greater in a relative and an absolute sense than at any other time in its history. This could conceivably give the Kremlin a feeling of security and a surcease from its endless struggles with its neighbors. And yet, as Helmut Sonnenfeldt notes, "Paradoxically, the more that Soviet power grows and spreads, the more the Soviet sense of encirclement seems to increase."[48]

A major component of this sense of encirclement is China, a nation that has never abandoned its claims over territories in Soviet East Asia lost through "unequal and illegal" treaties with Tsarist Russia. One might argue that the major failure of the Brezhnev administration was its inability to heal the Sino-Soviet rift with Mao Zedong's successors. Collusion between China and the United States is only one of many Soviet fears. Almost certainly Moscow wants to avoid a nuclear war as much as the United States. The memories of 20 million dead in the second World War remain alive for the Soviet people as well as for their leaders.

Yet the Soviets are better prepared today than at any time in their history to challenge the West militarily should they choose to do so. The decade of the 1970s witnessed a steady widening of the gap between Soviet and United States general purpose (as well as nuclear) forces. A few figures will illustrate the difference. By the end of the decade, the United States armed forces numbered 2,022,000; the USSR had 3,658,000 people under arms. United States tanks numbered 10,500, roughly the same as a decade earlier; the Soviet Union had about 50,000 tanks (some obsolete) compared with 34,000 in 1967. The number of U.S. naval units reached a low of 180 major surface combat ships compared to 275 on the Soviet side.[49] Though these figures do not tell the whole story, they clearly indicate that the Soviet Union is in a position to back up its diplomacy with substantial military might.

The Soviet Union may be in a position to challenge the supremacy of the United States in military power, but it continues to be a considerably weaker power in overall economic measures. The gap in economic power is even greater when the strengths of both alliances are calculated, as table 8.1 shows:[50]

Table 8.1. Comparative Economic Strength, 1977

Category	United States	USSR	United States and allies	USSR and allies
Population (in millions)	217	259	759	379
GNP (in billions)	$1,887	$932	$4,907	$1,292
Per capita GNP	$8,704	$3,600	$6,348	$1,164
Electric power (in billion kilowatt-hours)	2,209	1,150	4,727	1,540

Source: Paul K. Cook, "The Political Setting," *Soviet Economy in a Time of Change*, p. 42

One can hope that Soviet aggression will be tempered by caution and even by a measure of prudence. Soviet spokesmen continue to speak of detente as one of the foundations of Soviet foreign policy. Prudent policies on the part of the United States may yet restore a measure of peace and stability in superpower relations, although the record to date cautions that there are limits to Soviet-

American detente. The limits are rooted in the profoundly different societies and political systems that gave birth to their foreign policies. Communism may not be a guide to Soviet behavior but it is a creed that continues to infuse Soviet policy with dynamism. It identifies a cause, defines the enemy, and inspires the faith. Without an enemy and a cause, there would be no justification for a Soviet claim to world leadership. Without the doctrine there would be no basis for the dictatorship of the Communist Party internally. Indeed, the whole logic of domestic repression is based upon a foreign threat. Thus, the very nature of the Soviet system sets limits on how far detente can go.

NOTES

1. *Pravda,* November 30, 1973.
2. *Pravda,* August 30, 1973.
3. Kissinger, *White House Years* (Boston: Little, Brown, 1979), pp. 617–631.
4. *New Times,* No. 32 (August, 1973).
5. This section draws on Kalb and Kalb, *Kissinger* (New York: Dell, 1975), pp. 453 ff.; and Robert H. Donaldson, "Soviet Union: International Views and Policies," in *1974 Yearbook on International Communist Affairs,* ed., Richard F. Staar, (Stanford: Hoover Institution Press, 1974), pp. 87–89.
6. Quoted in Kalb and Kalb, *Kissinger,* p. 488.
7. *SShA: Ekonomika, politika, idiologiia,* no. 12 (December, 1973).
8. *Pravda,* June 5, 1974, p. 1.
9. *Pravda,* October 18, 1974.
10. *Za rubezhom,* No. 38 (1975).
11. *The New York Times,* April 22, 1979.
12. *The Soviet Union and The Third World: A Watershed in Great Power Policy: Report to the Committee on International Relations, House of Representatives by the Senior Specialists Division, Congressional Research Service, Library of Congress, May 8, 1977* (Washington: U.S. Government Printing Office, 1977), p. 107.
13. *New Times,* "The People of Angola Are Not Alone," No. 2 (2 January 1976), p. 1.
14. *The New York Times,* January 8, 1976.
15. *Documents and Resolutions, 25th Congress of the CPSU* (Moscow, 1976), p. 40.
16. The test of the joint Soviet-American statement is in *Pravda,* October 3, 1977.
17. The text of the treaty is in *The New York Times,* March 27, 1979, pp. A14–16.
18. See Richard Remnek, "Soviet Policy in the Horn of Africa: The Decision To Intervene," in *Soviet Policy in the Third World,* ed., Robert H. Donaldson, (Boulder: Westview Press, 1980).

19. The article was written by I. Alexandrov, a pseudonym used in the Soviet press for articles reflecting official thinking.
20. *The New York Times,* November 8, 1978.
21. Ibid., February 19, 1979.
22. Quoted in Shahram Chubin, "Soviet Policy Toward Iran and the Gulf," *Adelphi Papers,* no. 157. Spring 1980 (London: Institute for Strategic Studies), p. 33.
23. Radio Moscow in Persian to Iran, 6 November 1979. *Foreign Broadcast Information Service, Daily Report 3,* no. 217, p. H2.
24. *The New York Times,* December 6, 1979, p. A18.
25. Ibid., April 26, 1980.
26. Ibid., January 6, 1980, p. El.
27. Hannah Negaran, "The Afghan Coup of April 1978: Revolution and International Security," *Orbis 23,* no. 1 (Spring 1979):100.
28. Vernon V. Aspaturian, "Moscow's Afghan Gamble," *The New Leader* (January 28, 1980), p. 11.
29. *The New York Times,* January 6, 1980, p. 2E.
30. Craig R. Whitney, "The View from the Kremlin," *The New York Times Magazine,* April 20, 1980, p. 91.
31. A. Petrov in *Pravda,* December 31, 1979.
32. There is some evidence that the Soviet analysis of the situation in Afghanistan was very similar to that regarding Czechoslovakia in 1968. See "World Communist Solidarity with the Afghan Revolution," *New Times,* No. 3 (January 1980), pp. 8-10.
33. *The New York Times,* January 24, 1980, p. 12.
34. Strobe Talbott, *Endgame, The Inside Story of SALT II* (New York: Harper and Row, 1979), p. 26.
35. This was its "B" version. Thomas W. Wolfe, *The SALT Experience* (Cambridge, Mass.: Ballinger, 1979), pp. 126-127.
36. Talbott, *Endgame,* p. 73. Brezhnev was incensed too by the ineptness of Carter's presentation. He made his proposals without any prearrangement with the Soviets and with considerable advanced publicity.
37. The text of the Treaty is in Talbott, *Endgame,* pp. 279-310. Also *The New York Times,* June 19, 1979.
38. Craig R. Whitney, "The View from the Kremlin," p. 33.
39. See Daniel P. Monihan, "The Politics of Human Rights," *Commentary 64,* no. 2 (August 1977):19-26.
40. William B. Husband, "Soviet Perceptions of U.S. 'Positions-of-Strength' Diplomacy in the 1970's," *World Politics 31,* no. 4 (July 1979):514.
41. *The New York Times,* August 4, 1977.
42. The distinction between totalitarianism and autocracy is developed in Carl S. Friedrich and Zbigniew Brzezinski, *Totalitarian Dictatorship and Autocracy* (Cambridge, Mass.: Harvard University Press, 1956).

43. A strong case is made by Frederick C. Barghoorn that a real detente with the West can be established only when the Soviet regime accepts the principles espoused by its dissidents. See Frederick C. Barghoorn, *Detente and the Democratic Movement in the USSR* (New York: The Free Press, 1976).

44. Robin Alison Remington, ed., *Winter in Prague, Documents on Czechoslovak Communism in Crisis* (Cambridge, Mass.: MIT Press, 1969), p. 415.

45. Pavel Litvinov, *The Demonstration in Pushkin Square* (Boston, Gambit, 1969), pp. 1-10.

46. Two useful analyses of the impending succession are R. Judson Mitchell, "The Soviet Succession: Who and What Will Follow Brezhnev?," *Orbis 23*, No. 1 (Spring 1979):9-34; and William G. Hyland, "Brezhnev and Beyond," *Foreign Affairs 58*, no. 1 (Fall 1979):51-66.

47. This analysis is based upon Holland Hunter, "Soviet Economic Problems and Alternative Policy Responses," in *Soviet Economy in a Time of Change*, Joint Economic Committee, 96 Congress, 1st. session, October 10, 1979, Washington, D.C.

48. "The Soviet Challenge," in *Setting National Priorities, Agenda for the 1980's*, ed., Joseph A. Pechman (Washington: The Brookings Institution, 1980), p. 358.

49. The figures in this paragraph are from The International Institute for Strategic Studies, *The Military Balance 1979–1980* (London: IISS, 1979), pp. 4, 5, 7, 10, and 92.

50. Paul K. Cook, "The Political Setting," *Soviet Economy in a Time of Change*, p. 42.

Annotated Bibliography

CHAPTER 1

Aspaturian, Vernon V. *Process and Power in Soviet Foreign Policy*. Boston: Little Brown, 1971. This is a large collection of essays, more than half of them by Aspaturian. There is some duplication here but also considerable information and insightful analysis.

Hoffman, Erik P. and Fleron, Frederic J., eds. rev. ed. *The Conduct of Soviet Foreign Policy*. Chicago: Aldine-Atherton, 1980. This is a collection of previously published essays covering a wide range of subjects.

Kennan, George F. *Russia and the West Under Lenin and Stalin*. Boston: Little, Brown, 1961. This is the best and most readable account of Soviet-Western relations from 1917 to 1945 in a single volume, replete with insightful observations on Soviet politics and how the West ought to manage its relations with the Soviet Union.

Mosely, Philip E. *The Kremlin and World Politics, Studies in Soviet Policy and Action*. New York: Vintage Books, 1960. This is a collection of essays by a scholar and statesman which, though it covers primarily the cold war years, has current relevance.

Rosser, Richard F. *An Introduction to Soviet Foreign Policy*. Englewood Cliffs, N.J.: Prentice-Hall, 1969. Rosser's book is a survey of the roots of Soviet foreign policy and its tactics.

Rubinstein, Alvin Z., ed. *The Foreign Policy of the Soviet Union*. New York: Random House, 1972. This is a collection of excerpts from Soviet writings and official pronouncements that explains the Soviet rationale for its own actions.

Schwartz, Morton. *The Foreign Policy of the USSR: Domestic Factors*. Encino, Calif.: Dickenson Publishing Co., 1975. Schwartz provides a useful survey of the domestic factors which determine Soviet foreign policy.

Triska, Jan F., and Finley, David D. *Soviet Foreign Policy*. New York: Macmillan, 1968. What makes this volume unusual is the use of behavioral research techniques in several of the chapters.

Ulam, Adam B. *Expansion and Coexistence: Soviet Foreign Policy 1917–1973.* New York: Praeger, 1974. This massive study, written with remarkable style and insight, is the best interpretive history of the subject, especially for the Stalin and Khrushchev periods.

Wesson, Robert G. *Soviet Foreign Policy in Perspective.* Homewood, Ill.: Dorsey Press, 1969. Largely historical in scope, this is a useful introduction.

CHAPTER 2

Carew Hunt, R. N. *The Theory and Practice of Communism, An Introduction.* New York: The Macmillan Co., 1957. Hunt provides an excellent survey and analysis of the principles of communist doctrine including the contributions of Marx, Engels, Lenin, and Stalin.

Feuer, Lewis S., ed. *Karl Marx and Friedrich Engels, Basic Writings on Politics and Philosophy.* Garden City, N.Y.: Doubleday and Co., 1959. This is a judicious editing of the most important writings that make up the core of communist ideology.

Goodman, Elliot R. *The Soviet Design for a World State.* New York: Columbia University Press, 1960. This scholarly analysis of communist writings reveals a pattern of expansionist tendencies which Goodman argues must be countered by a strong and unified West.

Leites, Nathan C. *A Study of Bolshevism.* Glencoe, Ill.: Free Press, 1953. This is a seminal study which examines the psychological and political premises of communist thinking as revealed in a large body of communist literature.

Lenin, V. I. *Imperialism, the Highest Stage of Capitalism.* In Robert C. Tucker, ed. *The Lenin Anthology.* New York: W. W. Norton, 1975. This essay is the classic statement of communist doctrine which explains why mature capitalism becomes imperialist.

Meyer, Alfred G. *Marxism, The Unit of Theory and Practice.* Cambridge: Harvard University Press, 1954. This is a brilliant analysis of Marxist theory, focusing on Marx as a social prophet, political revolutionary, and social scientist.

Meyer, Alfred G. *Leninism.* Cambridge: Harvard University Press, 1957. Meyer's study is an original and perceptive analysis that explains the Leninist adaptation of Marxist thought to the conditions of the early 20th century.

Stalin, Joseph. *Economic Problems of Socialism in the U.S.S.R.* New York: International Publishers, 1952. This is Stalin's last theoretical writing in which he forsees wars between capitalist states as the main cause of war.

Tucker, Robert C. *The Soviet Political Mind, Stalinism and Post-Stalin Change.* Rev. Ed. New York: Norton, 1971. Tucker's volume contains a dozen essays that explore the theoretical, psychological, and political bases of Soviet politics during and after the Stalinist period.

Wolfe, Bertram D. *Marxism, One Hundred Years in the Life of a Doctrine.* New York: The Dial Press, 1965. Wolfe's is a brilliant piece of scholarship that examines the ambiguous heritage of Marxism.

CHAPTER 3

Churchill, Winston S. *The Second World War.* Vol. 1, *The Gathering Storm*; Vol. 2, *Their Finest Hour*; Vol. 3, *The Grand Alliance*; Vol. 4, *The Hinge of Fate*; Vol. 5, *Closing the Ring*; Vol. 6, *Triumph and Tragedy.* Boston: Houghton Mifflin Co., 1948-53. Churchill has written invaluable first-hand accounts of the major wartime conferences, described in his inimitable Churchillian prose.

Dallin, Alexander. *The Soviet Union at the United Nations.* New York: Praeger, 1962. This is especially useful for its analysis of Communist conceptions of international organizations and its account of Soviet behavior in the early days of the UN.

Fischer, Louis. *The Road to Yalta: Soviet Foreign Relations 1941-1945.* New York: Harper and Row, 1972. Fisher's is a perceptive analysis, especially good in its accounts of the personalities and motivations of Stalin, Roosevelt, and Churchill, written in readable quasijournalistic style.

Kennan, George F. *Memoirs.* Boston: Little, Brown and Company, 1967. Kennan provides valuable recollections and interpretations, by the U.S. government's postwar Soviet "expert" and author of the containment doctrine.

Maddox, Robert James. *The New Left and the Origins of the Cold War.* Princeton, N.J.: Princeton University Press, 1973. This is a trenchant analysis of the works of the leading "revisionist" American historians of the postwar period.

Mastny, Vojtech. *Russia's Road to the Cold War: Diplomacy, Warfare and the Politics of Communism, 1941-1945.* New York: Columbia University Press, 1979. Mastny's study is a long-needed close examination of the wartime diplomacy of the USSR, employing new evidence from Soviet sources.

Mee, Charles L., Jr. *Meeting at Postdam.* New York: Dell, 1975. This is a lucid and critical account of the motivations and actions of the "Big Three" at the last wartime summit conference.

Paterson, Thomas G. *Soviet-American Confrontation: Postwar Reconstruction and the Origins of the Cold War.* Baltimore: Johns Hopkins University Press, 1973. An analysis directed especially at the economic dimension of the postwar Soviet-American relationship, this suffers from the general "revisionist" malady of insufficient attention to Soviet sources.

Ponomarev, Gromyko, A., Khvostov, V., eds. *History of Soviet Foreign Policy 1945-1970.* Moscow: Progress Publishers, 1973. This is an authoritative Soviet interpretation of Moscow's postwar foreign policy, devoid of documentation or self-criticism and very revealing of the Marxist-Leninist perspective.

Shulman, Marshall D. *Stalin's Foreign Policy Reappraised.* New York: Atheneum, 1965. Based on the thesis that Stalin's policy was undergoing change in the years immediately before his death, this is a lucid and original interpretation.

Yergin, Daniel. *Shattered Peace: The Origins of the Cold War and the National Security State.* Boston: Houghton Mifflin Co., 1978. Yergin provides a thorough analysis, written primarily from the standpoint of U.S. policymakers.

CHAPTER 4

Abel, Elie. *The Missile Crisis.* New York: Bantam, 1966. This is the best short account available, excitingly written by a perceptive and well-informed American journalist.

The Anti-Stalin Campaign and International Communism. A selection of documents edited by the Russian Institute, Columbia University. New York: Columbia University Press, 1956. This selection contains the full Englishlanguage text of Khrushchev's 1956 "secret speech" denouncing Stalin.

Dallin, David. J. *Soviet Foreign Policy after Stalin.* Philadelphia: Lippincott, 1961. Based on a close and insightful study of Soviet sources, this analysis is particularly detailed for the period 1953-57.

Horelick, Arnold L., and Rush, Myron. *Strategic Power and Soviet Foreign Policy.* Chicago: University of Chicago Press, 1966. Horelick and Rush provide a persuasive and well-documented analysis of Khrushchev's "missile diplomacy" from the launching of Sputnik through the Cuban Missile Crisis.

Khrushchev Remembers, with an introduction, commentary and notes by Edward Crankshaw, translated and edited by Strobe Talbott. Boston: Little, Brown and Company, 1970. *Khrushchev Remembers: The Last Testament.* Translated and edited by Strobe Talbott, with a foreword by Edward Crankshaw and an introduction by Jerrold L. Schecter. Boston: Little, Brown and Company, 1974. These two volumes contain the memoir materials dictated by former Soviet premier Khrushchev after his ouster; though unreliable as history, they are invaluable sources on Khrushchev's own perceptions and post-hoc justifications. The two volumes overlap in part, though the second contains more material concerning Khrushchev's foreign policy.

Mackintosh, J. M. *Strategy and Tactics of Soviet Foreign Policy.* New York: Oxford University Press, 1963. This is a dry and thorough account of the main directions of Soviet policy, with emphasis on the late 1940s and 1950s.

Medvedev, Roy A. and Zhores, A. *Khrushchev: The Years in Power.* New York: Columbia University Press, 1976. Although it contains relatively little material on foreign affairs, this is a rare view of Soviet politics "from the inside," by two well-informed Soviet dissident writers.

Tatu, Michel. *Power in the Kremlin: From Khrushchev to Kosygin.* New York: Viking, 1967. Long-time Moscow correspondent of *Le Monde*, Tatu is a most perceptive and well-informed "Kremlinologist," and this well-documented account contains much valuable material on foreign policy from the U-2 incident to the Six-Day War.

Wolfe, Thomas W. *Soviet Power and Europe 1945-1970.* Baltimore: Johns Hopkins University Press, 1970. Wolfe's is a well-documented and reliable analysis of Soviet military strategy and capabilities in Europe as they relate to Soviet foreign policy in the postwar period.

Zimmerman, William. *Soviet Perspectives of International Relations 1956-1967.* New York: Columbia University Press, 1969. This is an analysis of the continuities and changes in Soviet conceptualization of international politics during a critical period.

CHAPTER 5

Donaldson, Robert H. *Soviet Policy toward India: Ideology and Strategy.* Cambridge, Mass.: Harvard University Press, 1974. Donaldson traces the interrelationship between Marxist-Leninist doctrine and Soviet policy in a major Third World state.

Donaldson, Robert H., ed. *The Soviet Union in the Third World: Successes and Failures.* Boulder, Colo.: Westview, 1980. Twenty-one specialists assess the Soviet record in Asia, Africa, and Latin America, presenting a balance sheet of Soviet achievements and disappointments.

Freedman, Robert O. *Soviet Policy toward the Middle East Since 1970.* Rev. ed. New York: Praeger, 1978. This is a thorough and up-to-date examination of the USSR's activity in the Middle East in a crucial period for the region.

Goldman, Marshall I. *Soviet Foreign Aid.* New York: Praeger, 1967. Though now somewhat dated, this remains the best analysis of this important instrument of the Soviet approach to the Third World.

Goure, Leon, and Rothenberg, Morris. *Soviet Penetration of Latin America.* Miami, Fla.: University of Miami, 1975. Goure and Rothenberg provide a useful (though somewhat alarmist) survey of Soviet policy in this region in the later 1960s and early 1970s.

Jukes, Geoffrey. *The Soviet Union in Asia.* Berkeley, Calif.: University of California Press, 1973. Proceeding from the premise that the USSR is a major Asian power, this Australian scholar skillfully analyzes the various dimensions of the Soviet involvement.

Kanet, Robert E. and Bahry, Donna, eds. *Soviet Economic and Political Rela-*

tions with the Developing World. New York: Praeger, 1975. The twelve essays in this book, sketching various facets of the Soviet approach, were
originally presented at the 1974 Banff International Congress of Slavists.

Kanet, Roger, E., ed. *The Soviet Union and The Developing Nations.* Baltimore:
Johns Hopkins University Press, 1974. Kanet has collected ten essays surveying the various policy dimensions and geographical areas of the Soviet approach in the Third World.

Laqueur, Walter A. *The Struggle for the Middle East: The Soviet Union and the
Middle East 1958-1968.* Baltimore: Penguin, 1972. This is a brief and perceptive analysis by one of the leading specialists on Soviet Middle Eastern policy.

Lenin, Vladimir I. *The National-Liberation Movement in the East.* Moscow:
Foreign Languages Publishing House, 1957. This is a comprehensive collection of Lenin's essays and speeches on the "national-liberation movement."

Levesque, Jacques. *The USSR and the Cuban Revolution: Soviet Ideological and
Strategical Perspectives, 1959-1977.* New York: Praeger, 1978. Levesque's is
an analysis of the Soviet-Cuban relationship from the time of Castro's revolution, by a well-informed French scholar.

McLane, Charles B. *Soviet Strategy in Southeast Asia: An Exploration of Eastern
Policy under Lenin and Stalin.* Princeton, N.J.: Princeton University Press,
1966. Thoroughly documented, this account not only describes the Soviet
approach to Southeast Asia in the period before 1953, but also provides a
sound analysis of the doctrinal bases of Soviet involvement in the developing
world.

Rubinstein, Alvin Z. *Red Star on the Nile.* Princeton, N.J.: Princeton University
Press, 1977. This is an exceptionally thorough and well-informed account of
the long Soviet struggle to establish influence in Egypt.

_____ , ed. *Soviet and Chinese Influence in the Third World.* New York: Praeger,
1975. Rubinstein has put together a collection of essays by leading specialists
who seek to apply a common analytic framework in examining Soviet and
Chinese attempts to obtain influence in various areas.

Thornton, Thomas P., ed. *The Third World in Soviet Perspective.* Princeton,
N.J.: Princeton University Press, 1964. Thornton's is a collection of translated essays by leading Soviet academic specialists, with an excellent introduction analyzing the application of "creative Marxism-Leninism" to the
interpretation of the problems of the developing world.

CHAPTER 6

Borisov, O. B., and Koloskov, B. T. *Soviet-Chinese Relations, 1945-1970.* Edited
by Vladimir Petrov. Bloomington, Ind.: Indiana University Press, 1975. This

is a transition of a work of two Soviet scholars; it is interesting for its account of anti-Soviet tendencies in China before 1960.

Brzezinski, Zbigniew K. *The Soviet Bloc, Unity and Conflict.* Rev. ed. Cambridge, Mass.: Harvard University Press, 1967. This is an in-depth analysis of the transformation of the Soviet bloc from a satellite to a polycentric system. Particular attention is paid to the relationship between power and ideology.

Carillo, Santiago. *Eurocommunism and the State.* Westport, Conn.: Lawrence Hill and Co., 1978. This is an authoritative exposition by the head of the Spanish Communist Party of the Eurocommunist argument for an independent road to socialism.

Gati, Charles, ed. *The International Politics of Eastern Europe.* New York: Praeger, 1976. Gati has compiled a superb collection of essays analyzing Eastern Europe's politics from the perspectives of the Soviet Union, China, and the West.

Remington, Robin Alison, ed. *Winter in Prague, Documents on Czechoslovak Communism in Crisis.* Cambridge, Mass.: The MIT Press, 1969. This volume contains 72 documents, chronologically arranged, that describe the Czechoslovak reforms, the orthodox response, the Soviet rationale for its invasion, and the reaction within international communism: a valuable collection.

Salisbury, Harrison E. *War Between Russia and China.* New York: W. W. Norton, 1961. This is a popular book by a distinguished journalist which describes the forces on both sides that could bring the two communist giants to war.

Tokes, Rudolf, L., ed. *Eurocommunism and Detente.* New York: New York University Press, 1978. Tokes has brought together nine scholarly essays that examine the evolution of Eurocommunism in Italy, France, Spain, and Portugal, and assess the impact of the movement in general on relations between the Soviet Union and Western and Eastern Europe.

Ulam, Adam B. *Titoism and the Cominform.* Cambridge, Mass.: Harvard University Press, 1952. This is a scholarly yet fascinating account of Tito's break with Stalin. Ulam offers interesting speculation on the implication of Titoism for the West and the Soviet bloc.

Valenta, Jiri. *Soviet Intervention in Czechoslovakia, 1968.* Baltimore: Johns Hopkins Press, 1979. Valenta's study is excellent not only for its description of the invasion of Czechoslovakia but for its analysis of decision making in the Kremlin.

Zinner, Paul, ed. *National Communism and Popular Revolt in Eastern Europe.* New York: Columbia University Press. 1956. These documents give an authentic and detailed description of the events that led up to the revolutions in Poland and Hungary during 1956 and of the course each revolution took.

CHAPTER 7

Dinerstein, Herbert S. *War and the Soviet Union, Nuclear Weapons and the Revolution in Soviet Military and Political Thinking.* New York: Federick A. Praeger, 1959. Though now somewhat dated, this remains an impressive examination of the impact of nuclear weapons on Soviet thinking.

Edmonds, Robin. *Soviet Foreign Policy, 1962–1973; The Paradox of Superpower.* New York: Oxford University Press, 1975. A British diplomat provides a year by year and area by area description of the diplomacy leading up to detente.

Goldman, Marshall I. *Detente and Dollars, Doing Business with the Soviets.* New York: Basic Books, 1975. This is a readable discussion of the prospects and problems for American businessmen wishing to enter the Soviet market. The author's caution has proven well founded.

Kissinger, Henry. *White House Years.* Boston: Little, Brown, 1979. Though reflecting an American perspective, these authoritative memoirs contain a detailed description of the diplomacy that produced detente. This is an extraordinarily rich volume, covering the years 1969–1973.

Korbel, Josef. *Detente in Europe, Real or Imaginery?* Princeton, N.J.: Princeton University Press, 1972. This is a perceptive analysis that looks very skeptically at detente. Korbel concludes that detent is real though limited in nature and scope and that its durability is uncertain: rather prophetic.

Kulski, W. W. *The Soviet Union in World Affairs, A Documented Analysis 1964–1972.* Syracuse: Syracuse University Press, 1973. Organized topically, this analysis makes substantial use of Russian language materials and includes many lengthy excerpts from these sources.

Newhouse, John. *Cold Dawn, the Story of Salt.* New York: Holt, Rinehart and Winston, 1973. This account of Salt I is based upon extensive interviews. Though written primarily from the American perspective, it contains valuable details of Soviet diplomatic behavior.

Schwartz, Morton. *Soviet Perceptions of the United States.* Berkeley, Calif.: University of California Press, 1978. This is a good survey of current Soviet perceptions of the United States as reflected in publications of the USA Institute of the Soviet Academy of Sciences. The author finds more realism in current Soviet perceptions.

Sokolovskiy, V. D. *Soviet Military Strategy.* Ed. Harriet Fast Scott. New York: Crane Russak, 1975. This is an edited version with analysis and commentary of the writings of the late Soviet Marshal, one of the Soviet Union's leading strategic theorists. Scott usefully compares this edition with earlier editions.

United States Arms Control and Disarmament Agency. *Arms Control and Disarmament Agreements, Texts and History of Negotiations.* Washington, D.C.: 1977. A useful reference, this contains the texts of all agreements through 1977.

CHAPTER 8

Barghoorn, Frederick C. *Detente and the Democratic Movement in the USSR.* New York: Free Press, 1976. Barghoorn provides a perceptive analysis of the several different schools of dissenters in the Soviet Union; the author sees a real connection between Soviet repression and detente with the West.

Brezhnev, L. I. *Selected Speeches and Writings on Foreign Affairs.* New York: Pergamon Press, 1979. This useful reference contains materials on Soviet foreign policy not readily available in English. All of the statements or writings were made in the 1970s.

Clemens, Walter C. *The U.S.S.R. and Global Interdependence, Alternative Futures.* Washington: American Enterprise Institute for Public Policy Research, 1978. An innovative examination of the debate in the Soviet Union between advocates of detente and trade vs. those stressing an autarkist stance. Clemens favors Western strategies that encourage Soviet interdependence with the Non-Soviet world.

Library of Congress. *Soviet Diplomacy and Negotiating Behavior: Emerging New Context for U.S. Diplomacy.* Special Studies on Foreign Affairs Issues, Vol. 1. Washington: U.S. Government Printing Office, 1979. This is a massive and detailed history of the style, purposes and effects of Soviet diplomacy.

Talbott, Strobe. *Endgame: The Inside Story of Salt II.* New York: Harper and Row, 1979. This is a well-written account of the evolution of U.S. Salt II policy based on extensive interviews. The Soviet position is examined largely as a reaction to U.S. proposals.

United States Congress, Joint Economic Committee. 96 Cong. 1st. sess. *Soviet Economy in a Time of Change,* 2 vols. Washington: U.S. Government Printing Office, October 10, 1979. This is a compendium of papers that examine, in some instances exhaustively, every major facet of the Soviet economy. There is much useful material here for assessing the direction the Soviet economy will take in the 1980s.

Wesson, Robert, ed. *The Soviet Union: Looking to the 1980's.* Stanford, Calif.: Hoover Institution Press, 1980. These essays cover both foreign and domestic issues and offer a variety of perspectives of the future.

Wolfe, Thomas W. *The Salt Experience.* Cambridge, Mass.: Ballinger Publishing Co., 1979. This is a detailed and balanced analysis of the Salt I and II diplomacy. Wolfe perceptively probes the different objectives of the United States and the Soviet Union in arms control negotiations.

Index

About the Authors

Joseph L. Nogee is Professor of Political Science and Director of the Russian Studies Program at the University of Houston. He received his doctorate from Yale University and has taught at Yale University, New York University, Vanderbilt University and the Army War College. He has also been a visiting research professor at the Strategic Studies Institute of the US Army War College. His research activities have focussed on Soviet foreign policy particularly in the area of disarmament and arms control. He has authored, co-authored, or edited four other books as well as articles in professional journals.

Robert H. Donaldson is Professor of Political Science and Associate Dean of the College of Arts and Science at Vanderbilt University. He received three degrees from Harvard University. He has served at the Department of State as International Affairs Fellow of the Council on Foreign Relations and at the Strategic Studies Institute of the US Army War College as visiting research professor. He has written extensively on Soviet policy in the Third World. He has authored or co-authored four other books and monographs as well as numerous articles.